ULSTER POLITICS

1868–86

ULSTER POLITICS

The Formative Years, 1868-86

B. M. WALKER

The Ulster Historical Foundation
and
The Institute of Irish Studies

Published 1989
by the Ulster Historical Foundation
68 Balmoral Avenue
Belfast
Northern Ireland

and

The Institute of Irish Studies
the Queen's University of Belfast
8 Fitzwilliam Street
Belfast
Northern Ireland

ISBN 0–901905–40–2

Printed by Graham & Sons (Printers) Ltd.
51 Gortin Road
Omagh
Co. Tyrone

Cover
Designed by Wendy Dunbar

For Evelyn

ILLUSTRATIONS

Cover illustration: political cartoon of 1868 Belfast election (Linen Hall Library). The candidates are, from right to left, John Mulholland and Sir Charles Lanyon (on the front cover) and Thomas McClure and William Johnston (on the back cover)

CONTENTS

Contents

IV NATIONALISTS AND UNIONISTS DIVIDE

V CONCLUSION 255

ACKNOWLEDGEMENTS

I wish to record my thanks to the owners or custodians of the various collections of papers that I have consulted or used in the writing of this book: the late Maj.-gen. Sir Allan Adair, bt, the Earl of Belmore, Carleton, Atkinson & Sloan (solicitors), Most Rev. Joseph Duffy, D.D., bishop of Clogher, Miss A. G. G. Browne, P. A. Duffy & Co. (solicitors), Mrs J. A. Collinson, the Marchioness of Dufferin and Ava, Falls & Hanna (solicitors), the Marquis of Hertford and Warwick County Record Office, W. Johnston Esq., L'Estrange & Brett (solicitors), F. McKee Esq., Dr Anthony Malcomson, Deputy Keeper of the Records, Public Record Office of Northern Ireland, J. Murland & Co. (solicitors), Robert Lowry Esq., A. J. Sheat Esq., John Moore Esq., J. W. D. Pinkerton Esq., E. J. Saunderson Esq., the late Sir Knox Cunningham, bt, D. C. O'Neill Esq., the National Trust, the Marquis of Salisbury, the Duke of Devonshire, Mrs Gillian Beath Ingall, H. Chesley Boyd, Ulster Reform Club, Dr Joe McKinney Dundee, the Keeper of Western Manuscripts, Bodleian Library, the British Library Board, the National Library of Ireland and the archives department of University College, Dublin.

The staff of many libraries and record offices kindly gave me assistance over a considerable period of time: the Linen Hall Library, the Public Record Office of Northern Ireland, the National Library of Ireland, The Queen's University Library, Trinity College, Dublin, Library, the Belfast Central Library, University College, Dublin, Archives, and the newspaper room of the British Library.

Many friends and colleagues in the world of history and political science gave valuable help. For their comments on my manuscript at various stages I am very grateful to Professor Don Akenson, Professor John Whyte, Professor David Miller, Dr Harvey Cox, Professor George Boyce, Professor Jim Donnelly, Professor Sam Clark and Professor David Harkness. Colleagues in the politics department at Queen's, particularly Dr Paul Bew and Professor Cornelius O'Leary, gave much encouragement. Help and information over different matters was kindly provided by Professor Finlay Holmes, Professor J. C. Beckett, Dr W. A. Maguire, Professor Desmond Bowen, Dr Tony Stewart, Dr David Hayton and Mr Richard

Acknowledgements

Hawkins. At an early stage of my interest in Irish history and politics I received valuable support and advice from the late Rev. Liam Barbour, Rev. John Brown and Professor J. L. McCracken.

During the research and writing of this work I was much indebted to the Institute of Irish Studies at Queen's. I am very grateful to the former director, the late Rodney Green, and the present director, Professor Ronald Buchanan, for their constant encouragement and advice. Queen's also provided a generous grant towards the cost of this publication. Others who helped in the production of the original typescript include Mrs Felicity Haire, Mrs Betty Kirkpatrick and Miss Daphne Smyth, and I am extremely indebted to them.

Throughout my research and writing for this book my parents constantly supported and encouraged me. My wife Evelyn was a great help and patiently put up with all the strains of drawing the manuscript finally together. Others who kindly gave me hospitality during the writing of the book include John and Yvonne Healy, the Annaghmakerrig Centre, Co. Monaghan, and friends at Carlingford, Co. Louth, Carnlough, Co. Antrim, and in Co. Donegal.

I wish to record my thanks to members of the nineteenth century seminar group that met at Trinity in the early 1970s: Dr Robert Kirkpatrick, Dr Elizabeth Malcolm, Dr Roy Foster, Mr David Haire, Dr Jacqueline Hill, Dr Christopher Woods and Dr Vincent Comerford. I have always valued highly these discussions and the friendships that arose from them. I would also like to thank another member of that group, Dr Bill Vaughan, who not only shared with me many special insights from his pioneering work on the land question but also introduced me to the beauty and realities of the Ulster countryside, particularly Co. Fermanagh.

Finally, I want to record my greatest debt of all, namely, to the late T. W. Moody, who was chairman of the seminar group. Theo Moody taught me Irish history during my undergraduate and postgraduate days. He suggested to me the subject of this book, which reflected his life long interest in his native Ulster. He remained a formative influence and inspiration in the years of research that followed. I hope that this book will in a small way repay my debt to him.

INTRODUCTION

On the afternoon of 19 July 1886 the last result for an Ulster constituency in the general election of that year was announced.
T. W. Russell, liberal unionist, was declared the new member of
parliament for South Tyrone with a total of 3,481 votes against
3,382 for his nationalist rival, William O'Brien. The final outcome
was that the nationalists held 16 seats in the nine counties of Ulster
while the unionists won 15 and the liberal unionists two. For the
observer of politics in Northern Ireland today such results might not
seem surprising. In fact, however, this general election was the first
one in the province in which there was a straightforward fight over
the home rule question. The year 1886 marked the climax to a
period of great political change that began in 1868. During this time
the electoral scene in Ulster was transformed from a long-standing,
almost total, domination by the conservatives to a liberal–
conservative rivalry, and finally to a simple confrontation between
nationalists and unionists or liberal unionists. The party lines drawn
up in 1886 have remained basically unaltered ever since. Clearly
then the elections of these years are very important in the development of politics in Ulster, particularly in what is now Northern
Ireland.

This period is significant for another good reason. It witnessed
important changes in relations between the religious denominations
in the province. From 1868 growth occurred in political cooperation
between protestant and catholic electors. In his *New Ireland* (1877),
A. M. Sullivan remarked on the decrease of sectarian animosities in
Ulster. 'Every season it becomes more and more plain', he wrote,
'that Ulster Orangeman and Ulster catholic are equally desirous of
terminating a state of things which was the scandal of Ireland and
the reproach of Christianity.'[1] By 1881 there was widespread inter-
denominational voting at elections, but thereafter it decreased and
by 1886 this agreement had disappeared almost everywhere. Never
again has there been such a close alliance between the two groups as
occurred in these years. From this time on most catholics have been
nationalist and most protestants unionist.

These decades are important also because they saw a considerable
extension of the franchise, and party organisation took on radically
new forms. By 1885 the majority of adult males had the vote.

Introduction

The social and religious composition of the electorate altered significantly in these years. Party organisation developed from private, landlord-dominated structures to broad-based, voluntary associations, aided by professional agents and central bodies. The new organisational structures that emerged in 1885-6 have proved to be of considerable consequence for future political developments. During this time, owing to the changes in the franchise and party structures as well as the rise of popular and rousing issues, the population at large became involved in electoral politics to an extent not witnessed previously.

The years 1868-86 have proved to be a watershed in the history of Ulster, especially of the six counties which now make up Northern Ireland. The period witnessed key changes at elections and in the nature of party politics that have had very considerable influence right up to the present. The conflict that emerged at this time between the powerful forces of unionism and nationalism, with their associated religious divisions, led to partition in 1921 and has provided the basic source for the troubles today in Northern Ireland. Because of the conditions and developments of these years party politics in the province took on special features and characteristics which have had enormous consequences for the political life of the community in the twentieth century. New parties of course have emerged in the present century but in their spirit and organisation they owe a very great deal to the developments of these decades.

Important, however, as these years are in the development of Ulster politics, they have received only limited attention from historians or political scientists. The two main works on Irish electoral politics during this time, D. A. Thornley's *Isaac Butt and home rule* (London, 1964) and Dr Conor Cruise O'Brien's *Parnell and his party, 1880-90* (London, 1957; corrected ed. 1964), are concerned chiefly with southern-based nationalist movements. Dr K. T. Hoppen's recent book on Irish elections covers the whole period 1832-85 and all of the country.[2] Some studies of Ulster politics have dealt briefly with these decades, and a number of articles have looked at certain elections or specific topics during the period.[3] No single work has been devoted entirely to northern elections and political developments in the crucial years 1868-86.

This book aims to fill the gap. It seeks to show how and why Ulster politics changed. Its main line of enquiry will be to study the elections, to look at the issues and the parties involved, and to see how the voters behaved. The important social changes of the period are examined and their impact on the political scene is assessed.

Attention focuses too on the changes in electoral rules, such as the franchise and ballot acts, and on the growth of different types of party organisation. Activities of the Ulster M.P.s at Westminster are examined briefly and reference also is made to political developments in the rest of Ireland. A major concern of this study is to reveal, through a very detailed investigation, just how politics operated in practice: for example, we look at how landlord influence *actually* worked and at who *exactly* had the vote.

The book falls into a number of sections. The first examines the background. What type of society was to be found in Ulster at this time? What changes occurred and what were the most important divisions? The second section deals with electoral politics in 1868-74 when the conservative landowners continued to hold a virtual monopoly of the parliamentary representation of the province but now saw the birth of a challenge to their power from the liberals, a popular conservative element, and the home-rule movement. How do we explain this landed, conservative, dominance and why did this opposition make its appearance? The third section (1874 to mid-1885) is concerned primarily with the rise of the liberal party and the growth of interdenominational voting but also studies intra-conservative conflict and the activities of the homerulers. How do we account for such developments? The fourth section looks at the general elections of 1885-6 when the Ulster electorate divided along religious lines in support of the nationalists or the unionists. What are the reasons for the success of these two parties and the failure of the liberals? Finally, some observations are made about this period and its importance.

A wide range of contemporary sources, both printed and manu-script, has been consulted. Parliamentary papers and newspapers gave much valuable information. The two-volume memoirs of Thomas MacKnight, *Ulster as it is* (London, 1896), which recounted his experiences in Ulster while editor of the liberal *Northern Whig* between 1866 and 1894, provided a useful survey of the period. The correspondence of local politicians has been examined for relevant material, as also have been the letters of politicians in the rest of Ireland and in Great Britain. A special insight into the actual opera-tion of elections was provided by the routine, everyday papers of party agents and by the documents of organisations such as the Ulster reform club.

This book then provides a detailed analysis of a very formative period in Ulster politics. Thomas MacKnight, in the first chapter of his memoirs, recorded a conversation he had with a fellow train passenger at Portadown on his first arrival in the province in 1866 which he recalled later in an attempt to explain subsequent developments.[4] The point of the dialogue was that the religious conflicts of 1641 and the past still influenced people's thoughts and actions, and thus determined events in the present. A different view, but also with an historical emphasis, was taken by Paschal Grousset, a French journalist, who wrote a book entitled *Ireland's disease: the English in Ireland,* based on visits to the country in 1886 and 1887.[5] He argued that the contemporary political developments were the outcome of a national struggle which went back to the twelfth century. For MacKnight then, the occurrences of these years were seen as the outcome of a basic, long term religious conflict while for Grousset they were viewed as the result of a fundamental, historically rooted national struggle. Both saw the final shape of politics to emerge in 1885-6 as unavoidable.

In this study, however, it will be argued that the upsurge of sectarian politics and the growth of nationalist/unionist divisions was neither predetermined nor inevitable and that it was the special conditions and developments of these years that brought about this situation. The rise of nationalist and unionist movements, based on sectarian divisions, was a result of the changes in the electoral system, of the developments in contemporary society, and, finally, of the impact and consequences of the new party organisations and leadership which emerged. Developments of the time influenced greatly the character of the new political movements and divisions that appeared in 1885-6 and have remained largely unchanged until recently.

I ULSTER SOCIETY, 1861-91

CHAPTER 1 *Country and town*

Most travellers' descriptions of Ulster in the second half of the nine-teenth century drew special attention to the growth of the towns and the development of industry in the province. J. B. Doyle, for example, in his *Tours in Ulster*, wrote graphically of 'an intensely industrious manufacturing population'.[1] Such features, when com-pared to the rest of Ireland, were indeed notable, but it must be realised that until the early twentieth century Ulster remained a predominantly rural society where the majority of people lived in the countryside and were engaged in agriculture. The census reports show that in 1861 less than 15 per cent of the population resided in towns of 2,000 inhabitants or over, while thirty years later the figure had risen to just over 27 per cent.[2] Given this predominance of the agricultural interest among the population as a whole, it is appropriate to begin a survey of Ulster society with a look at the countryside.

Land, landlords, and tenants
In the last week of April 1859 a public dinner was held at Crumlin, Co. Antrim, by tenantry of the Pakenham estate to honour their landlord, Rev. A. H. Pakenham, and his brother, Lt-col. T. H. Pakenham, M.P. for the county. Toasts were given in honour of the queen, the prince consort, the Pakenhams, and their land agent and speeches were made in acknowledgement of the good landlord–tenant relations on the Pakenham estate. An address to the Paken-hams from the assembled tenants praised the family in fulsome tone:

> They have never forgotten that 'while property has its rights, it also has its duties'; and they have always been distinguished by their kindness and their consideration for the welfare of their tenantry. They have, from the first, recognised and sustained the just rights of their tenantry, and they have always continued to act in the same spirit, never having taken advantage of the improvements effected by them.[3]

This event is interesting for two reasons. First, it is indicative of the good landlord–tenant relations that existed in this part of Ulster from the early 1850s until the 1870s. Secondly, seen in retrospect, it

1

is valuable evidence of how dramatic the change in these relations was to be, even on so model an estate as the Pakenhams'. Many of those present had by the mid-1870s become fervent critics of the landlord system. Dr G. A. Hume, secretary of the dinner committee, emerged as a leader of tenant opposition in South Antrim.[4] Others, such as W. F. McKinney, voted against landlord candidates in the 1874 and 1880 general elections and did not hesitate to bring their landlord to the newly established land courts of the 1880s to seek rent reductions.[5]

Elsewhere in Ulster the picture was similar. Until the 1870s rural society was dominated by landlords whose position was largely accepted, although not everywhere so enthusiastically as at Crumlin. Even the farmers' protest movement of the years 1848-52 had not urged the downfall of the landlords but merely called for changes in tenurial relationships.[6] There were few who publicly demanded the abolition, as opposed to the reform, of the existing land system. A notable exception was James McKnight, editor of the *Londonderry Standard*, but his approach was often rather eccentric.[7] From the early 1870s, however, the position of the landlord was questioned increasingly widely, especially in the years 1879-82, and the deferential type of rural society that had existed was undermined and eventually destroyed. It is important, therefore, to explain this dominance, both economic and social, of the gentry, and to show how it was rejected finally.

As the 1871 census disclosed, only 19·29 per cent of the Ulster population resided in towns.[8] The remainder lived in the country-side where the land was owned by landlords and occupied by farmers, the great majority of whom held yearly tenancies. A parliamentary return of 1876 showed that almost 80 per cent of the land of Ulster was the property of only 804 landowners.[9] In the same year there were 190,973 occupiers of land, of whom just over 20 per cent farmed holdings above 30 acres.[10] About 18 per cent of the holdings in Ulster were held under leases, while the rest were yearly tenancies.[11] From the early 1850s until the late 1870s the farming community in general experienced growing prosperity due to increased pro-duction and rising prices.[12]

During our period then the landlords enjoyed considerable economic power and influence in the countryside. The largest estate in Ulster in 1876 was that of the third marquis of Conyngham, who possessed 122,300 acres in Co. Donegal, although, because much of this was poor land, its rateable valuation was only £15,166. In con-trast, the sixth marquis of Downshire in the same year had 70,143 acres in Cos Down and Antrim, with a valuation of £67,708. Both Conyngham and Downshire owned land elsewhere in Ireland. The Hertford property in South Antrim in the early 1870s comprised some 66,000 acres with a population of about 20,000. There were around 4,000 holdings, of which 1,000 were leasehold and the remainder tenancies on a yearly basis. The rent of the estate in 1871 was £58,000 per annum. At the other end of the scale there were landowners such as Major James Hamilton of Ballintra, Co. Donegal, whose property of 8,507 acres had a yearly rental of just over £2,000 in the 1870s.[13]

Many of the Ulster landed families were long established and well connected. Perhaps the most notable in our period were the Hamiltons of Baronscourt, Co. Tyrone. They owned 63,657 acres in Cos Tyrone and Donegal, acquired in the seventeenth century. The second marquis of Hamilton (1811-85) was created duke of Abercorn in 1868 and served two periods as lord lieutenant of Ireland. Five of his sons became M.P.s of either English or Ulster constituencies, while seven of his daughters married English or Scottish peers.[14] New families joined this landowning group. The Youngs of Galgorm Castle, Ballymena, Co. Antrim, were former Ballymena merchants who in 1850 acquired 1,649 acres from the earl of Mountcashel, through the encumbered estates court. The very successful linen manufacturing family, the Mulhollands, purchased in the 1840s a 6,769-acre estate at Ballywalter, Co. Down, where Charles Lanyon designed for Andrew Mulholland (1792-1866) a magnificent Italian palazzo-style house.[15]

The landlords occupied an important social position in the counties and, indeed, in many of the boroughs. Normally they acted as magistrates, served as members of the grand juries, and were the principal figures in the poor law boards of guardians on which they sat as ex-officio members. In addition they usually took a leading part in local affairs. An example was Sir H. H. Bruce, conservative M.P. for Coleraine (1865-74, 1880-85) and a prominent Co. Londonderry landowner. This description of him, which appeared in a Coleraine newspaper in 1880, illustrates the prominent social role often taken by the landlords:

> As lieutenant of the county he transacts an amount of official duties of which the public are completely ignorant. He is foreman of the County Derry grand jury, chairman of the lunatic asylum board, chairman of the Coleraine bench of magistrates, chairman of the Coleraine harbour commissioners, chairman of the Derry central railway, chairman of the Coleraine board of guardians, president of the academical institution,

president of the Coleraine building society, president of the farming
society, president of the mechanics' institute, president of the Bann
rowing club, etc. He does not merely occupy these public positions, but
he takes an active interest in each one of the institutions we have named
and by his presence adds to their usefulness and prestige.[16]

Relations between landlords and tenants have frequently been
portrayed as hostile, with the former cast as harsh and the latter as
faced constantly with eviction and high rents. Recent research on
the period 1850-79, particularly by Dr W. E. Vaughan, has thrown
important new light on the subject.[17] It has been shown that evictions
were infrequent, that rents were neither high nor often raised, and
that most tenants were not impoverished but enjoyed growing
prosperity. The above account of the tenants' dinner in Crumlin
showed how tenants expected (and, in this and many other cases,
received) certain duties and rights from their landlord. But if
landlord–tenant relations were not as bad as has sometimes been
imagined, it remains true, nonetheless, that there were sources of
tension between the two parties, particularly over the question of
security because tenure was often vague and ill-defined. The
growing prosperity from 1850 onwards only served to highlight this
insecurity.

In Ulster the tenants had certain long-standing rights, which were
known collectively as the Ulster custom. This gave northern farmers
security of tenure in return for a fair rent and allowed for compensation for improvements when holdings were given up. But these
rights were not defined by law, and the insecurity that this created
was a potential source of grievance. S. C. McElroy, a prominent
figure in the Route land reform movement in Co. Antrim in the
period 1870-1900, described the situation at the beginning of this
time in the following manner: in reply to a rhetorical question about
why there had been a land reform movement in north Antrim, he
stated:

> Ask the rivers why they run to the sea — it is the potency of their being,
> the soul that is in them. Evictions were few and far between; one eviction
> would terrify a whole neighbourhood. It was the same with rackrenting,
> the same with unfree sale. The tenant held by the will of the landlord;
> the evil of the time was uncertainty of tenure, uncertainty of rent, and
> uncertainty of sale of tenant right.[18]

Nonetheless, it should be remembered that, deficient as the
Ulster custom was, it gave more security to northern farmers than
that enjoyed by farmers elsewhere in Ireland.[19] Many southern
tenants also had customary rights of tenure but these tenurial

arrangements were even less systematic and formal than in Ulster. At the same time it is worth noting that there were more leaseholds and larger farms generally in the three southern provinces than in the north.[20] The benefits of rising agricultural prices were enjoyed equally by southern and northern farmers, and the prosperity of counties such as Kildare and Meath were on a par with the wealthiest northern counties, as reflected in such matters as the level of housing standards.[21]

In the late 1840s and early 1850s the land question had aroused strong interest among tenant farmers in Ulster as well as in the rest of Ireland. The agrarian movement that appeared failed to achieve reform, however, and the issue was relegated to the background owing to the growing prosperity of Irish farming after 1853 and the unlikelihood of change. Interest in the subject picked up in the second part of the 1860s, perhaps as a result of expressed concern on the Irish land question from several English politicians such as Gladstone and John Bright. From 1867 tenant right meetings began to be held in Ulster and in other parts of Ireland.[22] .

The Irish land act of 1870 failed to improve matters.[23] It provided legal recognition of the Ulster custom in Ulster and well established tenurial practices elsewhere. In practice, however, its weaknesses dashed hopes and added to the spread of the land reform movement. As early as April 1870 James McKnight, editor of the *Londonderry Standard*, wrote to Gladstone: 'Already the notable deficiencies of the bill, as contrasted with popular hope . . . have begun to excite among the people a spirit of embittered discontent.'[24] Problems arose over the fact that there was no uniform Ulster custom. Attempts to define it in the courts embittered landlord–tenant relations since each of the parties had different views on what their rights were. Moreover, the act did not protect leaseholders. In regard to the new law, S. C. McElroy commented: 'In fact its failure brought rights more prominently to the footlights.'[25]

On 19 November 1869 the Route tenants' defence association had been formed at Ballymoney, and it was followed in the early 1870s by a number of other tenant groups such as the Down farmers' union, established in May 1872 to 'preserve tenant farmers in their rights.'[26] By October 1873 there were at least five tenant right associations in Co. Londonderry.[27] In January 1874, delegates from twenty-nine tenant right organisations, nineteen of them based in Ulster, attended a national conference in Belfast. The speakers strongly criticised the 1870 land act, and resolutions were passed that defined the Ulster custom as embracing continued occupancy

at a fair rent as well as free sale, and a call was made for its full legislation throughout the country.[28]

Several points are worth noting about these Ulster tenant right
associations. First, they were composed of fairly well-to-do farmers.
Describing events after the inaugural meeting of the Route association, S. C. McElroy noted: 'In the evening a great soiree was held
in the town hall . . . the assemblage embraced the flower of the
middle classes.'[29] Second, in their origins they were essentially
moderate bodies, which respected the right of landlords to own land
and profit from it. A public letter about the aims of the Down
farmers' union in 1872 indicated that this organisation sought to
improve the position of the tenant and 'at the same time to secure
to the landlord well paid rents and create over the country a
prosperous tenantry'. Likewise in Co. Monaghan, the Farney
tenants' association was established in the early 1870s to agitate for
improvements to the tenants' lot, but still it respected the rights of
landlords (as did most tenants' associations in the rest of Ireland in
the 1860s and 1870s).[30]

The movement for land reform continued to grow during the
1870s. New tenant right associations were formed, such as the
Monaghan tenants' defence association, set up in August 1875.[31] In
Co. Antrim the various tenant right bodies joined together in the
Antrim central tenant right association in June 1876.[32] The campaign
for reform was given fresh impetus by the agricultural depression
that struck the Irish countryside, beginning in 1877. A decline in
farm prices and a series of poor harvests resulted in considerable
distress. Although not so badly affected as Connacht, Ulster did not
go unscathed. In Co. Donegal the situation was most serious, while
in Cavan, Fermanagh, Monaghan, and Tyrone, certain areas were
hard hit.[33] Elsewhere conditions were better, but all over the province by 1880 farmers had experienced falling incomes.[34] The land
league was formed in Mayo in late 1879, but it had little impact in
Ulster before mid-1880. Tenant right associations, however, continued to swell in numbers.

This rising wave of discontent and organised activity over the land
question continued unabated throughout 1880 and into 1881.
During these two years there was a high number of evictions in
Ulster but fewer agrarian outrages than elsewhere.[35] Not only did
the tenant right organisations persist in demanding fair rents, free
sale, and fixity of tenure (the 'three Fs')[36] but from the autumn of
1880 the land league spread to many parts of the province. There
was considerable cooperation between branches of the land league

and tenant right associations, as Sir Thomas Bateson, a prominent northern landowner and conservative, lamented to Lord Salisbury in late December 1880:

> A few weeks since the land league invaded Ulster. Up to that moment rents were cheerfully paid without even a murmur. Now all that is changed. The league operates in concert with the central radical tenant right association, and the result is a general strike on the part of the tenants — men who voted for the conservatives last April are now openly fraternising with democrats, who six weeks ago they would not have touched with a long pole, and the wave of communism has spread like wildfire. The demand is 25, 30, and in some cases 50 per cent permanent reduction of rents on the plea of low prices caused by American importation.[37]

At land meetings in late 1880 and during the first half of 1881 in the north the speakers from the various parties, including home rulers, dwelt almost exclusively on the land question.[38] Throughout the same period liberal and nationalist politicians cooperated in the tenant right movement, although there were certain signs of tension.[39] Meetings were organised, sometimes by landlords, against the land league, which was accused of being tainted with republicanism, but even those meetings could not entirely ignore the land question.[40] A meeting held in Co. Monaghan in December 1880 to protest against land league activities was described by one of its supporters as a 'tenant right anti-land league Orange meeting'.[41] In December 1880 the Orange emergency committee was set up to combat the league, while a group of landowners formed the property defence association. Nevertheless, the activities of the northern tenant right movement played a crucial role in persuading Gladstone to introduce his 1881 land act.[42]

By the end of 1881, however, serious divisions had appeared within the ranks of the land movement. These were a result of differences in the aims and methods of the organisations involved, the increase of distress in the south and west, and internal political conflict. The northern tenant right associations tended to be more moderate than the land league, and called for the rights of tenants while the league demanded the abolition of landlordism.[43] In the southern provinces, where distress was worse than in the north and where the land league was strongest, the league organised action against the collection of rents and against evictions. Gladstone's land act of 1881 gave fair rent, free sale, and fixity of tenure to tenants but met with differing responses from the two wings of the tenant movement and their political supporters.

Most of the tenant right associations in the north were allied closely to the liberals and declared their approval of this liberal act.[44] Parnellite leadership of the land league, however, took a hostile attitude towards the new legislation and at a convention of the league in mid-September the land act was strongly criticised. The league continued its meetings and activities. In October Parnell was arrested and shortly afterwards the land league was declared an illegal organisation. After its suppression the ladies' land league carried on its work. Parnell and his followers were eventually released from jail and in October 1882 they formed the Irish national league with the main object of national self-government, and other secondary aims that included reform of the land laws.[45] During the second half of 1881, however, cooperation between land league branches and tenant right associations had declined. There is little evidence of goodwill between the national league and the tenant associations.

This collapse in sympathy between the different wings of the land movement is seen clearly in the columns of the *Impartial Reporter* in Enniskillen. Under the editorship of W. C. Trimble, a strong supporter of tenant right, the paper expressed considerable sympathy with the land league in Fermanagh up to August 1881 and urged cooperation among all involved in seeking reform. But on 11 August, in response to a violent speech by a prominent member of the land league at a meeting in the county, the paper stated that the land league in Fermanagh had been on the old lines of tenant right and warned that it should not advance any further. A week later the paper welcomed the land act and from this time on became increasingly critical of Parnell, his advocacy of land reform and self-government openly on the same platform, and his increased militancy as seen in the 'no rent manifesto'. On 22 December Trimble chaired a meeting in Enniskillen to revive the Fermanagh farmers' association which had lapsed in face of the land league.[46]

Nonetheless, in spite of these divisions, concern with the land question remained alive in rural Ulster. In the years that followed, tenants sought rent reductions in the new land courts; and peasant proprietorship, along with the exclusion of leaseholders from the benefits of the 1881 land act, became salient issues. Organisation continued among Ulster farmers to promote their demands, though clearly at a slower pace because some of the most important aims had already been achieved. In January 1883 the Ulster land committee was formed as a central body representing the various tenant-right associations in the province.[47] The national league sponsored a campaign in the north in 1883, and a number of branches were set up, but rapid growth did not come until 1885 and 1886.

The Ashbourne act of 1885 gave important new facilities for land purchase, although many regarded them as inadequate. From their inception the Ulster tenant right organisations had tended to be more moderate than the land league, but by 1886 both supported the compulsory sale of estates. The northern tenant righters, however, saw peasant proprietorship as a long-term process, and in the meantime they sought to advance the farmers' interests. In its memorial to Gladstone in 1886, the Antrim central tenant right association declared: 'The terms of the Ulster plantation settlement were intended to secure to the tenants the occupation of their holdings at easy rents.'[48] The national league, on the other hand, demanded an immediate end to landlordism, and asserted that the landlords had stolen the land from the people. One speaker, at a meeting of the Donoughmore branch of the national league in November 1885, assured his listeners that 'the land they lived on once belonged to their ancestors free of rent and free of burden, possessed in joint ownership with the chiefs of Donegal.'[49]

In spite of organisational fissures and ideological differences among northern tenants, their relations with landlords everywhere underwent dramatic change. The position of the gentry in society had been challenged. H. H. McNeile, a Co. Antrim proprietor, lamented their lost status to Lord Cairns in February 1882. 'Where a year ago there was good feeling and courtesy', he observed, 'there is now a defiant take-what-you-can, you-are-lucky-to-get-anything sort of feeling, even among the best of the tenantry.'[50] On boards of guardians the exclusive leadership of the gentry was questioned and the right of farmers to a share of power asserted. Landlords still retained prominent positions on these boards and in local affairs generally, but the extent of their dominance had been irrevocably questioned by the farmers throughout Ulster, who had developed a new political and social consciousness of their own, with profound consequences, thanks to the agrarian issue.[51]

During the period from the early 1850s to the mid-1880s, organised political activity among tenant farmers was greatest in Co. Londonderry. Special circumstances help to explain the high level of agrarian unrest in this county. By the middle of the nineteenth century over half the land in Co. Londonderry was still owned by the London companies under the original grants of the plantation of the early 1600s. In the eighteenth century the companies had leased their estates to middlemen and, when these leases expired during the early nineteenth century, the companies sought to pursue a more rigorous estate policy.[52] For example, the Salters' and Ironmongers' companies took active steps in the 1860s to limit the occupier's right to sell his tenant right for its full market value. After a revaluation in 1872, the Skinners' company raised rents on their estate, as the Salters' company had already done in the 1850s and 1860s.[53] These steps by the companies caused considerable popular resentment.[54]

Finally, mention must be made of the labourers in the Ulster countryside. In 1871 they numbered 194,097, of whom half were indoor farm servants and half were agricultural labourers who lived in cottages that belonged to farmers or landlords.[55] Although in 1871 their numbers were greater than those of the farmers (157,898 in 1871) they were a declining section of the rural population. By 1892 there were 111,151 labourers compared to 129,667 farmers.[56] During the second half of the nineteenth century their conditions changed for the better but by the 1890s the quality of their houses and the level of wages were still in need of considerable improvement. In spite of their deprivations there was no sign of serious resentment between the labourers and either the landlords or the farmers.[57] Labourers in Ulster took little part in the conflict between landlords and farmers and did not benefit from the change in legal relations between these two parties. Indeed in some cases standards of dwellings and wages for labourers were better under landlords than farmers.[58]

Towns, industry, and local urban politics
While Ulster society in the late nineteenth century was predominantly rural, there were nonetheless many flourishing towns in the province. The best example was Belfast which W. M. Thackeray had described in 1842 as 'hearty, thriving, and prosperous, as if it had money in its pocket and roast beef for dinner'.[59] The 1868 *Chambers Encyclopaedia* commented: 'The general aspect of Belfast is indicative of life and prosperity, exhibiting all the trade and commerce of Glasgow and Manchester, with far less of their smoke and dirt.' Twenty years later Belfast was officially designated a city. The population increased from just under 100,000 in 1851 to over a third of a million at the end of the century: indeed Belfast grew faster than any other urban centre in the British Isles in the second half of the nineteenth century.[60]

The drive and spirit of Victorian Belfast is well illustrated by R. J. Welch's photograph of the grand trades arch that was erected in Donegall Square for the visit of the prince and princess of Wales in 1885.[61] Around the edge of the arch were the words 'Man goeth forth unto his work and to his labour until the evening' and 'Trade is the golden girdle of the globe.' Other slogans proclaimed 'Employment is nature's physician' and 'Temperance is a girdle of gold .' Models of a steam engine, a loom, and a ship on the arch represented the great industries of engineering, linen, and shipbuilding that were the basis of Belfast's remarkable growth and prosperity. By 1881 there were nearly 75,000 people employed in the industries of Belfast.[62]

Although Belfast was exceptional in the extent of its growth, other towns in Ulster, especially in the north-east, also witnessed expansion and rising prosperity, thanks chiefly to the linen industry. The urban centres most affected were Ballymena, Lisburn, Lurgan, Portadown, Coleraine, Newry, and Derry. Even smaller towns, such as Killyleagh and Castlewellan in Co. Down, often had the benefits of a substantial linen mill located in their area. Industrial communities gathered round factories at places such as Drumaness and Shrigley, Co. Down, Bessbrook, Co. Armagh, and Sion Mills, Co. Tyrone. Bessbrook, for example, was a village built by the Richardson family (prominent quakers) for their mill workers, and had various amenities such as a school, recreational hall, and library, but, thanks to the Richardsons, no public houses.[63]

This economic development in the north of Ireland caused a substantial growth in the number of industrial workers. By the 1880s, however, there was still relatively little trade union organisation apart from engineering unions, which seem to have been mainly concerned with protecting their position from other workers.[64] The growth of Belfast and these towns had another important outcome, as Professor J. L. McCracken has pointed out, namely an increase in the prosperity and numbers of the middle classes:

> The development of industry and business brought wealth to some and a considerable degree of comfort to many others. The leading businessmen had their country estates or their fine houses along the shore of the lough, the less opulent their substantial terrace houses built farther and farther from the centre of the towns as transport improved. New opportunities opened up for white-collared workers in business, insurance and banking, and the older professions expanded remarkably: there were two to three times as many more doctors, lawyers, teachers, and clergymen in Belfast at the end of the century as there had been thirty years before.[65]

Some of these merchants and industrialists were from established families such as the Richardsons of Lisburn and Bessbrook, but many were new arrivals, particularly linen manufacturers, who appeared about 1850 and, like T. A. Dickson of Dungannon, were to prosper greatly in the early 1860s due to the linen boom caused by the American civil war.[66]

The benefits of manufacturing industry in Ulster, however, affected not only the towns, but also the surrounding countryside. The cultivation of flax for the linen business greatly benefited northern farmers. The growing towns and expanding factories gave the rural population good markets for their produce and alternative means of employment. The industrial and commercial prosperity of Ulster helped most of the province to escape the worst effects of the great famine and to suffer less subsequently from population decline, caused by the move from tillage to pasture and the consolidation of farms.[67] The population as a whole fell by only one third between 1841 and 1911 while in the rest of the country it declined by one half.[68] Thanks particularly to the growth of Belfast, the north east of the province found alternative employment for many of those leaving the land: in the rest of the province, however, there was also a considerable population decline.[69]

Little of this industrial and urban expansion occurred in the rest of Ireland. There were, of course, important centres of population and of commerce such as Dublin and Cork. But there was no industry to compare with the linen and shipbuilding industries in the north. Many of the towns declined in population although there was expansion in the Dublin area, and in Leinster a higher percentage of the inhabitants lived in towns than in Ulster.[70] The professions, however, increased in numbers as in Ulster. A point worth noting in regard to the economies of Ulster and the other provinces is that in its growth as the major industrial centre in the country Belfast was less connected with the internal economy of Ireland than with raw materials from Great Britain and export markets there and elsewhere in the world.[71]

An important urban development in the nineteenth century was the appearance of locally elected bodies to deal with municipal affairs. Several acts of the late 1820s and 1830s gave towns the right to have elected boards of commissioners or councillors to look after certain local matters; the scope of their duties was enlarged by further acts. From the 1830s towns in Ulster came increasingly to avail of these powers of local government, with important consequences. The boards gave townspeople valuable political experience. An examination of the names of local commissioners in the Ulster towns in the middle 1860s shows many who later became deeply involved in parliamentary politics and in the tenant right associations.[72] Also, as commissioners sought to increase their powers, this sometimes brought them into conflict with the gentry, who still had an important say in local matters. At an enquiry into local government in 1877 Edward Gardner, chairman of the Downpatrick commissioners, expressed dissatisfaction that the board of guardians had control over certain matters in the town such as the sanitary arrangements, about which he believed the guardians knew nothing: 'they are generally country gentlemen, particularly the ex-officio guardians'.[73]

In Enniskillen conflict broke out in the late 1840s between the earl of Enniskillen and the town commissioners over the ownership of some corporate property. The principal individual involved was John Collum, who had obtained from the commissioners the lease of part of this property, claimed by the earl.[74] Collum and his sons were to be bitter rivals of the earl of Enniskillen and his family in the parliamentary elections from 1850 to 1880. But while these developments in local government and the rise of new merchant and professional families in the towns sometimes brought the townspeople into conflict with the local landowners or the neighbouring gentry, it should be realised that often the townspeople and the local 'lord of the soil' remained on amicable terms. This was especially the case in Lisburn, where many accounts tell of the liberality of the proprietor, Sir Richard Wallace, and his good relations with the commissioners and inhabitants.[75]

Local government affairs in Carrickfergus developed rather differently from elsewhere.[76] By the mid-1860s there was bitter hostility in Carrickfergus between the town commissioners and the freemen, a numerous body, over the question of ownership of common land. This caused a number of expensive court cases and the matter ended only when M. R. Dalway, a leading townsman and supporter of the freemen in the conflict, was appointed chairman of the board of commissioners in early 1874 and given the power to arrange for the letting of the land to certain of the freemen. However, the popularity that Dalway had gained among the freemen up to this point disappeared owing to his method of distribution of the land. A petition signed by 300 freemen in complaint against his actions was sent to the lords of the treasury. Dalway was elected as M.P. for the town in 1868 and 1874, but defeated in 1880.

This survey of the Ulster countryside and towns in 1861-91 reveals a number of important cleavages; certain of these assumed a special significance during our period. These included social divisions between landlords and tenants, gentry and business and professional people, and manufacturers and workers. There were sectional differences between the prosperous, industrialised north-east of Ulster and the rest of the country, and between the northern farmers with their Ulster custom and farmers elsewhere who had less security. Some of the conflicts to emerge from these divisions, such as that between landlord and tenant, would clearly have important consequences for politics.

CHAPTER 2 *Religion*

When W. M. Thackeray visited Belfast in 1842 he noted that there were 'violent disputes' between the different parts of the Christian church over various issues. Not only did protestant and catholic quarrel with each other, but presbyterians and members of the Church of Ireland were engaged in argument.[1] Had Thackeray returned twenty-six years later, at the beginning of our period in 1868, he would again have found heated controversy between the denominations over the question of the disestablishment of the Church of Ireland. By 1870 this issue had been settled but there remained conflicts between the various churches. Religious divisions with their inter-related social differences continued to have an influential bearing on the life of the people of the province and are the subject of investigation in the first part of this chapter. Education and the press are also looked at because of their religious dimension.

Religious divisions
Ulster is often thought of as a predominantly protestant region. But in 1861 it was 50·5 per cent catholic. By 1871, however, the catholic percentage of the population had fallen to 48·9 and twenty years later it stood at 46·0. This fall was due to the fact that most industrial expansion was in the east of the province where protestants predominated. Of the protestants in the province, the presbyterians were the largest single group, and members of the Church of Ireland were the next biggest. In 1871, for example, presbyterians were 26·1 per cent, members of the Church of Ireland 21·5 per cent, methodists 1·6 per cent, and others 1·9 per cent.[2] There was considerable variation in denominational distribution within the province, as can be seen in tables 1a and 1b.

1a: Percentage distribution of denominations in the Ulster counties (excluding parliamentary boroughs), 1871.[3]

denominations

counties	cath.	C. of I.	pres.	meth.	others
Antrim	23·5	18·6	53·2	1·1	3·7
Armagh	46·9	32·9	16·1	2·6	1·6

counties	cath.	C. of I.	pres.	meth.	others
Cavan	80·4	15·1	3·6	0·7	0·2
Donegal	75·7	12·1	10·6	0·8	0·5
Down	30·4	21·8	43·2	1·3	3·2
Fermanagh	55·9	37·9	1·9	4·1	0·2
Monaghan	73·4	13·6	12·1	0·4	0·5
Tyrone	55·6	22·7	19·7	1·4	0·6
Total	51·1	20·6	25·3	1·3	1·7

Some important observations can be made from these figures. While there were members of each main denomination in every county, the counties can conveniently be divided into several types. First there are the three counties of Antrim, Down, and Londonderry, where not only were protestants a clear majority, but presbyterians made up the largest protestant group. Secondly, there are the three mid-Ulster counties of Armagh, Fermanagh, and Tyrone, where protestants accounted for slightly over or slightly under 50 per cent, but members of the Church of Ireland were the most numerous protestant section. Finally, there are the three counties of Monaghan, Cavan, and Donegal where catholics formed a substantial majority and members of the Church of Ireland and presbyterians made up similar numbers in two but not in the third.

In the parliamentary boroughs there were also marked differences in religious distribution, as can be seen in table 1b.

1b: Percentage distribution of denominations in the Ulster parliamentary boroughs, 1871.

counties	cath.	C. of I.	pres.	meth.	others
Armagh	52·4	33·8	10·3	2·6	0·9
Belfast	31·9	26·6	34·5	3·9	3·1
Carrickfergus	10·6	17·3	58·1	3·7	10·2
Coleraine	21·5	34·4	35·8	3·7	4·7
Derry	54·8	20·3	21·6	1·1	2·3
Downpatrick	44·4	31·9	20·7	1·4	1·5
Dungannon	55·2	30·0	12·3	2·0	0·5
Enniskillen	56·1	35·9	3·0	3·9	1·1
Lisburn	23·0	50·5	19·7	4·0	2·9
Newry	64·0	18·4	13·2	1·4	3·0

In Armagh, Newry, Derry, Dungannon, and Enniskillen catholics were in a majority; in Belfast and Downpatrick they were present in substantial numbers, although not a majority; and in Carrickfergus,

Coleraine, and Lisburn their proportions of the populations were small. Protestants, however, made up over two-thirds of the population of Belfast, which had more than twice as many people as all the other Ulster parliamentary boroughs put together.[4] Presbyterians were a majority in Carrickfergus, and the largest protestant group in Belfast, Coleraine, and Derry. Members of the Church of Ireland numbered over half only in Lisburn but formed the biggest single protestant denomination in Armagh, Downpatrick, Dungannon, Enniskillen, and Newry. Methodists were not numerous in any of the towns, and in Lisburn alone were they as much as 4 per cent of the population. Other denominations numbered 10·2 per cent in Carrickfergus, for reasons that are not clear, but elsewhere they were not significant.

Besides these variations in distribution there were important social and economic differences between the denominations. To illustrate this point, table 1c gives a number of the more significant male occupations in the 1871 census and shows the proportions of each religious group in these categories.

1c: Percentage of each denomination engaged in various occupations in Ulster, 1871 (males only)[5]

	total	cath.	C. of I.	pres.	meth.	others
	879,805	48.9	21·4	26·2	2·2	1·9
professional						
civil service	758	33·1	36·7	24·1	3·6	2·5
magistrates	132	7·6	80·3	9·8	0·8	1·5
police	2,979	57·4	30·7	10·4	2·8	1·9
clergy	2,043	27·1	33·5	28·8	7·2	3·4
lawyers (solicitors and barristers)	311	14·1	57·2	22·5	1·3	5·1
teachers	3,006	39·5	28·3	28·2	2·0	1·9
domestic						
hotel keepers/ publicans	2,216	55·5	18·8	24·0	0·5	1·2
domestic servants	4,470	46·3	32·7	19·3	0·8	0·9
commercial						
merchants	1,539	22·3	25·5	41·2	5·8	5·2
commercial clerks	3,405	15·9	28·2	43·1	6·1	5·0
shopkeepers (branch undefined)	3,328	59·7	17·6	20·0	1·8	0·8

	total	cath.	C. of I.	pres.	meth.	others
agriculture						
proprietors	904	24·2	48·2	22·2	2·1	3·2
farmers	157,898	52·9	17·1	27·4	1·4	1·2
agricultural labourers[6]	99,718	57·3	20·5	21·0	0·5	0·6
farm servants (indoor)	94,379	63·1	14·8	20·6	0·7	0·7
industrial						
workers in linen manufacture	25,371	30·4	29·8	35·5	1·7	2·7
weavers	12,756	26·6	34·5	34·4	2·6	2·0
workers in shipbuilding	1,064	16·9	28·0	49·2	2·7	2·2
workers in iron manufacture	1,023	25·4	29·0	38·5	4·0	3·0
engine and machine making and selling	1,352	25·3	26·7	40·2	5·2	2·7

Useful as these statistics are, however, they must be supplemented
with information from other sources to give a proper picture of the
social and economic differences between the denominations. First,
the agricultural section may be looked at because it was the largest
one. As the general report in the 1871 census remarks, the statistics
for proprietors give a false impression as they include very minor
owners of land.[7] In fact the proprietors of the vast bulk of Irish land
were nearly all Church of Ireland. In Ulster there were no major
catholic or presbyterian landowners and even among the smaller
landowners there were few who did not belong to the Church of
Ireland. Catholics and protestants were represented among the
tenant farmers in roughly similar proportions to their numbers in
the population but, generally speaking, the larger and better farms
were held by protestants. Where presbyterians were present they
tended to occupy more prosperous farms than members of the
Church of Ireland.

These points are well illustrated in a study, by Mr Jack Johnston,
of the Clogher valley in South Tyrone, an area with a population
numbering around 22,000 in 1871, of whom just over 50 per cent
were catholic, slightly over half of the remainder were presbyterian,
and the others belonged to the Church of Ireland.[8] Members of the
Church of Ireland included nearly all of the landowners and also
many poor parishioners in the small farmer group but few in the
large tenant farmer group. In 1860, of 37 occupiers in the Clogher

valley with a rateable valuation of £60 or more, only one was a catholic. The presbyterian community included most of the wealthiest tenant stock, as can be seen from the fact that they were strongest in the highest rated electoral divisions.

Other commentators, both contemporary and modern, have confirmed this view that in Ulster the landowners were nearly all Church of Ireland, the larger tenant farmers tended to be presbyterian, and the medium-sized and smaller farmers usually Church of Ireland or catholic.[9] In a description of the part of Co. Donegal where he was brought up in the 1870s, Stephen Gwynn commented: 'The presbyterians were strong middle-class farmers and shopkeepers; the gentry were without exception of the Irish Church; and the gentry ruled the country absolutely, with the assistance of the rectors.'[10] Certain qualifications, however, must be borne in mind when considering these general statements about rural society. While the best farms tended to be held by protestants, and the poorest farms by catholics, society in the Ulster countryside cannot be viewed simply as consisting of well-to-do protestants and impoverished catholics, for several reasons.

In the first place, the best farms were relatively few in number, Church of Ireland farmers often had medium or small-sized farms, and there were many medium-sized farms held by catholics. In the whole of Co. Tyrone in 1870 there were only 565 holdings at £50 and over, out of a total of 35,331; yet in 1871 there were in the county 24,314 farmers of whom 5,257 were presbyterian.[11] In Clogher and elsewhere farms occupied by members of the Church of Ireland tended to be smaller than those held by presbyterians.[12] An indication of the number of catholic medium-sized farmers can be found in the figures for the county franchise, which required a person to occupy land valued at over £12: underrepresented in proportion to their ratio in the population, catholics were nonetheless present in significant strength. Catholics in 1881 in Tyrone were 55·5 per cent of the population and 26 per cent of the electorate: in Antrim the respective figures were 22·7 and 19 per cent.[13] Studies of both Monaghan and Fermanagh in the nineteenth century show numbers of substantial catholic farmers.[14]

Secondly, there were many protestant labourers. As we can see in the percentage of each denomination among the agricultural labourers in 1871, catholics, who were 48·9 per cent of the Ulster population, were over-represented among the labourers with a percentage of 57·3, and among the indoor farm servants with 63·1 per cent. The protestants were proportionately under-represented but still constituted a considerable proportion of the labourers and farm servants. Members of the Church of Ireland were 21·4 per cent of the population and 20·5 per cent of the labourers. However, presbyterians were 26·2 per cent of the population and 21·0 per cent of the labourers, while methodists were 1·6 per cent of the population and 0·7 per cent of the labourers. This disparity between protestant and catholic in the rural labouring population is mainly explained by the larger number of protestants engaged as workers or as weavers in the industrial section.

The fact that the landowners were nearly all Church of Ireland was probably an important influence on the attitudes of farmers, although specifically religious matters were not referred to on land reform platforms. It may be noted that tenant right activity was keenest among presbyterians and catholics.[15] Presbyterian ministers, such as N. M. Brown of Limavady, and catholic priests, such as J. P. O'Boyle of Saintfield, played an influential part in the tenant right movement and frequently appeared on the platform together at land meetings.[16] There does not seem to be any known instance of Church of Ireland clergy taking part in tenant right or land league activity. Some of the tenant right activists in Fermanagh belonged to the Church of Ireland, as did a number of supporters elsewhere, but compared with other denominations members of the Church of Ireland were not greatly involved in this movement. The religious difference between landlords and many of the tenants, therefore, was probably an additional element in the hostility between farmers and landlords.[17]

At the same time mention must be made of the rivalry that could sometimes manifest itself between catholics and protestants over the occupation of land. At the meeting of the Fermanagh county grand Orange lodge on 20 November 1879, a resolution from a district lodge was read out to draw the attention of Orangemen 'to the efforts which Roman Catholics are too successfully making for the purchase of farms and estates of protestants in Ireland' and to urge steps to be taken to counter these efforts.[18] On the other hand, in Coleraine in 1863 the local St Vincent de Paul society expressed concern that landlords were taking protestant tenants in preference to catholic ones and urged that money be allocated to help needy local catholic farmers.[19]

Nonetheless, in the land reform movement there was considerable cooperation between protestant and catholic farmers. The tenant right associations in Ulster in the 1870s were strongest in north-east Ulster and among presbyterians but there was considerable catholic involvement.[20] Some associations in southern and western Ulster, such as the two main Monaghan tenant organisations, were predominantly catholic with a strong catholic clerical leadership.[21] There was widespread cooperation between tenant right associations and local branches of the land league in 1880 and 1881. Although the land league was strongest in catholic areas,[22] there is evidence that in many districts protestants did join it.

In Co. Armagh, shortly before his arrest in early 1881, Michael Davitt spoke at a land league meeting after which a local correspondent noted, perhaps with some exaggeration, 'Orangemen that day joined the league in vast numbers.'[23] This, however, was not an isolated incident. The *Impartial Reporter* in Co. Fermanagh on 12 December 1880 remarked: 'One of the signs of the times is the union of Orangemen, protestants, and catholics in accepting the league in Derrygonnelly.'[24] Two Fermanagh Orange lodges had their warrants cancelled because of land league activity by their members.[25] As regards Co. Monaghan, Rev. D. C. Abbot wrote: 'most of the presbyterians, and younger methodists, and I may say all the Romanists go in the "whole length of the unclean animal" with the land league.'[26] The correspondence of landlords, agents and their associates underscores the pervasive reality that farmers of all denominations and political backgrounds were uniting behind the banner of agrarian reform.[27]

During the second half of 1881, however, divisions appeared in this protestant–catholic cooperation, thanks to the different attitudes of the land league and most of the northern tenant associations to the new land act. Disagreement over this matter led to the breakdown of the alliance of these two wings of the local land movement and consequently a decline in the unity of protestant and catholic farmers. By late 1881, as the example of Co. Fermanagh shows, most protestants had left the land league, and they shunned also the new national league formed a year later.[28] In some areas catholics continued to be involved in tenant right associations but in others they were attracted eventually to the national league.

In June 1882 Sir Thomas Bateson was able to give Lord Salisbury a very different description of the situation from that of eighteen months earlier (see above p. 7).

> I have just come back from the north of Ireland. There has been a considerable change in the feelings of the better class of liberal presbyterians since the Kilmainham treaty and the Dublin assassinations. The same applies to the democratic presbyterian farmers. They approved rightly

[sic] of the spirit of communism which transferred 25 per cent of the landlords' property to the tenant farmers but they are greatly alarmed at the nationalisation scheme of Mr Davitt and his confederates. They think that confiscation should not be extended to their class or rather in favour of the class below them. They hold that communism has been pushed far enough, and there seems to be a growing feeling that the policy of the national party is to stamp out the English garrison, and make Ireland a purely R. Catholic country. There is throughout Ulster a growing distrust of the R. Catholics on the part of the protestant farmers, and with the exception of the ruinous cutting down of rents by the land commissioners, things are, from what I can gather, better than they were a few months ago. I speak of the protestant districts of Ulster only.[29]

There is no other evidence that fear of land nationalisation was an important factor in the collapse of protestant farmer support for the land league and the national league. But the close association of these bodies with nationalist aims resulted in the alienation of most northern protestant tenants.[30] On the other hand, many catholics were attracted to the new political stance of the land league and national league and were happy to support them, although in some areas like Co. Monaghan this did not happen on a significant scale until mid-1883.[31]

A further source of tension between catholic and protestant tenant farmers arose in the 1880s over the land league and national league demand that land should be returned to the ownership of the 'people'. This aroused fear among protestant farmers that they would be dispossessed and their land given to catholics, although this was strongly denied by the national league.[32] Some of the landlords shared this fear. Sir Thomas Bateson forwarded to the marquis of Salisbury in 1886 a letter from a landowner in South Down, Major W. J. Hall, of Narrow Water Castle, Warrenpoint, who said that the national league branch in his area had held a ballot for his land and intended to leave him only an eight-acre mountain farm to live on; a further meeting of the league decided to change their plans and instead to give him only a second-class boat ticket to England, after his land was redistributed.[33]

Attention may now be turned to some of the other groups in table 1c. In the professional section, members of the Church of Ireland were considerably over-represented in most of the principal categories in proportion to their size in the population. But this situation was changing as presbyterians and catholics increased their numbers in many of these categories. By 1891 there were in Ulster 480 lawyers of whom 22·3 per cent were catholic, 38·3 per cent Church of Ireland, and 29·2 per cent presbyterian. By 1891 the number of clergy had increased by only 16 but out of the total catholics had grown to 31·7 per cent, presbyterians had slipped slightly to 26·2 per cent, and members of the Church of Ireland had fallen considerably to 28·4 per cent.[34] Church of Ireland members predominated among the magistrates as they did among the part-time justices of the peace who were not recorded in the census report but, according to a later parliamentary return, 72·6 per cent of the Ulster J.P.s in 1884 belonged to the Church of Ireland, while 14·0 per cent were presbyterian and 8·5 per cent catholic.[35]

Resentment was often felt in catholic and presbyterian circles about the predominance of Church of Ireland persons in official positions such as the magistracy.[36] The liberals tried to appoint more presbyterians and catholics to these posts. In the case of the selection of J.P.s difficulty was encountered because of the customary requirement that magistrates should be substantial occupiers or landowners. Accepting the point about the need for more catholic and presbyterian magistrates, Thomas O'Hagan, lord chancellor, commented in a letter to James McKnight of Derry in 1870:

> This matter of magisterial appointments is very difficult especially in the north where the social status of the Roman Catholics and even of the presbyterians makes many selections of fit persons often impracticable . . . I do not think that your Derry politicians or some of the northern liberal journals do justice to the government, certainly there is a most genuine desire to give confidence in the administration of justice by the appointments of fair and impartial men.[37]

In a letter to John Harbison of Cookstown about the appointment of catholic magistrates, O'Hagan remarked that he had turned down a Mr Fay in Co. Cavan for such a post because, although he earned two or three thousand pounds a year, he was in the retail trade, and the government wished to avoid recommending such persons 'on the ground of the danger of influence being exerted by customers and others'.[38] One of the Fay family subsequently became home rule M.P. for Co. Cavan.

The domestic, commercial, and industrial sections of the census figures for Ulster in 1871 reflect also interesting differences between the denominations, compared with their proportions of the population. Catholics were over-represented among hotel keepers and publicans while members of the Church of Ireland were over-represented among domestic servants. Catholics were more numerous among the general shopkeepers than the other denominations, while presbyterians predominated among commercial clerks. In the industrial section protestants were over-represented in proportion to their numbers in the population, partly because they were most numerous in the east of the province, where such industries predominated. Besides being a high percentage of categories such as weavers and workers in linen manufacture, protestants were pre-eminent among the skilled crafts like shipbuilding and engineering. In contrast, catholics were over-represented among semi- or non-skilled workers.

If we look more closely at this protestant dominance of skilled crafts, it soon becomes clear that it is in fact a presbyterian dominance. Comparing the proportion of the denominations of workers in shipbuilding, iron work and machine work, based very largely in Belfast, with the proportions of these denominations in the Belfast population in 1871, (see tables 1b and 1c), members of the Church of Ireland are represented in a proportion roughly equal to their strength in the population, but catholics are under-represented and presbyterians over-represented. This presbyterian dominance of skilled jobs is undoubtedly a result of their markedly higher literacy: in 1871 in Belfast, of persons aged five years and upwards who were illiterate, the figure for catholics was 28·1 per cent, Church of Ireland members 14·0 per cent and presbyterians only 7·4 per cent.[39] Differences between the denominations in educational standards did drop eventually, but their early lead gave protestants, especially presbyterians, a dominance in these new, growing industries, which family tradition, closed work practices and, (in particular after 1885-6), membership of organisations such as the Orange order, helped to maintain.

The merchants in Ulster at this time were predominantly protestant but, in this instance as well, presbyterians were the largest section while members of the Church of Ireland were only slightly higher in proportion to their numerical strength in the population and catholics were under-represented. The census report does not give separate figures for industrialists and manufacturers but the picture here was probably similar. A survey of the leading businessmen, merchants, industrialists, and manufacturers illustrates further this picture of the religious composition of this important group. A few were catholic such as William Ross of the Clonard mills in Belfast, which employed 500 hands in the 1860s. Some were members of the Church of Ireland, including men at the top of the group like the linen manufacturers John Mulholland and William Ewart and the shipbuilder E. J. Harland. The biggest single group, however, seem to have been presbyterian, including men such as the linen manufacturer J. S. Brown and the shipbuilder Harry Workman. The Richardsons of Bessbrook were quakers.

From the evidence of this material, then, and the individual county census reports it is clear that catholics were over-represented at the lower end of the socio-economic scale and under-represented at the higher level. Throughout the Ulster counties they were over-represented among labourers and small farmers and under-represented among the gentry, merchants, and the professions. An exception to this general picture was Cavan where the catholic proportion of the population, 80·4 per cent, was greater than elsewhere. Here there were a number of minor catholic landowning families such as the Deases, and in 1884 there were as many catholic J.P.s in the county as in all Cos Donegal, Monaghan, and Fermanagh together.[40] In 1871 there were in Co. Cavan 11 lawyers, 51 merchants, and 72 clergy who were catholic out of a total male population of 70,479, in contrast to Donegal with its population of 106,080 males of whom 3 lawyers, 48 merchants, and 83 clergy only were catholic.[41]

In the Ulster towns also catholics were over-represented among the poorest section of the population. Because of their lower socio-economic position, a high municipal franchise, and the absence of a ward system which in certain places meant that the majority party could take the vast majority of seats, catholics played a minor role in the new local town councils and commissions in the province. At the inquiry into local government in 1877 it was revealed that while catholics were nearly one-third of Belfast's population there were only 2 catholics on a council of 40 and in Derry where catholics were a majority of the population there were just 2 catholic councillors out of a total of 24.[42] Elsewhere there were more catholics on town councils,[43] but usually their share of these posts was smaller than their share of the population. This was a serious source of grievance among catholics.[44]

At the same time it must be realised that in the towns there was a growing number of catholic tradesmen and professional people and there were many protestants who stood outside the principal social categories. This was clearly the case in Belfast. There were five catholic lawyers in the town in 1871 and twenty-nine two decades later; over the same period the percentage of Belfast merchants who were catholic rose from 22·3 to 30·8 per cent.[45] Catholics were over-represented among general labourers in the town as in 1871 they were 42·8 per cent of the total although only 31·9 per cent of the population, but this still left 57·2 per cent of the labourers who were protestant.[46] Because of their greater absolute numbers there were far more protestants than catholics in Belfast in semi-skilled or unskilled manual operations.[47] If we look more closely at this question we find again that presbyterians often were better off than members of the Church of Ireland. The latter in 1871 were 26·6 per cent of the town's population and 29 per cent of the general labourers, while the former were 34·5 per cent and 26·1 per cent respectively. As one modern historian has remarked, members of the Church of Ireland as a group 'could have found a basis for feeling under-privileged had they any ideological stimulus to seek one'.[48]

The comparative socio-economic positions of the various denominations in Ulster may be usefully contrasted with the situation outside the province. In the rest of Ireland religious divisions among the population were very different from thóse in Ulster. Whereas 51·1 per cent of the Ulster population in 1871 were protestant, the figure for the other provinces was 10·0 per cent in 1871; the vast majority of these were members of the Church of Ireland.[49] Although a minority in the three southern provinces, pro-testants owned most of the land before its transfer to the tenants as a result of the various land purchase acts. They dominated the pro-fessions and commerce.[50] Where they were present in the country-side as tenant farmers, protestants tended to own the larger farms.[51]

By the 1870s, however, a number of catholics had bought landed estates, and catholic participation in the professional and com-mercial life of the country was already quite significant and growing rapidly. They were the chief element in most of the town councils outside Ulster.[52] These developments were much more marked in the southern provinces than in the north, partly because of the higher proportion of catholics in the south. Although protestant farmers owned the better farms, they were often so few in number that there was a very large section of prosperous catholic tenant farmers. Another important difference between the two parts of the country was that, whereas in Ulster there was a sizeable and labouring element among the protestants, this was not so in the rest of Ireland. Outside Dublin and Cork, relatively few protestants belonged to this group.[53]

So far our study of the religious divisions within society has been largely a statistical and factual one, concerned primarily with the size and distribution of the various religious denominations and the social and economic differences or similarities between them. Attention must now be turned to an examination of differences in attitudes and outlook of the denominations in religious matters as they related to each other and to public affairs. These differences were of considerable importance to the contemporary situation because, partly as a result of diverging social backgrounds, their religious viewpoints were concerned with more than purely theological matters and significantly affected their approach to events. We shall look first at the catholics and then at the protestants.

For catholics in Ulster, as in the rest of Ireland, the nineteenth century was a time of considerable organisational growth and spiritual revival, as they sought to rebuild after the deprivations of the penal laws. During this time churches and schools were constructed at an ever increasing rate and the numbers of the priesthood increased markedly.[54] Important new devotional practices were introduced to Irish catholicism in the decades after the famine.[55] The authority of the bishops over their clergy and catholic affairs was strengthened. Changes caused by the Vatican council of 1870 were taken up enthusiastically by the Irish catholic church. Irish bishops had favoured the movement in the council for acceptance of papal infallibility and it was quickly accepted by Irish catholics.[56]

Exactly what effect these changes had on the attitude of Irish catholics towards protestants it is difficult to say. The changes in devotional practice no doubt tended to emphasise the differences in spiritual matters between catholics and protestants and to give catholics more of a separate identity.[57] Probably the declaration of papal infallibility adversely affected catholic views on a broad Christian church including different viewpoints. Certainly catholic tolerance of the protestant stand on theological matters seems to have improved little in this period. The catholic-owned newspaper, the *Anglo-Celt*, in 1868 described the Church of Ireland as 'founded and maintained by swords and bayonets' while the *Weekly Examiner* in 1886 called it 'the alien church'.[58] In 1885 the catholic bishops petitioned Gladstone to make the Church of Ireland change its name; the nationalist M.P., T. M. Healy, later supported the bishops' case in parliament.[59]

Specific catholic grievances against the existing system were varied. Many catholics were concerned about the continued establishment of the Church of Ireland as the state church, because its members were only 11·96 per cent of the Irish population in 1861. This was seen as part of the earlier system of protestant domination with its restrictions on the social and political activities of catholics, which had been largely, but not altogether, removed by the 1860s.[60] Catholics welcomed the disestablishment of the Church of Ireland

in 1870 but regarded other facets of 'protestant ascendancy' as still
in existence.

Grievances in a local context were seen in the protestant dominance of official positions, and discrimination against catholics by
some protestant-controlled town councils and poor law boards of
guardians.[61] The electoral procedures of certain councils and boards
of commissioners kept catholics from taking a full part in the new
local town government.[62] Restrictions against catholics in the
United Kingdom as a whole were felt in things such as the limited
number of the catholic clergy in the armed services, the religious
test at Oxford and Cambridge universities, and the ecclesiastical
titles act. In evidence about the last named act in 1867 before a
select committee of the house of commons, the Ulster born
Thomas O'Hagan, then a barrister, remarked on how the act
tended to 'separate the R.C. hierarchy from the civil government'.[63]

A further cause of bitterness among many catholics in Ireland was
the attitude taken by protestants and the British government
towards catholic temporal affairs in Europe.[64] The local catholic
press gave widespread and sympathetic coverage to the struggles of
the pope and the church authorities in various countries, especially
Germany and Italy, against hostile nationalist and state forces,
which often had British support. As Dr R. V. Comerford has
pointed out, public demonstrations in Ireland in 1870, for example,
in support of France in the Franco-Prussian war, largely because
France supported the papacy, evoked greater enthusiasm in the
catholic community than did political meetings, such as those for
fenian amnesty.[65] In a letter to Lord Dufferin in 1871, Bishop Patrick
Dorrian of Down and Connor expressed the wish that Gladstone's
views on foreign affairs were better formed 'as he could thus more
easily avoid stumbling on such phrases as 'Italian despotism', whatever that may mean'.[66] Dr James Donnelly, catholic bishop of
Clogher, wrote in 1883 of the government 'headed by Gladstone,
enemy of catholicity and friend of Garibaldi'.[67] This concern was
reinforced by annoyance over the overtly protestant occurrences
which sometimes took place in parliament such as the introduction
of C. N. Newdegate's motion for the inspection of convents in England and the protestant stance on civil and religious affairs often
adopted by English politicians.[68] Another important grievance in
this period for the catholic bishops involved the education question.
(See below, pp. 33-4, for further discussion on this.)

In spite of these problems the second half of the nineteenth century saw the growth of a new self-confident spirit among Ulster

catholics. This was especially so in Belfast which was under the charge of Bishop Patrick Dorrian of Down and Connor from the mid-1860s.[69] At his funeral service in 1885, glowing reference was made to how twenty years earlier he had taken over a very weak catholic structure with few priests and churches, and transformed it:

> What do we see now? We see the city dotted over, as it were, by magnificent catholic churches. . . . We have now, I think eight catholic churches, which for beauty and magnificence are second to none. We have six convents, in which every want that flesh is heir to is provided for. We have forty priests in the town instead of three and we have a community of men of the Congregation of the Passion who not only edify the people here, but by their missions throughout the country spread religion and piety among the people elsewhere.[70]

Besides such institutional improvements, which were plainly evident in other dioceses, catholics in general benefited from the growing prosperity in the countryside and towns. Their numbers among the professional and business community increased markedly in the late nineteenth century. Such changes led to a new confidence.

For protestants also the second half of the nineteenth century was a time of considerable reorganisation and spiritual growth. Because of earlier advantages the protestant churches were not so involved as the catholic church in the construction of new churches and schools, but the growth of industrial Belfast brought special problems for all the protestant denominations, and for the Church of Ireland disestablishment created a great organisational challenge. Two characteristics of Irish protestantism in this period are especially noticeable. First, all the churches continued to be distinguished by their evangelicalism, a development aided, although not started, by the religious revival in the north in 1859. Secondly, by this time the main churches were marked by a fairly conservative orthodoxy; this was seen in the presbyterian church by the triumph of Rev. Henry Cooke and his followers and in the Church of Ireland by the new church constitution of the 1870s which set up that body on relatively narrow low-church principles.[71]

Again, as in the case of the catholic church, it is difficult to assess precisely the effect of these developments. Given that these low-church features of Irish protestantism emphasised differences between protestant and catholic viewpoints in spiritual matters and that the firm establishment of a conservative religious orthodoxy made people more opposed to the idea of a pluralist Christian church and society, it is very likely that these developments made protestants less tolerant towards catholics. Probably the growing conservatism within Irish protestantism made protestants more conservative in general outlook.[72] The reaction of protestants to catholicism could often be harsh. The protestant-owned *Bally-shannon Herald* began its editorial on 19 June 1880 with the question 'Is the pope a man of sin?' It answered in the affirmative. Certain clergymen and ministers such as Thomas Drew and Hugh Hanna were often very abusive in their sermons about catholicism.[73]

To protestants the existing social and religious system appeared rather differently than it did to catholics. Contributory to this were the disparate social positions between catholics and protestants in Ireland and also the fact that while protestants were a minority and catholics a majority in Ireland, catholics were a minority and protestants a majority in the United Kingdom of Great Britain and Ireland. This latter fact was seen as justification for the establishment of the Church of Ireland. Not only in Ireland but also in Great Britain, however, many protestants shared a distrust of catholics on religious grounds and this affected their approach to catholics in other matters.

At the beginning of the nineteenth century the character of the constitution and government of the United Kingdom had been largely protestant. During the century this protestant character of the state was progressively altered by measures such as catholic emancipation and the admission of Jews to parliament.[74] Among protestants in Great Britain a more tolerant and pluralist view of society eventually came to be widely held.[75] But concern about catholicism remained strong in Great Britain, as exemplified by the 1851 ecclesiastical titles act which was not repealed until 1871.[76] Even men like Gladstone were suspicious of and concerned about catholic claims, as seen in his 1874 pamphlet on the recent Vatican decrees. Gladstone wrote: 'the Rome of the middle ages claimed universal monarchy. The modern church of Rome has abandoned nothing, retracted nothing.'[77]

By the 1860s the idea of a pluralist religious society had taken less hold among protestants in Ireland than among those in Great Britain. Suspicion of catholicism remained a strong force among Irish protestants, who looked on catholic claims and the reorganising catholic church as part of an aggressive ultramontane movement which was seen as hostile towards them.[78] The declaration of papal infallibility was regarded as a religious and political challenge.[79] The growing power of the catholic bishops and clergy concerned many Irish protestants.[80] For example, liberal Belfast protestants were alarmed by Bishop Dorrian's opposition to an institute for protestant and catholic working men on the grounds that they should not meet for arranged discussion and debate.[81] Catholic clerical intervention in elections in the early 1870s and, particularly, in the 1885-6 period, greatly aroused protestant fears.[82] This suspicion of catholicism was widespread among Ulster protestants, although its intensity differed between people, as did views on how the state should deal with catholic interests.

Some argued that equality for all denominations was a desirable state of affairs and that protestants and catholics could live together in peace.[83] This view was felt especially among presbyterians, many of whom objected to the establishment of the Church of Ireland. Others, however, believed that to upset the existing social, political, and religious structures would inevitably lead to power for catholics who would use it in an arbitrary manner against protestants.[84] This line of argument usually contended that society could be dominated by either catholics or protestants but not by both on equal terms. To people who held these views, evidence of catholic aggression was seen not only in the activities of the catholic church in Ireland but also in the conflict (followed keenly in the local press) between civil governments and catholic authorities in different parts of Europe such as Italy and Germany. In 1874, for example, a meeting was held by protestants in Carrickfergus to 'express sympathy with the emperor of Germany in his present struggle with ultramontane Jesuits'.[85]

This second line of argument was firmly held by spokesmen of the Orange order. In the 1860s the order was weak in Ulster. Its rank and file seem mainly to have been small farmers and labourers, both town and country.[86] Members of the gentry were often associated with the order but the names of those on Orange platforms in this period suggest that the gentry played a limited part in the organisation.[87] The movement seems to have been strongest in Cos Armagh, Tyrone and Fermanagh. Numbers in the order expanded in this period, however, especially from the early 1880s onwards. The gentry began to play a much more important role. Up to this time the order seems largely to have been Church of Ireland in composition and the Church of Ireland clergy were the principal clerical element, but many presbyterians now joined, including ministers, well-to-do tenant farmers, and townspeople, particularly from 1885.[88]

So far our attention has focused on protestant–catholic division, but mention must be made of intra-protestant conflict. As already noted, there were marked differences in the social profiles of the presbyterian and Church of Ireland communities. Although Rev. Henry Cooke in the 1830s had urged an alliance of the two denominations, many presbyterians remained hostile to the Church of Ireland, as Dr Richard McMinn has pointed out.[89] In part, this hostility arose from religious objections. W. F. McKinney, a presbyterian tenant farmer of Sentry Hill, Carnmoney, writing in the late 1870s, remarked caustically on 'the nonsensical, unscriptural customs that are still practised in the Church of Ireland.'[90] It was also caused by radical opposition to an establishment of which 'the land-lord class and the Church of Ireland were seen as two aspects of the one thing.'[91]

For the presbyterian community as a whole, the second half of the nineteenth century was a time of considerable progress which saw the building of new churches and schools and the growth in prosperity of its farming and business members. All this gave a new self-confidence to presbyterians and a desire among some to question the high social and political status of Church of Ireland adherents. Even after disestablishment of the Church of Ireland in 1870, many presbyterians still felt that undue favour was given to anglicans in official appointments such as the magistracy, the police, and the education boards. In 1880 the presbyterian *Witness* stated: 'From the very highest official to the lowest, there is a disposition to keep episcopacy in a position of ascendancy.'[92]

We began this chapter by remarking that if Thackeray had returned to Belfast in 1868 he would have found great debate among the churches over disestablishment. Relations between the denominations were not all hostile, of course. In the same year at Ballynahinch the catholic bishop of Dromore, Dr J. P. Leahy, thanked the persons 'both Roman Catholic and protestant' who had generously subscribed towards the new church in the town.[93] J. A. Rentoul, in his biography, recorded the good relations between the different clergy in Donegal in the 1870s and 1880s. He described how Dr Daniel McGettigan, when catholic bishop of Raphoe, had regarded his father, a presbyterian minister, as 'a co-worker engaged with him in a common war, though fighting under different regimental colours.'[94] A. M. Sullivan jun. recalled how a Church of Ireland rector forbade the flying of flags on his church, to avoid giving offence to his catholic neighbours.[95] In the rural community, farmers of all denominations commonly gave each other assistance at harvest time.[96] But still religious divisions were of considerable consequence, not only because of the social divisions that accompanied them, but also because of the differences in attitude of the denominations to each other and various aspects of society. The significance of these differences spread beyond church matters to other areas of importance such as education and the press.

Education

Two main points can be made with regard to the state of education in this period.[97] The first is that standards of literacy continued to improve considerably. By 1861 30 per cent of the Ulster population, aged five years old and upwards, were illiterate but thirty years later the figure was just 15·4 per cent. So our period covers the key stage at which the vast majority of adults were fully literate for the first time. In fact the 1871 census records the first time that just over half the people in Ulster aged 20 or over could both read and write: by 1891 the figure stood at nearly 90 per cent.

The second point is that there were considerable differences between the denominations in the levels of literacy, as can be seen in the figures for those aged five years old and upwards. In 1871 in Ulster 39·8 per cent of catholics were illiterate, while for those who belonged to the Church of Ireland, the figure was 18·7 per cent, for presbyterians 9·8 per cent, for methodists 7·6 per cent, and for others 7·7 per cent. In succeeding years the rate of illiteracy fell and the differences between the denominations became less although throughout this period it remained much higher among catholics than protestants and also greater for members of the Church of Ireland than presbyterians. By 1891, 24·0 per cent of catholics were illiterate compared with 11·4 per cent of Church of Ireland members, 5·7 per cent of presbyterians, 4·9 per cent of methodists, and 4·5 per cent of others. Throughout the nineteenth century presbyterians had higher literacy standards than both members of the Church of Ireland and catholics. Cultural and religious factors probably lie behind these high presbyterian literacy figures.

There were also significant differences between the denominations in the field of higher education. Of those described in the 1871 census for Ulster as engaged in 'superior' education (excluding students at Queen's College, Belfast), 19·9 per cent were catholic, 25·2 per cent Church of Ireland and 55·8 per cent presbyterian. At Queen's College, Belfast, in 1871, there were 12 catholics, 74 Church of Ireland members and 285 presbyterians.[98] These last figures are not a true representation of the number of people in the province in receipt of university education, because many members of the Church of Ireland and catholics (and some presbyterians) tended to go to colleges or universities outside Ulster.[99] However, of those who attended universities and other colleges in Ireland in 1871, 44·4 per cent were catholic, 36·1 per cent Church of Ireland, and 19·5 per cent presbyterian.[100]

Control of education was an issue of considerable controversy between the churches. At the primary level the national school system had been set up on a non-denominational basis but by the 1860s the system had become largely denominational in practice. The government also attempted to promote non-denominational secondary and university education. This met with strong opposition from the catholic bishops, who wanted full control over the education of catholics which they saw as necessary for the maintenance of their faith. In 1874 Bishop Patrick Dorrian of Down and Connor warned Belfast catholics that mixed schooling would lead to their children being educated as 'mongrels'.[101] The intermediate education act of 1878 was fairly well received by catholics but university education remained a problem.

The attempts made in the 1860s, 1870s and 1880s by various governments to provide university education for catholics, such as Gladstone's proposals of 1873, met with little support and the catholic bishops condemned them for their failure to give what the bishops regarded as their due say in the control of university education.[102] In 1873 all religious tests in Trinity were removed but the college failed to find favour in catholic eyes. The university education act of 1879, which set up the Royal University of Ireland and provided indirect endowment for the catholic university of Dublin, was seen as a help to catholic needs, but still insufficient.

This issue was strongly felt by catholics, partly because in a society that many catholics regarded as hostile to their interests, full control over catholic education was viewed as vital. Elsewhere in Europe also, conflict arose between catholic bishops and governments over university education, so the Irish situation was not simply the result of Irish conditions.[103] On the other side, many protestants in England and Ireland felt that the catholic demands were unreasonable. Especially among Ulster presbyterians and English nonconformists there was strong opposition to funding a denominational system.

The press
Attention must be paid now to the Ulster newspapers at this time. In contemporary press directories, newspapers were usually classified according to their political viewpoint and 'religious principles'.[104]

As these directories show, presbyterian and Church of Ireland views and conservative and liberal interests were well represented in the press, while catholic views and home rule interests were much less prominent. But the degree of representation in the press for the different groups varied between areas, and the numbers of papers supporting catholic and home rule views increased at this time. Denominational differences between presbyterian and Church of Ireland papers became less marked over the period, especially from 1885. The number of newspapers grew in Ulster during these years, clearly as a result of the rise in literacy and increased political activity.

Throughout this time there was a wide range of newspapers in Belfast. Several of these supported catholic interests. The *Belfast Morning News* was a moderate catholic paper which was founded in 1855. It was liberal in political sympathies until about 1882 (although by this time it had become increasingly critical of liberal policies), when it was bought by E. D. Gray of the *Freeman's Journal* and became nationalist. Another catholic newspaper in this period was the *Northern Star* later called the *Northern Star and Ulster Observer*, which W. J. McKenna established in 1868. McKenna, however, came into conflict with Bishop Patrick Dorrian, as he had on an earlier occasion over a different newspaper, and the newspaper closed in 1872.

With Dorrian's backing the *Ulster Examiner* commenced publication on 14 March 1868. Its opening editorial proclaimed:

> In the *Ulster Examiner*, the catholics of Belfast and Ulster will have a recognised organ of catholic opinion which will be sincerely and zealously devoted to their interests. . . . We have yet faith in the imperial parliament, and believe, with all sensible and reflecting men, that the grievances under which we labour can be redressed by the means which the constitution affords.[105]

On 21 March the paper carried a letter from Bishop Dorrian who gave it his support: the bishop commented 'Of your politics I need not speak. They will be catholic.' The *Ulster Examiner* backed the liberals for the next few years and then the home rulers. It also ran a weekly edition, the *Weekly Examiner*. Both papers were bought out in the early 1880s by E. D. Gray, who merged the daily paper with the *Morning News* but kept the *Weekly Examiner* in existence.

The *Belfast Newsletter* was the chief conservative paper in Belfast and throughout the province; it was pro-Church of Ireland although frequently it made appeals to protestants in general. The *Northern Whig*, which was sympathetic to the presbyterian cause, was the leading liberal paper in Belfast and the rest of Ulster. Both papers

ran weekly editions, the former the *Weekly News* and the latter the
Weekly Whig. *The Belfast Evening Telegraph*, started in 1870, was
protestant and conservative in its sympathies. The *Banner of Ulster*,
founded in 1842 'to advance the interests of the presbyterian
church',[106] ran until 1870 and in its place in January 1874 the *Witness*
was established. These two papers were first and foremost concerned with presbyterianism, but often general news topics were
covered, in particular the tenant right issue, over which they
strongly supported the farmers. After the 1885 general election and
the split in the liberal party, nearly all the liberal papers in Ulster
became liberal unionist.

In Cos Down and Antrim, there were various local newspapers,
which represented the different interests in many of the towns. Only
in Newry, however, was there a pro-catholic and nationalist paper
in this period, the *Belfast and Newry Standard*. In Armagh the
Ulster Gazette and *Armagh Guardian* were pro-Church of Ireland
and conservative. At the same time the two papers had sympathies
with the tenant farmers and could be critical of the conservative
party in the county. The *Armagh Herald* was formed in 1880 by local
conservatives but soon afterwards collapsed. In Co. Tyrone the
main paper was the *Tyrone Constitution* which was conservative and
pro-Church of Ireland. Another Tyrone conservative paper, the
Tyrone Courier, was established in 1880. The *Tyrone Herald*, pro-
catholic and nationalist, was not founded until 1892.

In Co. Fermanagh the principal paper throughout these years was
the *Impartial Reporter* which was pro-Church of Ireland (although
often critical of the church) and in the 1860s moderately conservative, but in the 1870s and 1880s it became increasingly pro-tenant-
right and against the landlords. In the late 1860s and early 1870s the
Enniskillen Advertiser ran as a liberal newspaper that addressed
both catholics and protestants. In March 1880 the *Fermanagh Times*
was started by a number of local conservative gentry; its opening
editorial declared it would defend 'those constitutional principles
which had been so zealously and consistently maintained from time
immemorial by the inhabitants of the county.'[107]

In the city of Derry there were three principal newspapers in
this period as well as a number of minor papers which appeared
briefly. The *Londonderry Sentinel* was pro-Church of Ireland and
conservative: an editorial on 20 September 1879, commemorating
the fiftieth anniversary of the paper, stated that it had originally
been founded 'to create an organ in the public press by which the
sentiments of constitutionalists and protestants should be vigorously

ventilated and their interests defended', and this was still its purpose.[108] The *Londonderry Standard* was a pro-presbyterian and
liberal paper and also the main upholder of tenant right in the province under the editorship of James McKnight (1801-76). It was
strongly opposed to both the landlords and the catholic clergy. On
21 March 1868, for example, the paper remarked that 'the civil
liberty as established by William III, has been taken from the
people of Ireland by the priests and the landlords.' The third main
Derry paper was the *Londonderry Journal* which was pro-catholic
and presbyterian during the 1860s and 1870s and then mainly pro-
catholic from 1880; its politics were liberal until 1880 when it
became strongly nationalist and changed it name to *Derry Journal*.
In Coleraine the *Coleraine Chronicle* was presbyterian and liberal in
sympathy. After the defeat of a conservative in the 1874 general
election, the *Coleraine Constitution* was set up by a number of conservatives, including both presbyterians and members of the
Church of Ireland.

   In Co. Donegal, during this time, there were two newspapers, the
Donegal Independent and the *Ballyshannon Herald*, both of which
were pro-Church of Ireland and conservative; a nationalist and pro-
catholic paper, the *Donegal Vindicator*, appeared for the first time
in 1889. In Co. Monaghan, the *Argus* and the *Northern Standard*
were also conservative and pro-Church of Ireland. *The Peoples'
Advocate* was established in the county in the 1870s on a catholic,
liberal and pro-tenant-right basis; it became nationalist in the 1880s.
In Co. Cavan, however, besides the conservative and pro-Church of
Ireland *Cavan Weekly News*, there was the *Anglo-Celt* which was
pro-catholic liberal in the 1860s, and subsequently a supporter of
home rule. In 1865 the *Nation* newspaper described the *Anglo-Celt*
as a 'genuine catholic paper' and stated that it had shown itself 'a
vigorous and fearless exponent of catholic opinion.'[109]

   Clearly the spread of newspapers and the growth of education, at
all levels, were of great importance for the population in Ulster as
elsewhere in Ireland. Together with political changes such as the
increase in the franchise, they created new conditions of public
awareness and involvement. In his account of Irish society and
politics, written in 1877, A. M. Sullivan observed these points and
remarked how the people were awakening.[110] At the same time it is
perhaps worth noting that in these two key areas of social development denominational divisions were strongly in force. Such
characteristics in themselves did not automatically cause sectarianism
because, as Sullivan also noted, protestant and catholic farmers

were cooperating on the land question; but still, this did mean that religious divisions continued to be a major, rather than a minor, part of the new consciousness.

CHAPTER 3 *The voters and the constituencies*

In an account of politics in Derry city after the 1884 reform act, T. M. Healy described to the house of commons the great activity at revision sessions in the city and the close watch kept on voters: 'in fact the voter was so closely watched that if a man got drunk and was put in the cells for twenty-four hours he was objected to and probably lost the franchise.' He also stated that 'in Derry every man, woman and child understood the franchise act.'[1] Undoubtedly revision sessions were very strongly contested during this period in Derry because of the way the two political sides in the borough were evenly balanced. But from 1868 onwards, as political debate in Ulster increased, the franchise laws and voter registration became objects of widespread interest throughout the province.[2]

We have already studied the different groups that made up Ulster society, but we must now investigate how far they were actually enfranchised. A variety of laws relating to the number of constituencies, the franchise, and the registration of voters significantly affected the character of politics in Ulster. Changes introduced in the years under review had important consequences for the outcome of elections. We must examine not only what this legislation stated but how it operated in practice. The simple question at the heart of the matter is 'who had the vote?' From detailed information gathered in answer to this question, it will be possible to achieve a better understanding of the outcome of the elections.

In contrast to England, where the parliamentary reform act of 1867 made a great impact, Ireland was little affected by the parallel Representation of the People (Ireland) Act of 1868. The number of constituencies agreed at the act of union, with the minor changes of 1832, survived unaltered. This meant that, in spite of great difference in population size, each of the nine Ulster counties had two M.P.s. Nine boroughs in the province each returned one M.P., while a tenth, Belfast, elected two M.P.s. The boundaries of Belfast, Newry, and Derry, however, were extended by the 1868 act. The country franchise remained, as laid down in 1850, confined to adult males who occupied property with a rateable valuation of at least £12, and to some categories of leaseholders and freeholders. In the boroughs, because of the new law, the occupier franchise was

39

extended to those with property valued at 'over £4': a lodger
franchise was also introduced. No changes were made in the other
minor borough franchise qualifications.

In practice, the electoral qualifications meant that in 1881 the
vote in the Ulster counties was restricted to 18 per cent of the adult
males or 4 per cent of the whole population.[3] There was, however,
variation among counties in the proportion of persons who held the
vote, thanks to the economic and social differences between areas.
This ranged from nearly 22 per cent of adult males in Antrim and
Down to nearly 9 per cent in Donegal. The vast majority of these
county electors were farmers, and because of the £12 rateable
valuation qualification most were well-to-do. An observer at the
Co. Antrim by-election of 1869 commented on the 'respectability
and enthusiasm of the farmers coming in to vote': they were distinguished . . . for great respectability and quietness as well as wealth
and intelligence.'[4] Approximately 40 per cent of the adult males
classified as farmers in the 1881 census were electors. Some county
electors lived in towns within the county, but such voters were not
numerous, except in Down and Antrim where they were around
5 per cent in 1874. County Antrim contained many voters who
belonged to the Belfast district: in 1880 the figure was put at 1,472
out of 11,701 electors.[5]

In the boroughs the picture was different but also varied. Due to
the 1868 act the number of electors in northern boroughs increased
considerably and the social character of the electorate broadened.
Observations by a speaker in Coleraine in November 1868 that
power now lay in 'the hands of the mechanics and working classes'
were exaggerated, but the act did enfranchise large numbers of
skilled artisans and working men.[6] Overall the electorate in Ulster
boroughs increased by 131 per cent between 1866 and 1868, and
thereafter continued to grow steadily — a reflection of the rising
prosperity of the Ulster towns. Excluding Belfast and Carrickfergus,
the proportion of adult males in the northern boroughs who had the
vote in 1871 was 25 per cent. In Belfast, where the growth of the
electorate was very marked after the 1868 reform act, 35 per cent of
adult males could vote by 1871; their numbers included many newly
enfranchised industrial workers. Carrickfergus had a special freeman franchise, which meant that in 1871 57 per cent of adult males,
including labourers, fishermen, and other social groups not
enfranchised elsewhere, were on the electoral rolls.[7] There were
considerable differences in the sizes of boroughs from towns like
Downpatrick and Dungannon with around 4,000 inhabitants in

1871, but each returning one M.P., to Belfast with 174,412 inhabitants and only two M.P.s.[8]

So far we have been concerned with only the numbers and the social composition of those who had the vote in the period between 1868 and the reforms of 1884-5. Attention must also be paid to the religious composition of the electorate. This was clearly affected not only by the variations between constituencies in denominational distribution but by differences in the social and economic positions of the denominations. In the countryside, as already observed, protestants tended to own the larger farms.[9] In the towns, the professions, the main commercial positions, and the skilled crafts were dominated by protestants. The result was that in this period catholics were usually under-represented in the electorate, in relation to their numbers in the population. Protestants, especially presbyterians, were over-represented. From contemporary analyses it is possible to gain valuable information on comparative denominational voting strengths. Exact figures for religious composition of the population have been noted earlier.[10]

As regards the boroughs, the protestants had a majority on all the electoral rolls and presbyterians were usually in a strong position. In Dungannon protestants were 46 per cent of the population in 1881 and 58 per cent of the 1880 electorate.[11] In Armagh 48 per cent of the 1871 population and 68 per cent of the 1876 voters were protestant.[12] More detailed breakdowns are available elsewhere. In Belfast presbyterians were 34 per cent of the population in 1881 and 52 per cent of the 1880 electoral register: in contrast members of the Church of Ireland were 29 per cent of the population and 21 per cent of the register in the same year.[13] In Derry and Newry in 1871 presbyterians numbered 22 and 13 per cent, respectively, of the population, while in 1868 they formed 41 per cent of the Derry voters and 26 per cent of the Newry electors.[14] Members of the Church of Ireland at this time formed 20 per cent of the population and 21 per cent of the electorate in Derry, and 18 per cent of the population and 24 per cent of the voters in Newry. Figures are unavailable for elsewhere, but from our knowledge of denominational distribution members of the Church of Ireland were strong in numbers among the voters of Armagh, Lisburn, Downpatrick, Enniskillen, and Dungannon, as were presbyterians in the Coleraine and Carrickfergus electorates.

During this period catholics were clearly under-represented in the boroughs in relation to their numerical strength in the population. It is worth noting, however, that the 1868 act increased the numbers of catholic voters. In Belfast, where catholics were nearly a third of the population in 1871 but only a quarter in 1881, they were around 16 per cent of the electorate in 1864 and 19 per cent in 1868 and 1880.[15] They were 64 per cent of the population of Newry in 1871, 39 per cent of the voters in 1866 and 45 per cent in 1868. In Derry city catholics were 55 per cent of the population in 1871 and 38 per cent of the electoral rolls in 1868. In Armagh city they were 52 per cent of the population in 1871 and 32 per cent of the electorate in 1876. In Dungannon catholics were 54 per cent of the population in 1881 and 42 per cent of those eligible to vote in 1880.

Only in Cos Donegal, Monaghan, and Cavan were catholics a substantial proportion of the electorate. In the 1870s and early 1880s, the voters in the first two counties were divided roughly equally between protestant and catholic, while in the third catholics had a slight majority.[16] There were few presbyterians in Cavan but in Donegal and Monaghan there were probably equal numbers of presbyterians and members of the Church of Ireland. In sharp contrast, presbyterians were a substantial proportion of the voting registers in Cos Down, Antrim, and Londonderry.[17] They were 52 per cent of the Down electorate in 1878, 65 per cent in Antrim in 1880, and 46 per cent in Londonderry in 1881. In the same years, of those qualified to vote, 22 per cent in Down, 19 per cent in Antrim, and 24 per cent in Londonderry were catholic. Figures for members of the Church of Ireland were 25 per cent, 16 per cent, and 30 per cent respectively. See above, p. 15, for the relative strength of these denominations in the population of the counties.

Denominational figures are unavailable for the Armagh and Fermanagh electorates but it is clear that in both counties protestant voters were more numerous than catholic, and Church of Ireland members were numerically more significant than elsewhere on the registers. Given the general distribution of denominations in these counties it is clear that there were hardly any presbyterian electors in Fermanagh and fewer in Armagh than Tyrone. In 1881 the electorate for Co. Tyrone could be divided approximately as follows: 26 per cent catholic, 32 per cent members of the Church of Ireland, and 42 per cent presbyterian.[18] Here again the voters were predominantly protestant but members of the Church of Ireland were present in large numbers.

The reforms of 1884-5 drastically reshaped the constituencies and the electorate. As a result of the 1885 redistribution act, the counties were arranged into divisions, roughly equal in population, with one M.P. being returned for each of the 27 divisions. The boroughs were abolished as separate constituencies except for Newry, Derry, and

Belfast; the first two each retained one M.P., while Belfast had four
M.P.s, one for each of the four divisions into which the borough was
divided. The vote was now extended by the Representation of the
People Act, 1884, to all adult male householders; sons living with
parents and indoor servants were still excluded.

As a consequence of the franchise changes in 1884 the constituencies in Ulster witnessed major changes in the proportion of
males with the vote and in the social and religious composition of
the electorate. The average was now 64 electors for every hundred
adult males in the population.[19] Some contemporaries and recent
commentators believed that the act placed power in the hands of the
agricultural labourers. But it must be remembered that indoor
servants (half the labouring population) were excluded and in fact
many small farmers were enfranchised. Still, the labourers were an
important new section of the electorate.

The denominational breakdown of the voters was roughly similar
to that of the population. A parliamentary return of 1884-5 gives the
religious breakdown of each new parliamentary constituency.[20]
Catholics comprised about 60 per cent of the electorate in twelve
county divisions, while protestants constituted around 60 per cent
or more in ten, leaving five where protestant and catholics were
fairly evenly balanced. In Newry there was a clear catholic majority,
while in Derry and West Belfast the numbers of protestant and
catholic were evenly balanced, and in the three other Belfast
divisions protestants had a large majority. Presbyterians and
members of the Church of Ireland were variously distributed among
the constituencies. Under the new franchise, catholics were slightly
disadvantaged because a higher proportion of indoor servants, who
did not have a vote, was catholic. At the same time the redistribution
of seats retained Newry, with its small electorate, as a separate constituency, which improved the catholic position.

All this electoral legislation applied equally to the rest of Ireland.
The 1868 act, however, had less effect in Leinster, Munster, and
Connacht than in Ulster, because there were fewer properties of the
required value of 'over £4'.[21] In the counties, roughly similar proportions of adult males (mostly farmers) were enfranchised, although
as in Ulster there was marked variation between counties. A
considerable difference existed, however, in the religious composition of the electorates in Ulster and the other provinces. The
vast majority of constituencies outside Ulster before 1885 had substantial catholic majorities, although protestants usually had a
stronger position in the electorate than their proportional strength

in the population, thanks to their generally higher economic position.[22] After 1885 this advantage ceased for protestants and, indeed, they had less influence in the southern constituencies than their overall numerical strength (around 10 per cent) would suggest, because they were widely distributed.

Although women were debarred from the franchise during this period the subject aroused little public controversy. The leading proponent of the issue in Ulster was Isabella Tod, one of the women who signed the first female suffrage petition that was sent to the house of commons in 1866. Meetings were held of the North of Ireland women's suffrage association in the 1870s and again in the 1880s, but there is no evidence of the matter impinging seriously on the political issues of the day.[23] Isabella Tod was the author of a private pamphlet sent in 1884 to Ulster M.P.s, entitled *Women and the new franchise bill: a letter to an Ulster member of parliament* (Belfast, 1884). These efforts, however, failed to raise any significant public controversy on the subject. Lack of educational and other facilities for women, various legal disabilities, and the existence of a franchise based on property were important factors in preventing female protest about the absence of the franchise for women.

Finally, mention must be made of the registration of voters. Following changes in the registration laws, introduced in 1850 and updated in 1885, the Irish system was reasonably fair and efficient. Basically it was run by the clerks of the poor law union, and the revision courts were conducted by official revising barristers who were chairmen of the quarter sessions. It was generally agreed that these officials did their work well. Increased political activity in Ulster from the late 1860s, however, gave the revision sessions extra importance, and from this time on the registration courts attracted growing attention from party supporters.[24]

Activities of registration agents were sometimes significant for the outcome of elections. While the electoral system did not offer the same opportunities for manipulating the registers as in Great Britain (thanks to the low number of property electors), there were still a number of ways in which an active registration agent could affect the electoral register in the party's favour. He could see to it that all his supporters with the necessary qualifications were on the electoral lists, and he could object to his opponent's followers who were incorrectly listed. In addition an agent could usefully study the lists to know the allegiances of the electors and so assist party organisation at election time. Sir John Ross described the conservative agent in Derry in the late nineteenth century in the following manner:

> In a closely fought seat everything depends on the registration agent. In Derry this official was a very remarkable man, Mr Daniel Holland. The population of the city exceeded 40,000 and it was said that he knew, by appearance and name, every one of them. I never met anybody among them whom he did not know.[25]

At the same time, the importance of these agents should not be exaggerated. Where only one party was present at the revisions sessions advantages could be gained, although there were limits to this owing to the rules of the registration system. Again, increased activity by one party usually led in the end to a growth in activity by opponents. Further, although one might reckon on so many supporters on the register, there was no guarantee that they would vote as expected. This was especially so in Ulster before 1885: a witness to the 1874 parliamentary enquiry into Irish registration explained that it was often difficult to tell the political complexion of northern farmers.[26] After 1885 such identification became fairly simple, with religious labels usually denoting party loyalties, although there were exceptions. Of course, mistakes could occur, as T. M. Healy related in an amusing account of his brother's efforts on the nationalist side in West Belfast at the revision courts of 1885 in opposition to the conservative agent, Wellington Young:

> Devices by claimants on both sides to secure votes on shaky titles were common, and an old nationalist, who had never had a vote, was inspired to claim, through the tory solicitor, as an Orangeman.
>
> Surnames in Belfast gave no certain clue to religion or politics, and the old fellow got into the witness chair under Wellington Young's auspices. He took him through his qualifications, walking delicately, and when he finished, my brother did not cross-examine. The revising barrister, Milo Burke, allowed the vote.
>
> 'Have I got it safe?' asked the claimant 'Yes', said the Judge. 'Is that true, Mr Wellington Young?' 'It is.' 'Is that right, Mr Healy?' 'It is.' 'I can't be struck off now?' 'No, no,' said Burke. 'Go down.' Leaving the box, he turned round to Young with a scornful laugh, shouting, 'Another vote for Parnell!'[27]

So we have seen that the laws affecting the franchise, the constituencies and registration had an important influence on the composition of the electorate. Only certain sections in society had the vote. This differed considerably between constituencies and over the whole period, as new laws changed the make up of the voters' rolls. Clearly these aspects of the electoral system would be of great importance for the outcome of elections. Several other notable changes occurred in this system, namely the ballot act of 1872 which gave secret voting, and the corrupt practices act of 1883 which severely limited expenditure at elections. The real significance of these acts will be assessed in the course of our study of Ulster politics in 1868-86.

Thus, within Ulster society, and in comparison with the rest of Ireland, there were important divisions. These included social, sectional, and denominational cleavages, and clearly they were significant for the elections during our period. From this survey alone, however, it is not possible to detect an inevitable, final, political outcome to these divisions; in fact several were possible. For example, a straight political conflict could have emerged between Ulster, both protestant and catholic, and the rest of the country, thanks to the differences in industry and tenant right. An all-important division might have developed between gentry on the one side and farmers (protestant and catholic) on the other. A deep rivalry could have appeared with both presbyterians and catholics ranged against members of the Church of Ireland. Poor catholics and poor members of the Church of Ireland might have combined against better-off presbyterians. Yet while several such divisions were politically important for a time, in the end none of them materialised in a permanent way. What finally emerged in Ulster was a basic conflict between protestants, of all denominations and social classes, and catholics of all sections. The political developments of the years under survey, 1868-86, involved the crucial alignment of Ulster politics and society along these sectarian lines.

The last point to be made about the developments in Ulster during these decades is that together they add up to a fundamental change in the very nature of society. In many ways modern Ulster society assumed its chief characteristics, social, economic, and religious, in these decades. In this period the main shape of the settlement of the land question was decided: a process had begun which would make the Ulster countryside a society of small owner-occupiers. Belfast became a city. For the first time, the vast majority of adults could read and write, and well over 50 per cent of adult males had the vote. A wide range of papers provided the population with access to new political ideas and options. All this gave the period a particular significance and would provide the political developments of the time with a unique setting.

II TORIES SUPREME

CHAPTER 4 *The 1868 general election*

Before 1868, Sir John Ross remarked in his memoirs, the inhabitants of Derry were 'peaceful, quiet, God-fearing folk'. In that year, however, 'the demon of party politics appeared, and since that time has reigned triumphantly. . . . '[1] Although the author slightly exaggerates the condition of his native city, both before and after 1868, his comments do capture the impact of the events of 1868 in Derry and also in a number of key northern constituencies. This year saw the first appearance of a strong liberal challenge to the existing order, and signs of important social division in conservative ranks. At the same time, 1868 was the final general election in both Ulster and the rest of Ireland at which the liberals and conservatives were the sole parties. As regards Ulster specifically, it was also the last general election at which the parliamentary representation was still dominated by the conservative landed interest. For these reasons 1868 can be regarded as both the beginning and the end of important periods in the electoral politics of the province.

Throughout the whole country in 1868 politics continued to be strongly influenced by the leading landed families and by local concerns.[2] But ever since the rise of issues in Irish politics in the early decades of the nineteenth century and the appearance of party labels from 1832 onwards, there had been political differences between Ulster and elsewhere.[3] Repeal in the 1830s and 1840s, for example, was backed by none of the northern M.P.s. Catholics, among whom support for repeal was mostly found, were not strong enough or sufficiently organised in any Ulster constituency to create an electoral impact on this matter. Among northern protestants there was little enthusiasm for O'Connell's movement. Certainly few of the presbyterian republican sympathies of 1798 had survived. Charles Gavan Duffy wrote of the northern presbyterians in the 1830s that they knew 'no more of Tone and Russell than of the Gracchi'.[4]

With the collapse of the repeal movement in the late 1840s, the two major political groupings in Ireland were those of liberal and conservative. During the 1850s and 1860s, in spite of some agrarian protest, the Ulster constituencies, with their predominantly

47

protestant electorates, returned landlord M.P.s who were mainly conservative and 'upholders of the *status quo* in church and state'.[5] Elsewhere, besides some areas where there was a strong protestant electorate or where particular conservative families were especially influential, the constituencies usually returned M.P.s who were liberal, although in the late 1850s and early 1860s significant sections of southern catholic opinion did swing briefly to the tories.[6] Under the name liberal could usually be grouped 'all those who wanted extensive reforms, whether constitutional, or ecclesiastic or economic'.[7] The liberals included many landlords who had clearly adapted successfully to their constituents' interests. At this stage politics did not centre around the question of repeal or home rule. At the 1865 general election the Ulster constituencies returned 2 liberals and 27 conservatives, compared with 56 liberals and 20 conservatives in the rest of Ireland.

During the months of 1868 prior to the general election in November, the main topic of political interest throughout Ireland was the prospective disestablishment of the Church of Ireland. Although the subject had aroused some public interest at earlier general elections, it became a matter of wide controversy only after Gladstone's announcement in 1867 of his intention to introduce legislation on the issue — as well as to withdraw the *regium donum*, which was paid to some presbyterian clergy, and the grant to Maynooth College. At meetings on the issue, and in the press, supporters of disestablishment argued that the members of the Church of Ireland were a minority in Ireland and it was wrong, therefore, that their church should be established. Opponents of disestablishment, on the other hand, argued that as anglicans were a majority in the whole of the United Kingdom it was appropriate that the Church of Ireland should be the official state church.

To many, however, disestablishment was seen as something more than simply the question of the legal position of the Church of Ireland. For example, T. G. Peel, a leading Armagh conservative, in a letter to the *Belfast Newsletter* in September 1868, remarked:

> We feel it is not a mere question of whether this or that protestant church shall be in the ascendant or otherwise. Our religion, our venerated constitution, our liberty — civil and religious — are at stake; therefore we are resolved to stand together and defend them, as our fathers did before.[8]

Not all protestants were against disestablishment. Many presbyterians in fact supported the measure, as was seen most clearly in the columns of the *Banner of Ulster*. Shortly before the election in

Belfast its editorial commented:

> And now, presbyterians of Belfast, . . . your fathers submitted to be
> hunted, like partridges on the mountains, rather than bow their heads to
> the yoke of prelacy. Will you now vote for its continued ascendancy?[9]

Among the catholic population of Ulster there was support for
disestablishment, although there appears to have been little
organisation among them to promote this object. As with many protestants, the matter was sometimes viewed as more than simply a
narrow theological issue. The *Ulster Examiner* in an editorial in
March 1868 declared: 'Every protestant church is looked upon by
the catholic peasant as a monument of former tyranny; every glebe
land he regards as a badge of conquest, the plunder of his fore-
fathers.'[10] The catholic archbishop of Armagh, Dr Michael Kieran,
in a public letter written shortly before the general election, stated
that 'the established church was forced on this country at the point
of the bayonet.'[11]

Other matters aroused public opinion in the months prior to the
general election. The subject of the fenians and the release of
members of the organisation, imprisoned for their part in the
abortive rising in 1865, was another issue of public concern. A
movement was started to procure an amnesty for fenian prisoners
but while it received considerable support outside Ulster it won little
backing in the province.[12] The question of the repeal of the party
processions act, which forbade all public demonstrations and
marches, was a special point of grievance among some Orangemen
in Ulster who felt that the act was operated unfairly against them
and that their M.P.s had not sufficiently opposed the measure in
parliament. In July 1867 William Johnston, from Ballykilbeg, Co.
Down, had defied the ban on parades and led an Orange demonstration at Bangor. He was imprisoned for two months for this
action in early 1868 but emerged from jail to continue his protest
against the act.

During 1868 there was little sign of agrarian unrest. In September
Isaac Butt delivered a lecture in Limerick that strongly criticised the
Irish land system. The lecture was widely reported in the press, and
shortly afterwards Rev. Thomas Drew, a prominent Belfast conservative and Orangeman, wrote to the papers to congratulate Butt
on his comments. In a subsequent public letter to William Johnston,
Drew vehemently denounced the landlords in the north of Ireland,
attacked their control of the parliamentary representation of the
province, and criticised the quality of the M.P.s: 'too often we are

presented with persons born never to rise above a billiard room or a dog kennel.'[13] Drew's letter caused considerable controversy when it appeared but it failed to arouse any widespread protest against the land system or landlord M.P.s.

Overall in Ulster in 1868, the general election did not cause great political activity, but there were important signs of new political unrest. Co. Monaghan, where a liberal opposed two conservatives, was the only contested county. In Newry and Derry, however, liberals strongly challenged the conservatives. In Carrickfergus an independent conservative stood in opposition to the former conservative M.P., in Belfast two conservative candidates of the Belfast conservative society faced a tough challenge for the constituency from an independent conservative and a liberal, and in Enniskillen the sitting conservative member was opposed by a liberal. In the remaining constituencies 20 conservatives and one liberal were returned unopposed.

Election addresses of the candidates in Ulster reflected the issues of the day.[14] Disestablishment was the main matter of concern. Most conservatives simply stated their opposition to the idea of disestablishment; some saw it as an attack on the 'protestant constitution of these realms' which would lead to anarchy, while a few accepted the need for some reform of the Church of Ireland. A small number of conservatives also declared their support for land reform. The liberals proclaimed their backing for disestablishment, put forward their belief in religious equality and advocated land reform. In the rest of Ireland the issues and the parties involved were similar to those in Ulster. There was, however, much greater backing for disestablishment and the liberals were far stronger in the three southern provinces than in the north.[15]

At this stage each of the Ulster counties returned 2 M.P.s and each of ten boroughs returned 1 M.P., except for Belfast which was represented by 2 M.P.s. In constituencies with 2 M.P.s, electors had 2 votes but, of course, needed only to cast one of them (a course of action known as plumping). The secret ballot had not yet been introduced and, at contested elections, voters attended polling stations to openly cast their votes. In the case of contested elections voting proceeded immediately after nominations which were public affairs and usually involved speeches from the candidates. By 1868 polling lasted only one day but during a general election voting occurred in constituencies on a number of different days. The worst aspects of electoral corruption, as witnessed earlier in the century, had been removed, thanks to various corrupt practices acts. There were still no limits, however, on what politicians could spend on elections.[16]

The counties

The fact that only one of the Ulster counties was contested in 1868 shows how the existing social and political structure of the country-side went unchallenged at this time. All the county representatives elected in 1868 either owned land themselves or were the relatives of proprietors of estates in the constituencies for which they were returned. Every one of them belonged to the Church of Ireland. Electoral matters were usually arranged in the first instance by the leading landed families in each county, although secondary land-lords and important local interests were also consulted. If elections occurred (and fewer took place in Ulster than in the rest of Ireland in the years 1832-68) tenants normally voted with their landlords, a consequence mainly of the dominant position of the landed gentry in rural society. In addition, also, to the bulk of the electors the political views of the M.P.s were acceptable, or at least not so unac-ceptable as to arouse serious opposition.

This state of affairs is well illustrated by a survey of the Ulster counties in 1868. In most constituencies there was very limited political activity, apart from some canvassing prior to the election. The revision sessions occurred quietly with little sign of political excitement. No selection or endorsement of candidates took place and sitting members simply announced their intention to stand again, usually in their election addresses. In the two cases where former M.P.s stood down, Armagh and Monaghan, new landed candidates came forward without any public selection procedure. There were no formal political associations, except in Armagh. Candidates themselves arranged any organisation that was necessary. Of the eighteen M.P.s elected in 1868, seventeen were labelled as conservative and one as a liberal (in Co. Cavan).

A more detailed study of each county will help to show how the system operated in practice. In Co. Antrim in 1868 the two sitting members were Rear-admiral G. H. Seymour and the hon. Edward O'Neill. Seymour never lived in the county at any time but he was a second cousin of the marquis of Hertford, owner of around 66,000 acres in south Antrim.[17] O'Neill's father was the proprietor of 64,163 acres in mid Antrim.[18] The comments of an observer in 1858 were still true a decade later: 'in former times the Hertford interest returned one M.P. and Lord O'Neill the other and . . . the two interests combined to assist each other.'[19] In their election addresses and in speeches at nomination both candidates stated their opposition to disestablishment. O'Neill argued that protestants were a majority in the United Kingdom and disestablishment threatened the constitution. Mindful no doubt of the strong presbyterian electorate in Antrim, O'Neill also made a point to say that he would oppose withdrawal of endowments to presbyterian clergy.[20]

In Co. Down the Londonderry and Downshire families had emerged as the dominant proprietorial interests in the county, after having fought off other families in the early nineteenth century and tenant right supporters in the 1850s. In correspondence about Down politics in the 1850s, Lord Londonderry, owner of 32,554 acres in north Down, referred to the 'family seat for the county in which we have so large a stake and in which I have myself spent so much.'[21] By 1868 the Londonderry interest was represented by Lt-col. W. B. Forde who owned an estate of 19,882 acres at Seaforde, Co. Down. The other M.P. for Down, Lord A. E. Hill-Trevor, was uncle of the marquis of Downshire, whose lands around Hillsborough extended to 64,356 acres.

In addition to opposing disestablishment both candidates in Down took care to placate their presbyterian electors by stating opposition to the withdrawal of the *regium donum* and Hill-Trevor also said that he would support any necessary reforms of the Church of Ireland. At the nominations Hill-Trevor declared that he represented the people of all denominations of the constituency.[22] Forde had previously been challenged by William Johnston to pledge his opposition to the party processions act. Forde refused and stated in reply: 'I cannot see how any man is to go into parliament as an independent member having to pledge himself to the crotchets of every elector.'[23] The Orange element that Johnston represented was not a major force among the respectable farming electors of north-east Ulster at this stage, and Forde could afford to ignore his appeal. The nominations were rowdy but no opposition appeared.

In Co. Londonderry political affairs were arranged by a number of prominent landed interests, in particular the families of Bateson, Dawson and Waterford, and also some of the London companies that held land in the county, such as the Irish Society. In the 1850s strong tenant right and presbyterian opposition challenged these arrangements and in 1857-9 a tenant right liberal candidate held one of the seats, the only time a 'popular' candidate won an Ulster county seat in this period.[24] In 1868, however, the two unopposed conservative candidates were R. P. Dawson, whose father owned a 2,618-acre estate at Castledawson in the county, and Sir F. W.

Heygate, bt, a native of Essex who had married the only daughter and heir of Conolly Gage, proprietor of the 5,507-acre Bellarena family estate in Co. Londonderry. Compared with elsewhere the estates of the two M.P.s were small owing to the important interests of the London companies.

Both candidates in Londonderry showed themselves sensitive to possible causes of dissent among their constituents. In their address and nomination speeches they took care to balance defence of the Church of Ireland with a determination 'to watch and guard the interests of our presbyterian fellow protestants'.[25] Dawson even stated that he wished there were more presbyterian M.P.s from Ulster. They also dealt with the land question. Dawson declared: 'No man is more desirous than I am of securing to the really improving tenant legitimate repayment for any additional value imparted to the land by expenditure of his money and labour.' Heygate called for better living conditions for the labourers; both advocated reform of the grand jury system.

In Co. Tyrone the Abercorn and Belmore families controlled the representation of the country with little opposition from other landed interests or tenant right protest of the early 1850s. The more senior of the two unopposed candidates in 1868 was the rt hon. H. T. Lowry Corry, first lord of the admiralty, who had held the seat since 1825 and was uncle of the earl of Belmore, proprietor of a 14,359-acre estate in Tyrone. The other candidate was the rt hon. Lord Claud Hamilton, brother of the duke of Abercorn, the owner of 47,615 acres at Baron's Court, Newtownstewart. In their addresses both strongly denounced disestablishment, which Lowry Corry saw as unjust and a subversion of the protestant constitution; Hamilton also opposed attempts to abolish the *regium donum* and called for improvements in intermediate education. Neither candidate mentioned the land question but at the nomination Lowry Corry said that he would support tenants' security and compensation for improvements.[26]

Of all the Ulster counties, Fermanagh had witnessed less challenge to the leading landowning families than any other. No contested election at all occurred in the constituency between 1830 and 1868. The families of Brooke, Archdale, and Enniskillen arranged the representation of the county with little difficulty. The senior candidate in 1868 was Capt. M. E. Archdale, a prominent Orangeman, owner of Castle Archdale and 27,410 acres in Fermanagh, and M.P. for the county since 1834, when he succeeded his uncle who had sat for Fermanagh from 1806. The other candidate was Lt-col. the hon.

H. A. Cole, second son of the earl of Enniskillen, proprietor of a 29,635-acre estate at Florence Court in Fermanagh.

In his address Cole merely stated that his principles were those that he had always held. Archdale said that he was an advocate of civil and religious liberty and would support protestant institutions as their destruction would lead to anarchy. At the nomination Archdale repeated these points, declared his friendship towards catholics, praised the Orange order, and also called for compensation for tenants' improvements. Cole was again brief and simply declared his agreement with Archdale.[27] Neither candidate mentioned the *regium donum* but then presbyterians were not numerous in Fermanagh.

For a brief period shortly before the election it seemed that there was some feeling in the county that local M.P.s were not very active in their duties. This unrest was led by J. G. V. Porter, a landowner from Belleisle, Co. Fermanagh, one of whose particular objects was to obtain government action over the frequent flooding of the Erne. In October it was reported in the press that Porter had been asked to stand for the county with independent support. Porter, however, was a rather eccentric character, whom the *Impartial Reporter* described as the 'onward, forward (we had nearly written froward), fidgetty, maggoty, yet blunt and fearless J. G. V. Porter of Belleisle', and his opposition failed to materialise.[28]

In the counties discussed so far all the principal landowning families were conservative. In Co. Armagh, however, there were liberal landowners such as the Charlemont family, and their candidate held one of the county seats with a conservative from 1832 until 1857, when the arrangement broke down and two conservatives were elected in a rare contested election. From 1832 until 1868 Lt-col. Sir E. W. Verner, whose family owned a 5,436-acre estate near Moy in Co. Armagh, occupied one of the seats as a conservative. On 11 August 1868, however, an announcement appeared in the *Armagh Guardian* from Verner's son William, who stated that as his father intended to retire at the next election he planned to stand for the seat, encouraged by many promises of support. Subsequently Sir E. W. Verner published an address that announced his retirement and recommended his son.

There is no report in the press of a meeting to select the new parliamentary candidate but obviously the matter was arranged privately and satisfactorily between the Verner family and the main political interests in the county. There was no sign of any protest and William Verner was elected unopposed. The other conservative candidate was Sir J. M. Stronge, proprietor of the 4,404 acres at Tynan Abbey in Co. Armagh and related by his brother's marriage to the liberal Charlemont family. This liberal connection may have prevented opposition in the county to Stronge from liberal interests but it did not stop him from stating in his address his 'firm attachment to the protestant constitution in church and state'. He declared his intention to protect the established church and also the presbyterians' *regium donum*.[29] A county conservative association did exist but it seems to have played no role in electoral affairs in 1868 apart from the attendance of its secretary, T. G. Peel, at the revision sessions.[30]

In Co. Donegal the parliamentary representation was controlled by the conservative Conolly and Abercorn families. Between 1832 and 1868 there were only two electoral challenges and both were unsuccessful. Thomas Conolly was the senior member in 1868. Twenty years earlier he had succeeded on his father's death to 130,000 acres in Donegal and in the following year he took over one of the county parliamentary seats that his father had held since 1831. The other sitting member was the marquis of Hamilton, first son of the duke of Abercorn who owned a 15,942-acre estate in Co. Donegal. Both men had their main homes out of the county, Conolly at Castletown House in Co. Kildare and Hamilton at Baronscourt in Co. Tyrone, but they were well regarded as Donegal landlords.[31]

In their election addresses Conolly and Hamilton opposed disestablishment but, no doubt conscious of the sizeable catholic electorate in Donegal, did so not primarily on grounds of defending the Church of Ireland or protestantism but instead because they thought it would upset the existing constitutional position and eventually shake 'the foundations of society'. Hamilton promised to give attention to the land question in parliament. At the nomination, both candidates specifically addressed the catholic voters and appealed for their support against disestablishment on the lines that it was a revolutionary move which not only threatened their protestant fellow countrymen but would endanger society. Conolly mentioned their 'free constitution' under which each group enjoyed the 'free exercise of their own religion'.[32]

A contest in fact had seemed a distinct possibility in Donegal for a time. In September a meeting of liberals in Donegal town asked Lord Francis Conyngham, son of the marquis of Conyngham, to stand on liberal principles. He agreed but then withdrew after his father stated that he would 'much dislike' to see him 'disturb the

county by contesting it'.[33] Besides parental disapproval there were
other good reasons for Conyngham not to contest Donegal, as an
editorial in the *Londonderry Journal* pointed out: 'Donegal is a
large county. The man who intends to contest it must be prepared
for hard work, with a purse long enough to stretch from St John's
Point to Inishowen Head.' In addition a candidate needed 'a
thoroughly liberal programme — one alike acceptable to presbyterians, liberal churchmen, and catholics. . . .'[34]

In Co. Cavan the leading landed interests were the Saundersons,
Annesleys, and Farnhams. Also influential in the county was the
Dease family, one of the few significant catholic landed families in
Ulster. M. O'R. Dease unsuccessfully stood as a liberal in 1857
against the two conservative members for Cavan. Capt. E. J.
Saunderson was more fortunate when he was elected liberal M.P.
for the county in 1865 without a contest. The fact that the retiring
conservative was an uncle of his may have helped bring the change.
Saunderson, owner of 12,362 acres at Castle Saunderson in Co.
Cavan, stood again in 1868. The other sitting member was the hon.
Hugh Annesley, brother of Earl Annesley, whose main estate was
at Castlewellan in Co. Down but who also owned a 24,221-acre
property in Cavan. Col. Annesley was a distinguished soldier:
Thom's directory, 1869, noted that he 'was severely wounded at the
Cape and at the battle of the Alma'.[35]

In his address Annesley stated that he would support the Church
of Ireland and also any well considered reforms of that body.
Saunderson, however, declared that he would give only independent
backing to a liberal government and would oppose disestablishment,
although he believed anomalies in the church's position should be
removed. He argued that land tenure reform was a matter of first
importance, and urged that tenants should be properly compensated
for improvements.[36] Saunderson's position on disestablishment
caused dismay among members of the catholic clergy and electors,
many of whom in the past had organised in support of the liberal
cause in the county. In July a meeting was held in Cavan town under
the presidency of Dr Nicholas Conaty, catholic bishop of Kilmore,
and a liberal county club, independent of Saunderson, was established, which consisted of catholic clergy and laity from each parish.
Although the club secretary did some work at the revision session,
and criticism of Saunderson's stand was voiced in the *Anglo-Celt*, no
real opposition emerged.[37] Indeed the club avoided a direct attack
on Saunderson, perhaps because he was still after all a liberal and
there was no alternative candidate.

In Co. Monaghan, the only county contested in 1868, the dominant proprietorial interests were the Leslies, Shirleys, and Forsters, who were conservative, and the Rossmore and Dartrey families, who were liberal. Affairs were usually arranged fairly amicably between them although a bitter electoral contest had broken out in 1865. In July 1868 an election address appeared in the Monaghan press from S. E. Shirley, whose father, a former Co. Monaghan M.P., was owner of 26,386 acres around Carrickmacross. He announced his intention 'as the only son of one of the largest landholders in the county' to stand at the next election as a conservative and a strong supporter of the protestant and British constitution which he now saw as under threat.[38] By early August the two sitting M.P.s, the conservative Col. C. P. Leslie and the liberal Lord Cremorne, had also announced their intention to come forward again for the seats.[39] Col. Leslie, whose father had been M.P. for Monaghan (1801-26), was proprietor of a 13,621-acre estate at Glaslough, Co. Monaghan. Lord Cremorne was the eldest son of the earl of Dartrey, who lived on the 17,345-acre family property at Dartrey, Co. Monaghan.

Although a liberal, Cremorne was against the disestablishment of the Church of Ireland. A series of letters in favour of Shirley and against Cremorne, written by John Madden, another county landowner and prominent Orangeman, now appeared in the *Northern Standard*.[40] He argued that as a conservative Shirley was much safer on the disestablishment question than Cremorne. On 18 August a meeting of county magistrates and property owners was called to decide between Cremorne and Shirley, in order to avoid a contest, but this failed to achieve anything. Finally on 10 October, an address from Cremorne appeared which stated that he planned to retire because he feared the disturbances which might arise from a contested election and also because 'under the present exceptional circumstances, my prospects are not such as I can confidently rely upon for success.'[41] Subsequent comments in the press suggested that the circumstances referred to were that Cremorne had lost the backing of the catholic clergy and laity, who had assisted him in 1865, because he would not support disestablishment.[42]

Shortly after this the press reported that the catholic clergy in Monaghan were seeking a new liberal candidate. By the first week in November, William Gray, a protestant hotelier from Ballybay, Co. Monaghan, was in the field as a liberal candidate, although it is not clear who asked him to stand.[43] Gray does not seem to have had much active assistance from either liberal proprietors or catholic clergy, nor did he have connections with the Belfast-based Ulster liberal society. In his address he stated that he would vote for dis-establishment, support fair rents and fixity of tenure, and back Gladstone.[44] The result of the election was Leslie 3,130, Shirley 2,785, and Gray 960 votes. The conservative press attributed the defeat of Cremorne and Gray to the work of John Madden and also the non-intervention of the catholic clergy.[45] The liberal press blamed Gray's failure at the poll on his late candidature and reported the activity of bailiffs and land agents in the conservative cause on polling day.[46]

The boroughs
There was much greater political activity in the Ulster boroughs than in the counties in 1868. Indeed this had consistently been the case since 1832. While proprietorial interests were still dominant in the majority of boroughs, these interests had sometimes been strongly challenged, usually over local matters, and occasionally defeated. In most places politicians, especially among the dominant conservatives, still relied on their own efforts to organise both for revision courts and for election campaigns, although a small number of party organisations were active. While purely local issues and conflicts continued to be a source of electoral rivalry in 1868, a more organised opposition than had been seen before appeared during the year. The franchise changes of 1868 had created new oppor-tunities in the boroughs and the revision sessions were heavily contested in the run-up to the general election.[47]

Central to this new challenge was the work of the Ulster liberal society, founded at a private meeting in the Royal Hotel, Belfast, on 4 August 1865, shortly after the general election of that year. According to confidential early papers of the society it was estab-lished because of frustration at the lack of liberal success in Ulster, which was put down to neglect of the registry and inadequate organisation.[48] The society's aims were to 'unite on a common plat-form all sections of the liberal party in the province of Ulster', to foster public opinion in the liberal cause, and to assist with regis-tration. An annual minimum subscription of £1 was fixed but members were encouraged to give more.

From the early lists of members we can see that the society con-tained some of the local liberal landowners, such as the earl of Charlemont. Its main membership, however, included a large range of manufacturing, business, and professional people from all over Ulster. The majority were presbyterian but there were also some catholics, such as Bernard Hughes, the well known Belfast bakery owner, and some members of the Church of Ireland, such as the solicitor C. H. Brett. Within a short time the society had a full-time secretary, A. M. Mitchell, and by the revision sessions of the 1868 he was present, with local liberals, not only in Belfast but at every borough except Downpatrick, Armagh, and Carrickfergus.[49] The names of all the liberal borough candidates in Ulster in 1868 are to be found in the lists of original members of the Ulster liberal society.[50]

During 1868 the liberals mounted a major challenge in Belfast against the conservatives, who now found themselves faced with special problems because of the franchise changes. By 1868 proprietorial interests counted for very little in the borough. Prior to 1832 parliamentary representation had been controlled by the borough's owner, the marquis of Donegall. But because of the collapse of Donegall power (due largely to heavy gambling debts)[51] and the appearance of new social forces in the throes of the rapid expansion of the town, reform and constitutional parties emerged in the 1830s and 1840s. Eventually in September 1842 the Belfast conservative society was formed, and from this time on the conservatives dominated the boroughs politics, both parliamentary and local.[52] Potential rivalry between presbyterians and Church of Ireland members was usually avoided by having a conservative candidate from each denomination for the two Belfast seats.

Opponents of the conservatives were not so well organised and had a number of ad hoc associations. In 1865, however, following another liberal defeat at the general election, the Belfast liberal association was formed, shortly after the establishment of the Ulster liberal society, and both groups were clearly closely linked. By 1868 the liberals had greatly improved their organisation in Belfast and were well represented at the revision sessions. Their electoral prospects were now enhanced considerably by divisions, both social and denominational, within the conservative ranks. For all parties concerned, the situation in Belfast by the general election was greatly changed by the reform act which expanded the numbers who had the vote, particularly among working men.

Rumours of the retirement of one of the two sitting Belfast conservative M.P.s, S. G. Getty, had been rife since mid-1867. The prominent Orangeman William Johnston, a minor Co. Down landowner and member of the Church of Ireland, announced in September 1867 his intention to stand for Belfast at the next election, principally on the issue of the party processions act, to which he believed the local conservative M.P.s had not sufficiently objected.[53]

His imprisonment in March 1868, following a protest march in 1867, led to an upsurge of support for him. As Thomas MacKnight observed, 'the most enthusiastic admirers of the imprisoned violator of the party processions act were among the Orange artisans of Belfast', and on 4 March 1868 a large number of them met in the Ulster Hall in Belfast to declare sympathy with Johnston.[54] The united protestant working men's association of Ulster was set up to return Johnston to parliament.

From mid-July 1868 the Belfast conservative association held private meetings to choose candidates for the forthcoming elections. The views of Johnston and his working-class supporters were ignored in the selection procedure. Finally in September Sir Charles Lanyon, a leading architect and one of the sitting M.P.s, and John Mulholland, head of the prominent Mulholland linen firm, emerged as the chosen candidates, in spite of the fact that (contrary to the practice of selecting a presbyterian as one of the conservative candidates), both were members of the Church of Ireland. A committee was set up to run their campaign.

After Johnston's release from jail in May 1868, he began his election campaign. At his meetings, made up largely of Belfast working men (many to be newly enfranchised by the reform act), resentment was expressed that the local conservative organisation had refused to accept him as a candidate. The chairman of one such gathering remarked: 'We conceive that the time has arrived when we shall be no longer their slaves, and that we now shall have a little of the fruits of our labour for ourselves.'[55] The right of the Belfast Orangemen and working men to put forward their own candidate was proclaimed. Johnston frequently spoke of how he stood for 'the protestant working men of Belfast' and how he was determined to maintain conservatism 'as long as it maintains protestantism, and no longer'. Johnston at the same time stated: 'Men must learn to know that to be an Orangeman is not to cease to be an Irishman, having at heart the interests of his country', and urged tolerance towards catholics.[56] He denounced the party processions act and advocated land reform, but was silent on disestablishment and other social issues. Lanyon and Mulholland insisted at their meetings that they had been properly selected.[57] They frequently stated their opposition to disestablishment and also said that they represented the working men of Belfast. Presbyterian support was sought by denunciation of any future removal of the *regium donum* and by reference to the resolution of the presbyterian assembly on disestablishment.

On 19 August 1868 a selection meeting of the Belfast liberal association was held. A resolution was passed that invited Thomas McClure, a presbyterian Belfast merchant, to contest the constituency in the liberal interest.[58] McClure accepted, and in early September his address appeared.[59] An executive committee was formed to organise his election campaign. On this committee were many merchants and manufacturers such as the catholic Bernard Hughes and the presbyterian J. G. Biggar, Robert McGeagh, and Thomas Sinclair.[60] Canvassing and meetings were arranged. At his meetings McClure spoke strongly for disestablishment of the Church of Ireland.[61] Presbyterian ministers were frequently on his platform and the opinion was often voiced that Belfast needed a presbyterian representative.[62] At the same time McClure talked of his desire to unite catholic and protestant behind the liberal banner. He also mentioned his belief that Belfast needed a merchant as one of its representatives.

On 17 November the nominations were held but had to be postponed until the next day due to disorder, caused mainly by the interruptions of John Rea, an eccentric Belfast solicitor. Before the polling had proceeded very far it was apparent that Johnston and McClure were in the lead, and so Mulholland retired from the contest in order to try to consolidate the conservative support behind Lanyon. This failed, however, to change matters and the result was Johnston 5,975, McClure 4,202, Lanyon 3,540, and Mulholland 1,580. Some useful insights into the nature of the candidates' support can be found in an examination of the details of the voting, which, because the secret ballot had not yet been introduced, were published after the election. (Plumpers, it can be noted, are single votes given for one candidate although in a two-member constituency, such as Belfast, electors had two votes.)

2a: Belfast poll: number of plumpers for each candidate and intervotes between candidates[63]

plumpers	Johnston	1,310
	McClure	1,815
	Lanyon	109
	Mulholland	43
intervotes	McClure and Johnston	2,307
	McClure and Mulholland	102
	Lanyon and Mulholland	1,247
	Lanyon and Johnston	2,108
	Johnston and Mulholland	198

Clearly a substantial amount of intervoting occurred between the supporters of Johnston and McClure, a step that brought considerable advantage to both candidates. As evidence of the strong feeling in presbyterian circles in favour of disestablishment and the liberal party we may observe that out of the 17 presbyterian ministers who can be identified in the printed poll book for the 1868 Belfast election, 7 voted only for McClure, 3 for McClure and Johnston, 1 for Johnston alone, 1 for Lanyon and Mulholland, and 4 abstained.[64] Also, as further proof of the social division within the conservative ranks caused by the election it can be noted that districts of Orange working men largely backed Johnston while in commercial and wealthier residential districts there was greater sympathy for Lanyon and Mulholland.[65] Clearly, new presbyterian and working-class dissent had created for the conservatives a difficult situation of which the liberals were able to take advantage.

In Derry, an expanding city where proprietorial interests were diffuse, the liberals also mounted a strong challenge in 1868. A popular local figure and a liberal, Sir R. A. Ferguson had sat as M.P. for the city from 1831 to his death in 1860, with no real opposition. The seat was then won by the conservative William McCormick; five years later he stood down to be replaced by another conservative, Lord C. J. Hamilton. Although Hamilton did not have significant property interests in Derry, he was well connected. Second son of the duke of Abercorn, he had one brother who was M.P. for Donegal, another brother who sat for Middlesex, and an uncle who sat for Tyrone. By 1868 the city had both a liberal association and a conservative committee.[66]

The first mention of a possible contest in the city during 1868 occurred in late May when it was reported that Richard Dowse, Q.C., would come forward as a liberal against the sitting conservative M.P.[67] He arrived in Derry on 14 July 1868 and met members of the liberal association, who accepted his candidature. On 27 July Lord C. J. Hamilton announced his intention to stand again. Both candidates belonged to the Church of Ireland. Matters quietened down from early August until mid-October, when the two candidates returned to the city and began to hold meetings and canvass. The result of the election was that Dowse received 704 votes and Hamilton 599. In his victory speech at the declaration of the poll Dowse thanked the clergy for their help and named Dr Francis Kelly, catholic bishop of Derry, and a presbyterian minister, Rev. William McClure. Hamilton in his speech attacked some presbyterian ministers for their part in his defeat and said they were 'likely soon to be taught a lesson which they will not easily forget'.[68]

Whether or not it resulted directly from these words of Hamilton we may note what happened to one presbyterian minister in the city, as his son Sir John Ross, bt, recorded later in his memoirs:

> The Sunday following the election brought a dreadful experience. Our church was more than half deserted; the congregation, resenting the defeat of their hero, Lord Claud, against whom my father had voted, had decided to leave the church. This was a terrible blow to my mother and the family, as it meant a serious diminution in the slender stipend on which the manse was kept going.[69]

As regards political organisation at the election it can be observed that on the liberal side there was a local liberal association which helped at the polls. After the election it was revealed that the Ulster liberal society subscribed substantially to the funds of this body, and the central liberal association in Dublin had lent one of their organisers to the Derry liberals during the election.[70] Subsequently a petition was brought against Dowse which alleged bribery, intimidation, and undue clerical influence, but none of these allegations were proved.[71] On the last issue no evidence at all was presented, but it is clear that catholic clergy and presbyterian ministers helped the liberal organisation. On the conservative side Hamilton had the assistance of a local committee and other groups such as the Londonderry working men's protestant defence association; this last-named body seems to have had no important social or political difference with the other conservative bodies, unlike the Belfast association. In Hamilton's case it also transpired later that money to help his cause had come from outside the city, namely the Carlton club.[72]

2b: Derry poll: votes for each candidate by religion[73]

	Dowse	Hamilton	unpolled	total
Church of Ireland	13	275	20	308
presbyterian	163	259	75	497
nonconformist[74]	27	43	31	101
catholic	501	22	40	563
total	704	599	166	1,469

From the evidence of a poll book published after the election, it is clear that the liberal voters were mainly catholic and the conservative mainly protestant. Most of Dowse's protestant supporters were presbyterians, although the bulk of the presbyterians supported Hamilton. As regards the importance of the franchise reform of 1868 it is clear that, since it increased the number of catholics on the register and these largely backed the liberal, the reform was of vital importance.

In Newry there was also a straightforward liberal–conservative contest. The principal proprietor in the town was the earl of Kilmorey but his political interest had been frequently challenged in the past, sometimes with success. D. C. Brady, the only catholic elected to parliament from an Ulster constituency before 1874, was M.P. for the town, 1835-7, and William Kirk held the seat as a liberal between 1852 and 1859. On 27 July 1868 Lord Newry, grandson and heir to the earl of Kilmorey, was selected at a meeting of conservatives in the borough as candidate in place of A. C. Innes, the sitting conservative member, who had intimated that he would not stand at the next election.[75]

Around the same time it was disclosed that William Kirk, a presbyterian merchant and the former liberal M.P. for the town, would come forward as a liberal candidate. At a meeting of liberals on 31 July in Newry, those present pledged themselves to support Kirk and it was reported that he had wide catholic and presbyterian backing.[76] The conservative *Newry Telegraph* described Kirk as the nominee of the Ulster liberal society,[77] although there is no direct evidence about this apart from the fact that A. M. Mitchell from the society assisted the Newry liberals at the revision sessions and Kirk was a founder member of the society. Both candidates canvassed and held meetings for a time in August; they then stopped until November, when they recommenced their campaigns.

At the nomination Kirk concentrated in his speech on disestablishment, which he strongly supported; he advocated the principle of religious equality. Lord Newry spoke about conservative foreign policy, and stated that the main issue was not disestablishment but the land question. On the subject of religious equality he believed that such a thing was impossible: some must go up and others down; if let, catholics would go up and protestants down, because catholics were more numerous.[78] The result of the contest was Kirk 386, Lord Newry 379.

2c: Newry poll: votes for each candidate by religious denomination.[79]
Those with valuation between £4 and £8 are given in brackets.

	Kirk		Newry		unpolled	
Church of Ireland	9	(1)	174	(45)	7	
presbyterian	30	(1)	171	(25)	9	
catholic	341	(102)	11	(7)	10	(3)
methodist	1	(1)	16	(4)	3	
independent	1	—	7	(2)	1	
quakers	4	—	0	—	2	—
total	386	(105)	379	(83)	32	(3)

The printed poll book for the election gives valuable insights into voting behaviour in Newry. First, it shows that, as in Derry, the liberal support came mainly from the catholics, with only a limited amount of protestant backing, chiefly from the presbyterians. But, small as this protestant liberal vote was, it was of great importance for Kirk. At the same time the table illustrates that the conservative electors were mostly protestant. Of the catholics who voted conservative, quite a few lived in property owned directly by the Kilmorey family.[80] Secondly, the table demonstrates clearly once again the significance of the franchise reforms in 1868. Of the new electors a higher proportion were supporters of the liberal than the conservative candidate. Thirdly, of the protestants who voted for the liberals few were in the lower rateable valuation group. As a more detailed study of the polling reveals, twenty-five of the protestants who backed the liberal held property valued at £20 or over. These liberal protestants were mainly merchants, solicitors, and shopkeepers.[81]

In Carrickfergus there was no organised liberal opposition to the sitting conservative M.P. but strong protest came from other quarters. Thanks to its special freeman franchise the borough had the socially broadest electorate in the whole country. Carrickfergus, however, was well known not for any populist or democratic leanings but rather for the corruption of its politics: indeed, the constituency was disenfranchised between 1833 and 1835 because of extensive bribery and venality. After the decline of the Donegall interest in the 1830s, the Downshires, owners also of great estates in Down and Wicklow, wielded the main proprietorial influence. They were able, in spite of frequent opposition, to control not only the parliamentary representation but also the town commission, which itself held considerable land in the borough.

Information about the 1868 election at Carrickfergus is unfortunately scarce, because no pre-1880 Carrickfergus paper has survived and reports about the election are scanty in the Belfast press. It seems clear, nonetheless, that the main political issues of the day counted for little. In his address, dated 10 October, the sitting conservative member, Robert Torrens, declared his intention to come forward at the next election and stated simply that his politics were well known to everyone.[82] Three days later M. R. Dalway, a local proprietor, issued an address which said that he also intended to stand at the request of a number of electors.[83] The only point of policy that Dalway made in this address was to state his determination to uphold the protestant religion and his belief that considerable reform in the established church would be conducive to this end. At the nominations neither candidate discussed policies at length. The contest resulted in the election of Dalway with 669 votes against 407 for Torrens.

Light can be cast on the Carrickfergus poll from other evidence. Undoubtedly Dalway's victory was connected in large part with the struggle of the freemen with the town commissioners over the commons land.[84] At the local elections of commissioners in 1867 Dalway and his friends had stood unsuccessfully: it was reported after the 1868 contest that at the nomination speeches his supporters had denounced in strong terms the commissioners and landlords.[85] Following the conclusion of the 1868 polls one of Dalway's supporters spoke of the 'victory they had obtained over the nominee of the town council'.[86] We may also note that the agent of the marquis of Downshire was on Torrens' committee.[87] Thus it is probable that the Carrickfergus contest was mainly the result of local dissatisfaction caused by the struggle over commons land.

Subsequently a petition was lodged against Dalway's return on grounds of bribery, intimidation, and treating, but none of the charges were proved, although it was shown that after the results were announced the Dalway side supplied a considerable amount of whiskey for celebration. This could have been embarrassing for Dalway, who was a leading temperance reformer, but it was claimed that his sister, not himself, was responsible.[88] It was also revealed at this election enquiry that Dalway had received funding from liberal sources, which had also assisted him at the revision sessions.

A straight liberal–conservative struggle occurred in Enniskillen in 1868, after certain complications caused by local factors. In a tradition that stretched back to the late seventeenth century the Coles, earls of Enniskillen, successfully controlled the parliamentary representation of Enniskillen.[89] Opposition in the 1850s and in 1865 from a local family, the Collums, which originated in a dispute over some town property,[90] failed to upset their position. In 1868 the election campaign began on 6 August with a meeting of electors in the town court house, at which the hon. J. C. Cole, sitting M.P. for the borough, announced his intention to retire at the next election. Then, according to the *Impartial Reporter*, 'he also said his brother, the earl of Enniskillen, did not wish his son, Lord Cole, in his extreme youth, to aspire to the honour and begged to introduce Lord Crichton for their favourable acceptance in his stead.'[91] A motion was put to the meeting in Crichton's favour, and was

accepted amidst considerable uproar. The following day a deputation from the meeting presented Lord Crichton, eldest son of the
earl of Erne, with a request to stand for parliament. Crichton agreed,
and at another gathering the following day he expressed his views as
a conservative and was accepted as candidate.

Both meetings of electors, however, had been interrupted by a
local conservative, W. A. Dane, who claimed that affairs concerning
the new representative had not been handled properly. Dane then
announced his intention to stand for election 'to test the independence of the conservative party'.[92] From the middle of August
onwards both candidates canvassed the electors as conservatives.
On 15 October John Collum, a prominent local solicitor, published
an election address as a liberal. The *Enniskillen Advertiser* commented on his candidature: 'he has been for fifteen years the
permanent candidate for Enniskillen in opposition to nomination',
a reference to his stand at several previous elections as a conservative and then a liberal against the Enniskillen family.[93] All candidates belonged to the Church of Ireland.

Nomination took place on 18 November. Shortly before it, however, Dane withdrew, explaining that he feared his continued candidature might harm the conservative party and that Lord Crichton
had assured him that he was not the nominee of any clique.[94] At the
nominations Collum and Lord Crichton reiterated the points made
in their addresses. Lord Crichton called disestablishment 'the first
step of the onward march of communistic and socialistic ideas' and
made a plea for the defence of the protestant faith, while Collum
remained evasive on the disestablishment and education questions,
but emphasised: 'The question you have to decide is whether this
town is to remain a pocket borough or not.'[95] When the poll ended
the result was Lord Crichton 171 and Collum 141, with 3 votes for
the hon. Charles Crichton and 1 for the hon. A. L. Cole (the last two
were put forward at the nomination without their consent). In a
speech that followed the declaration of the poll one of Collum's
helpers, Jeremiah Jordan, thanked those who had voted for Collum
and implied that between 20 and 30 of them were protestants and
the rest catholics.[96] The small number of presbyterian electors in
Enniskillen was undoubtedly a key factor in the liberal failure.

Crucial to the conservative position in Enniskillen, however, was
the candidature and last-minute withdrawal of Dane. Dane had
claimed that he stood in protest against improper means of selecting
the conservative candidate. Other evidence, however, indicates
that there was more to his actions than this. On 5 February 1868

Lord Mayo asked the viceroy, Lord Abercorn, to find a government post for Dane, a matter that he said Lord Enniskillen's family had raised with him many times.[97] He enclosed a letter from Lt-col. the rt hon. T. E. Taylor, M.P., Irish conservative whip, which stated that Dane was an important conservative supporter in Enniskillen of long standing who in 1865 had become estranged from the Enniskillen family:

> To secure his good offices, it became necessary that we should promise to endeavour to get for him some . . . professional place in the event of our coming into power. Mr Dane has not failed on several occasions since 1866 to remind me that he remained unprovided for, and I am satisfied that if nothing is done for him before the general election we shall lose Enniskillen.[98]

In another letter, the rt hon. H. T. Lowry Corry, M.P. for Tyrone, warned of the danger of a direct refusal to Dane and suggested that his ill health could be used as an excuse not to give him a post: 'the fact is . . . with gout . . . he has spent half his time in bed for years.'[99]

All was to no avail and Dane proceeded with his candidature. Had he persevered in this it is likely that the fears of Taylor and Lowry Corry would have been realised and the seat lost to a liberal through a divided conservative vote. His last-minute withdrawal was of great importance. Dane himself explained that he had done so to avoid a split in the conservative support. We may note, however, that on 10 December 1868 the *Enniskillen Advertiser* carried a report that Paul Dane, son of W. A. Dane, had been appointed clerk of the crown in Co. Wicklow. In view of the earlier correspondence with Lord Abercorn, it is very likely that his withdrawal was connected with this appointment.

Dungannon was another good example of a borough where the local proprietor had maintained a strong political position. In an historical account of the constituency, written in 1885, the earl of Belmore described how the Ranfurly family had effectively controlled the town's parliamentary representation from 1695: 'Down to 1874, in every generation, one or more members of that family (twelve in all) have at some time or other represented the borough of Dungannon'.[100] The family representative in 1868 was Col. the hon. W. S. Knox, uncle to the earl of Ranfurly. In his address he spoke of 'the affectionate regard that has for many generations subsisted between the inhabitants of Dungannon and my family'. He repudiated any 'feelings of intolerance' but avowed his attachment to the established church.[101] At the revision sessions a local solicitor, Henry Kelly, had handled the conservative interest; we know from his accounts that he was commissioned for this work by the earl of Ranfurly.[102] In most other small boroughs the conservative registration agents would likewise have been employed by the local proprietor.

A contested poll seemed a possibility to the very last in Dungannon in 1868. T. A. Dickson, a local presbyterian merchant, collected pledges of support for a liberal candidate, James Brown of Donaghmore, Co. Tyrone, but a week before the nomination his candidature was dropped. In a letter to the *Northern Whig* Dickson explained that he had put Brown forward because he was 'mainly influenced by the desire of removing from the presbyterians the stigma of not having presbyterians in parliament'. But Knox meantime had received the backing of Dr C. L. Morell, moderator of the presbyterian general assembly and a local Dungannon minister, and so Dickson felt that he could not continue with his plan.[103] Two other liberal candidates issued addresses in November but then withdrew. At the uncontested nomination where he was proposed by Morell, Knox took good care to support the *regium donum*, although the subject had not been mentioned in his address.[104]

In Coleraine proprietorial interests were not so singular as in Dungannon but there was also a strong presbyterian section among the electors, which the sitting conservative M.P. had to deal with carefully. The Beresford family and the Irish Society were the two principal landowners of the town but differences in politics had led to bitter contests between them in the 1830s and in 1843 the main proprietary interests were successfully challenged by John Boyd on conservative and presbyterian lines.[105] Apart from 1852-7, Boyd held the seat until 1862 when on his death he was succeeded by Sir H. H. Bruce, bt, the owner of some property in Coleraine but a major landowner in Co. Londonderry. Bruce was not opposed in 1868, but his actions during the year show that he was concerned to work for local support, which could not be taken for granted.

His election address stated that he would maintain all the protestant churches in connection with the state, referring here of course to the establishment of the Church of Ireland and the presbyterians' *regium donum*.[106] At the nominations he was introduced as 'a landlord and a resident gentleman well known in the neighbourhood'. Bruce then explained his actions over the Monsell burial bill, about which he had been criticised by some presbyterians. He opposed disestablishment on the general grounds that it would dissociate religion from the state. Local matters such as the navigation of the Bann were also mentioned.[107] While the Coleraine newspaper reports during the second half of 1868 show presbyterian

criticism of Bruce, they also reveal how he played a prominent part
in public affairs. For example, he attended the Coleraine and Route
horticultural society show where he came second in the competition
for 'three head of celery'. He was present at the races of the Bann
rowing club, of which he was president.[108] Four years later he gave
a grand banquet to his constituents in Coleraine.[109]

In the other uncontested boroughs in 1868, Downpatrick,
Armagh, and Lisburn, proprietorial interests were also important
but pressures from the voters were rather different. In all three,
presbyterians were neither numerous nor influential, and catholics
were a significant number of the electorate in Downpatrick and
Armagh, but not in Lisburn. The Ker family had purchased the
greater part of Downpatrick in the early 1830s, and from 1835 to
1865 members of the family or their nominees represented the town
with little opposition. In 1865 William Keown became M.P., and he
stood again in 1868. Described in the press as the second largest
owner of property in the borough, Keown stressed in his address
and at the nominations that he sought to be reelected as an independent member but at the same time thought that a conservative
government was best for the county.[110] Only in passing did he
mention his opposition to disestablishment. The *Down Recorder*
reported that during a canvass of Downpatrick in September
Keown was promised the support of the rector, two presbyterian
ministers, and the parish priest, so clearly he had adopted, probably
deliberately, a vague political position to avoid arousing
opposition.[111]

In Armagh the main political influence was that of the Church of
Ireland primate but his power had been on the wane since the 1832
reform act. Local notables, both liberal and conservative, had contested the constituency, which possessed a conservative society,
founded in the 1830s; under its secretary, T. G. Peel, the main purpose of the society seems to have been to supervise the registration
in the conservative interest.[112] The conservative candidate in 1868
was John Vance, a Dublin merchant and former Dublin M.P., who
had been asked to take the seat at a by-election of 1867 in the
absence of a suitable local candidate. Vance's address said that he
would go to parliament unpledged, but stated that the main issue of
the next parliament would be whether or not the protestant constitution and institutions were maintained.[113] At the nomination he
only briefly mentioned disestablishment but said that the *regium
donum* should be increased. He thanked the Armagh conservative
society for its work. No opponent to Vance emerged apart from one

Patrick McMahon, described by a contemporary as 'a great deal more mad than drunk',[114] who created such a disturbance at the nomination that he was forcibly removed.

Lisburn was owned entirely by the Hertford family. Successful opposition to them, however, had arisen in the 1850s from some local manufacturers and merchants but in 1863 a nominee of the family, E. W. Verner, regained the seat. Verner, who stood again in 1868, was a member of the prominent Orange Verner family of Armagh and brother of the new M.P. for Co. Armagh. Introduced as 'the member of a family long identified with true protestantism' by his seconder, Verner attacked the catholic church, which he saw as hostile to free governments, and he advocated rights for tenants.[115] Lisburn had also a local conservative society, concerned primarily with registration. Neither this nor the Armagh society (both of which were probably formed because of the absence of a strong, resident proprietor) showed signed of activity at election time.

Summary of results
Compared with the election results of 1865, the final outcome of the 1868 general election in Ulster showed slight, but significant, political change. Of the 29 M.P.s returned for the province, 25 were conservative and 4 (3 in urban seats) were liberal, compared with 27 conservatives and 2 liberals (both in rural seats) three years earlier. Of the county members (1 liberal and 17 conservatives) all were owners or relatives of owners of substantial estates in their constituencies. Of the 8 conservative borough M.P.s, only John Vance, a Dublin merchant, came from a non-landed background. The Carrickfergus M.P., M. R. Dalway, was a minor landowner in the town but had won the seat in opposition to the leading proprietorial interests. William Johnston in Belfast was a Co. Down landlord, although his estate was a very small one. All the other borough conservatives were connected with or had the backing of the main proprietorial powers in their constituencies. In sharp contrast, however, the three liberal borough M.P.s consisted of two merchants and a queen's counsel.

As regards the educational and religious backgrounds of the Ulster M.P.s, we may note that all the conservatives, apart from Johnston, were educated privately or at English public schools, and around half had received a university education at Oxford or Cambridge. Johnston attended a local diocesan school and then went to Trinity College, Dublin: the hon. Edward O'Neill also attended

Trinity. Of the liberals, Saunderson was educated privately, Dowse at Dungannon Royal School and Trinity, McClure at Royal Belfast Academical Institution, and Kirk at a local school. Every conservative belonged to the Church of Ireland, as did Saunderson and Dowse, but not McClure and Kirk, who were presbyterian. The names of all the liberal borough M.P.s can be found in the lists of founding members of the Ulster liberal society in 1865.[116]

During the election campaign political organisation had clearly been arranged differently by the two parties. On the conservative side organisation had revolved around the candidates and their families, and there was little sign of political societies or associations apart from the rather feeble Armagh and Lisburn societies and the more active Belfast and Derry associations. On the liberal side, however, there was the Ulster liberal society with its important registration activities and local associations in Belfast and Derry, all of which had played an important part in the liberals' campaign.

In the rest of Ireland in 1868 the political divisions of conservative and liberal also remained the most important ones, although in different proportions to Ulster: 14 conservatives and 62 liberals were returned to parliament compared with 20 and 56, respectively, in 1865. Thus the total Irish representation, which had consisted of 47 conservatives and 58 liberals three years earlier, now stood at 39 conservatives and 66 liberals. Liberal politics, particularly on the question of disestablishment and also, to a lesser extent, land and education reform, had found considerable support in the three southern provinces, with their strong catholic electorate, while conservative policies, especially anti-disestablishment, had found most backing in Ulster. Those conservatives returned for seats outside Ulster came from constituencies with a substantial protestant electorate, such as Co. Dublin, or where conservative families, such as the Bruens in Co. Carlow, retained their influence. Of the 76 M.P.s outside Ulster, a significantly higher number, especially among the liberals in the boroughs, were from professional and mercantile backgrounds, although the majority (52) were still from landed backgrounds and around half (39) were protestant.[117]

The conservatives had no significant formal political organisation outside Dublin and Cork and seem to have relied during the election on the efforts of their landed candidates and families. The liberals, likewise, had little structured party organisation but many in the counties occupied leading positions among the landowners which they used to advantage. In certain areas, however, liberal candidates had the support of tenant associations and county political clubs.

The catholic clergy were also an influential force in the liberal camp, either as a significant interest to be dealt with, or as the means of providing organisational assistance.

The contemporary liberal press tended to attribute the conservative success in the north in 1868 to 'landlordocracy and territorial influence'.[118] In a sense this was true: most of the M.P.s came from the leading landowning families, which was an important factor in their election. But the absence of political activity in all but a few of the Ulster constituencies suggests there was little real opposition to their political and social role, and their policies seem to have been acceptable by and large in the protestant-dominated constituencies. At the same time the general election had shown evidence of unrest and the beginning of political protest from a number of quarters. Two developments in particular, the growth of the liberals and internal conflict within conservatism, had revealed that new forces were at work in Ulster politics.

Richard Seymour Conway, fourth marquis of Hertford, was undoubtedly the grandest and also the least known locally of all the great landowning magnates of Ulster. His estate in south Antrim at the beginning of the 1870s comprised 66,000 acres with a population of about 20,000 and a rental of £58,000 a year. There were no less than 1,000 electors on the estate out of a total of just over 10,000 for the county.[1] But the fourth marquis visited Ireland only twice as he chose to spend most of his time in Paris where he lived in the Chateau Bagatelle on the Bois de Boulogne. He was a friend of the emperor Napoleon III and amassed a magnificent art collection which eventually formed the main part of the Wallace collection at Hertford House in London.[2] This Hertford connection with Co. Antrim suddenly became of direct relevance to Ulster politics in 1869 with the death in the middle of the year of Rear-admiral G. H. Seymour, the family member of parliament for the county.

The contested by election which followed witnessed a continuation of the Hertford position in Co. Antrim, but it deserves special attention because of the extensive information about the election which has survived. Revealing Hertford family papers, together with evidence from an unusual libel court case, give a unique insight into the political power and influence of Ulster landlord M.P.s in this period. At the same time the material reveals the first appearance of growing tenant right protest which was soon to spread throughout the province and to create a new political protest in the rural constituencies.

Co. Antrim, 1869

On 21 July 1869, the day after Seymour's demise, a private meeting was held in London to arrange his parliamentary successor.[3] Present were Major-general F. H. Seymour, brother of the late M.P. and eldest son of Admiral Sir G. F. Seymour, heir presumptive to the marquis of Hertford; Dean J. W. Stannus, principal agent of the Hertford Antrim estate; and Lord O'Neill, owner of the second largest Antrim estate after the Hertfords', and father of the other M.P. for the county. O'Neill was informed of the wish of the Seymour family to put forward Capt. H. de G. Seymour, General Seymour's eldest son, for the seat. He agreed and the following day

Stannus wrote to the marquis of Hertford to inform him that Capt. Seymour would stand as the family candidate unless he heard to the contrary.[4]

From London Capt. Seymour then posted his address to the Antrim newspapers along with letters to the leading county landlords to seek their support.[5] After the admiral's funeral he proceeded to Ireland and arrived in Co. Antrim on 9 August. Meantime, Sir R. S. Adair, a landowner from Ballymena and member of the Ulster liberal society, had been selected by the society to stand as a liberal candidate.[6] The possibility of another proprietor coming forward as a conservative was averted, partly through fear that the liberal would win on a split conservative vote and partly in acknowledgement of the dominant position of the Hertford interest. Resentment among landlords and tenants at family absenteeism was appeased by promises from Seymour to reside at Lisburn. He visited local landlords and addressed gatherings of supporters. Adair also held meetings and canvassed.

In his address Seymour took the line of a moderate English conservative on the issues of the day.[7] He stated that his principles led him to 'deprecate' the disestablishment of the Church of Ireland, which he saw as 'injurious' to religion and to the security of property. By this stage the Irish church bill had already been passed by parliament and would come into operation at the end of the year. Seymour made no mention of the land question. But he was soon made aware of strong feelings on these matters, and quickly responded. After a public meeting in Belfast his uncle observed privately: 'we see that in future much more business about "William III" and "No surrender" must be put in'; as regards tenant right he observed that 'all over the county that is the question'.[8] By the nominations Seymour had given strong declarations of support for protestantism and land reform.[9] In his address and speeches Adair concentrated on the land question. The elections ended in a sizeable victory for Seymour, who received 5,588 votes against Adair's 2,294.

Subsequently this election was cited as an example of the coercive power of the landlords. Thomas MacKnight, editor of the *Northern Whig*, described it in 1896 as showing 'the utter want of independence on the part of many of the sturdy tenant farmers of Ulster'.[10] Samuel McElroy, in his account of the land reform movement in Antrim, wrote that 'cohorts of tenants were marched to the poll, having the aspects of slaves'.[11] But in 1872, when members of the Stannus family filed suit against the *Northern Whig* for allegations that they had used their position as the agents of Lord Hertford for improper political purposes over the previous twenty-two years, the judgement went in favour of the Stannuses.[12] Only a small number of examples were cited in court for the whole of this period in which coercion had been used. No such evidence could be furnished for the 1869 by-election.

At the same time, the contest showed the influential role played by landlords in politics. During the election proceedings W. T. Stannus, son of Dean Stannus, denied in a speech at Lisburn that coercion was employed, but went on then to say:

> Is it to be counted as a crime, in the nineteenth century, for a landed proprietor who is supposed to have an interest in the welfare of his tenants, when he knows a person whom he thinks would make a suitable representative, to use all his legitimate influence on his behalf?[13]

The attention paid by Seymour to the gentry during the campaign was an acknowledgement of their position and power. The proprietors expected to give a lead and the tenants accepted their right to do so, mainly, it seems, in recognition of the social and political role of the landlords. Seymour had also to be aware of landlord sensitivities, in particular the annoyance about the non-residence of his predecessors.

It would be wrong, nonetheless, to dismiss entirely the coercive element in landlord–tenant relations. During the 1872 court case, although no examples were given of coercion in 1869, it was pointed out that all the Hertford bailiffs canvassed actively for Seymour. Witnesses claimed that it was generally understood that tenants would vote for the estate office candidate. One person who testified made the valid point that the support for Seymour of all but 14 out of 940 voters from the Hertford estate constituted an abnormally high preference for one candidate. Even if the bailiffs did not threaten prospective voters, tenants may well have feared adverse consequences if they defied their landlord's wishes. One witness, a Hertford tenant, gave evidence of this feeling in court:

> At the last County Antrim election I voted for Seymour, and I would rather not have gone, for I was not fit. I have got some notices to quit. I would have voted for a liberal man if I durst [*sic*], but I was afraid to do it, for fear Mr Stannus would throw me out of my wee place.[14]

Eviction was not really very likely, as the past record of the Hertford estate showed, but to go against the landlord's wishes could result in loss of the landlord's goodwill. Acceptance of the landlord's role would allow what a lawyer for the Stannus family in 1872 euphemistically called 'reciprocity of benefits'. In those small number of cases of coercion actually proven on the Hertford estate, tenants were punished by the removal of certain rights that were dependent on landlord goodwill. The absence of the secret ballot did produce a degree of subservience, but it was not a major factor; even after 1872 there was not complete secrecy of voting.[15] Much more important was the deferential society that existed in the countryside.

In addition, of course, the landlord party could afford a large organisation; in fact Seymour spent just over £9,000 in 1869.[16] Most of his helpers were paid for their work. Over 500 men were hired as canvassers, clerks, messengers, drivers and agents. When the election began the Seymours expected that the marquis of Hertford would pay for the contest as he had on previous occasions. But no order was received from Hertford to this effect and after attempts failed to charge the costs to Hertford's account, loans had to be arranged with banks in Lisburn and London. Matters were further complicated by the death of the marquis and by his will, which left his fortune to an illegitimate son, Richard Wallace. The Seymours contested the will and after lengthy legal proceedings did finally manage to reach a suitable settlement with Wallace, although the latter acquired nearly all the Irish estate.[17]

The Antrim by-election, however, shows that even a well financed candidate from the right landlord background usually could not ignore the particular concerns of the electors whose votes he sought. There had to be a sensitivity on the part of a candidate towards local feelings and a certain identity of political interest between the candidate and electors. We have seen how in response to objections to the family's absenteeism Seymour promised to reside in Lisburn against his own personal wishes; W. T. Stannus was later to offer the consolation that there was at least 'a good pack of harriers in the neighbourhood'.[18] It was observed how during the election Seymour adapted his views to take a stronger line on support for protestantism and land reform. Because of his soundness in these matters, together with his elaborate organisation, considerable landlord support, and distinctive family background, Seymour was able to capture the seat.

Thus in Co. Antrim, which seems to have been fairly typical of the Ulster counties, landlords in this period enjoyed considerable influence over their tenants. This influence was a result of their social position and economic power, but it was also dependent on the identity of political interest between landlords, tenants, and the candidate and his policies. Now this was to be challenged. Beginning with the Antrim by-election of 1869, and probably originating in the hopes raised by Gladstone in the liberals' recently declared aim to change the Irish land system, and encouraged by organisations such as the Ulster liberal society, the question of agrarian reform increasingly became a matter of concern on the hustings. It would lead eventually to the undermining of the landlords' power and the collapse of the political interest between them and their tenants.

Derry city, 1870

The next by-election in Ulster, however, was for a borough seat, and there was no sign of dissatisfaction with Gladstone. By early February 1870 it was rumoured that Richard Dowse, M.P. for Derry city, would soon receive a government post. On 11 February the *Londonderry Sentinel* reported that Dowse had been appointed solicitor general for Ireland and so had vacated his seat. The paper also carried the address of a conservative candidate, Robert Baxter, an English solicitor and member of the Plymouth Brethren, along with that of Dowse, who stood again for the constituency. During the election campaign it was claimed that Baxter had been asked to stand by leading merchants and gentry of the city and also that the person responsible for Baxter's appearance was Lord Claud Hamilton, now M.P. for King's Lynn, who gave his assistance to the conservative candidate.[19] At the nominations Dowse was proposed by Rev. Prof. Richard Smyth, moderator of the presbyterian general assembly.[20]

The result was Dowse 680 and Baxter 592, which was roughly similar to the 1868 poll when Dowse's voters numbered 704 and Hamilton's 599. As the figures in the table show, the liberal retained the bulk of the catholic vote and the conservative the greater part of the Church of Ireland electorate. The percentage of presbyterians who voted liberal was not very different from the 1868 figure, although the number of presbyterian non-voters had grown. An increase in the number of Church of Ireland electors on the register, due apparently to successful conservative registration helped the conservative position.[21]

3: Votes for each candidate by religion[22]

	Dowse	Baxter	unpolled	total
Church of Ireland	15	301	40	356
presbyterians	143	245	125	513
nonconformist	14	31	44	89
catholic	508	15	40	563
total	680	592	249	1,521

During the campaign for the Derry by-election Gladstone's Irish land bill was introduced to parliament on 15 February. In the debates and the voting that ensued on the proposed legislation the four Ulster liberals, as expected, backed it.[23] More surprising, however, was the reaction from the Ulster conservatives. Shortly before the second reading of the bill, Sir F. W. Heygate wrote to Disraeli to say that 'the general feeling among Ulster members appears to be that it will be highly inadvisable to make any strong remarks against the bill in the present state of Ireland.'[24] Several Ulster conservatives criticised the bill on grounds such as the difficulties in defining the Ulster custom, but at the vote for the second reading 14 Ulster conservatives voted for it and 10 abstained.[25] Clearly the Ulster conservatives were concerned about public opinion in the north over this question. Paradoxically, however, the failure of this land act dashed expectations and contributed significantly to the growth of the agrarian movement.

Newry and Co. Monaghan, 1871
At the end of 1870 and the beginning of 1871, another by-election occurred in an Ulster borough, which resulted in a conservative winning a liberal seat and can be seen as evidence of the continuing power of proprietorial interests in the boroughs. William Kirk, liberal M.P. for Newry, died on 21 December 1870. By the end of the month Viscount Newry, defeated candidate in 1868 and eldest son of the chief proprietor in the town, had published an address that stated his intention to stand but made no specific references to policy apart from the hope that all parties would unite and return him to promote the prosperity of the town.[26] No liberal candidate appeared, although attempts were made to find one, and at a meeting between Lord Newry and the principal liberals an agreement seems to have been reached to accept him. While there was no doubt that he was a conservative the issues of the day were played down. He was nominated without opposition.[27]

By the time of the Monaghan by-election of July 1871 an important political development had taken place in the form of the appearance of the home rule movement in Dublin.[28] Several rather different elements made up this new movement. First, there were liberals who felt that Gladstone's policies as enunciated at the 1868 general election had not materialised sufficiently. Dissatisfaction was felt in particular over the 1870 land act, which was regarded as very inadequate, and over lack of action on the education question;

the government's amnesty of certain fenian prisoners was regarded as too limited by some liberals. Secondly, there was a group of conservatives who believed they had been betrayed by the disestablishment of the Church of Ireland. A third element was made up of nationalists, both constitutionalist and fenian. These groups came together at a meeting at Bilton's Hotel in Dublin, May 1870, to form the Home Government Association with the object of self government for Ireland. By July 1871 the association had expanded and contested some by-elections but at the same time faced growing tension between the disparate elements within its own ranks.

The Co. Monaghan by-election was the first in Ulster since the foundation of the association. The cause of the contest was the death of Col. C. P. Leslie on 26 June. By the beginning of July John Leslie, brother of the deceased M.P., had issued an address in which he stated that his family's principles were well known and, if returned, he would promote the interests of Ireland and the empire.[29] An election address was also issued by John Madden, who was the owner of a 4,644-acre estate at Hilton Park, Clones, in the county, an Orangeman, a former active conservative, and now a member of the home government association.[30] He declared that Ireland would be the better for home rule and ended with the statement: 'Let us forget old enmities. Irishmen should work together for the one object — the good of old Ireland, our common country.'[31] By early July, however, Madden decided not to go forward for election, partly because of opposition from certain catholic quarters, especially Cardinal Cullen, who looked on Madden and the other 'Orange' home rule candidates with distrust.[32] On Madden's withdrawal, the home government association determined not to let the election go uncontested, and they put forward in mid-July Isaac Butt, the lawyer and Church of Ireland member, born in Co. Donegal, who was the leader of the movement. His address was a general one and its main point was to urge the protection of tenant right.[33]

Limited organisation seems to have taken place on Butt's side because of his late appearance, although reports said that he had the help of some of the catholic clergy.[34] There was also a third candidate in the person of a Dublin catholic lawyer, John McMahon, who stood as a liberal but withdrew at the nominations. Leslie stated that he had Ireland's interests as much at heart as Butt and wanted civil and religious liberty for all men. Butt himself was not present. His proposer declared that Butt's principles were in favour of home rule, and mentioned no other issues.

We want something to bring back the spirit of the country taken from us by the British house of commons. We want something to put us forward in a proper direction, as a people and nation that had vitality in them.[35]

The outcome of the polling was Leslie 2,538, Butt 1,451. Butt had arrived too late on the scene to be really effective but clearly there was some support for home rule among the population.

Derry city, 1872

The Derry city by-election was the first in Ireland after the passage of the ballot act which not only introduced secret voting but also abolished public nominations. The 1872 contest resulted from the elevation of Richard Dowse to the position of baron of the exchequer. Although this appointment was made only in October, earlier rumours of such a step had caused the various parties to make preparations. In August, John Ferguson, a home ruler originally from Belfast but resident in Glasgow, arrived in the city to organise home rule support. In correspondence to Isaac Butt he described attempts to win catholics away from the liberals and to set up a local home rule organisation: 'we want the whole thing done this month and the entire catholic party pledged to support home rule at this election.'[36] On 26 August at a home rule meeting in the city, J. G. Biggar, presbyterian president of the Belfast home rule association, was accepted as home rule candidate.[37] On 13 September, a home rule association was set up in Derry.[38] In October, when Dowse's resignation was announced, Biggar confirmed his intention to contest the seat and issued an address that declared his backing for home rule, 'by which I mean an Irish parliament to legislate in Ireland for Irish affairs', and supported fixity of tenure.[39]

The conservatives had also made early arrangements. On 5 August, a large meeting was held in Derry in response to a circular from Samuel MacDermott, secretary of the local conservative association.[40] A London presbyterian solicitor, C. E. Lewis, who was present and spoke to the gathering, was asked to stand as a conservative for the election that many expected to occur soon. Lewis issued his address on 10 August, but on 29 August, another address appeared from a local merchant, Bartholomew McCorkell, who called himself a progressive constitutionalist.[41] McCorkell, whose candidature arose out of resentment that a local Derry candidate had not been selected, remained in the field until one day before polling when he retired, in order (he claimed) to avoid a conservative split.[42] In his address Lewis declared himself a moderate conservative, said he would uphold the constitution, the protestant character of which he regarded as inviolate, and stated his opposition to denominational elections.[43] John Rea, the eccentric solicitor from Belfast, also issued an address but did not follow it up.

The liberals were not so quick as the others to select their candidate. By the end of August the rt hon. Christopher Palles was spoken of as the likely candidate because the liberals would need a law officer in the commons in place of Dowse. Palles was solicitor general and a catholic, both of which facts had important consequences in Derry. On 7 October 1872, Dowse described to Lord Hartington his efforts in support of Palles and some of the difficulties he had encountered:

> I have been using all my influence in favour of Palles in Derry and what I confess I did not expect, the opposition is with the R. Catholics. The protestant liberals say that much as it goes against their grain to have a R. Catholic for member, as they have never wavered in their allegiance to Mr. Gladstone, they will accept a R.C. law officer for his sake. The R. Catholic bishop on the contrary is sullen and will not support him. I have made an effort to try and change him but the solicitor general must be up and doing if he wishes for a seat. . . . To find the liberal presbyterians willing to accept a R.C. should encourage any man.[44]

By the end of October it was clear that Palles had been agreed to as liberal candidate, but not until 26 October was it reported that Dowse had accepted a judgeship. On 6 November Palles arrived in Derry where he was greeted by W. H. Dodd, secretary of the Ulster liberal society, and local liberals.[45] The catholic hostility mentioned by Dowse was a result of the resentment felt in some quarters towards Palles because of his pronouncements in his official legal capacity against clerical intervention at the Galway election petition trials. The catholic *Northern Star* and the catholic bishop of Down and Dromore, Dr Patrick Dorrian, bitterly attacked his candidature, and at home rule meetings he was vilified: A. M. Sullivan stated that he had 'betrayed his country and his God'.[46]

On 7 November, Palles issued his election address.[47] He urged the electors to support Gladstone by voting for him, and pointed to the church, land, and ballot acts as evidence of what Gladstone and the liberals had done for Ireland, but made no mention of the education question. For a time Dr Francis Kelly, the catholic bishop, and his clergy seem to have remained undecided as to whom they would endorse but by 14 November they had begun to back Palles.[48] By this stage it was known that Palles supported denominational education,[49] a factor that may have helped influence the catholic clergy in his favour. On the eve of the election the clergy gave Palles their full support: Ferguson, writing to Butt after the election, remarked: 'The screw was put on for the last three days. The priests went from house to house and our very leaders had to give up Biggar and vote for "a good catholic".'[50] Kelly was one of the proposers of Palles's nomination.

The result was Lewis 696, Palles 522, Biggar 89, and McCorkell 2. The Derry election was the first in Ireland after the ballot act, and so an accurate breakdown of the voting as in 1868 and 1870 is impossible. But it can be observed that, compared with the 1870 results, the liberals had lost support to the conservative, and since it is unlikely that any catholics changed allegiance to the conservative it is clear that a considerable section of the liberal presbyterian vote must have done so. Other sources confirm this view and point to Palles's backing for denominational education as the cause of this withdrawal of support.[51] Another point we may note from this election is the lack of success of the home rule candidates. Liberalism was still an important force in Ulster, even if it had lost some of its presbyterian votes over the educational question. The new ballot act does not seem to have had much consequence for the voting, but the ending of speeches at nomination caused a quieter election than formerly.

Co. Armagh and Lisburn, 1873

On 13 January 1873 the *Belfast Newsletter* carried a report of the rumoured death of Sir William Verner, bt, M.P. for Co. Armagh; the paper also stated that Verner had been ill for some time, and that twelve months previously, when he had contemplated vacating the seat, his brother E. W. Verner, M.P. for Lisburn, had been adopted as conservative candidate by the Co. Armagh grand Orange lodge. Two days later Verner's death was confirmed. On 22 January an address appeared in the papers from E. W. Verner which announced the giving up of his Lisburn seat and his proposal to stand for Co. Armagh. He stated that he had received a requisition the previous year to stand — a reference no doubt to the Co. Armagh G.O.L. He declared his determination to support, as his brother and father had done, the principles of the constitution of 1688. Verner also said that his family had always encouraged the industrious tenant, and promised to back the right of tenants while doing justice to the landlords.[52]

On the same day that Verner announced his intention to vacate his borough seat, a meeting was held in Lisburn under the auspices of the Lisburn conservative registration society to select a candidate for the town.[53] A letter was read from Sir Richard Wallace, who had succeeded to nearly all the Co. Antrim estate of the late marquis of Hertford, which included Lisburn. In reply to an earlier letter from the society, asking him whether he would stand for Lisburn if Verner gave up the seat, he answered in the affirmative. He further added that he was a 'thorough conservative' in politics. A letter from Fred Caproni, Wallace's new Lisburn agent, also gave assurances that Wallace was a conservative.

This extra concern about Wallace's politics arose from the fact that little was known about him apart from his reputation as a philanthropist and art collector, and for a time after his succession to the Hertford estates a false rumour had circulated in Lisburn that he was a catholic, which caused considerable disquiet in the town.[54] The meeting passed a resolution in favour of Wallace, which was then posted to him. On 31 January Wallace's address appeared. He referred to the request for him to stand and remarked: 'My personal interests are identical with your own, and my political principles are strictly conservative.' He urged economy in public expenditure and promised to carry out his duties faithfully.[55]

Affairs proceeded in both constituencies with little fuss. In Co. Armagh John Rea handed in nomination papers but withdrew, and Verner was elected without a contest. On 14 February, Wallace arrived in Lisburn on his first visit to the town and was given a great civic reception. He announced his intention to take up residence in the county. Apart from John Rea, who turned up again and sought nomination unsuccessfully, there was no opposition to Wallace. The *Northern Whig* welcomed him as very different from the normal run of Irish conservatives and a noble benefactor of his country.[56] The *Belfast Newsletter* delivered an ecstatic eulogy on his election:

> The great interest Sir Richard, as lord of the soil, now possesses in the borough — his princely munificence, self-sacrificing philanthropy, and large-hearted benevolence — would not fail to command for him the sympathy and attachment of such a constituency as Lisburn; while his attachment to conservative principles especially commends him to that large class of the electors through whose fidelity and zeal the cause of conservatism has secured so many triumphs in the borough.[57]

Co. Tyrone, 1873

Neither the Armagh nor the Lisburn by-election showed signs of the growing unrest over the 1870 land act. Tenant farmer protest, however, was now to become very obvious at the Tyrone by-election of April 1873, caused by the death on 6 March of H. T. Lowry Corry, a member of the Belmore family. Like the 1869 Antrim by-election, this contest deserves an in-depth study because of extensive manuscript sources that have survived, in this case from the Belmore family. A week after Lowry Corry's death, while discussions as to his successor were taking place among the local gentry, the county grand Orange lodge of Tyrone held a meeting at Killyman in Co. Tyrone and J. W. Ellison Macartney was recommended as a suitable candidate for the seat.[58] Ellison Macartney, although not an Orangeman, was a barrister who lived on his wife's property of 3,468 acres at Clogher, Co. Tyrone, while he also held a smaller estate in Co. Antrim.

From reports of the meeting it is clear that Ellison Macartney's selection occurred partly because of Orange dissatisfaction with gentry domination of the parliamentary representation, but mostly because of unrest over the land question.[59] By this stage the party processions act was no longer a cause of Orange dissatisfaction: it was repealed during 1872. In his election address Ellison Macartney pledged that as 'a staunch protestant' he would give general backing to the conservatives and that he opposed denominational education 'tending, as it must, to erect another barrier of separation between Irishmen'. Pointedly, he declared that he would support amendments to remove deficiencies in the land act.[60]

The Belmore family now also put forward a conservative candidate in the person of Capt. the hon. H. W. Lowry Corry, brother of the earl of Belmore. R. C. Brush, the Belmore land agent, on hearing of Ellison Macartney's selection, privately made suggestions to the earl about his brother's address:

> The points your lordship's brother, Capt. Hon. H. Corry, will have to stand to, to gain the majority of interests are: the fact of being a protestant, moderate conservative, upholder of tenant right, such as is fair and has been acknowledged on the estate, opposed to sectarian education — and with these safeguards the family influence and respect in the county will have great weight.[61]

In response to Ellison Macartney's challenge and the advice he had received, Lowry Corry published an address in which he promised to maintain the 'glorious constitution' and to back non-denominational education. He referred to the rights of tenants on the family estates and said that he intended to secure the interests of tenants, both yearly and leasehold.[62] Under normal circumstances such an approach would have been sufficient, but letters from various quarters now warned of the rise of agrarian discontent.

The candidature of Ellison Macartney caused concern not only to the Belmores but also to other leading Ulster conservatives. The 1870 land act had been supported in parliament by most Ulster conservative M.P.s in response to local feeling, but these new developments were upsetting. A private letter from Col. the hon. W. S. Knox, the Dungannon M.P., on 15 March from London to the earl of Belmore, warned that 'unless the landed proprietors of Ulster are to abdicate in favour of low Orange democracy, it is of the most vital importance for Ulster generally that Mr Ellison Macartney should be fought to the death.' After receiving Lowry Corry's address, however, Knox expressed great concern over his proposals for land reform: 'I take my stand firmly on the settlement of 1870, and a peg further I will not go for a seat in parliament.'[63] But if to Knox and others at Westminster this response to the Ellison Macartney challenge seemed to go too far, to Lowry Corry in Tyrone it was very apparent that it was essential.

Reports from helpers and the questions from his own supporters at meetings about his views on the land question indicated that he faced a real threat from Ellison Macartney's candidature.[64] His opponent established a vigorous election campaign, canvassed electors and addressed meetings. A committee to assist him was organised early on. Ellison Macartney's appeal arose from both the tenant right issue and Orange discontent. A handbill to advertise a meeting in Cookstown proclaimed:

> John Ellison Macartney, the tenant right candidate and people's representative, will be present and explain his views on tenant right, as it should be and will yet be. Tenant farmers and independent electors, be true to your own interests, and protected by the ballot, vote for the true friend of the county. Come out in your thousands!!, and show the grand jury that you will be slaves no longer to a clique, but are determined to return the man of your choice.[65]

At this Cookstown meeting on 24 March, attended by catholic priests and presbyterian ministers, Ellison Macartney spoke at length on the land question and nothing else: he stated that the 1870 act had not defined sufficiently the Ulster custom, and called for tenant right for leaseholders at the expiration of their leases. At the end of the proceedings a resolution was passed supporting him as the tenant right candidate. Two days later at a meeting at Stewartstown, where no catholic priests were present, he said that he had been asked to stand for the county by an Orange deputation upon 'steadfast, protestant principles, as no other man holding any other would have been invited by the Orangemen of Tyrone'. He then dealt with the land question.[66]

Lowry Corry also addressed meetings and canvassed, with the help of a committee. An elaborate organisation was set up for each barony, special trains were arranged to transport voters on polling day, and lists of local supporters were printed to give confidence to other persons to vote the right way, 'when they see the respectable neighbouring farmers, on whose judgment they rely, supporting Captain Corry'.[67] This was the first contested county election in Ulster after the ballot act, and instructions were issued to agents to give voters tally cards which they were to request back after the poll; if they returned them, the agents were to record them on their lists as Lowry Corry supporters, and if they handed the cards to the opposite side, they were to be marked down with a different sign.[68]

Besides this organisation Lowry Corry and his brother made efforts to divide the Orange support of Ellison Macartney. The earl of Belmore urgently contacted Mervyn Stewart, grand master of the Tyrone orangemen, and the earl of Enniskillen, grand master of the Orange lodge of Ireland, for their help. At the beginning of the contest both refused to assist him and stated that in recent years the gentry had ignored the Orangemen, who were now going their own way.[69] By 25 March, however, Stewart was reported as 'getting disgusted' with Ellison Macartney and his 'radical supporters', and for fear of the consequences of victory by a tenant and independent candidate he and Lord Enniskillen used their influence in Lowry Corry's favour.[70] The Tyrone grand lodge finally decided that it should be left to each Orangeman to decide how to vote.

The Belmores also contacted neighbouring landlords to seek their support. Y. H. Burges, however, replied to the earl of Belmore to criticise the way the election affairs had been handled:

> I cannot in frankness conceal from you my regret that the gentlemen of the county did not call a meeting of electors, and there endeavour to have no conflicting interests in the choice of a candidate. What can be more hurtful, what more anti-conservative, than by slighting the 'populus' through not even making an appearance of consulting them, to raise a split in these days between landlord and tenant? The 'democratic Orangeman', though he may call himself a conservative in Ireland, would be radical in England.[71]

Other landlords were more encouraging. J. F. Lowry wrote:

> Get the sheriff to give the longest day, that landlords may talk to their tenants. I got Brown to write to his steward, who is an Orangeman of the lowest orders, last night. He answers all the tenants are with Brown.

Major Lindsay went down last night, and Capt. Smyley says he will do all
he can at Castlederg. I believe it is on the cards, if pressure is put on. I got
Mrs Ogilby to telegraph to her husband to stay in the country and see
every tenant. If you could get Crossle to go about and harangue the
Orangemen, it might turn the tables and show them the priests are
boasting of the alliance of the Orangemen and Romans. Robert will call
together his district, and satisfy them that all the heads are against such an
alliance. . . . Blacker is now writing to his agent to work his Drumquin
area.[72]

Efforts were made to frighten away Orange backing from Ellison
Macartney by emphasising his catholic support. Copies of a letter
from a catholic priest in favour of Ellison Macartney were widely
distributed, a member of Lowry Corry's committee declaring: 'we
consider the more that Mr Macartney's cause is identified with the
Roman Catholics, the less the Orangemen will like it, and that much
more good will result from the letter than harm.'[73] By the final stages
of the campaign the outcome was uncertain. Several supporters
of Lowry Corry reported a good response to him, but others were
less optimistic and emphasised the importance of the land question.
On 5 April R. C. Brush, the Belmore agent, expressed his grave
concern to the earl of Belmore:

I sincerely wish Monday's election was over, resulting in a favourable
majority, but no one can ever guess at the probable result of the ballot.
This end of the country is in heavy force against anyone of a landlord
class, and matters will run very close here, but I hope for a better majority
in the upper end. Several land cases and acts that would better have been
left alone for some little time, have in these Dungannon three baronies
caused a feeling of democratic antagonism to landlord influences I hardly
expected had taken such deep and decided root. . . .[74]

The polling took place on 7 April. The outcome of the contest was
Lowry Corry 3,139, and Ellison Macartney 3,103. Corry and
his friends greeted the results with relief. Sir Thomas Bateson
remarked: 'Tyrone was too close to be pleasant, but if Macartney
had carried it no county in Ulster would have been safe.'[75] Clearly
the whole election had revealed serious new problems for the
conservatives. One Lowry Corry supporter warned the earl of
Belmore:

The democratic Orange tenant right vote, under the ballot, is much more
potent for mischief than I anticipated, and it will require all the prudence
and energy of the conservative party to steer the north out of the most
serious complications at the coming dissolution. A much larger proportion
of the registered electors came to the poll than was expected, and I fear
the R. Catholic vote on the whole was decidedly unfavourable.[76]

For the conservatives' opponents the outcome of the election was also looked upon with satisfaction in spite of their defeat. A Co. Tyrone solicitor, in a letter to Isaac Butt, commented: 'Our election here has given tenant right a great position in this county and even the landlords have to cry "tenant right".'[77]

As regards the denominational breakdown of the poll, it is not possible to give a completely accurate analysis because of the ballot. But it is clear that Ellison Macartney, as tenant right and independent candidate, had considerable support from both protestant and catholic quarters. This development, no doubt, stemmed partly from the ballot act, although because of the tally card system that law did not bring full secrecy. Much more importantly, this political protest was the result of the way in which rising feeling over the land issue had upset traditional social and political relations in the countryside. Clearly the identity of interest between the dominant conservative families and the electorate was coming under strain.

During 1874 Gladstone introduced to parliament legislation to deal with the other important area of his Irish policy — education. In February, he brought forward an Irish universities bill that sought to establish an Irish national university with affiliated colleges, consisting of Trinity, the queen's colleges, the catholic college, and Magee College, with an overall governing body. Ulster conservatives opposed the measure because they believed it supported denominational education, while of the Ulster liberals Thomas McClure backed it and E. J. Saunderson abstained.[78] The majority of Irish liberals opposed the proposed legislation because it did not do enough for catholic education. Gladstone also lost support from English liberals who regarded the bill as a concession to denomi-nationalism. The result of this opposition was the defeat of the measure and consequently the downfall of Gladstone's ministry.[79]

On the eve of the 1874 general election, the parliamentary representation of Ulster numbered 2 liberals and 27 conservatives, compared with 4 liberals and 25 conservatives in 1868: the conservatives had regained two borough seats. The conservative M.P.s, drawn almost entirely from the Church of Ireland landed gentry, still monopolised the northern seats with traditional methods of organisation. But there were now clear signs of challenge from a number of quarters. From presbyterian, catholic, and Orange ranks as well as from urban, professional, mercantile, and farming sections, opposition had emerged to the existing order. The failure of the land act and the universities bill helped to fuel this discontent. Protest had appeared in the country and towns, from within the ranks of conservative supporters as well as from opponents. The Ulster liberal society had proved itself able to represent much of this unrest but the home rule movement had now emerged to provide another political focus for this opposition. When parliament was finally dissolved, two questions must have been prominent in people's minds in Ulster. How would the conservatives respond to these challenges? How effectively would the new political movements organise and direct this upsurge of protest?

III LIBERALS ADVANCE

CHAPTER 6 *The 1874 general election*

The growing political excitement in the province was strongly reflected in the general election of 1874. Contests occurred in every county and in 7 out of 9 boroughs in Ulster. An editorial in the *Ulster Examiner* proclaimed: 'Never, we believe, within the recollection of living men were so many seats contested in this province.'[1] In fact, never at *any* previous general election had such a large number of northern constituencies witnessed a poll. In the rest of Ireland also the dissolution of parliament in early 1874 was the cause of heated political activity. Throughout the whole country there were two main issues that held the attention of the electorate, home rule and land reform. This former subject, however, which aroused widespread interest and support in the three southern provinces, gathered little backing in Ulster. In contrast, the land question was a matter of great interest throughout the north and provided the key issue around which a strong opposition would challenge the old order.

Dissatisfaction over Gladstone's land act and its operation had grown unabated from 1870. On 20-21 January 1874 a national tenant right conference was held in Belfast under the auspices of the Co. Antrim tenant right associations.[2] In all, thirty tenant right organisations were represented, including nineteen from Ulster, mainly from Cos Antrim, Down, Londonderry and Tyrone. Among those present were the conservative M.P. William Johnston, the liberal M.P. Sir Thomas McClure, and the Rev. Isaac Nelson of the Belfast home rule association. Resolution were passed which condemned the 1870 land act as inadequate and called for various reforms, including the establishment of the three Fs. Farmers were urged to elect representatives who supported these points.

By early 1874 the home rule movement in Ireland had undergone considerable development and growth since its foundation.[3] To gain wider backing it had allied home rule to other issues, principally land reform and denominational education. In November 1873 a large conference was held in Dublin at which the home rule league was formed out of the old home rule association. In Leinster, Munster, and Connacht local societies were established in support of the movement and a number of farmer's and political clubs had come out in favour of its aims.[4] Some home rule associations were formed in Ulster in affiliation with the central Dublin body before the general election, most notably at Belfast in April 1872, Derry in September 1872, and Cavan in September 1873.[5] But while these and a few other home rule organisations were set up in the province before 1874, they were neither numerous nor effective.

Unlike the Ulster liberal society, the central home rule association in Dublin refused to take an active role in either establishing local branches or giving any such bodies advisers on registration or financial aid for such matters. In a letter to an Armagh supporter in 1873, the Dublin secretary rejected pleas for help in these areas on the grounds that 'this association cannot undertake to look at the registry in any place. Such a proceeding would be altogether outside its province.'[6] Hugh Heinrick, an assistant to the secretary, did visit Fermanagh and Tyrone in 1873 but managed only with great difficulty to locate a group of supporters in Tyrone.[7] There is no evidence of tenant right associations backing home rule as occurred elsewhere. At the home rule conference in Dublin in late 1873 just around thirty of the 1,000 ticket holders were from Ulster and nearly half of these belonged to Belfast.[8]

In only two Ulster constituencies were there home rule candidates. In Co. Cavan two home rulers faced a liberal while in Monaghan one home ruler opposed two conservatives. Two conservatives and a liberal contested each of Cos Down, Antrim and Armagh while two conservatives and two liberals fought for Cos Londonderry and Donegal. In Co. Tyrone the two sitting conservative M.P.s were challenged by J. W. Ellison Macartney, who campaigned on an independent conservative tenant right platform. Likewise in Co. Fermanagh two conservatives were opposed by two independent conservative tenant right candidates, conveniently described as liberals by the contemporary press. In each of Armagh, Coleraine, Derry, Dungannon, Enniskillen, and Newry a liberal challenged a conservative. Three conservatives and one liberal ran for the Belfast seats while two conservatives contested Carrickfergus.

In their election addresses the conservatives sometimes referred to defence of the union or of protestantism.[9] Capt. the hon. H. W. L. Corry, Co. Tyrone, for example, stated: 'As a conservative I shall always seek to maintain the integrity of this great empire; and, as a protestant, I shall use my utmost endeavours to uphold our glorious constitution, granting at the same time to every man the fullest civil and religious liberty.'[10] But there was less reference to such religious and constitutional matters than in 1868, and the land question took a prominent place in addresses. In some cases, as in Tyrone, the tory candidates made specific recommendations (such as tenant right for leaseholders at the expiration of current agreements), but usually they contented themselves with general comments, referring perhaps to good relations with tenants on their own estates. The borough candidates paid less attention to the land question than county candidates and emphasised issues such as opposition to denominational education and support for existing institutions. Frequently, especially in the boroughs, candidates stated their concern for local interests.

Among liberals in the Ulster counties the agrarian issue was clearly the principal topic in their addresses. F. W. McBlaine, candidate for Co. Armagh, declared: 'The battle of tenant right is being fought all over Ulster. Armagh will nobly bear its part in the glorious struggle.'[11] They called for reforms such as 'fair rent' and 'free sale' or for backing of the resolutions of the Belfast tenant right conference. The liberal borough candidates, except for Taylor in Coleraine, also supported land reform. Other issues in liberal addresses included reform of grand jury laws but educational matters were avoided. For the three home rule party candidates home rule was the main topic in their addresses. J. G. Biggar in Cavan declared: 'This country, in my opinion, can never rise from her present state of stagnation until she has once again a native parliament.'[12] But the land question also figured in their addresses, while Biggar and C. J. Fay in Cavan (although not John Madden in Co. Monaghan) declared their support for denominational education.

Outside Ulster the main issue of the general election was home rule. In the addresses of the home rule candidates, many of whom had been liberals formerly, this matter figured most prominently, followed by the land question; fixity of tenure and fair rents were popular demands. Denominational education and an amnesty for all political prisoners were the two next most popular subjects, after which came grand jury reform and defence of the pope against Italian nationalists. The liberals in the other three provinces sought moderate amendments to the land act and denominational education. Southern conservatives were less favourable towards land reform than either the liberals or the home rulers, but a number of them did support denominational education.

The counties
Throughout the Ulster countryside proprietorial interests were
challenged. In most constituencies the land question was the issue
which aroused this political unrest but in a couple of counties home
rule was also important. Tenants' associations (all formed since
1868) played a vital part in organising and directing this agrarian
opposition. Although the various parties had been represented at
the Belfast land conference it soon became clear that most of these
associations were supporters of the liberals. There was still relatively
little activity at county revision sessions, but we know that at least
in the case of Co. Antrim the secretary of the Ulster liberal society
had advised farmers on registration prior to 1874; also revision
sessions in Co. Londonderry were keenly contested in 1873.[13] The
public excitement that the land issue created would test not only old
loyalties but long-standing methods of organisation. New types of
organisation and interest groups, especially the tenant right groups
and their liberal links, actively challenged the traditional tory landlord control of the Ulster counties.

   This assault on proprietorial interests by tenant right and liberal
forces was especially strong in Cos Antrim, Down, and Londonderry (all with sizeable presbyterian electorates). In Co. Antrim
meetings of tenant associations had taken place several times during
1873 to organise for the return of a tenant right candidate at the next
election, and the Ulster liberal society had been approached for its
help and advice on the matter. A meeting of representatives of Co.
Antrim tenant right organisations was held on 27 January 1874 in
Ballymena to select a candidate. Several local men were proposed
but turned down the nomination. Eventually on 1 February the
Route tenant association received a telegram from Charles Wilson
(a presbyterian, formerly of Broughshane but now resident in
England and the possessor of a large fortune made in Australia)
which stated that he would stand on liberal and tenant right principles.
A meeting of deputies of Co. Antrim tenant associations approved
of his candidature on 2 February.[14]

   In Co. Down an advertisement in the press on 29 January from
officers of the Co. Down tenants' association warned people not to
commit their vote to the conservatives, as a tenant right candidate
would shortly come forward. On 30 January a large meeting of
representatives from all districts of the county was held to select a
candidate to contest the county on liberal and tenant right principles.
James Sharman Crawford, son of the well known reformer William
Sharman Crawford, a presbyterian and land agent on his brother's

estate, was chosen.[15] At a meeting of the Co. Londonderry tenant farmers' association in Derry on 28 January Rev. Professor Richard Smyth of Magee College, a key liberal figure at previous elections in the city and county, was selected. A second candidate, Hugh Law, Q.C., a Church of Ireland member and solicitor general, was chosen by the Kennaught tenant right defence association on 30 January.[16]

For the conservatives in these counties, selection of candidates followed a procedure that was different from the liberals' but had worked successfully in the past. In Co. Down, where the former M.P.s sought reelection, addresses were issued that stated their intentions to stand and listed their political views, apparently without any form of selection. In Co. Antrim it had become known by the end of January that Seymour would not stand again and meetings of Co. Antrim gentry were held in Belfast on 29 and 30 January. James Chaine, a Church of Ireland landlord and manufacturer from Larne, was finally selected.[17] The other former conservative member for Antrim, the hon. Edward O'Neill, published his address without any new selection procedure.

In Co. Londonderry, selection of the conservative candidates proved more difficult. On 27 January, the *Londonderry Sentinel* reported that Sir F. W. Heygate, bt, would not stand for reelection owing to ill health. Two days later the address of R. P. Dawson, the second former M.P. for the county, appeared. At this stage Rev. Professor Richard Smyth was the only other candidate in the field and it seems that the Londonderry conservatives contemplated just putting forward Dawson in order to avoid a contest. With Law's appearance at the end of the month, however, R. J. Alexander, a minor Church of Ireland landowner from Portglenone, Co. Antrim, came forward, apparently as the result of a meeting of landlords in Belfast. Dawson was not prepared to face a contest and withdrew on 2 February. The next day J. B. Beresford, land agent to the marquis of Waterford, was selected as the second conservative at a gathering of gentry in Coleraine.[18]

In these three counties the liberals conducted vigorous election campaigns. The land question was clearly the main issue. Liberal headquarters in Co. Down were situated in Belfast. From the papers of their agent, C. H. Brett, we can see how he coordinated the work of committees throughout the county, organised canvassing and meetings, sent posters and circulars to different parts, appointed personation and polling agents for election day, and, where no liberal organisation existed, contacted local supporters to organise committees.[19] Tenant associations in the county gave considerable assistance to the liberals. Brett's correspondents included farmers' leaders such as Joseph Perry, a farmer of over 100 acres from Downpatrick; William Hurst, a linen manufacturer from Drumaness; and Edward Gardner, a solicitor from Downpatrick. Frequent newspaper advertisements assured people that the ballot was secret.[20]

Neither conservative in Down had mentioned the land question in their original addresses but they subsequently issued a joint letter that denied rumours that they wished to repeal the land act, and stated that they would support any measure to 'facilitate the carrying out of the measure in the spirit in which it was intended.'[21] A particular local court case that ensued from the land act was frequently cast up during the campaign against one of the conservatives, Col. W. B. Forde.[22] William Johnston spoke at conservative meetings where concern was expressed for farmers' rights; Johnston's assistance was regarded as especially valuable because of his tenant right connections.[23] Local landlords and agents convassed tenants in the conservative cause. D. S. Ker of Ballynahinch, for example, issued a printed letter to all his tenants to urge them to support Forde and Hill.[24] The final outcome of the poll was Hill-Trevor (conservative) 5,029; Sharman Crawford (liberal) 4,814; and Forde (the defeated conservative) 4,683.

In Co. Antrim the liberals started with the initial drawback of a delayed selection of candidate, in spite of efforts to organise the county in 1873 for the next election. Also Wilson had the disadvantage of being little known and names such as 'returned convict' were circulated about him.[25] Nonetheless, the liberals conducted a strong campaign, held many meetings, and carried out an extensive canvass, with tenant associations playing a large role.[26] A local conservative landowner, H. H. McNeile, wrote at some length to Lord Cairns about Wilson and his campaign. After describing him caustically as 'a vulgar rich squatter of farmer origin and connection', he commented:

> It is said he is a poor performer but he has very busy partisans, well organised through the tenant leaguers and he has the sympathies of a vast number of the tenant class, who have only just had their appetites whetted by the land bill — and who believe that Wilson's return will go far to get them further important slices of their landlord's property.[27]

In face of this strong liberal challenge, the conservatives in Antrim mounted a vigorous defence. William Johnston's assistance was again sought for public meetings. County proprietors, such as

Sir Richard Wallace, played an important part in the campaign, speaking to their own tenants and assisting elsewhere.[28] In his letter to Lord Cairns during the election H. H. McNeile described his own work on the conservatives' behalf and the challenge that had now emerged:

> I spent Friday and Saturday among my tenants, in a house to house canvass, and I saw nearly all — I found a sympathy for Wilson's views — a gross ignorance of the real position of the landlord and tenant question, and an almost universal willingness to vote whichever way I wished. I did not go to the Glens, but I sent a letter to each voter on my property, asking his support for my tenants. 'Free sale' and 'fixity of tenure' are now the demands — Orangeism, education, and all general politics are entirely neglected.[29]

The final result in Co. Antrim was 4,356 votes for the conservative Chaine, 4,142 for the conservative O'Neill, and 4,009 for the liberal Wilson. Although a defeat for the liberals, the result was an improvement in their overall position from 1869.

In Co. Londonderry it was the conservatives who faced the initial disadvantage of delay in finding candidates. Dawson's sudden withdrawal, when it became clear there would be a contest, caused great consternation in the tory ranks; after the election Dawson felt obliged to write a public letter to excuse his actions.[30] Throughout the campaign and afterwards, the lack of organisation on the conservatives' part was commented on by local newspapers.[31] The liberals conducted a widespread campaign assisted by tenant organisations; presbyterian ministers were especially active in Co. Londonderry in the liberal cause.[32] Several of the London companies announced that they did not wish to influence in any way their tenants at the election, which may have benefited the liberals.[33]

The liberal candidates made a special point of declaring their support for Gladstone as the statesman who had introduced the first land reform. Later, Law wrote to Gladstone:

> My chief recommendation to the electors of Londonderry Co. was my being one of the law officers connected with your government — and during my public canvass through the country I found that your name always evoked an enthusiastic cheer from my hard-headed Ulstermen.[34]

The liberals Smyth and Law received 2,988 and 2,701 votes respectively and the conservatives Alexander and Beresford 1,747 and 1,402 respectively. This result marked the liberals' greatest success in the province during the general election. Clearly the extensive activity of the Londonderry tenant right associations helped their cause. But in contrast to Down and Antrim they faced a less effective, badly organised, conservative force. Again, their candidates in Londonderry and Down were well known individuals while their representative in Antrim arrived late on the scene and was not widely known.

In Cos Tyrone, Armagh, and Fermanagh, where presbyterians were not as numerous, the land question was also important but there were signs of social divisions within conservative ranks. In Co. Tyrone the poll was contested by three conservatives. Shortly after the announcement of the dissolution, it was reported that J. W. Ellison Macartney, the defeated candidate in the 1873 by-election, who was on a visit to Rome, intended to return to contest the seat on conservative and tenant right principles.[35] He arrived in Omagh on 30 January and a committee was set up to organise his campaign.[36] Meanwhile, at a private meeting of Co. Tyrone gentry in Omagh on 26 January, it was decided that the rt hon. Lord Claud Hamilton and Captain the hon. H. W. Lowry Corry, the two former conservative M.P.s, should run again for the constituency and a joint committee was set up to help them.[37] Their candidature was then publicly announced.

Suggestions now came from several quarters, including Disraeli, that as all three candidates were technically conservative and Ellison Macartney was reported as the strongest candidate, it would be advisable for either Lowry Corry or Hamilton to retire in order to avoid a conservative defeat or even perhaps the election of a liberal because of a split conservative vote.[38] Hamilton hoped that Lowry Corry would step down as he was the junior M.P. but Lowry Corry was reluctant to do so, partly because of all the money he had recently spent to win the seat.[39] Also Ellison Macartney's candidature was viewed with great alarm by the Tyrone gentry and other Ulster conservatives. At a meeting of the joint electoral committee on 3 February, the day of the nomination, it was finally decided that both Lowry Corry and Hamilton would stand. Lowry Corry's later description of the meeting to his brother expressed the concern felt about Ellison Macartney:

> With the exception of Lord Claud and Greer, the opinion was unanimous that I could not withdraw, and when he threatened to do so himself, he was told that in the case of [his] doing so, somebody else would be put up to oppose Macartney. This brought him to his bearings, and Knox has written to say that I did everything I honourably could to carry out the wishes of the head of the conservative party, but it would have ruined the prospects of the party in Ulster, if we had given in before a single election was decided.[40]

On 29 January the election address appeared of a home rule candidate, B. Finnigan, but in spite of some canvassing his candidature failed to materialise.[41] The main subject during the campaign was the land question. All three candidates made similar remarks in their addresses on this matter.[42] They advocated amendments to the land act and specified tenant right for leaseholders as well. But clearly Ellison Macartney had the backing of the tenant right movement in the county. At a meeting in support of him on 31 January, a speaker stated that Ellison Macartney accepted fully the resolutions of the Belfast tenant right conference and declared that electors now had the chance to throw off 'the fetters that had bound them for ages, the slaves of a combined aristocracy.'[43]

On 10 February a letter addressed to the tenant farmers and catholic electors of Tyrone, from a Joseph Smyth of Omagh, appeared in the *Northern Whig*. It urged them to return Ellison Macartney. This was followed in the same column by another letter from three persons in Cookstown who described themselves as catholic members of the Cookstown tenant league committee; they expressed their confidence in the tenant right principles of Ellison Macartney and recommended people to vote for him. At the same time Ellison Macartney was able to hold valuable Orange support. Although Lowry Corry was nominated by the grand master of the Tyrone Orangemen, Ellison Macartney later said that he had come forward as the chosen candidate of Tyrone Orangemen, and their assistance at the election was referred to by a correspondent in the *Belfast Newsletter*.[44] The outcome of the poll was Ellison Macartney 4,710, Corry 3,173 and Hamilton 2,752. This result reflected a considerable increase in Ellison Macartney's vote since the by-election, especially among protestants, as a result of the growth in concern over the land question.

In Co. Fermanagh there were four conservative candidates in the field. The contemporary press called two of them liberals but this was only correct in so far as they opposed the representatives of the leading proprietoral interests; they were not supporters of the liberal party. J. G. V. Porter, a county landowner involved in various local enterprises, who had protested about the representation of Fermanagh in 1868, called several meetings during January in Enniskillen to discuss the forthcoming election. Then Porter issued an address, which said that he intended to stand for parliament and stated his views.[45] At the same time one of the sitting M.P.s, Capt. M. E. Archdale, announced at the end of January that he would not

go forward for the constituency again, and his brother W. H. Archdale issued an address in his stead.[46] The other former M.P., the
hon. H. A. Cole, then declared his intention to stand. Finally on 31
January a fourth candidate, Capt. C. R. Barton, a minor Fermanagh
landlord, published an election manifesto.[47] All candidates were
members of the Church of Ireland.

In their election address Cole and Archdale concentrated on constitutional and religious matters. Cole warned that home rule meant
repeal of the union and dismemberment of the empire. He declared
himself an Orangeman and warned of attempts being made to sow
dissension among Orangemen. In his address Barton declared that
he was a protestant and an Orangeman and his sympathies were
with the tenant farmers. He criticised the land act, called for complete security of tenure, and said that if returned to parliament he
would work for the interests of all: 'What I claim of liberty for my
protestant and Orange, I claim for my Roman Catholic countrymen.' Porter also called for the amendment of the land act and
urged that land registries be set up in every town. He attacked
Orangeism as a closed society with no open discussion. His own
principles, he declared, were in accord with William III's principles
of civil and religious liberty, but Orangeism in 1874 was 'as contrary
to the prince of Orange, as Jesuitism to the divine words of Jesus'.[48]
Clearly the land issue was involved in the election as well as the
subject of Orangeism.

All the candidates canvassed and held meetings throughout the
constituency. Barton and Porter contested the election separately
while Cole and Archdale worked together. The final result of the
voting was Cole 2,285, Archdale 2,205, Porter 1,546, and Barton
1,111. Although Porter and Barton won considerably fewer votes
than the other two, the gap between them in support among the
electorate was not as great as the voting would suggest. Porter's and
Barton's supporters plumped largely for their own candidate.[49] Had
they given their second vote to the other, as Cole's and Archdale's
did, the figures would have been much closer.

In Armagh likewise there were signs of Orange division but in this
case there was also a proper liberal candidate. On 30 January the
local press carried a statement of retirement from Sir J. M. Stronge,
bt, and also an address from M. C. Close that announced his intention
to stand in Stronge's place.[50] Close was a former M.P. for the
county, and a member of the Close family which owned an estate at
Drumbanagher. No report appeared of a meeting to select Close,
but it was probably arranged between the gentry, the Co. Armagh

conservative society, and the Co. Armagh grand Orange lodge, the last named having played an important part in the selection of the candidate in the 1873 by-election.[51] The other former M.P., E. W. Verner, simply issued his address without a public reselection procedure. Then on 2 February at a meeting of Co. Armagh farmers' clubs in Newry F. W. McBlaine, a protestant barrister, was selected to stand as a liberal candidate for the county.[52]

Both conservatives had stated in their addresses their desire to improve landlord–tenant relations.[53] But, indicative of the rapidly growing unrest about the land question, a letter appeared in the newspapers from T. G. Peel, a leading Orangeman and secretary of the Armagh county and borough constitutional societies, in which he pledged his word that both candidates were in favour of tenant right and would seek amendments to the land act, so that protestant landlords and tenants could be

> on such terms as men like them, living together in the face of a bitter and deadly foe, ought to be on. . . . I appeal to you, fellow electors, to be true to your religion, your bible, your country, your family, and yourselves, by voting for Verner and Close on Saturday next.[54]

Subsequently the *Belfast Newsletter* paid tribute to the role played by the Orange order in the Armagh conservative organisation.[55]

The late start for the liberals' campaign in Armagh undoubtedly damaged their electoral position. McBlaine was selected only a day before nominations and therefore little was known about him. After the polls he published a letter in the press that regretted that he had not had more time to get to know the electors and so disprove some of the rumours that had circulated about him, such as that he supported home rule.[56] The outcome of the election was a sharp liberal defeat: McBlaine received only 1,673 votes while Verner won 3,527 and Close 3,496. These elections in Armagh, Fermanagh, and Tyrone all showed how widespread was the concern over the land question. No liberal had been returned for any of the three counties, due partly to the lack of suitable candidates and effective organisation, but unrest had clearly surfaced even in Orange circles, which the conservatives had faced with varying degrees of success.

In the three remaining counties, Cavan, Monaghan, and Donegal, all of which had large numbers of catholic voters, electoral affairs proceeded rather differently from elsewhere, especially in the former two constituencies. In Cavan town, on 26 January, a meeting of around twenty persons connected with the home rule movement in the county was held to select candidates for the forthcoming election. It was agreed to invite J. G. Biggar, a presbyterian merchant and member of the Belfast home rule association, and P. McC. Fay, a local man, to stand. That same evening Rev. Peter Galligan, C.C., issued a circular requesting priests, curates and electors of each catholic parish to assemble in Cavan on 30 January to choose candidates in favour of home rule and denominational education.[57] On 28 January Biggar's address appeared in the *Freeman's Journal* and he began to canvass. The meeting on the 30th took place in the catholic college in Cavan and it was agreed to back Biggar and another member of the Fay family, C. J. Fay, a catholic solicitor who worked in Dublin.[58]

Opposition to the home rule candidates was slow to appear. On 30 January the *Cavan Weekly News* printed a letter from Captain E. J. Saunderson, former liberal M.P. for the county, which stated that at the request of friends he had rescinded his earlier intention not to stand. At this stage Lt-col. the hon. Hugh Annesley, the other former member, who was a conservative, indicated that he would not contest the seat, and no effort seems to have been made to find someone to replace him. In contemporary newspapers Saunderson was called a liberal but in his address he said that he would vote independently in parliament and made no commitment to reforms on either land or educational matters.[59] Prior to the election he appears to have alienated catholic support by some of his statements at the Church of Ireland synod, and also his opposition to disestablishment had not been well received.[60]

In his address Biggar strongly advocated home rule, stated that denominational education must be 'wrung' from the next government, and declared the 1870 land act to be a 'delusion, a mockery, and a sham'. At the nomination Biggar and Fay were proposed by Dr Nicholas Conaty, catholic bishop of Kilmore, and on polling day catholic clergy took an active part in his campaign.[61] Saunderson was proposed at the nomination and assisted in his campaign by some of the gentry. The result was Fay 3,229, Biggar 3,079, and Saunderson 2,310. In a later assessment of the election, the *Cavan Weekly News* attributed Saunderson's defeat to the activity of the catholic clergy on the home rule side (a point also made by the *Nation*) and the failure of some conservatives to support Saunderson.[62] This conservative opposition was probably a result of Saunderson's comments on the Orange order during a speech in the house of commons against repeal of the party processions act. He stated that where he lived it would be hard to know of the existence of the Orangemen 'but for their persistent use of large drums'.[63]

In Co. Monaghan the home rule campaign went somewhat differently to that in Co. Cavan. On 31 January the *Northern Standard* carried election addresses from S. E. Shirley and John Leslie, the two former conservative M.P.s, and John Madden, the Monaghan landowner and member of the Church of Ireland who had stood as a home rule candidate in 1871 but withdrew before the poll. While declaring himself in favour of home rule, Madden made no mention of the education question and passed only very reserved remarks about land reform. Madden's reserve on these issues had already weakened his support. In late January, he had met the committee of the county home rule association but the meeting had not gone well because of his standpoint on land reform. Madden had also tried to gain the support of Dr James Donnelly, catholic bishop of Clogher, but Donnelly had declined to commit himself publicly.[64] At the beginning of February W. T. Power, a local landowner from Annaghmakerrig, Newbliss, issued an address as a liberal but then withdrew on 7 February.[65] This obviously helped Madden's chances and the local home rule movement now decided to back him.

Madden's conducting agent was an Orangeman but he appears to have received only limited protestant support. A letter in the *Northern Standard* of 7 February, from the grand master of the Co. Monaghan grand Orange lodge, stated that Orangemen had a duty to oppose home rule, which would only be the first step towards the dissolution of the United Kingdom. The editorial in the paper on the same day said it hoped that no protestant would vote for home rule, and quoted a passage from the *Ulster Examiner* that asserted that the few protestants in the home rule movement could have little say in it.[66] If Madden won poor Orange backing, he also received little official clerical aid. The catholic bishop and clergy retained reservations about him, apparently because he would not compromise on education.[67] Donnelly, unlike Conaty in Co. Cavan, did not propose him at the nominations and there is much less evidence than in the other constituency of clerical assistance for him in his campaign. The two conservatives in their campaign seem to have received the usual landlord help. The result was Leslie 2,481, Shirley 2,417, and Madden 2,105. In a letter to Isaac Butt after the election, Madden commented on the lack of catholic support:

> Had the people in Farney voted honestly as they led me to believe and as they said they would do, there would have been no trouble and I should have been at the head of the poll. I got as I calculate from 600 to 700

protestant votes certain — the failure of the catholic vote in Farney defeated me.[68]

Organisational problems and divisions within the ranks of his followers were clearly important factors in Madden's defeat and calls were to be made subsequently for a new conservative organisation.[69]

In Co. Donegal no significant home rule organisation or candidate emerged and the principal centre of opposition to proprietorial interests lay in a number of tenant right associations. In January various meetings of farmers' organisations were held to select candidates. After several persons declined nomination, the brothers Evory and Tristram Kennedy, members of the tenant right movement in the 1850s in Donegal, emerged on 31 January as the chosen candidates. One brother was a doctor and the other a barrister; both belonged to the Church of Ireland.[70] The two former conservative members, Thomas Conolly and the marquis of Hamilton, issued their addresses without any formal reselection procedure.

Both liberals and conservatives conducted vigorous election campaigns. In his election address the marquis of Hamilton had declared his support for the Ulster custom in regard to leaseholds and yearly tenancies. Public pressure on this now obliged him and Conolly to issue a joint public letter in early February to confirm that they both stood firmly by this position.[71] Tenant associations helped the liberals in their campaign and catholic clergy were noticeably present on liberal platforms as were presbyterian ministers.[72] The result was a very close one. Hamilton received 2,102 votes, Conolly 1,866, Evory Kennedy 1,826, and Tristram Kennedy 1,757. The outcome in Donegal, Cavan, and Monaghan showed how proprietorial interests in the counties were threatened not only as a result of the land question but also as a consequence of the home rule movement. The success of home rule in Cavan, but not, however, elsewhere, reflected the good organisation of the movement in a county with a catholic majority among the electorate and also the party's ability to capture full catholic support.

As regards denominational support for the different parties, newspaper reports indicate that, generally, catholic electors supported the liberals while members of the Church of Ireland backed the conservatives, although there were exceptions in some areas.[73] One source estimated that in Co. Down about 7 per cent of the votes of Sharman Crawford, the liberal, came from members of the Church of Ireland, while about 9 per cent of the conservative Forde's votes were given by catholics.[74] The presbyterians were divided but large numbers of them joined catholics in voting for liberal candidates, as the results in Antrim, Down, and Londonderry clearly show. Ellison Macartney won substantial backing from both catholics and protestants, including some Orangemen.[75] Porter, in Fermanagh, probably received a joint protestant–catholic vote. In Cavan the home rule candidates obtained apparently only catholic votes, but in Monaghan the home ruler seems to have secured some protestant support as well.[76]

The boroughs

In the Ulster boroughs in 1874, the land question was clearly not as important as in the counties. At the same time, interest in this subject in the community at large did draw attention to the prominent role that landed proprietors often played in the parliamentary boroughs. Social and political dissatisfaction at the position of the gentry in the towns had already surfaced in 1868 in a number of boroughs and it was now to spread to even more. A survey of the revision sessions in 1873 reveals the presence of the new Ulster liberal society secretary, Mathew Wylie, and local agents at most of the boroughs, while the conservatives in the boroughs continued to rely largely on local landlord assistance.[77] Although broader issues were of importance in some constituencies, in others local issues and rivalries continued to be significant.

Lisburn and Downpatrick were the only boroughs in which conservative members representing proprietorial interests were returned unopposed. In late 1873 John Mulholland, unsuccessful conservative candidate for Belfast in 1868, had purchased the Ker estate in Downpatrick, making him the largest property owner in the town.[78] Consequently William Keown, the sitting member, declared his intention to retire from parliament. Mulholland published an address and was elected without a contest, or any real show of opposition. A subsequent report in the *Down Recorder*, 21 March 1874, noted, as evidence of the new proprietor's interest in the welfare of the tenants on his Downpatrick estate, that he had placed at their disposal the service of his 'magnificent red bull Maximum Gwynne'.[79]

In Lisburn matters were arranged somewhat similarly. Since his election in February 1873, Sir Richard Wallace had strengthened his position as proprietor and M.P. In September 1873 he made an extended visit to Lisburn, when he donated liberally to the town charities and bought two paintings from a local artist, Samuel McCloy, for his famous art collection.[80] There were no liberal agents at the borough revision sessions of 1873 and the *Northern Whig* in its report on the registration remarked that Lisburn was becoming a 'kind of Happy Land' in which party politics would be unknown.[81] But while there was general support for Wallace, there was no doubt that he was a conservative, as he made clear in a speech after the election. At his nomination Wallace was proposed and seconded by prominent members of the Lisburn conservative society.[82] Lack of protest in these two boroughs can be attributed to the low number of presbyterian voters, the popularity of the new owners, and the absence of prominent local opponents.

Developments were rather different in Coleraine, Dungannon, and Newry, where conservative political interests found themselves under a strong attack from able liberal opponents backed by presbyterian and catholic forces. In Coleraine the poll was between the former conservative M.P., Sir H. H. Bruce, bt, and a liberal, Daniel Taylor, a local presbyterian merchant. For a time there was a third candidate, Leslie Beers, who in his address urged that 'under the banner of Orangeism, temperance, and reform, the true friends of religious, social, and political progress should rally.'[83] After a brief period Beers retired, claiming that he did not want to split the conservative vote. His candidature arose apparently because a number of Coleraine Orangemen felt that Bruce had snubbed them.[84] In their addresses both Taylor and Bruce made general comments on the need for land reform. Bruce referred to foreign policy and Taylor to temperance and defence of local interests; the former was clearly a conservative supporter while the latter said that he would back Gladstone's government.[85]

An indication of some of the social and religious tensions involved in the election can be seen in an editorial of the liberal *Coleraine Chronicle* on 31 January. First it stated: 'Leaving party politics out of account altogether, it is preeminently desirable that a town of such important commercial relations should be represented by a merchant.' Then it went on about Taylor:

> He is the representative of interests, the importance of which cannot be ignored. Above all he is a presbyterian. By electing him Coleraine will confer an invaluable service on the presbyterian church. We complain of being treated as hewers of wood and drawers of water. Why? Because we have not risen above political drudgery; because we have not prized our birthright. For a mess of conservative pottage it has been ignominiously sold; and it is a glorious sign that presbyterians are beginning to adopt broad independent principles and are espousing a candidature so highly fitted to blot out a reproach and rectify a wrong.

The result of the poll was Taylor 227 and Bruce 160. The *Northern Whig* stated that Taylor had been returned by a united presbyterian and catholic vote.[86] While this was no doubt so, it is well to remember the Orange discontent that may have caused some Orangemen to abstain or even support Taylor.

The election in Dungannon was fought between the former conservative M.P., Col. the hon. W. S. Knox, and T. A. Dickson, a presbyterian liberal who was, according to one newspaper account, 'the most extensive merchant, manufacturer, and employer of labour in the district'.[87] In their addresses, Knox said that he had voted for the second reading of the land bill, while Dickson stated that he would give hearty support to amendments to the 1870 act.[88] Knox referred to his family connection with the borough, and Dickson claimed that he had been asked to stand by a deputation of electors. Knox declared that he would resist any attack on the protestant faith and the supremacy of the crown. Dickson announced that he gave full endorsement to the liberal party.

Both candidates canvassed, Knox being escorted by the earl of Ranfurly's agent.[89] Details are scarce about the election campaign, but probably there were present the same social and religious tensions as in Coleraine. In 1868 Dickson had organised opposition to Knox on the grounds that presbyterians did not have their fair share of the parliamentary representation. As an indication of merchant and shopkeeper resentment against the domination of the Ranfurly family it may be noted that the *Tyrone Constitution* accused Dickson of arousing the middle class against the upper class.[90] Dickson won with 121 votes to Knox's 109. As in Coleraine, the liberal victory was acclaimed as the result of joint catholic–presbyterian voting.[91]

In Newry a large meeting of conservatives on 29 January invited Lord Newry to stand for reelection, an invitation that he accepted. On the same day the liberals held a selection meeting. Their first choice was Benjamin Whitworth, a prominent liberal from Drogheda, who declined to stand, and the next day his brother William, a Church of Ireland merchant, was selected.[92] Both candidates carried out extensive canvassing and held several public meetings. Whitworth declared his strong appeal for the actions of Gladstone and the liberal government, urged amendments to the land act, and called for certain matters of local interest to be dealt with in Ireland, not at Westminster. He declined to mention the education issue. In his address Lord Newry had merely stated that his principles were conservative. At the nomination Whitworth was proposed by a catholic and a presbyterian.[93] The result was Whitworth 459 and Newry 455 votes, which undoubtedly reflected catholic and presbyterian support for the liberal.

In Carrickfergus the leading proprietorial interests were also defeated but this time by an independent conservative candidate and for special local reasons. G. A. C. May, a queen's counsel, described in the press as the candidate of the marquis of Downshire (the leading landlord of the town), stood against the former M.P., M. R. Dalway.[94] May called himself a conservative who would protect the protestant constitution, while Dalway said that he would act independently but support measures to uphold the protestant religion.[95] More importantly, May said that he would look after local interests, while Dalway remarked that he had just become chairman of the Carrickfergus commissioners and would devote his time to the improvement of the town. Clearly what was at issue was still the question of the rights to commons land and the feelings of the freemen on this.[96] The outcome was a victory for Dalway who received 628 votes against May's 452.

In Armagh and Enniskillen the conservatives faced liberal candidates but did not have to worry about presbyterian opposition or an Orange split. In Enniskillen the election opened with the issue of addresses from the former conservative M.P., Viscount Crichton, and two liberals, Jeremiah Jordan and Capt. L. J. Collum.[97] Crichton declared his opposition to home rule. Jordan, an Enniskillen methodist merchant, described himself as 'one of yourselves and one of the common people' and said that he would support whichever party favoured the tenants. He then withdrew in favour of Collum. In his address Collum, son of John Collum, the longtime opponent of the earl of Enniskillen, stated that he would seek amendments to the land act, particularly in relation to town tenants, and declared that his own interests in the borough were greater than those of Crichton (who owned property in Lisnaskea and was only related by marriage to the earl of Enniskillen).

This rivalry between Crichton and Collum contained a certain degree of social conflict, as was revealed in the editorial of the liberal *Enniskillen Advertiser* on 5 February. It asked whether or not Enniskillen was to remain the appendage of one family, to be handed from one brother to another. It urged support for Collum, who had more local interests, and said that the people had the opportunity to throw off the Cole domination of the borough. The result of the vote, however, was Crichton 192 and Collum 172. According to one report Collum's backing was mainly catholic and

Jordan claimed that the conservatives had held the seat by the use of the cry 'protestantism in danger'.[98] The social division revealed during the election does not seem to have affected the other division of protestant and catholic in the community.

In Armagh G. L. Cochrane, a local solicitor, stood as a liberal against John Vance, the former conservative M.P. In his address Cochrane declared that he came forward as an 'unpledged and independent representative' who had been asked to stand by a number of voters because 'they consider that my family and local connections would render me a more fitting representative of this town, than anyone who is in no way identified with it, either by property or otherwise.'[99] This last remark was a reference to the fact that Vance was a Dublin merchant. Vance countered these comments at a meeting in Armagh on 29 January when he claimed that Cochrane had been asked to stand by a numerous body of catholics and a mere handful of protestants.[100] Vance had the support of the borough conservative society although there is no information on its actual role in the election. The outcome of the poll was Vance 325 and Cochrane 214.

The absence of a significant presbyterian electorate in Enniskillen and Armagh had probably damaged liberal opportunities in these two boroughs, and also in neither constituency had the conservatives faced a split Orange vote. But in Belfast and Derry in 1868 the liberals had benefited from a valuable presbyterian–catholic alliance in both, and a divided Orange electorate in the former. By 1874, however, these liberal advantages had been diminished. The sudden dissolution of parliament found the Belfast conservatives in a well organised position. The divisions of 1868 had been overcome. In early 1873 the Orange and protestant working men's association and the Belfast conservative society were amalgamated into a new conservative association with an elaborate selection procedure, whereby the conservative candidates were selected by the organisation's committee and then put to a general meeting of the association for its consideration.[101] On 23 January 1874 a large gathering of the association, mindful no doubt of presbyterian interests, approved of the choice of J. P. Corry, a presbyterian shipowner and merchant, as a conservative candidate at the next election, along with William Johnston, who had already been accepted as an official candidate.[102]

With the announcement of dissolution several days later, the conservatives quickly set about the work of organisation. Ward committees were established and an extensive canvass and a series of public meetings were conducted. Both candidates visited firms such as Harland & Wolff to address the workers. On 29 January the grand Orange lodge of Belfast met and declared its support for the two conservatives. Orange halls were often used as meeting places and for housing the local conservative committees. The Irish temperance league announced its backing for Corry and Johnston. On 29 January the presbyterian constitutional association came to an agreement with the conservative association over the choice of candidates, in spite of some earlier disagreement.[103] In their speeches Corry and Johnston dwelt at length on their opposition to home rule and their support for conservatism and protestantism. At a meeting on 29 January Johnston declared:

> You will stand up for conservative members, because they are pro-
> testants. I would not ask you to support conservative candidates if they
> ceased for a moment to conserve protestantism and conservatism. And
> the conservative that would not stand for protestantism is not a conser-
> vator of the British constitution.[104]

The liberals were slower to launch their campaign. On 27 January a representative gathering of the liberal committees of the five wards of Belfast was held in the rooms of the Ulster liberal society in Belfast. Thomas McClure, the former M.P., was reselected. Liberal meetings were now held in the borough, and the local ward committees organised a canvass and other election work. On 27 January the presbyterian liberal association appointed persons to support McClure's candidature in the different presbyterian churches. On 30 January the Ulster catholic association in Belfast passed resolutions that approved of McClure and recommended catholics to back him. Meetings of different branches of the catholic association took place on 1 February to make arrangements to canvass catholics on McClure's behalf.[105] In his speeches McClure described how he had worked in parliament with the liberal party, which had dealt with the Irish church question and the land problem. He extolled the religious equality and fair treatment which he said the liberals had brought about for the benefit of presbyterians and catholics. McClure did not deal with the education question.[106]

In Belfast at this time there was a home rule association, but it seems to have lacked both strength and purpose, as it made no effective impact during the election. This inactivity may well have been related to the fact that home rule had made headway only among some Belfast catholics, who were anyway a small section of the electorate. By 1874 home rule in Belfast had already become closely associated with catholicism in the minds of many catholics and protestants, in spite of efforts by individuals to prevent this. At a meeting of the Belfast association on 31 December 1873 impassioned pleas were made that Irishmen should forget past differences and support home rule. The *Ulster Examiner* the next day exclaimed: 'What we earnestly wish is that in our land there should be no distinction of creed, no distinction of race, that all should be Irishmen'.[107]

But a month later, in an editorial on how catholics should vote at the election, the *Ulster Examiner* commented:

> When speaking to the catholic body, of course we include the home rulers, for, with an almost inappreciable exception, the home rulers of Belfast are thorough and enthusiastic catholics. There are, of course, a few protestants and presbyterians, but the numbers are so insignificant that their influence cannot and should not weigh in the determination of the policy to be adopted.[108]

On 3 February the paper reported on a meeting of the association which was addressed by its chairman, the presbyterian minister Rev. Isaac Nelson. First, it reminded the readers that there were just five presbyterians in the association and then rebuked Nelson for his statement that if religious principles clashed with the cause of one's country, then the former should be disregarded: 'We think ... that religious principles should be put before any opinions, even conscientiously held, with regard to the rights and liberties of one's country.' The *Examiner* denounced Nelson, 'who at last has shown the cloven foot', and claimed that it was the true and only representative of the home rule party in Belfast. These comments of the *Examiner* had been closely observed by the conservative press. On 5 February the *Belfast Newsletter* stated:

> Home rule is simple Rome rule, and, if home rule were accomplished tomorrow, before that day week Rome rule would be evident. The 'enthusiastic catholics' would do in all Ireland as they are doing in Belfast with the few protestants who were foolish enough to join that association and they would tell you loyal men that you had no rights at all, no voice at all, no claim on the country at all.

The fourth candidate in 1874 in Belfast was John Rea. In his usual eccentric style Rea issued a series of political addresses to 'the eleven thousand protestants of the English garrison of Ulster, now resident in Belfast, and in possession of the parliamentary franchise for the borough', but did little in the way of political campaigning. He declared his intention 'probably with some thoroughly anti-papal colleague, such as the Garibaldian General Chambers, or Mr James Anthony Froude' to contest Belfast 'against the English tories and their "natural allies" the Irish papish priests'.[109] Polling occurred on 5 February. Rea came to an early ignominous fate when he was seized outside a polling station by a group of men and dropped into a heap of mud. The final result was Corry 8,412, Johnston 8,176, McClure 4,096, and Rea 506 votes.

Thus clearly the conservatives had healed the divisions of 1868 and established a firm majority in the Belfast electorate. McClure wrote afterwards to Gladstone and remarked that he was 'overwhelmed by the influence and organisation of the Orange party now more formidable than ever'.[110] Thomas MacKnight also commented to Gladstone: 'We are badly beaten in Belfast at the general election, because the dissolution was unexpected, and, with existing dissensions between catholics and presbyterians there was no time to organise the party and banish our difficulties.'[111] The advent of the home rule movement and its growth among the catholic population had caused friction between presbyterian and catholic liberals.[112] Although McClure had the backing of many presbyterian ministers, his support for the universities bill, as well as his refusal to take a strong stand on temperance, had lost him presbyterian votes.[113] Besides these weaknesses on McClure's side and the fact that he had no longer the second vote of Johnston's followers, McClure's defeat reflected the considerable success of conservatism among the protestants of Belfast and the way in which it had reorganised in face of Orange and presbyterian objections.

In Derry also the conservatives were able to prevent either presbyterian or Orange defection from damaging their electoral strength. The fact that the conservative candidate, C. E. Lewis, first elected for the city in 1872, was a presbyterian himself was helpful. Lewis had the backing of the Derry working men's protestant defence association and after the election he paid tribute to the efforts by his supporters, 'above all . . . the exertions of the working men of Derry'.[114] Lewis described himself as a moderate conservative who agreed that improvement was needed in relation to the land question and education, but reserved his judgement on these matters until he saw what the government proposed.[115] He also advocated the abolition of income tax. The conservatives conducted a vigorous election campaign which contrasted with a less effective one run by the liberals.

On 28 January it was reported in the press that a meeting had taken place between the Derry home rule association and the local liberals about the selection of a candidate.[116] Nothing seems to have come directly from this meeting but by the end of the month the

liberals had persuaded Bartholomew McCorkell, a prominent presbyterian city merchant and candidate at the 1872 by-election, to
stand. The home rule party seems to have concurred in this choice.
In his address McCorkell declared that he stood as an independent,
he sought amendments to the land act, and he promised to promote
the development of the city.[117] The result was a victory for Lewis
with 744 votes against 715 for McCorkell. For the liberals this was
actually an improvement on their 1872 performance and, indeed,
they won more protestant electors than two years previously, as the
Londonderry Sentinel lamented,[118] but still it did reflect the success
of the conservatives in adjusting to meet local demands.

Summary of results
For the 29 Ulster seats, 21 conservatives, 6 liberals, and 2 home
rulers were elected in 1874 compared with 25 conservatives and 4
liberals in 1868.[119] Of the 18 county M.P.s, 13 were conservatives, all
of whom were the owners or related to the owners of the principal
estates in their constituencies, except for J. W. Ellison Macartney,
who was a landlord but possessed little property in his constituency.
The 8 borough conservatives consisted of 3 who were the chief
proprietors in their boroughs, a shipowner, a merchant, a solicitor
and 2 minor landowners. James Chaine, Co. Antrim, and John
Mulholland, Downpatrick, were prominent landowners but had
important links with linen manufacturing. Of the conservatives, 2
were presbyterian and the remainder members of the Church of
Ireland.
     Of the 3 liberal county M.P.s, one was a land agent, one a queen's
counsel, and one a presbyterian minister and professor. The 3 liberal
borough M.P.s were all merchants, 2 belonging to the constituency
they represented and the other coming from a town elsewhere. Of
the liberals, 4 were presbyterian and 2 members of the Church of
Ireland. One of the home rulers was a solicitor and the other was a
provisions' merchant. Fay was a catholic and Biggar a presbyterian
who became a catholic in 1877. All of the conservatives, except
William Johnston, were educated privately or at English public
schools, while the liberals, the home rulers, and Johnston attended
Irish schools such as Dungannon Royal School. About half the conservatives went to Oxford or Cambridge, while one liberal went to
Trinity and one to Glasgow University. Ellison Macartney attended
university in Germany.
     Thus the number of M.P.s from other than landed, Church of
Ireland, and English public school background had increased

markedly among the Ulster M.P.s. These developments were most obvious among the liberal and home rule M.P.s, but they were also apparent among the conservatives. Hopes expressed in catholic circles[120] prior to the election that they would be able to return many of their own members to parliament had failed to materialise in a significant way, but similar hopes in presbyterian circles were realised considerably. After the general election the *Witness* commented:

> We must confess our joy that the presbyterian church is to have this share in the representation. For one thing, the fact indicates an improvement in the social status of presbyterianism, which is noteworthy. It can now take its place side by side with any of the churches, fearing no comparison of its ministers or its people with those of any other body.[121]

The 1874 general election with its high number of contested elections witnessed more political organisation than had existed in 1868. For the conservatives organisation remained chiefly in the hands of the candidates and their families, who hired agents, formed committees, and availed of other landlords' assistance. Only in Belfast and Derry is there evidence of conservative political associations at work, although party organisations existed in Armagh, Co. Armagh, and Lisburn but did little. For the liberals, the Ulster liberal society had provided valuable pre-election help at the revision sessions, especially in the boroughs. In the boroughs, committees were formed at election time and only Belfast and Derry seem to have had permanent liberal associations. In the counties, however, the liberal cause was given important assistance by the tenant right associations. There was little sign during the election of effective home rule organisation except in Co. Cavan, where the organisation seems to have been a rather loose one, led by a number of catholic clergy.

In the rest of Ireland outside Ulster, 12 conservatives, 4 liberals, and 58 home rulers were returned, compared with 14 conservatives and 62 liberals in 1868 (Cashel and Sligo were disfranchised in 1870). The total Irish representation in 1874 consisted of 33 conservatives, 10 liberals, and 60 home rulers. These overall results contrasted sharply with the 1868 results when 66 liberals and 39 conservatives had been returned; it represented a dramatic defeat for the liberals, and meant that for the first time ever a majority of Irish representatives had been elected who sought a change in the constitutional arrangements between Great Britain and Ireland. Of the M.P.s from constituencies outside Ulster the number of landowners had sunk from 52 in 1868 to 35 and of protestants from 39 to 28. The 16 liberals and conservatives were predominantly from landed and protestant background. At the same time, the number of members from a catholic and professional or mercantile background had increased, especially among the home rulers, of whom only 23 had important landed interests.[122]

Conservative and liberal organisation in 1874 outside of Ulster was mainly limited still to Dublin and Cork, while elsewhere it was dependent on gentry support. The home rule party had the assistance of a number of home rule clubs, sympathetic farmers' associations, and catholic clergy.[123] The home rule organisation, however, was not well developed; it was not based on a new organisation challenging a liberal one, but depended on public opinion, which made existing associations sympathetic towards it and persuaded many former liberal M.P.s to join its ranks.[124]

Thus the home rule party, with its policy of home rule coupled with extensive land reform, denominational education, and minor issues such as amnesty of fenians and support for the pope, achieved very considerable success in the three southern provinces. But it had made little headway in the north. Where home rule was put forward, as in Monaghan, without any of the other objectives of the home rule party, it achieved little endorsement from anyone. Where it was put forward with these other aims, as in Co. Cavan, it received support from catholics but not from protestants: in Belfast, where a candidate was not actually put forward but a home rule association did exist, the movement also had largely, although not wholly, catholic backing.

Significant developments, however, continued to take place among the Ulster representation. The social split in the conservative ranks in Belfast had been settled for the time being, but social divisions had now appeared in the conservative ranks in the country owing to the growing agrarian unrest. J. W. Ellison Macartney had defeated the leading proprietary interests in Co. Tyrone with former conservative as well as liberal support, and division within Orange ranks had posed a serious threat in several more counties, especially Co. Fermanagh. The conservatives, with their strong position in society and relatively effective organisation, had been able to hold on to thirteen of the eighteen county seats, partly by advocacy of land reform, but they now faced a growing social and political challenge. An anonymous correspondent in 1875 warned a friend of the Belmores in Co. Tyrone:

> The people in this county are at present undergoing a sort of educational process to the effect 'that the Belmore family take no interest in the people of their county', and this is forced on them as a reason not to

support Col. Corry at the next election for this county.[125]

In the boroughs they had also lost to the liberals in three cases, but they had retained Belfast and Derry on a strong protestant vote with policies of support for the constitution and the empire; in both these latter cases it may be noted that they put forward a presbyterian candidate.

The Ulster liberals continued to grow in strength with their three borough and three county seats. In the boroughs the nature of their success indicates both religious and social dissatisfaction with the political representation. The vote of the presbyterian liberals seems largely to have stemmed from resentment at the Church of Ireland gentry domination of the parliamentary representation, while the catholic liberal vote probably arose from similar grounds and may also in places have been a protest against the protestant control of local government affairs, of which the conservative M.P.s and their supporters approved.[126] The presbyterian, professional, and merchant character of the liberal M.P.s reveals religious and social discontent among these particular sections with their Westminster members.

The most significant factor, however, in this liberal growth was the success of the liberals in the counties among the farmers. After the general election H. de F. Montgomery commented: 'In Ulster the constituencies with the help of the ballot emancipated themselves to a great extent from the dictation of the small sets of tory landlords which hitherto completely managed all elections in our counties.'[127] While the ballot act may to some degree have helped the liberals, what was much more important was the fact that under the new social pressures in the countryside the common political interest between landlords and tenants, and conservative M.P.s and electors, was breaking down. The liberal party, with its expanding organisation based on the tenant associations, now provided the political leadership for this new rising protest.

CHAPTER 7 *By-elections, 1874-80*

For Gladstone, according to Thomas MacKnight, the liberal successes in Ulster in 1874 were a source of cheer.[1] Elsewhere, however, the election results gave few reasons for happiness to the liberal leader and a conservative government was established at Westminster for the next six years, during which time little legislation of direct importance to Ireland was passed in the houses of parliament. Although the government's foreign policy aroused considerable interest and sympathy among many Ulster protestants, as evidenced by various well attended conservative and Orange public meetings in 1878 and 1879 ,[2] politics in the province still continued to be dominated by the land question. The down-turn in Irish agriculture after 1877 helped to fuel what was already a situation of deep unrest in the countryside.

In the immediate aftermath of the general election, however, political attention focused on the issue of party organisation. Poor conservative organisation in Co. Monaghan during the election had aroused local criticism. The *Northern Standard* on 14 February urged that a county constitutional association should be set up to look after registration and the selection of parliamentary candidates:

> Such a course, if adopted, would give the people an interest in working for the candidates selected which could be secured in no other way. The time has passed when such an association could be confined to the aristocratic element. Recent events fully prove that the rank and file of our communities are the only real power in the state.

On 19 February a meeting was held in the county to establish the County Monaghan conservative and constitutional association.[3]

This feeling of the need for broader conservative organisation was also expressed elsewhere. Shortly after these Monaghan events, which had been noted with approval in the *Belfast Newsletter*, a similar course of action was started in Co. Down by supporters of Hill-Trevor and Forde. On 18 July, after several months of preparation, a large preliminary meeting of the Co. Down constitutional association was convened and steps were taken for the organisation of local committees.[4] In Co. Antrim similar moves were made and by July the county constitutional association was active. Local branches were formed, such as that at Ballymacash, established on 6 July.[5] E. S. Finnigan became full time secretary to both the Cos Down and Antrim associations. After their defeat in Coleraine a meeting of conservative electors was held in the town at which it was decided to set up a borough constitutional association; a full-time agent was also appointed for this organisation.[6] A prime responsibility of the associations and their officials was supervision of the revision sessions in the conservative interest.

Among the liberals, as well, organisational growth occurred after the 1874 general election. On 25 February 1874 at a meeting of Donegal liberal electors the Donegal tenant right and liberal association was established.[7] Local committees in the form of district tenant right associations were to be set up with an annual subscription of 10s. for members and 2s. 6d. for associates. In other parts of Ulster tenant right associations were formed, especially in Down, as for example at Clough in June 1874, and in Antrim, as at Crumlin in March 1874.[8] The leading role of well known liberals, such as Joseph Perry and Edward Gardner of Downpatrick, in the formation of these organisations indicates the close link between the liberals and the tenant right associations. In Co. Antrim the various tenant right groups joined together into the Antrim central tenant right association in June 1876,[9] although each still retained its separate identity; Lord Waveney was president of this central organisation and of the Ulster liberal society. Registration activities of the Ulster liberal society secretary now spread to the counties.

Reorganisation among the home rulers in Ulster was slower than among the other parties. The Dublin-based home rule league, the central body of the home rule movement, appears to have included only a limited number of northerners, a fact related partly to the distance of Dublin from Belfast and also the annual membership subscription of £1 and upwards.[10] In a letter of early 1875, John Martin, the secretary, remarked: 'As to Ulster, I count six representatives from that province in the council of 1874 — the two M.P.s for Cavan Co.; Mr. John Madden, Clones; W. McCloskey, Derry; Rev. I. Nelson, Belfast; Rev. P. O'Reilly, P.P., Kingscourt.'[11] In the period after the general election there is evidence of some activity by local home rule groups in Ulster, as seen for example in the home rule meeting in Cootehill, Co. Cavan, in August 1874, and in the activities of the Ballyshannon home rule association.[12]

Yet these local associations do not seem to have had much success in organising a strong movement, partly because of lack of support from the home rule league in Dublin whose only assistance to local associations was to supply the occasional speaker. The secretary of the Newry home rule association, in a letter to Butt in October

1876, asked him to address a meeting in Newry as 'we meet with great opposition here, the people is (sic) almost dead to anything national, the thing has been neglected here for a considerable time. By you giving us a lecture . . . would do us a great deal of good.'[13]

On 23 November 1877 a conference was held in Belfast of representatives of the different home rule associations in Ulster.[14] The Ulster home government association was established as a body embracing all those who sought 'autonomy for Ireland'. A committee of 25 was set up with representatives for each home rule branch. Special attention was to be given by the local societies to registration. In spite of this attempt to put some energy into the home rule movement in the north, there seems to have been little change in the situation, although the Ulster home government association did play a small role in subsequent elections. So far as registration went, there is no evidence of participation by local home rule associations or the Ulster central body. An Ulster catholic registration society was set up in 1875 in Armagh but its agents appeared only briefly at revision courts in Armagh.[15]

Armagh city, 1875

The first by-election in Ulster was caused by the death in late September 1875 of the Armagh city M.P., John Vance. Within a short time of his death, addresses appeared from two conservatives, W. S. B. Kaye, LL.D., a local Church of Ireland barrister, and Capt. G. de la P. Beresford, son of the Church of Ireland primate.[16] Beresford stated that his views were the same as those of the late member for the city and that he was a warm supporter of the government. Kaye also said that he was a conservative and was in favour of the Ulster custom, especially at the expiration of leases. Both candidates canvassed, but only Kaye seems to have held public meetings. Kaye frequently emphasised his support for tenant right and insisted that he had the backing of the main body of Armagh conservatives; T. G. Peel, city coroner and secretary of the borough and county conservative societies, and an important figure in the Orange order in Co. Armagh, was a speaker at Kaye's meetings.

This contest between two conservative candidates was now given a new aspect by the attitude and action of the Armagh city catholics, who numbered about 180 out of 596 electors. At a meeting of catholics on 27 September, where the principal speaker was Father P. J. Byrne, administrator of the cathedral parish, a resolution was passed which stated that as neither candidate had anything to offer catholics on the question of home rule or denominational education,

catholics should abstain from the poll. Resolutions were also passed
stating that catholics were excluded from any say in the city's affairs,
that more should have the vote, and that steps should be taken to
organise the catholic vote and see to the registers.[17]

On the day of polling, however, another meeting of catholics
decided to vote against Kaye, even though he was regarded as a
tenant right supporter, because he was closely associated with T. G.
Peel who was strongly disliked by Armagh catholics.[18] This decision
was an unexpected one but may well have been deliberately left
until the last minute for tactical reasons. The result was Bereford
278 and Kaye 247. According to a report in the *Ulster Gazette*
around 170 catholics voted for Beresford plus 108 protestants, while
Kaye's supporters were all protestants.[19] After the contest an
election petition trial was held owing to allegations by Kaye. He
claimed that Beresford had used corrupt methods to win the poll,
such as providing ample quantities of free alcohol for electors and
arranging for the Armagh militia to go on a long route march to
keep some Kaye supporters among its members away from the poll.
All this was proved to be untrue and it turned out that Peel had
manufactured these allegations to try and persuade Beresford to
back a relative of his for a local job of clerk of the crown in return
for dropping the charges.[20]

Enniskillen and Co. Donegal, 1876

The appointment of Viscount Crichton as lord of the treasury
resulted in a by-election in Enniskillen in February 1876. Crichton
stood for reelection and in his address urged the electors to support
him as a sign of their sympathy for the government in its domestic
and foreign policies.[21] For a time it seemed that Crichton might face
an opponent in the person of David McBirney, the Dublin owner of
the Belleek potteries, but this failed to materialise and Crichton was
returned without a contest. While this borough by-election passed
with little fuss, the next by-election, which was for a county, would
reveal the growing protest in the Ulster countryside over the land
question. Politicians of all parties were well aware of this and even
as early as June 1874 the conservative M.P. for Co. Donegal, the
marquis of Hamilton, had written to Disraeli's secretary to urge that
the conservative party take action on the matter: 'I am convinced in
my mind that if the present government do not do something in the
way of amending the Land Act themselves, that at the next election
the few remaining conservative seats in Ulster will go also.'[22] But
this position received no support from the government, and several

bills introduced by Ulster conservative M.P.s failed to obtain government backing. Liberal bills likewise did not achieve anything.

Hamilton's words would now be tested at the by-election that followed the death of his fellow M.P., Thomas Conolly, on 10 August 1876, after a long illness. Within a week of his death election addresses had appeared in the papers from William Wilson, a presbyterian solicitor from Raphoe, who stood as a conservative, and Thomas Lea, a congregationalist manufacturer and former M.P. of Kidderminster, as a liberal. From subsequent reports, it seems that a number of Donegal liberals had met several months before Conolly's death to consider a liberal candidate and on the recommendation of Prof. Richard Smyth, M.P. for Co. Londonderry, had contacted Lea who had agreed to stand in the liberal interest.[23] How Wilson was selected is not clear. Addresses also appeared from another conservative and liberal, but both candidates withdrew to avoid splitting their respective party votes.[24]

In his address, Wilson stated that he was a native of the county, that he would seek amendments to the land act so as to secure the benefits of the Ulster custom both for leaseholders and for yearly tenants, and that he supported reform of the grand juries. He declared himself a liberal conservative and said he would back the conservative government, although he retained the right to act independently when necessary. Lea in his address advocated free sale of farms, fair rents, and the full legislation of tenant right. Both Lea and Wilson canvassed and held meetings.[25]

Division threatened the liberal ranks, however, at an early stage of the campaign. On 22 August a long letter appeared in the *Ulster Examiner* from Rev. M. H. Cahill, C.C., of St Patrick's, Belfast. In this he alleged presbyterian tyranny and claimed that the presbyterian liberals did not heed catholic interests, especially over education and the Belfast burials' question. He stated that catholics would support a presbyterian liberal but presbyterians would not back a catholic liberal. On 17 August a meeting of the catholic bishop of Raphoe and his clergy was held in Donegal.[26] At the meeting it was decided that although dissatisfied with both candidates they felt Lea was the more eligible and a circular was released that recommended that all the clergy let this be known to the people 'with a view to guiding them in their choice'.

In his campaign Wilson had the support of the local landlords.[27] Lord Enniskillen, in a letter to the earl of Belmore on the eve of polling, remarked: 'Lord Hamilton writes me word that every vote will be required in Donegal. Your agent, Benson, and his father have votes. Pray telegraph to them to go, as the time is too short to write.'[28] In spite of earlier difficulties catholic clergy assisted Lea, as did some presbyterian ministers.[29] At the nomination, Wilson was proposed by two tenant farmers, while Lea was put forward by two merchants, one a catholic and the other a protestant.[30] The result was a conservative victory: Wilson obtained 1,975 votes against Lea's 1,876. The conservatives' choice of Wilson, a local presbyterian who backed tenant right, was clearly an important factor in their success and showed how they were adapting to the new political demands. The rather unenthusiastic support for Lea among Donegal catholics, as well as the fact that he was relatively unknown, were probably factors that weakened Lea's position. As regards the home rule movement and the election, the comment of the *Ulster Examiner* was that home rulers in Donegal had no organisation, no programme, and no leaders, for which the paper blamed the home rule league in Dublin.[31]

Belfast, Co. Down, and Co. Londonderry, 1878
On 18 March 1878 the Belfast papers reported that William Johnston had been offered a government post as an inspector of Irish fisheries and would retire from the representation of the borough in order to accept the position. Three days later Johnston confirmed this at a meeting of the Belfast conservative association where he said that the appointment had been offered to him without any solicitation;[32] in fact Johnston had sought a government post for a number of years, owing to his poor financial position, and he and others had frequently written to Disraeli on the matter.[33] Following this meeting the committee of the association met to select a candidate. Two names were put forward — William Ewart, a very prominent Belfast linen merchant and manufacturer who was chairman of the conservative association, and Robert Seeds, LL.D., a Belfast-born queen's counsel who worked in Dublin. Ewart and Seeds were both members of the Church of Ireland but not Orangemen. Ewart was chosen by a large majority and was subsequently accepted as the party candidate at a general conservative association meeting on 26 March.[34]

Election addresses appeared now in the press from Seeds and Ewart, both of whom declared themselves to be conservative.[35] Each candidate had an election committee and addressed public gatherings. At Seeds's meetings speakers said that Ewart had been selected by a small clique and that Seeds was the choice of all independent protestants and Orangemen.[36] While this protestant side to the election campaign of Seeds was well apparent, so also was the social aspect. Seeds argued that the main question was 'the rights of the working man' and mentioned various social issues which he urged needed attention such as compensation for industrial injuries. Some Orange lodges declared their support for Seeds and he had the open assistance of the Belfast grand master, William McCormack.[37] Ewart at his meetings asserted that he was the properly chosen candidate of the Belfast conservative association in which working men had a large representation, and that he sought to represent every class. With one exception, all the district Orange lodges in Belfast declared that they backed Ewart. William Johnston let his support for Ewart be known.[38]

Neither of the two other parties, the liberals and the home rulers, took an active part in the election, apparently seeing no advantage in doing so. The Belfast liberal association had, in fact, collapsed after the 1874 general election. At a meeting of Belfast home rulers on 28 March, a decision was made to advise all party followers to refrain from voting.[39] Shortly before polling, however, the *Northern Whig* suggested that the liberals should give some support to the followers of Seeds in their assertion of 'independence against the conservative party'.[40] The result of the contest was Ewart 8,241 and Seeds 4,895; over 7,000 electors remained unpolled. Who voted for Seeds is not exactly clear. The *Belfast Newsletter* claimed that not less than 2,000 catholics supported Seeds, but it is unlikely this was so in view of the hostility to Seeds among home rulers and the catholic press.[41] It also claimed that many liberal protestants voted for Seeds, but only a very limited declaration of support had come from liberal circles and after the election the *Northern Whig* said that few liberals had backed him.[42] Probably Seeds's vote represented a considerable protestant working-class sympathy for him.

The announcement of the death of James Sharman Crawford, M.P. for Co. Down, on 29 April 1878, came as a complete surprise to the people of his constituency. In spite of this, the liberals were quick to choose a new candidate because they had expected Lord A. E. Hill-Trevor, the other county M.P., to retire due to ill health and had already made arrangements for the selection of a liberal candidate. A committee, appointed some time before by a meeting of representatives of tenant right associations, had asked W. D. Andrews, LL.D., a unitarian barrister from Comber who was a member of a prominent liberal family, to come forward in the liberal

interest.[43] Andrews had agreed but on Sharman Crawford's death
had suggested that a brother of Sharman Crawford should stand.
He refused, however, and Andrews consented once again to contest
the county in the liberal cause. At a meeting of liberal representatives
from different districts of Co. Down on 3 May in Belfast, under the
chairmanship of Sir Thomas McClure, the selection of Andrews was
approved.[44]

In his address Andrews stated that his views on tenant right and
grand jury reform were well known; he would support the land bill
introduced by the late member for the county, which sought to give
further protection to tenant right, irrespective of office rules or the
existence of a lease, and to secure freedom of sale and fair rents.[45]
Committees were set up to assist Andrews. Throughout the county,
meetings were arranged at which prominent liberals such as T. A.
Dickson spoke, as well as tenant right leaders and presbyterian
ministers.[46] At these gatherings, speakers denounced the previous
domination of the representation of the county by the Downshire
and Londonderry families and stated that now the tenant farmers
had the opportunity to assert their own cause.

Before Sharman Crawford's death the conservatives, also, had
initiated arrangements to select a conservative candidate for the
next election in the county. A committee set up by the conservative
association had asked Col. W. B. Forde to stand, but he refused and
it had been planned to hold a meeting to choose another candidate
when the vacancy occurred. On 3 May a meeting of delegates
of the conservative association connected with the different
polling districts was held under the chairmanship of Lord A. E.
Hill-Trevor.[47] The name of Viscount Castlereagh, son of the
marquis of Londonderry, the second largest landowner in the
county, was put forward and he was selected as party candidate.

In his address Castlereagh stated that he was a conservative and
would support the government.[48] He remarked that the land
question was the most pressing issue, and declared his backing for
the just rights of farmers. Support for Castlereagh now came from
the Irish temperance league because of a reply of his to a letter of
the league on temperance matters.[49] During the campaign the
government announced that they would give a second reading to
Hill-Trevor's leasehold bill. At his meetings speakers stated that the
Londonderry estates in Co. Down had always recognised fully the
Ulster custom.[50] Committees were set up to canvass electors and
organise for polling. The bill for this came to a colossal £14,000,
probably the largest sum spent on an Irish election during 1868-86;

this was charged to Lord Londonderry.[51]

A new element of the election campaign was added by the Ulster home rule association. The minutes of the organisation in the election period were later revealed in a letter from its secretary, J. C. Quinn, to the press during the 1880 general election. A deputation from the association approached Castlereagh and put to him questions on the home rule and education questions, to which they believed they received a sympathetic response. On 14 May the Ulster home rule association urged electors to vote for Castlereagh.[52]

The outcome of the polling was Castlereagh 6,076 and Andrews 4,701; the total electorate was 12,814. Compared with the 1874 result the liberal vote had slipped only slightly while the conservative vote had increased. Conservative efforts at the registration courts clearly had paid off, as several sources acknowledged at the time.[53] The expensively oiled conservative election machine, with E. S. Finnigan as agent, had proved effective in bringing out supporters: opponents even alleged that 'one invalid turned up from Nice'. Their candidate had appealed successfully to many sections of the electorate. Castlereagh subsequently denied that he had promised support to the views of the Ulster home rule association. Hill-Trevor's leasehold bill failed to secure a passage through parliament.

Three days after the death of Professor Richard Smyth, M.P. for Co. Londonderry, on 4 December, a meeting of county conservatives took place in Coleraine, at which S. M. Alexander, a Church of Ireland landlord from Limavady, was selected. At the same time a meeting of liberals was held in Ballymoney, when a presbyterian, Sir Thomas McClure, bt, a manufacturer and former M.P. for Belfast, was chosen as liberal candidate.[54] In his election address McClure stated that he would support measures to secure to tenants the full benefit of the land act and would also advocate land purchase by tenants.[55] He deplored the conservatives' foreign policy and supported the liberals, who, he said, had given religious equality, freedom for voters through the ballot, and security for farmers. Alexander, in his address, declared his approval of the government's foreign policy, urged economy in public expenditure, and stated that he would back whatever measures might be necessary to help carry out the principles of the 1870 land act.[56]

Both candidates canvassed and held meetings. On 7 December a gathering of catholic electors in Limavady and the surrounding district took place, after which a circular was sent to parish priests in the county.[57] This declared that the time had come for catholics to vote together as one body to have their grievances redressed and their voice more effectively heard. The clergy were urged to tell their parishioners not to connect themselves with either party until the catholic body in general had thought about the matter and, at a future conference of catholic delegates, had decided how they should vote. Whether or not these delegates met again is not clear but the first meeting certainly indicates the growing political awareness of catholics. Although the parish priest in the Waterside district of Derry city urged people to vote for Alexander because he was a good landlord, there were many more examples of their attendance at McClure's meetings.[58]

On 17 December the papers carried a manifesto from the Ulster home rule association which said that they had put their views to the two candidates and had received the best reaction from McClure. They recommended McClure to home rule supporters, although somewhat reluctantly:

> The limited state of the franchise precludes us from putting forward a candidate who would really represent the interests of Ireland, and, under these circumstances, the only alternative left us is to support the least objectionable candidate who is undoubtedly Sir Thomas McClure.[59]

At McClure's meetings, where presbyterian ministers were well in evidence, the main topic was the land question.[60] Speakers remarked on how the conservatives had changed their views on the subject, and the point was often made that the conservatives backed a government that had opposed amendments to the land laws. At Alexander's meetings support was declared for the government's foreign policy and comment was passed on the liberals' lack of policy on education.[61] Alexander emphasised the good landlord–tenant relations on his own estate and said that he would back legislation to amend the land act.

The result of the election was McClure 2,479 and Alexander 1,878 votes. Compared with the 1874 result these figures showed the conservatives had slightly improved their position. Still the liberals were very pleased at the outcome, especially at this time: 'It will do much', commented Mathew Wylie, 'to revive the hopes that were so dashed by the Down defeat.'[62] Poor organisation by the conservatives may have been a factor in their defeat but what was clearly most important was the growing belief that only the liberals could bring land reform; the *Londonderry Sentinel* (21 December) saw the conservative defeat as 'owing to the prejudice of tenant farmers, who have been instilled with the belief that liberal legislation alone will grant a satisfactory settlement of the land question'.

Co. Donegal, 1879

By late 1879 the conservative government had still failed to introduce new land legislation in spite of the action of Ulster M.P.s of all
parties to attempt to bring forward reforms in parliament. The Co.
Donegal by-election of 1879 was a result of the death of Charles
Wilson. Election addresses quickly appeared in the papers from
Thomas Lea, the unsuccessful liberal in 1876; D. B. McCorkell,
presbyterian barrister from Derry, a conservative; and Lord
Mountcharles, Church of Ireland son of the marquis of Conyngham,
an extensive Co. Donegal landowner, who also was a conservative.[63]
Before long, Mountcharles retired to avoid splitting the vote. In
their addresses the two remaining candidates both stated that they
would support amendment to the land act to obtain for the tenant
security of tenure and free sale, and would urge an extension of the
Bright clauses in the land act on land purchase. Lea said that the
conservatives had done nothing about the land question while in
office, and he mentioned the growing depression in the country.
There is no information in the papers about formal selection of the
candidates, but in both cases meetings of electors subsequently gave
them their support.[64] Each held rallies and canvassed widely.

In early December a letter appeared in the papers from Philip
Callan, home rule M.P. for Dundalk, which accused Lea of support
for the Newdegate bill for the inspection of convents and of
opposition to tenant right reform and denominational education.[65]
These charges were strenuously denied by Lea.[66] Callan, however,
arrived in Derry to continue his attack on Lea, motivated apparently
by the wish to earn government gratitude.[67] A catholic priest from
St Johnston in Donegal announced support for McCorkell because
of the liberal views on education and because the conservatives had
helped restore the pope to Rome after he had been driven out by
Napoleon; in his statement he also reminded people that Lucifer
was the 'first liberal'.[68] Apart from this priest, Lea seems to have had
the general support of the catholic clergy.[69] Shortly before the
polling day the Ulster home rule association issued an address
which said that they had not put forward a candidate because of the
limited franchise, but of the two candidates they found Lea the
more satisfactory, especially on the land question.[70] A number of
presbyterian ministers spoke on behalf of Lea at public gatherings.[71]

The result was Lea 2,313 and McCorkell 1,630. Compared with
the result of the 1876 by-election these figures reflected a fall in the
conservative and a rise in the liberal poll. In an attempt to account
for the conservative defeat, the *Londonderry Sentinel* drew

attention to the widespread feeling in the farming community that
only the liberals could bring land reform.[72] The other M.P. for Co.
Donegal, the marquis of Hamilton, estimated that the opposition of
Lord Gifford to a leasehold bill introduced by Ulster conservative
M.P.s in parliament had lost them 300-400 votes.[73] In both the
Donegal and Londonderry by-elections of 1878 and 1879, the
catholics seem generally to have supported the liberals, while the
degree of presbyterian backing for the liberals was steadily growing.[74]

Thus, by the eve of the 1880 general election, the political
character of Ulster representation was unchanged from 1874.
An intermediate education act of 1878 had been welcomed by
the population at large. But the demand for land reform and the dissatisfaction among the electorate with their existing parliamentary
representation continued to grow. The increase in attention given
to the land question and the consequent cooperation between
catholic and protestant farmers had clearly brought a new spirit into
politics. In his *New Ireland* (published in 1877) A. M. Sullivan noted
that, apart from Belfast and some other towns, there had been a
marked decline in sectarian feeling. He commented: 'Every season
it becomes more and more plain that Ulster Orangeman and Ulster
catholic are equally desirous of terminating a state of things which
was the scandal of Ireland and the reproach of Christianity.'[75] The
political impact of these developments would now be made clear in
the general election of 1880.

CHAPTER 8 *The 1880 general election*

'The question of the hour', declared the *Fermanagh Times* on the eve of the 1880 general election, 'is a sad one — destitution. It is echoed from the Giant's Causeway to the Cove of Cork. Go where we may, throughout Ireland, to-day, we hear the wail of distress for food.'[1] By March 1880 the situation in the countryside was one of severe depression, due to bad harvests in 1878 and 1879 and the competition of agricultural goods from America. By the general election, a rising wave of tenant unrest, led by tenants' associations both new and old, was apparent throughout Ulster. All this had important political implications. In correspondence to Disraeli's secretary, Montague Corry, in early 1880, the marquis of Hamilton, M.P. for Donegal, lamented:

> There is only one subject that these tenant farmers in the north of Ireland at the present time care about — and that is the land question. It is all-absorbing to them. They care little about general policies or foreign policies, but the whole of their thoughts absolutely and without exception is concentrated upon the land.[2]

During the 1880 election in Ulster all the county seats and every borough, except two, were contested. In Cavan two home rulers opposed a conservative; in Antrim, Down, Fermanagh and Tyrone two tories stood against a liberal in each constituency; and in both Monaghan and Londonderry two conservatives confronted two liberals. In Armagh three conservatives faced one liberal, and in Donegal one conservative opposed two liberals. Among the boroughs, Lisburn and Armagh were the only uncontested seats. In Coleraine, Dungannon, Derry, Enniskillen, and Downpatrick a liberal faced a conservative. Finally, in Belfast three conservatives and one liberal fought for the two seats while in Carrickfergus two conservatives contested the single seat.

In the address of nearly every county candidate the land question was the primary issue. The two home rulers renewed their pledge to support fixity of tenure at fair rents and the principle of peasant proprietorship as well as home rule and denominational education. In their manifestoes the conservatives usually endorsed the government's foreign policy but nearly all dwelt at great length on their desire for agrarian reform. They often urged greater security for the tenant farmer, and a few expressed approval for land purchase.

Some liberals attacked the government's foreign policy, but all of them concentrated on the agrarian issue. They called for the three Fs, and a number demanded peasant proprietorship.

In the boroughs, the addresses of conservative candidates emphasised support for the government, in particular its foreign policy. John Mulholland, Downpatrick, declared his backing for a ministry 'which has upheld the honour of the empire, preserved peace, and defended the constitution'. Several conservatives endorsed the government's educational policy, while a number declared that they would look after local interests. In neither county nor borough addresses of conservatives did the subject of defence of protestantism feature greatly. Among the liberal candidates in the boroughs the government's foreign policy and the land question were the two most important issues. They spoke out strongly against the existing foreign policy, which in the view of T. A. Dickson, Dungannon, had led to bloodshed. Most also spoke of their determination to preserve the integrity of the empire. None mentioned education, except Taylor in Coleraine, who said that he backed the government on this issue.

In the election addresses of candidates in the three southern provinces, the main issues were the land question, home rule, and the government's policies. Among home rulers demands for land reform figured prominently: most candidates called for the three Fs and many demanded peasant proprietorship. Home rule was forthrightly advocated and many also called for denominational education. A number in their addresses declared support for C. S. Parnell; this reflected the struggle at the polls between the radical members of the home rule party, who were strongly anti-landlord and led by Parnell, and the more conservative section under Isaac Butt's leadership. The liberal candidates announced their sympathy for land reform, although usually not so specifically as the home rulers. The conservatives declared their backing for Disraeli's policies, especially in relation to foreign affairs. They seldom referred to the land question. Some liberals and conservatives stated their sympathy for denominational education.

The counties

In 1880 proprietorial interests in the Ulster counties faced a major challenge. Dissatisfaction over the land situation was greater than ever before. In addition, farmers were organised in associations that were extremely vocal, determined, and more numerous than in

1874. The social position of landlords was now questioned in a manner rarely seen and this was bound to have important political consequences. By 1880 also, in contrast to 1874, the Ulster liberal society had done more effective work in the counties, especially in the revision courts. During registration in 1879 the society's secretary, Mathew Wylie, gave assistance to local agents in Cos Antrim, Down, and Londonderry.[3] There were also liberal agents at the revision sessions in Cos Donegal and Monaghan.[4]

These developments had not occurred without a conservative response. In Down and Antrim the secretary of the two county constitutional associations, E. S. Finnigan, had been active at the registration courts.[5] More importantly, Ulster conservative M.P.s kept up their efforts to persuade the conservative government to respond positively to the situation. The marquis of Hamilton, M.P. for Donegal, in a letter to Disraeli's secretary, Montague Corry, in early 1880 warned of the growing tenant unrest and bitterly complained that the government had done nothing about it: 'I must tell you plainly, it is of no use to hide it — the govt are extremely unpopular in the north of Ireland.'[6] Clearly in response to this, the government, shortly prior to dissolution, announced its consent to the second reading of Ellison Macartney's leasehold bill. Sir Stafford Northcote wrote to Hamilton to assure him of the government's good intentions in the matter.[7]

During the election, a high level of political activity spread throughout the countryside. Candidates held well attended public demonstrations and extensive canvassing was carried out. The conservatives had the active assistance of many of the landlords and the backing of a few county constitutional associations. Conservative candidates strongly declared their support for land reform, and copies of Northcote's letter to Hamilton were often read out at meetings as evidence of the government's good intention. The liberals in their campaigns had the assistance of the various tenant right associations. The land question was by far the main issue in their speeches and addresses. Macartney's bill was attacked as insufficient, and protestant and catholic farmers were urged to unite to support the liberals, who alone, it was claimed, could achieve reform. At the liberal meetings catholic priests and presbyterian ministers were well in evidence. Local home rule associations played little direct part in the election, except in Cavan.

At the previous general election in Cos Donegal and Monaghan the conservatives had been relatively successful in dealing with opposition, but six years later they faced a more serious threat. In his correspondence with Montague Corry, Hamilton forwarded a letter from a Co. Donegal landlord who warned of the deteriorating situation in the county due to the land problem: tenants were losing sympathy with their landlords, and catholic and protestant farmers were coming together in the tenant right cause.[8] He remarked: 'Day by day that fear of popery which alone kept the presbyterians loyal is decreasing — you are now losing them by the hundred for they now consider the land question the all-important one.'[9] These charges were of considerable importance to the electoral scene, as Hamilton ruefully admitted: 'it makes me very unhappy and uneasy as the whole political aspect of these northern parts is gradually altering.'

Soon after the dissolution of parliament, Thomas Lea, the sitting liberal M.P. for Donegal, let it be known that he intended to contest the constituency again, and groups of liberals and tenant farmers indicated their support for him. For a time the liberals planned to put forward only one candidate but the policy was changed and eventually it was announced in late March that Rev. John Kinnear, presbyterian minister from Letterkenny and a prominent tenant righter, had agreed to stand.[10] On the conservative side a meeting of county supporters was held on 13 March and it was decided to put forward only the marquis of Hamilton, in the hope that the liberals would nominate just one candidate.[11] Although this hope was not realised, the conservatives did not run a second candidate.

In their speeches the liberals dealt almost exclusively with the land question. Kinnear frequently called for the creation of a peasant proprietary as well as the more immediate object of the three Fs.[12] At a meeting of catholic clergy on 30 March at Raphoe it was decided that the clergy would not pledge themselves to any side but would back the party of their own choice. At the liberal meetings, however, catholic clergy were frequently present as were a number of presbyterian ministers.[13] Besides trying to reassure the electors of his concern about the land question, Hamilton attempted to make himself as popular as he could in the constituency over other matters, such as support for a local railway project, about which he wrote to Lord Beaconsfield.[14] The result, however, was Lea 2,274, Kinnear 2,015, and Hamilton 1,954 votes.

In Co. Monaghan on 7 January 1880 John Givan, a presbyterian solicitor from Aughnacloy, Co. Tyrone, whose wife had Monaghan connections, addressed a meeting of liberal electors and expressed his willingness to contest the county on tenant right principles.[15] A month later, at a well attended county meeting of liberals in the catholic church in Castleblaney, it was resolved to accept the candidature of Givan and a Co. Monaghan landlord, Sir W. T. Power.[16] By early March, however, Power had decided not to stand and the committee of the county liberal association held a representative county meeting at Castleblaney on 16 March, at which William Findlater, a presbyterian solicitor and merchant from Dublin, was selected.[17] Another candidate, Charles Russell, Q.C., a catholic, originally from Co. Down, was not adopted, for reasons that cast an interesting light on some of the tensions in the liberal camp. In a letter to Gladstone six years after the event Russell remarked: 'The catholic bishop, Dr Donnelly, urged upon me the fact that the so-called protestant liberal vote could not be depended on for a catholic candidate. My enquiries satisfied me that this was correct, and in the result I did not stand.'[18]

After a meeting of the Co. Monaghan conservative and constitutional association in mid-January 1880, it was announced that the two sitting members for the county, Sir John Leslie and S. E. Shirley, would stand at the next election.[19] Both the conservative and liberal sides in Monaghan had the assistance of local party associations during the campaign. The liberal candidates had the active aid of bodies such as the Farney tenants' defence association. At liberal meetings and demonstrations, there were often present catholic clergy and sometimes presbyterian ministers; Dr James Donnelly, the catholic bishop of Clogher, and his clergy played a leading role in the liberal campaign.[20] Leslie and Shirley canvassed and held meetings with the support of local landlords.[21] The result was a liberal victory: Givan secured 2,818 votes, Findlater 2,545, Leslie 2,117, and Shirley 2,099. In both Donegal and Monaghan the catholic vote, plus significant presbyterian backing, had turned the election results in the liberals favour.

Co. Cavan, where the catholic electorate was larger and home rule organisation greater than elsewhere, was the only Ulster county contested by home rule candidates in 1880. According to a notice that appeared in the *Nation*, 20 March, a meeting was held in the Farnham Arms hotel, Cavan, chaired by Dr Francis O'Reilly, P.P. The meeting was supposed to be a preliminary one for a larger county assembly, but because time was short before the election and Fay and Biggar, the sitting M.P.s, had their full confidence, it was 'resolved that we, the bishop, priests, and people of County Cavan, hereby pledge ourselves to support their candidature at the forthcoming election'. On 29 March, Fay and Biggar, both of whom were catholic, arrived in Cavan. After a visit to the catholic bishop, Dr

Nicholas Conaty, they then commenced to canvass and hold public meetings. During their campaign the two candidates received considerable organisational assistance from the catholic clergy, and at the nomination both were proposed by Dr Conaty.[22]

For a time it seemed that the election would be uncontested. Major E. J. Saunderson, defeated liberal candidate in 1874, rejected the idea of standing. In a letter to his wife, 25 March 1880, he commented: 'I saw John in Dublin. He says that had I stood for Cavan I should probably have got in as the people were anxious that I should try again. I am not such a fool.'[23] But on 26 March an election address appeared in the local press from Capt. S. H. Maxwell, heir presumptive to the Farnham estates in Cavan, who stood as a conservative; he was a member of the Church of Ireland. He canvassed and held public meetings. His uncle, Lord Farnham, was reported as having entertained large numbers of landed gentry, no doubt in order to gain their assistance at the election. At the nomination, Maxwell was proposed by local landowners.[24] The result was Fay 3,097, Biggar 3,061, and Maxwell 2,233 votes. Little plumping occurred between the conservative and the home rulers, and reports suggest that most of the catholics supported the latter and most of the protestants the former.[25]

In Cos Armagh, Tyrone and Fermanagh, conservative interests faced not only a strong liberal challenge but dangerous internal conflicts. Within a week of the announcement of the dissolution of parliament, there were three conservatives in the electoral field in Armagh. They were M. C. Close, the former member; St John Blacker, a landlord with some local connections but whose main estate was in Co. Kerry; and Sir William Verner, bt, a local landowner and nephew of the other former M.P. for the county. In their election addresses, the three candidates, all of whom were Church of Ireland, declared their support for constitutional principles and land reform. On the latter issue, Verner went further than the other two and not only backed Macartney's bill but called for the three Fs and advocated measures to help tenants purchase their own land.[26]

Besides differences over views on the land question, there was also conflict between these candidates over methods of selection. Verner stated that in late 1878 he had been requested by a deputation of tenant farmers to stand at the next election on principles of conservatism, protestantism, and tenant right, and this request was renewed at a meeting of farmers at Kilmore on 13 February. Verner and his friends protested that his selection was a defiance of the 'wire pullers in Armagh' — a reference to P. G. Synott, deputy

grand master of the Co. Armagh grand Orange lodge, Rev. Thomas
Ellis, county grand chaplain, and T. G. Peel, deputy grand
secretary and secretary of the borough and county constitutional
associations.[27]

Peel, Synott and Ellis claimed that Verner had refused to meet a
deputation from the county grand lodge to answer their questions
prior to the selection of a conservative candidate. Blacker was then
adopted as candidate after two large meetings of conservatives,
including local gentry, with the recommendation of the county
grand lodge. Verner's candidature reflected dissatisfaction with the
existing control of selection of conservative candidates and a determination to put forward an independent candidate with strong
views on the land question. Supporters of Verner claimed that
Blacker had been nominated in an effort by T. G. Peel to maintain
his position as 'patron' of the constituency.[28]

The election developed a new aspect with the appearance of a
liberal candidate, J. N. Richardson, a quaker and linen manufacturer
from Bessbrook, Co. Armagh. On 15 March a conference of tenant
farmers had taken place in Portadown and a resolution was passed
that asked Richardson to stand as a liberal and tenant right candidate.[29] Four days later it was reported that he had accepted the
invitation. At his meetings Richardson had broad catholic and protestant, but mainly presbyterian, support.[30] A public letter written
to W. E. Forster, chief secretary, by Armagh liberals after the
election included the names of Rev. Jackson Smith, a prominent
Armagh presbyterian minister, and Dr Daniel McGettigan, the
catholic primate.[31] The result of the election was Richardson 2,738,
Close 2,654, Blacker 2,275, and Verner 1,781 votes. The split conservative vote undoubtedly helped the liberal candidate.

In Co. Tyrone, the main issue was the land question. One contemporary noted on 3 April: 'nobody here I am afraid cares a button
for anything except the three Fs. . . .'[32] At the previous general
election, conservative proprietorial interests had suffered a defeat
at the hands of J. W. Ellison Macartney. This time they took the
wise precaution of acknowledging him as an acceptable conservative
candidate and put forward only one other candidate, Lord Claud
Hamilton, who had been beaten in 1874. A liberal candidate
emerged after some delay. How he was selected is unclear but on 20
March an advertisement in the local press signed by T. A. Dickson,
M.P. for Dungannon, announced that E. C. Litton, a Church of
Ireland barrister with family connections in Tyrone, had consented
to stand on liberal principles.[33]

In his campaign Litton was assisted by Dickson and James Brown of Donoughmore, a well known presbyterian liberal and tenant righter. In a letter to Lord O'Hagan after the election John Harbison, a prominent catholic tenant right leader from Cookstown, described the activity of himself and other Tyrone catholics at the elections and also some of the religious tensions in the liberal side:

> We had a very sharp contest in Tyrone, I was asked to second Mr Dickson's nomination of E. F. Litton for our co[unty], but I advised, knowing how easily bigoted feelings were generated, to keep my co-religionists in the background, but I joined as one of the assentors and threw all the influence I possessed into the scale. I am confident there was not a score of catholics in Tyrone but plump'd as it is called for Litton . . .[34]

By 1880 Ellison Macartney had lost the catholic support which had helped him in 1874, owing mainly to his vote for Newdegate's bill for the inspection of convents.[35] He now directed himself entirely to the protestant electorate. A newspaper report of a meeting of Ellison Macartney's in Omagh on 27 March described how he said that:

> he would not desert his colours — his colours were the true blue colours — orange and blue. Some would like to mix orange and green, but he was not in favour of that. He was in favour of liberty and of conscience, an open bible and no surrender.[36]

At the same time, he took care to emphasise the land question and the importance of his leasehold bill.[37] Ellison Macartney succeeded in holding one of the seats with 3,826 votes but Hamilton, who received 3,470 votes, was defeated by Litton with 3,511.

In both Armagh and Tyrone the liberals had won seats but in Fermanagh they were less successful. The liberal cause in Fermanagh may have suffered because their candidate was the eccentric J. G. V. Porter of Belleisle. A meeting of tenant farmers, which included Orangemen and catholics, was held in Enniskillen on 10 March. Resolutions were passed that urged that a tenant farmer should be their representative and that a fund should be set up to defray his expenses. A committee was formed to select a candidate and six days later it reported back to another meeting that a farmer candidate could not be found but they recommended Porter, a candidate in 1874, who had already issued an address that stated his 'loyal and liberal principles' and made a strong declaration of support for tenant right. This recommendation was accepted although somewhat reluctantly.[38]

To assist Porter's campaign, committees were set up and a canvass organised. He had the support of various local tenants' associations although there is evidence that they were not entirely behind him. A letter from the secretary of Ederney tenants' association, written on 20 March and published in the press in early April, accused him of vagueness on the land question. At a meeting at Belleek he was queried by catholics about his attitude to education.[39] On the conservative side, W. H. Archdale, former M.P., issued his address shortly after dissolution of parliament and, following the hon. H. A. Cole's statement that he would not recontest the seat, Lord Crichton, former M.P. for Enniskillen, declared his intention to stand for the county. At their meetings the conservatives spoke of their advocacy of tenant right and attacked Porter for his peculiar views and inconsistencies: he was accused of having criticised both Orangemen and catholics in the past.[40] The press carried reports of statements of support from various Orange lodges for both Archdale and Crichton.[41]

The outcome of the election was Archdale 2,479, Crichton 2,443, and Porter 1,835 votes. In what was probably a correct assessment of the situation in Co. Fermanagh, the *Belfast Morning News* commented about Porter: 'he had no support but independent farmers, as he had not always agreed with any party, either Orange or catholic, and this affected him greatly, besides he had to fight the whole landlord interest.'[42] In Cos Tyrone and Armagh, the liberals benefited from significant presbyterian support along with a high catholic vote. Absence of a substantial presbyterian vote in Fermanagh undoubtedly harmed this cause. From a reading of the columns of the *Impartial Reporter* (with its presbyterian editor, W. C. Trimble) it is clear that Porter had some protestant backing, but the important role played by the gentry in the Orange order in Fermanagh probably prevented a serious division in Orange ranks, as seen in the other two counties.

In the three remaining counties, the conservatives faced a sustained liberal attack, which drew on the large presbyterian electorates of these constituencies. In Co. Londonderry, following the news of the dissolution of parliament, the two members for the constituency wired to Derry their intention to stand for reelection. Subsequent liberal and tenant right meetings approved of their candidature.[43] On 13 March the *Londonderry Sentinel* reported that S. M. Alexander, defeated candidate at the 1878 by-election, would stand again as a conservative. No other conservative candidate was put forward. In his address and speeches Alexander took an advanced

position on the land question.[44] Not only did he support measures to
give tenants full security but he backed measures to enable occupiers
to become proprietors. Law also advocated a peasant proprietary,
while both he and McClure spoke of the liberals as the only true
friends of the farmers. McClure emphasised that the 'the desire of
the liberal party was to place all classes and creeds on an equality.'[45]

The liberals had an effective system of local committees throughout the county, assisted by Mathew Wylie, secretary of the Ulster
liberal society, and various tenant associations gave important
help.[46] John Harbison of Cookstown later described the effort put
into the contest by a number of Londonderry catholics:

> My brother James and his family among others lent valuable aid in Derry,
> his son John the attorney who was acting professionally for that side put
> his heart and soul in the work. He had tried his hand a few months ago in
> Donegal for Mr Lea which inspirited him, then seeing that Mr Alexander
> was set up to oust Mr Law if possible a considerable number of catholics,
> knowing that the presbyterians would stand by Mr McClure, acted so as
> to put Mr Law foremost. . . . [47]

Law was a member of the Church of Ireland while McClure was
presbyterian, which explains this presbyterian preference for
McClure. The result was a liberal victory. Law and McClure received
3,012 and 3,112 votes respectively while Alexander won only 2,107.

The election campaigns in Antrim and Down can be considered
together because of the similarities between them. There were
strong tenant organisations in both and also, unlike elsewhere,
efficient county constitutional associations. For tactical reasons the
liberals ran only one candidate in Down, where the main liberal and
tenant right body was the Down tenants' association. Representatives from this body approached a number of possible candidates
and finally, on 15 March, it was reported that Major John Sharman
Crawford, a presbyterian landlord, another son of the late William
Sharman Crawford, had agreed to stand.[48]

In Co. Antrim the selection of the liberal candidate was a long-
drawn-out process. For several years before 1880, joint meetings of
the Antrim tenants' associations had been held to choose a candidate for the next election.[49] The leading light in all this organisation
was S. C. McElroy, president of the Antrim central tenant right
association, a body formed in 1876 from representatives of all the
Antrim farmers' groups. In early 1879, he sought the help of Lord
Waveney, president of both the Ulster liberal society and the
central tenant association, to ask him to persuade Charles Wilson,

the defeated liberal candidate of 1874, to stand: 'While the matter remains unsettled, I cannot use the platform for the advancement of liberal interests. I am still of opinion that Mr Wilson can carry the county, and the gain of even one seat would be of much value to the liberal party.'[50] At a meeting in May 1879 it was announced that Wilson had agreed to come forward again. In early March 1880 Samuel Black, a substantial presbyterian tenant farmer from Randalstown, Co. Antrim, was also requested by the central association to contest the county in the liberal interest. On 15 March he formally accepted.[51]

Among the conservatives, selection of candidates was at its most efficient in Co. Down. On 12 March a large gathering of electors was held in Downpatrick under the auspices of the Co. Down constitutional association.[52] For several days it had been rumoured that one of the former members, Lord A. E. Hill-Trevor, would not stand again. This was confirmed at the meeting and his nephew, Lord A. W. Hill, heir to the Downshire title and estates, was proposed and accepted along with the other former member, Lord Castlereagh. In Co. Antrim, within a week of the dissolution of parliament, election addresses were issued by James Chaine, the former M.P. for the county, and Edward Macnaghten, Q.C., brother of a prominent north Antrim landlord; the other former Antrim M.P., the hon. Edward O'Neill, had meantime indicated that he would not stand again. Macnaghten's candidature seems to have been something of a surprise to the county conservatives. But, after other Antrim gentry such as Sir Richard Wallace had turned the nomination down, a meeting of conservative landlords and tenants from each district in the county accepted Macnaghten on 17 March.[53]

In their addresses and speeches, the liberal candidates declared their backing for the three Fs. Black said that he would welcome the creation of a peasant proprietorship.[54] The liberals had the full assistance of the local tenant right associations. A considerable number of presbyterian ministers were on liberal platforms as were some catholic priests, such as Rev. James O'Laverty of Holywood.[55] Insight into liberal organisation in Co. Down can be gained through the private papers of C. H. Brett, who was once more the liberal agent in Co. Down.[56] From a central committee office in Belfast he maintained contact with local liberals who were organised under central committees for large areas, such as in Newtownards for the Ards, and local committees at places like Portaferry. He provided leaflets, assisted with speakers for meetings and gave advice about

electoral matters. Through their offices he organised polling agents
and personation officers for polling day. His local correspondents
included prominent tenant farmers, solicitors and manufacturers.

The conservative candidates in the two counties also stressed
their support for further land reform. Ellison Macartney's leasehold
bill was mentioned frequently at meetings. Castlereagh and Hill
emphasised the good landlord–tenant relations on their own estates,
while Macnaghten said that he backed greater facilities for tenants
to purchase their holdings.[57] In the case of Down we can get an
interesting view of the conservative organisation from the evidence
given later at the Co. Down election petition trial, where charges
of undue influence and bribery were brought against the conservatives.[58] The chief organiser in the county was E. S. Finnigan,
secretary of the conservative associations of Down and Antrim, and
the charges applied mainly to him.

Under the aegis of the county association there were a number of
local committees, which looked after their own districts under
Finnigan's direction, providing canvassers, agents, and drivers, and
organising meetings. Although members of the committees often
provided their services free, the other election workers were usually
paid; charges that electors were given paid election work to secure
their votes were not proved in the court. Estate agents and bailiffs
were frequently on the committees and acted on election day for the
conservatives as did many landlords. Conservative organisation was
probably similar in Co. Antrim. The county constitutional associations helped to involve a fairly wide spectrum of local conservatives
in the selection procedure and aided at revision sessions. They
provided some voluntary assistance at polling time but still the conservatives relied considerably on paid help or landlord assistance.

At the trial an agent's letter, which was distributed during the
election by his son, was read to the court. After a reminder to his
tenants of what beneficent landlords the Downshire and Londonderry families were, the agent went on:

> Believing as I do, most conscientiously, that you will best serve the
> interests of the tenant farmers of Ireland, and gain for them the same
> blessings as you yourselves enjoy, by voting for Lord Arthur Hill and
> Lord Castlereagh, I earnestly beg of you to do so. . . . Mr Stewart, your
> landlord, will esteem your compliance with the request herein made,
> as a personal favour to himself.[59]

In this case, which seems to have been a typical example of landlord
influence at work, it was denied that intimidation was involved, and

no concrete examples were presented to disprove this denial. Indeed, in their final judgment the judges remarked that throughout the case there was not even a suggestion that the landlords treated their tenants unfairly in respect of electioneering affairs.

But while landlord influence in Down and elsewhere must be seen in this period as a matter of leadership and advice, there remained a very slight coercive element. Through the use of tally cards and also because votes were counted and declared in polling districts before an aggregate total was announced, it was possible for interested parties to have a rough idea of how people had voted. The fact that the landlord or some other party might learn how an elector polled and so withdraw his goodwill may have affected how people cast their votes. Although in the elections in general there is no evidence that this coercive element played an important part, it may well have operated to a slightly greater degree in Cos Down and Antrim than elsewhere, because of the particular activities of Finnigan.

The lack of complete secrecy in the voting system, due particularly to the tally card practice, was clear to many but not regarded as a serious weakness. In late February 1880, however, Finnigan had claimed that there were other ways in which a person's vote could be known and in a letter to the *Northern Whig* he said that it was easy to ascertain how an individual voted. He then arranged a meeting where, according to the *Belfast Newsletter*, he demonstrated how this could be done, although the paper did not state his means of doing it. His reported success was well publicised in conservative newspapers and thousands of copies of the article about his demonstration were widely circulated in Co. Down. Finnigan's opponents claimed that his purpose in doing this was to frighten the electors into believing that their landlords would know how they voted.

At the trial Finnigan stated that his claim about the ballot not being secret was based primarily on the fact that the ballot papers were numbered and so a person at the counting could discover how someone had voted if he knew his number. Finnigan argued that he had circulated information about this fault in the system in a spirit of reform.[60] But as this fault was hardly a serious one, and considering the publicity he deliberately aroused on the matter, it is clear that his action was a ploy to frighten gullible electors who might be concerned about their landlord knowing how they voted.

This latter view of affairs was taken by one of the judges, who reckoned in his judgment that Finnigan's actions amounted to a serious disturbance with the free exercise of the ballot which must have affected a number of people in their voting.[61] The third judge, however, took the view that the purpose of the ballot act had been to prevent intimidation of voters and as there was no concrete evidence of an elector having been threatened as a result of Finnigan's action there was no case against him.[62] Since the judges differed, the case against Finnigan was dismissed. Although Finnigan was, therefore, innocent of the technical charge of undue influence, it seems fair to accept the view of the first judge that his activity must have influenced some voters who feared the loss of their landlord's favour. The whole business served to emphasise the slight element of coercive influence that remained.

The result of the Co. Down election was Hill 5,873, Castlereagh 5,599, and Sharman Crawford 5,579 votes, while in Co. Antrim the result was Chaine 5,124, Macnaghten 5,936, Wilson 4,789, and Black 4,610 votes. The outcome of these elections, where four conservatives were elected contrary to trends elsewhere, needs further comment. First, Finnigan's tactic over the ballot in Down was important because, while it may not have affected many, it must almost certainly have affected twenty voters and this was the size of Castlereagh's majority over Sharman Crawford.[63] Secondly, it was pointed out that the Antrim electorate contained a high number of Belfast electors and most seem to have backed the conservatives; so the conservatives were not as successful among the Antrim farmers as the results might suggest.[64] The liberals were strong among the farmers in North, East, and Mid Antrim, where presbyterians were numerous, but weak in South Antrim, where there were many members of the Church of Ireland.[65]

Thirdly, the conservatives in both counties appear to have had an efficient organisation.[66] As has been noted, some attempt was made to broaden the selection procedure in both counties. In addition the conservatives spent considerably more on the election than the liberals: in Antrim the two conservatives had electoral expenses of £9,006 15s. 7d. The conservative expenses in the two counties were higher than in any other contest in Ireland.[67] Finally, landlord–tenant relations between the Downshire and Londonderry families and their tenants seem to have been especially good, as several witnesses at the 1881 commission into the land question bore testimony.[68] In Antrim, just before the election, Chaine presented a large quantity of potatoes to his tenants to alleviate their distress.[69]

Some interesting observations can be made about denominational support for the various parties in the counties. Numerous contemporary reports indicated that the liberals secured the support of most catholics and many presbyterians.[70] The conservatives must therefore have done especially well among Church of Ireland voters but far less well among presbyterians. Election results depended largely on the relative distribution of the denominations in the different constituencies. Since their share of seats in the counties had grown since 1874, it is clear that the liberals must have increased their presbyterian vote, besides holding their catholic backing. To show the exact extent of presbyterian support for the liberals, it is best to examine more closely some particular results. In these cases we can assume that there was no difference in turn-out between denominations, and cross-party voting, which was insignificant, can be ignored.

In Co. Derry, the liberals won about 60 per cent of the votes cast. Since catholics were 24 per cent of the electors this meant that the remaining 36 per cent, that the liberals won, represented over 70 per cent of the presbyterian vote, which was 46 per cent of the total. In Co. Antrim catholics numbered just under 20 per cent of the voters and so the remaining 25 per cent of electors who voted for the liberals accounted for just over half the presbyterians who polled. A similar picture of around half the presbyterians voting liberal emerges also in Co. Down and Co. Armagh. In Co. Monaghan, however, the percentage of presbyterians who voted liberal was lower at around 30 per cent and the figure was probably no higher in Co. Donegal. Taking the cross voting in Tyrone into account, around one quarter of the presbyterians plumped for the liberal, while another quarter gave one vote to the liberal and the other to the independent conservative.

The boroughs

In the boroughs in 1880, the conservatives also came under a sustained attack from the liberals. The Ulster liberal society continued to send its agent, Mathew Wylie, to many of the borough revision sessions, and other agents represented the liberal cause elsewhere.[71] In contrast to the counties, however, this liberal assault was largely unsuccessful. In part this failure was due to the conservative success in developing their organisation at local level from a narrow proprietorial base. The liberal challenge in the revision courts was met by conservative agents in most boroughs, while a number of new, or revived, constitutional associations broadened the conservative base among their followers and so brought wider involvement, which helped avoid division. Also important in the outcome of these elections was the fact that, unlike in the counties, where the land question was so important, the liberals did not have a major issue around which to unite their followers.

Lisburn and Armagh were the only uncontested constituencies in Ulster. The two former conservative M.P.s for these boroughs stood for reelection with no sign of opposition. In Armagh the divisions within the conservative ranks had been healed by the general election and Capt. C. de la P. Beresford had the endorsement of all conservative interests.[72] In Lisburn Sir Richard Wallace continued to grow in popularity with the electors. Starting in 1874 Wallace's agent granted, contrary to previous practice on the estate, generous building leases in the town, and work commenced on a splendid new residence in Lisburn for Sir Richard and his family.[73] After the nomination in Armagh and Lisburn the candidates expressed their support for policies of the conservative government. The existence of long established, if not very active, constitutional associations in both towns may have helped bring some feeling of local involvement.

Conservative efforts at reorganisation were very successful at the electoral contest in Coleraine. The two candidates were the liberal, Daniel Taylor, the former member, and the conservative, Sir H. H. Bruce, bt, defeated candidate in 1874. Some time before the election Bruce was presented with a petition, signed (it was claimed) by a majority of the electors, which asked him to contest the seat.[74] By the time of the poll Bruce had strengthened his position thanks to the efforts of the new local conservative society at the registration courts and to the donation of money to various presbyterian charities and other Coleraine concerns.[75] The Orange rift, which had harmed his cause in 1874, seems to have been healed, as seen by the speeches made in his favour at a Coleraine Orange banquet on 3 February 1880.[76] Both candidates issued typical party addresses although Taylor took the unusual step of backing the conservative government's educational policy. The result was Bruce 222 votes and Taylor 193, which represented a considerable reversal in comparison with 1874. Comment in the papers after the election paid tribute to the effective conservative organisation and Orange–conservative unity. It was also suggested that some catholics may have voted conservative out of sympathy for Beaconsfield and because they felt neglected by liberals.[77]

In Newry the two candidates were selected early on in the election

campaign at meetings of their respective supporters. On 11 March
P. G. H. Carvill, a local catholic barrister, was chosen as liberal
candidate at a meeting of liberals.[78] Lord Newry, perhaps in
acknowledgement of anti-proprietorial feeling, declined to come
forward this time and decided instead to contest the seat vacated by
his wife's father in Shrewsbury. Two days after the liberal selection,
Henry Thompson, a local wine merchant and member of the
Church of Ireland, was picked as candidate at a well attended conservative gathering.[79] The result was a liberal defeat. Thompson
received 587 votes and Carvill 557.

Various reasons were given subsequently for the liberal loss. It
was claimed that there had been a drop in presbyterian liberal
support for Carvill because he was a catholic, but this was denied
and it was argued that the liberal defeat was caused by a withdrawal
of catholic publican backing over the liberal connections with
temperance.[80] Possibly there was a loss of some catholic publican
votes and we may note a letter in the papers from Carvill, which
denied that he had lost presbyterian support because he was a
catholic.[81] But it can be observed also that he stated he had agreed
to stand only after he was assured of the vote of 45 protestants, and
these had in fact voted for him. In 1868, however, 45 protestants
had polled for the liberal and ensured his victory, but the electorate
had increased by 50 per cent since 1868 and if only around 45 protestants had backed Carvill this represented a proportional drop in
protestant liberal votes.

The conservatives were also successful in Carrickfergus. They
won the seat back from an independent conservative candidate who
had represented the borough since 1868, thanks largely to the
peculiar local circumstances of controversy over commons' land.
Since 1874, however, Dalway had fallen out of favour with many of
the freemen over his handling of the problem.[82] In 1880 he was
challenged for the borough by Thomas Greer, who was from Cork
but resided in the constituency; Greer married into the Carrickfergus Owden family, partners in the wealthy linen business of
Richardson, Sons, and Owden. It was later revealed that a conservative committee had been set up as early as 1878 to assist Greer's
candidature.[83] While both candidates were regarded as conservative
by the press, Greer was seen as the more orthodox, mainstream
candidate.

In his address Dalway said that he would continue to pursue his
independent line in parliament but he denounced home rule,
supported land reform, and promised, above all, to remain deeply

concerned about local affairs.[84] His opponent emphasised his backing for the government and expressed a hope that the borough would return to its former proper conservatism.[85] The result was Greer 591 votes and Dalway 554. These figures represent a considerable reversal in Dalway's position since the previous election. They undoubtedly reflect his loss of favour among the freemen and may also show the conservative success in putting forward a candidate not identified with landed proprietorial interests. An election petition subsequently revealed that paupers had been brought from the Larne workhouse to vote but the result was not overturned.[86]

In Dungannon, however, the conservatives did not regain their seat. In this case they do not seem to have developed any new approach to deal with their liberal opponents. The conservative candidate was once again Col. the hon. W. S. Knox, defeated candidate in 1874 and uncle of the earl of Ranfurly, chief proprietor of the town. In his address Knox emphasised his personal connections with the borough and the interest that the Ranfurly family had always taken in the constituency. He declared himself a conservative.[87] His opponent was the former M.P. for Dungannon, T. A. Dickson. In his address Dickson attacked the domination of the town by the Ranfurly family and emphasised that he was a thorough liberal supporter.[88]

The outcome was a liberal victory. Dickson won 132 votes and Knox 128. This result, however, did reflect a slight drop in support for the liberal candidate, compared with 1874. Opposition to the liberal stand on temperance was given as a reason for this drop in Dickson's vote.[89] A press report later suggested that Dickson's supporters had comprised 95 catholics, 25 presbyterians, 4 methodists, and 4 members of the Church of Ireland.[90] Subsequently the election was disallowed because of the disclosure at an election petition trial that an elector had been bribed by a Dickson aide to spend the day at Whiteabbey (with refreshments provided) to prevent him from voting for the conservative.[91] While proprietorial interests were unsuccessful in Dungannon, they were able to hold their own in Downpatrick and Enniskillen. Liberal forces had not succeeded in the past in upsetting the political arrangements in these two boroughs and the 1880 general election failed to witness the appearance of any new forces to undermine conservative proprietorial interests.

In Downpatrick the liberals had been looking for a candidate since 1879, but only a short time after the dissolution of parliament in early March 1880 was it announced that Alexander Fraser, a presbyterian banker from London, had consented to stand. In his address he advocated land reform and attacked the government's foreign policy.[92] On 17 March at a meeting of conservatives, the candidature of John Mulholland, the former conservative M.P., was approved. In his address Mulholland stated that he supported a conservative ministry that 'has upheld the honour of the empire, preserved the peace, and defended the constitution'. He reminded readers of the important measures that the government had passed for the advantage of the working classes.[93]

The result of the election was Mulholland 176 votes and Fraser 99. This marked liberal defeat appears to have been largely the result of defection from liberal ranks of both catholic and protestant support. One contemporary remarked: 'We had in Downpatrick as many as would have given a majority but our presbyterian and dissenting friends deserted us wholesale in the booths.'[94] There seems also to have been a loss of catholic votes for the liberals, possibly due to friction between local catholic and protestant liberals over education policy.[95] Finally the last-minute selection of an outside candidate undoubtedly harmed the liberal campaign.

In Enniskillen, following Viscount Crichton's declaration of retirement from the borough representation, Viscount Cole, son of the earl of Enniskillen, announced that he would stand and issued an address. A short time later it was reported that Capt. William Collum, another son of John Collum, 'after solicitation' had agreed to contest the seat as a liberal.[96] The election was probably just a further round in the fight between the Collums and the earl of Enniskillen, although Cole took a strong stand behind the government and its policies and advocated land reform, while Collum opposed these policies but strongly supported land reform.[97] The result was similar to 1874: Cole 198 and Collum 178 votes. In the two remaining boroughs, Belfast and Derry, proprietorial interests had long ceased to control conservative politics although in the former the conservative candidates faced rivalry from forces that regarded changes in the structure and concerns of conservatism as inadequate, as well as from the liberals.

In Derry city the news of the dissolution of parliament immediately brought forward two election addresses, the first from the former member, Charles Lewis, and the second from Adam Hogg, a presbyterian linen manufacturer, who had apparently been selected as liberal candidate at an earlier stage. Both candidates organised committees, conducted extensive canvassing, and held well attended meetings, assisted by their respective local associations. At one such meeting on 19 March, Hogg said that the land question was the main issue; other speakers went on to attack the conservative government for its domestic and foreign policies.[98] On 24 March Lewis challenged Hogg to state clearly his views on education and suggested that he was favourable towards home rule. Lewis's own programme was based primarily on support for the conservative government. Also he had the backing of the temperance movement, which in a public letter claimed that he was safer on the question than Hogg.[99]

The outcome of the election was a conservative victory. Lewis gained 964 votes against Hogg's 876. This result reflected a loss in liberal support, although a proper comparison with 1874 is not possible because of the increase in the electorate. After the election it was alleged in the *Northern Whig* that catholics in Derry had let the liberals down.[100] This was denied by catholic sources which stated that 727 out of a total 787 catholic electors backed Hogg which left 149 protestant liberal voters.[101] This figure of the 1880 protestant vote compared with 172 in 1870. Whether or not this 1880 figure is correct it is hard to say, but, remembering the growth of the electorate in these 10 years and given the general fall in protestant support for the liberals, it does seem clear that the protestant liberal vote had failed to grow.

In Belfast two important meetings in relation to the coming election took place on 10 December.[102] One was held by the general committee of the Belfast conservative association, at which the two former conservative M.P.s, J. P. Corry and William Ewart, were selected unanimously as the conservative candidates. The other was organised by the Belfast Orange and protestant workingmen's association, which had been formed after the defeat of Robert Seeds in 1878 and now declared its full backing for Seeds, who had said that he was prepared to stand again in response to an earlier request of the association. On 23 March, a meeting of Belfast liberals selected as their candidate John Shaw Brown, a presbyterian linen manufacturer.[103]

Corry and Ewart had a joint campaign with the assistance of the Belfast conservative association. At their meetings it was stated that they were large employers of men, and that the conservative association was a fully representative body. Both candidates spoke of their support for the government's foreign policy, which they believed had upheld the honour of the empire abroad.[104] Brown called for measures such as compensation for industrial injuries and land reform. He declared himself a liberal presbyterian 'anxious for justice to all classes of countrymen'. He backed free trade and opposed the government's foreign policy, although he said that he would protect the empire.[105] The Belfast liberal association had collapsed by 1880, but a liberal committee was formed to help Brown's campaign.

In his address and speeches also Seeds declared his backing for the conservatives and their policies, both domestic and foreign.[106] He mentioned acts that the government had introduced, such as the artisan's dwelling house act, and he promised to uphold the integrity of the empire. He said that he had come forward in response to the call of protestant working men, and would support the just claims of labour; he believed that the working classes did not have adequate representation in parliament. A committee was set up to assist Seeds in his campaign. The outcome of the poll was Ewart 8,132, Corry 7,683, Seeds 6,119, and Brown 5,122 votes.

The success of the two official conservatives over their opponents, however, was not as great as these figures suggest. Supporters of Ewart and Corry intervoted to a large degree whereas a higher number of their opponents' voters plumped for their candidates.[107] Had the supporters of Seeds and Brown intervoted to the same degree as Ewart's and Corry's, Seeds would have been first in the poll and Brown just a few hundred votes behind Corry. Several other comments can be made about the result. First, it shows the strength of conservatism, official and unofficial, in Belfast. Secondly, it demonstrates the continuing social divisions within the conservative ranks. Thirdly, it shows that the liberals had failed to make strong headway in Belfast, although the result was an improvement on their 1874 performance and was probably affected by the collapse of their organisation.

Summary of results
The results dramatically demonstrated how much the land question had upset the usual pattern of parliamentary representation in Ulster. For the province there were now 18 conservatives, 9 liberals and 2 home rulers, compared with 21 conservatives, 6 liberals and 2 home rulers in 1874.[108] Of the 18 county M.P.s, conservatives numbered 8, all of whom, except J. W. Ellison Macartney, were prominent landowners or related to the leading landowners in their constituencies. Ellison Macartney was also a landlord but his Co. Tyrone estate was a small one. The 10 borough conservative M.P.s consisted of 4 who were the principal proprietors in their boroughs,

3 merchants and manufacturers, a solicitor, and 2 minor landowners. Among the conservatives from substantial landowning backgrounds were two, James Chaine, Co. Antrim, and John Mulholland, Downpatrick, with important commercial connections. Of the total Ulster conservative representation, two M.P.s were presbyterians and the rest belonged to the Church of Ireland.

The 8 liberals elected for Ulster counties comprised 4 merchants and manufacturers, 2 queen's counsels, a solicitor and a presbyterian minister. The single liberal borough M.P. was a merchant. Of the Ulster liberals, 5 were presbyterians, 2 members of the Church of Ireland, 1 congregationalist, and 1 quaker. The 2 Ulster home rulers, both of whom were catholic, consisted of a merchant and a solicitor. All of the conservatives, except 2, were educated privately or at English public schools, as were 2 of the liberals. The remaining Ulster conservatives and liberals had been taught at local schools such as the Belfast Academy. The 2 home rulers also were educated in Ireland. The Ulster M.P.s included 9 who had attended university: 7 were conservatives, most of whom went to Oxford or Cambridge, and 2 were liberals who graduated at Trinity College, Dublin.

Thus by 1880 significant changes had occurred in the social, religious and educational character of the Ulster parliamentary representation. In 1868 25 Ulster M.P.s were from a landed background but by 1874 the number stood at 19, and by 1880 it had dropped to 15. In 1868 there were just 2 M.P.s who were not members of the Church of Ireland, by 1874 there were 8, and by 1880 there were 11, of whom 7 were presbyterian. Whereas all but 4 of the Ulster M.P.s in 1868 had been educated privately or at English public school, the number who received this type of education had fallen to 21 in 1874 and to 18 in 1880. M.P.s with a university background decreased from a half of the Ulster M.P.s in 1868 to under half in 1874 and just over a third in 1880.

Party organisation during the general election had been somewhat different from the previous general election. This was especially so on the conservative side. Although family influence and the assistance of landlords and their agents still played a very important part in the conservative organisation, a number of associations had come into being that played a new political role in the conservative organisation and electoral machinery. These associations had also provided valuable help before the general election at revision sessions. The liberals continued to have the assistance of the Ulster liberal society, but during the general election their organisation

depended on tenant associations and other groups such as the presbyterian and catholic clergy, as well as, in some areas, solicitors,
merchants and manufacturers. The only effective home rule
organisation during the election appeared in Co. Cavan, where the
catholic clergy played a significant role.

In the three other provinces 7 conservatives, 6 liberals, and 61
home rulers (including 25 Parnellites) were returned.[109] This compared with 12 conservatives, 4 liberals, and 58 home rulers in 1874.
The total Irish representation in 1880 consisted of 25 conservatives,
15 liberals, and 63 home rulers, while six years previously there had
been 33 conservatives, 10 liberals, and 60 home rulers. The social,
religious, and educational backgrounds of the southern liberals and
conservatives were relatively unaltered. A very significant change,
however, had taken place in the backgrounds of the home rule
M.P.s. Of the home rulers, only 8 now were landowners and 6 were
rentiers, while 40 were merchants or belonged to the professions, 2
were farmers, and 3 were of undefined occupation.[110] Of the home
rulers 51 were catholic: as 3 liberals were catholic, this meant that
for the first time a majority of the Irish M.P.s were catholic. Thus
among the M.P.s in the three southern provinces the number from
non-landed, professional, merchant and catholic background had
increased markedly.

Neither the liberals nor the conservatives outside Ulster seem to
have had much political organisation, apart from the efforts of
individuals. The home rule party had the assistance of tenant
farmers' associations, independent clubs, and home rule league
branches. Most significant of all, it had the help of the land league,
which was an important influence against landlord representatives
in the home rule party.[111] The catholic clergy also gave useful aid to
the home rule candidates.[112]

So the result of the general election was that the home rule party
consolidated its general electoral position in the three southern provinces; at the same time the home rule party witnessed a significant
drop in the number of landowning M.P.s within its ranks due to a
growing opposition to the social and political position of the landlords. But the only home rule success in Ulster was in Co. Cavan,
where the home rule candidates won the two seats on an almost
entirely catholic vote. In the rest of the province, in response to the
deteriorating agrarian situation, members of both the liberal and
conservative parties advocated land reform. With non-landlord
candidates, assisted by tenant associations and other interested
bodies, the liberals were able to win eight of the county seats in

Ulster, with a vote consisting of most of the catholic electors and many, sometimes over half, of the presbyterian voters.

The outcome of these elections showed that the sense of political identity between the Ulster landlord M.P.s and the tenant farmer electors was disappearing under the rising social and political discontent. Only the land reform views of the conservative candidates and the assistance of the new political organisations prevented an even greater liberal victory. The fact that most of these liberal protestant electors were presbyterian indicates a certain underlying religious tension between them and the landlords. The high proportion of presbyterian merchants and professional men among the liberal M.P.s indicates social conflict between these groups and the landed gentry. The earl of Charlemont in Co. Armagh, for example, looked on the liberal candidate for the county, J. N. Richardson, as an intruder and wrote to an acquaintance that it was 'a piece of demonstrative impertinence his coming forward at all'.[113] Although a patron of the original 1865 committee of the Ulster liberal society, Charlemont regarded the liberal movement that eventually emerged as a threat. For Charlemont there was the personal problem that in the 1860s he had decorated his house with busts of Gladstone, Bright, and other liberal heroes.[114] After disestablishment he performed the annual ritual of tarring these offending heads and no doubt the developments of the 1870s and 1880s made his annoyance all the greater.

The broad support by catholics for the liberals as shown in the county results reflects the existing social, political, and religious discontent among Ulster catholics against the former conservative parliamentary representatives. During 1880 some catholics may have backed the liberals only because there was no home rule alternative, but it is evident that others gave them their whole hearted support.[115] John Harbison, a prominent catholic liberal from Cookstown, remarked in a letter to Lord O'Hagan that the catholic liberals in Cos Londonderry and Tyrone 'wrought with extreme warmth and zeal' on behalf of the liberal candidates.[116] The liberal catholic newspaper, the *Belfast Morning News*, on 13 April described Parnell as an 'irresponsible agitator'. In the common interest of land reform, differences between presbyterian and catholic electors in other matters were put in the background.

In the boroughs, however, the conservatives, with their policies of support for the empire and the conservative party's domestic and foreign policies, were able to hold their own against the liberals. In Belfast social division within the conservative ranks continued to be a serious problem. The conservatives seem to have had mostly protestant and the liberals largely catholic backing, although in Belfast there was a significant joint presbyterian–catholic vote for the liberal candidate. Probably this political division of the electorate on sectarian lines merely reflected other social and religious divisions in the population of the boroughs. Seriously weakened in the counties, the conservatives nonetheless remained an important force in Ulster politics, especially among protestant voters in the boroughs.

The end of the general election brought no abatement in agrarian protest. From the autumn of 1880 the land league spread to many parts of Ulster and new tenant right associations were established. In this growing movement for land reform there was considerable cooperation between protestant and catholic farmers. Eventually, in response to the situation in Ireland, the government introduced a land bill, which became law in August 1881. In that same month, a by-election in Tyrone resulted in a resounding defeat for the conservative landlord candidate, one observer noting that 'the protestants as well as the Roman Catholics do not want an Orangeman or even a fenian if he is a gentleman or a landlord'.[1] From this time on, however, divisions appeared in the farmers' movement and much of the protestant–catholic cooperation ended.

While the land question continued to be the main issue in Ulster after the general election, the subject of party reorganisation was also a matter of considerable political interest. In the liberal press, criticism was voiced that at both central and local level liberal organisation was inadequate.[2] At a gathering of liberals in Belfast on 7 May 1880 a committee was set up to look into ways to improve their organisation in the province. At subsequent private meetings the committee members discussed the idea of forming a centre for liberals in Belfast and the secretary of the Manchester liberal association, B. L. Green, was invited to speak to them about the subject on 28 May.[3]

Green urged the formation of a club similar to the Manchester reform club, from which he claimed all the Manchester liberal organisations had sprung. Such a centre in Belfast, he suggested, 'would bring together the men of position and influence in the province'. After a discussion that included a debate on how broad the membership of this new body should be, a report was drawn up that recommended the creation of a Belfast centre on the lines of the Manchester club, to be called the Ulster reform club. A week later, a special committee was formed, consisting of eleven prominent liberals, which consulted liberal M.P.s and supporters in the province. It then drew up a plan to form a limited liability company to construct a building for the club which would have a planned membership of around 300, based on a ten-guinea entrance fee and an annual subscription of five guineas for Belfast members and three guineas for country members. An alternative scheme to have a larger membership and a cheaper subscription was rejected, in spite of pleas from the *Northern Whig* that the new club should not be exclusive. On 22 October members of the committee approached Lord Waveney, president of the Ulster liberal society, who agreed with the scheme. On their behalf he sent out a circular in early 1881 about the centre, which he said would 'greatly tend to strengthen and consolidate the party in Ulster'; prominent liberals were asked to join a provisional committee in order to get the club established.[4]

From a list of those who accepted Waveney's invitation an executive committee was formed and steps were taken to raise money and commence the construction of a grand club house in Royal Avenue. By early 1884 building work had progressed well and a membership list for the centre was opened. It was decided that there should be a management committee and also a general committee that would direct the club in political affairs. On 12 June 1884, when members numbered 287, a general meeting was held. Lord Waveney was elected president and J. S. Brown vice-president. The general committee included many of the most prominent businessmen in the province, such as W. J. Pirrie, Edward Hughes, and Adam Duffin, as well as professional men such as Alexander Caruth and C. H. Brett. There was only an occasional tenant farmer such as Samuel Black of Antrim. Plans for a formal opening were postponed until 1885 because of problems in getting a leading liberal from England to perform the ceremony. On New Year's Day 1885, however, the club opened for business.[5]

As regards other liberal organisation in this period, the calls made for strong local constituency organisations seem to have had a limited response. A committee, set up on 4 June 1880 to reorganise the liberal party in Belfast, held a number of private conferences and on 22 December 1880 convened a public meeting of Belfast liberals to deliver a report.[6] This occasion ended in disorder due to the interference of John Rea, but subsequent meetings seem to have taken place, and at the revision sessions of 1881 Mathew Wylie was reported as acting on behalf of the newly formed Belfast liberal association.[7]

In Co. Armagh on 28 September 1880 a meeting of J. N. Richardson's supporters was held at which many catholic priests and presbyterian ministers were present.[8] The Co. Armagh liberal registration association was formed. Shortly after this a public letter from persons who called themselves members of the liberal party in Co.

Armagh, and included J. N. Richardson, Dr Daniel McGettigan, the catholic archbishop, and Rev. Jackson Smith, an Armagh city presbyterian minister, was addressed to W. E. Forster, the chief secretary, inviting him to a banquet in the county in his honour.[9] Apart from this Armagh association there is little evidence of other local organisations being formed in this post general election period. By 1885, however, the Portadown liberal club, the Co. Tyrone liberal association, and the Roughfort liberal association had been established.

Among the conservatives, also, the opinion had been loudly voiced after the general election that new political organisations were required. In December the Ulster constitutional union was launched at a meeting in Belfast of conservatives from throughout Ulster.[10] Its president was the duke of Abercorn and its vice-presidents included all the conservative M.P.s and many of the peers in the province, along with county grand masters of the Orange order. The honorary secretary was Lord A. W. Hill and the acting secretary E. S. Finnigan. Its function was to act as a central body for the conservatives in Ulster and it was to be composed of delegates from each constitutional society or conservative organisation. Henry Kelly of Dungannon was advised that his local association should send two delegates to the union's committee, preferably one from the gentry and the other from the town: 'One of the two delegates ought to be a merchant, tradesman of Dungannon; even an artisan if an artisan has most brains.'[11] The union now assisted local associations with advice about registration and organisation.[12]

At the local level, also, steps were taken to set up new conservative organisations. On 5 April 1880 the Dungannon constitutional club was formed as a result of the conservative defeat.[13] In Co. Armagh the county constitutional association was reconstituted and reorganised at a meeting on 7 January 1881, which excluded T. G. Peel.[14] In Enniskillen also steps seem to have been taken after the general election to set up a conservative association and by early 1884 the association had its own club room.[15] Following the 1881 Co. Tyrone by-election a meeting was held under the chairmanship of J. W. Ellison Macartney, at which it was decided to form a new society to be called the Co. Tyrone protestant constitutional association, with the prime purpose of looking after registration.[16] By 1882 a Carrickfergus constitutional association was in existence.

In late 1881 the Ulster conservatives decided that a new central organisation was required, different from the union. At a meeting of conservatives, under the auspices of the union, on 17 October 1881 an address was delivered on party organisation by J. E. Gorst, secretary of the national union of conservative associations of Great Britain. According to the minutes of the union,

> Mr Gorst addressed the meeting, and explained the system of organisation existing in England; impressed upon those present the necessity for holding public meetings to educate the people, also the need of a central club for Ulster, and promised that if a constitutional club as an Ulster political centre was established that either Lord Salisbury or Sir Stafford Northcote, or both, would come to lay the foundation stone or open the club.[17]

It was decided to set up a constitutional club in Belfast and a committee was established to raise £6,000 in £1 shares in order to form a limited liability company which could purchase a building for the club, which would serve as a political and social centre for Ulster conservatives.[18]

At a meeting of the constitutional union on 8 September 1882 the decision was taken to purchase the Music Hall, May Street, for a club building. According to a newspaper account of the meeting, it was determined that the management of the club was to be vested in a committee of conservative representatives from each county and borough in Ulster, and in order 'to secure the Orange association a representative voice on the new organisation' it was arranged that the county grand masters and the Belfast grand master would be on the committee of management.[19] Efforts were made to find a prominent English conservative to open the club. Eventually Sir Stafford Northcote, bt, M.P., accepted and on 3 October 1883 the formal opening took place.[20]

The list of delegates present at the opening casts an interesting light on conservative organisation at this time.[21] There were delegates from thirteen constitutional associations, namely Belfast, Armagh city, Co. Armagh, Co. Monaghan, Co. Tyrone, Co. Antrim, Co. Down and Lisburn, Enniskillen, Dungannon, Newry, Carrickfergus, and Randalstown. There were representatives of the conservatives in Downpatrick, Lurgan, and Cos Donegal and Londonderry. The county grand lodges of Antrim, Armagh, and Down as well as the Belfast grand lodge were represented. Ten years previously there had only been constitutional organisations in Lisburn, Armagh, Belfast, and Derry.

After the general election nationalist organisation in the province seems to have largely collapsed, with the principal members disagreeing among themselves. On 10 July a letter appeared in the

Ulster Examiner from J. C. Quinn, honorary secretary of the Ulster home government association, in which he resigned his post because he said that he had lost hope of success by parliamentary methods. In October 1880 J. G. Biggar and Rev. Isaac Nelson, now M.P. for Co. Mayo, clashed in public over Nelson's absence from the Irish constabulary vote and also because of a speech by Nelson that criticised certain catholic clergy.[22] The association remained in existence for some time after this, but had little effect on the political scene. There is no evidence of local nationalist reorganisation having taken place in this post-election period. It may be noted, however, that catholic registration associations became active in both Derry and Newry during the early 1880s.[23]

Elsewhere C. S. Parnell continued to strengthen his position and in May 1880 became leader of the home rule party. In October 1882, however, the Irish National League was established in Dublin. Its first aim was national self-government, which Parnell defined at the inaugural meeting as 'the restitution to the Irish people of the right to manage their own affairs in a parliament elected by the people'; other aims were reform of the land laws, local self-government, extension of the parliamentary and municipal franchises, and the development and encouragement of the labour and industrial interests of Ireland.[24] The organisation of the league consisted of a central committee and local branches.

A number of delegates from Ulster were present at the inaugural meeting of the national league. Two months later it was reported in the *Irish Times* that there were 38 league branches in the province; this total was made up of 13 in Cavan, 8 in Tyrone, 5 in Down, 5 in Donegal, 4 in Fermanagh and one in each of the remaining counties.[25] From this time, however, there seems to have been little further expansion of the movement until the Monaghan by-election of July 1883 which resulted in the return of a nationalist, T. M. Healy. Following this by-election a campaign was mounted in the north, led by prominent members of the national league and the nationalist party, which established branches of the league in many parts of the province, particularly in catholic areas.[26]

Co. Londonderry and Dungannon, 1880

The first 2 by-elections in Ulster after the general election were fought on the same issues as the 1880 general election. The Co. Londonderry by-election, in the middle of May, was caused by the appointment of Hugh Law as attorney-general for Ireland. He stood for reelection and was returned without any sign of opposition. The Dungannon by-election arose from the unseating of T. A. Dickson on a petition after the general election. The judgement of the petition trial was announced on 10 May and on the next day, at a meeting of liberal electors in the town, James Dickson, son of T. A. Dickson, accepted a request to contest the seat. Col. the hon. W. S. Knox, defeated conservative candidate at the general election, indicated that he also would stand and shortly before polling day published an address in which he repeated his views of three months previous.[27] Dickson did not issue an address, as it was apparently well known that his views were the same as his father's.

Both candidates conducted a vigorous campaign. Although by this time the constitutional club had been formed in the borough, there is little evidence that it took an active part in the contest. The outcome (Dickson 132 and Knox 128 votes) was similar to the general election result. The denominational breakdown of the voting seems to have been no different from that in the general election, with around 45 protestants and 87 catholics in support of the liberal and about 128 protestants behind the conservative.[28]

Meanwhile in parliament attention had continued to focus on the land question. When the house of commons met after the general election, bills to legislate on the matter were introduced straightaway by Ulster conservatives, C. E. Lewis and J. W. Ellison Macartney, but their bill was rejected, as were subsequent measures from other M.P.s.[29] The government brought in emergency laws to deal with agrarian disturbances. Eventually on 7 April 1881 Gladstone introduced a land bill that granted the three Fs. The Ulster liberal M.P.s welcomed the new legislation and all voted for its second reading. More surprising, most of the Ulster conservatives also supported the bill and thirteen out of eighteen M.P.s backed its second reading; James Corry, Sir H. H. Bruce, Lord Castlereagh, and Viscount Crichton abstained while only Cole voted against it. The home ruler C. J. Fay voted for the bill but J. G. Biggar, in company with C. S. Parnell and some other home rulers, abstained because he regarded the measure as an unsatisfactory settlement of the land question.[30]

The Ulster M.P.s in fact, as Dr Frank Thompson has pointed out, played a major role in the introduction and passing of Gladstone's land bill.[31] Even before the general election Ulster liberals had pressed upon Gladstone the importance of granting the three Fs. Advisers warned that only such a measure would satisfy feeling in the north and prevent the disorder that had occurred elsewhere in Ireland.[32] The Ulster conservatives, conscious of the feeling among their followers, played a significant part in assisting the bill through parliament, in spite of opposition from the conservative party in general. On 29 August 1881 Sir Stafford Northcote acknowledged their role on this issue in a letter to Edward Gibson:

> If the Irish landlords, and especially the Ulster members, had taken a decided line against the bill, we could have stopped it or cut it down to nothing by action in the two houses. But this was impossible in the face of their determination to pass the measure, and I do not know that the conclusion is to be regretted.[33]

Co. Tyrone and Co. Londonderry, 1881

The immediate political consequence of the land act, however, was a by-election in Co. Tyrone because E. F. Litton, M.P. for the county, was appointed a commissioner of the new land court. Rumours of the likelihood of such an appointment had circulated the county since early August. In view of this a meeting of delegates from local land league branches in Co. Tyrone was held on 4 August.[34] Speakers condemned the land bill as insufficient, denounced Irish landlordism as an English garrison and urged its abolition, and stated that Ireland belonged to the Irish. The Ulster liberals were attacked for their connection with the government and its policies. A call was also made for a land league candidate at the by-election, but, in spite of this and the attitude towards the liberals expressed at the meeting, on the next day a deputation met T. A. Dickson, commonly rumoured to be a liberal candidate at the by-election, and gave him their support. On 13 August a gathering of tenant farmers in Omagh declared their backing for Dickson.[35] By this time it was known that Col. the hon. W. S. Knox would stand as a conservative; he later claimed that he had been asked to come forward by the Orangemen and tenant farmers of the county.[36]

On 20 August a notice finally appeared in the *Northern Whig* from Litton, announcing his retirement from the representation of Co. Tyrone, and the election began in earnest. In his address Knox declared the hope that the new land laws would strengthen the good relations between landlord and tenant, and expressed satisfaction about the clauses affecting leaseholders.[37] Dickson announced that he stood as an independent liberal and declared his opposition to the coercion laws of the government. He stated his views that the land act, although not perfect, was a 'noble instalment of justice to

the farmers of Ireland' and a monument to the genius of Gladstone.[38] By 24 August Dickson and Knox had been joined by a third
candidate, Rev. Harold Rylett, an Englishman who was unitarian
minister at Moneymore, Co. Down, and one of the main organisers
of the land league in Ulster. This followed an unexpected address
from C. S. Parnell, which appeared in the Dublin evening papers
on 23 August, advising his land league friends to withhold their
support until a land league candidate could be found to oppose
Dickson.

In his address Rylett stated that the election gave the electors a
chance to protest against the coercion policies of the government.[39]
He declared that he stood on land league principles and would
devote all his energy to make every Irish farmer owner of the land
that he tilled. Rylett's candidature was a surprise, not least to land
league supporters and probably to Rylett himself. Earlier, on 19
August, Rylett had actually sent a letter to the secretaries of several
land league branches in Co. Tyrone that claimed that the deputation
appointed at the late convention in the county had met Dickson,
who assured them that he was strongly as ever against landlord
tyranny, and so they were not prepared to oppose him.[40] Rylett's
candidature at this later stage was in fact the result of a sudden move
by Parnell who wished to embarrass the government, if not by a
nationalist victory, at least by spoiling the liberal vote and letting a
conservative win.[41]

The three candidates conducted vigorous campaigns. Knox
repeatedly declared his endorsement of the land reforms. He also
stated that he did not want catholics or 'fainthearted' protestants to
vote for him, and called on the loyal men of Tyrone to stick to their
principles. This specifically protestant appeal was repeated in a
leaflet in support of Knox entitled 'Reasons why no protestant can
vote for Dickson'.[42] It warned that Parnell's object of 'land for the
people' meant in the end taking land from protestants. In his
speeches Dickson queried Knox's sincerity on the land question and
said that he wished to appeal not to one particular section but to all
the tenant farmers whatever their creed or religion.[43] Parnell spoke
at Rylett's meetings, accused the Ulster liberals of connivance with
the coercion policies of the liberal government, criticised the land
act, and condemned sectarian bigotry. Unlike previous occasions
when he had spoken in the north, Parnell combined demands for
land reform with advocacy of self government: 'We never can
hope', he said at a meeting on 31 August, 'for really just laws until
we obtain a representative assembly, making its laws on Irish soil.'[44]

Rylett's late appearance in the campaign, however, had a harmful effect on the home rule vote because several land league branches, on the strength of his letter of 19 August, had pledged themselves to back Dickson and felt obliged to honour their pledges.[45]

The result of the election was Dickson 3,168, Knox 3,084, and Rylett 907 votes. These figures clearly represented a declaration of support for Gladstone and the land act, although Rylett's position had been weakened because of the mix up over his candidature. Several sources estimated that around 1,800 catholics out of the 2,300 on the register polled and, accepting Parnell's claim that Rylett's voters were nearly all catholic, this means that at least 2,200 protestants backed the liberal.[46] Parnell also claimed that 500 Orangemen voted for Dickson. This growth of protestant and even Orange support for the liberals and against landlord representatives was ruefully acknowledged in a letter of James Crossle, Sir William Verner's agent in Tyrone:

> It is too bad that what was once called protestant Tyrone could not return a protestant member. That low fellow Dickson was returned by pro-
> testants and I believe numbers of Orangemen voted against their grand
> master. The fact is the protestants as well as the Roman catholics do not
> want an Orangeman or even a fenian if he is a gentleman or a landlord.
> I look upon the event of this election as a death blow to protestantism.[47]

The Tyrone by-election marked the height of protestant–catholic alliance in the countryside. By the end of 1881 serious divisions had developed in the ranks of the farmers' movement. The northern tenant right associations and the land league each went their own way and much of the previous catholic protestant cooperation ended. The connection of the tenant right bodies with the liberals and of the land league with the nationalists was an important factor in this development. Northern tenants' associations expressed their approval of Gladstone's act as did the Ulster liberal society and the Ulster liberal M.P.s. But the Parnellite leadership of the home rule party and the land league assumed a different stance. Partly because of anger over other government measures and partly to appease his more revolutionary wing, Parnell adopted a hostile attitude towards both the land act and the liberals.

At the land league convention in September 1881 the new law was strenuously criticised, and the league persisted in its struggle against the collection of rents and in its opposition to the liberal govern-ment. As a result Parnell and the land league leaders were arrested in October 1881 and the organisation was banned. Eventually, after his release from prison, Parnell and others formed the Irish national

1 This photograph shows a scene that was not untypical of landed society in the 1860s. The third earl of Roden (1788-1870) and his family are viewed here at their home at Tollymore, Bryansford, Co. Down, giving blankets to the womenfolk of their labourers, c. 1865. Probably this was a relief measure during a harsh winter. A report in the *Down Recorder*, 10 October 1868, mentioned how another Co. Down landlord, J. W. Maxwell of Finnebrogue, assembled all his farm labourers in one of the farm buildings:

> and, after supplying each of them with a hearty draught of good ale, distributed among them sixty pairs of large heavy blankets, together with winter trousers for the sons, and dresses for the wives and daughters of the men.

To modern observers such action may appear patronising, but at the time, it was all part of a deferential, ordered and sometimes benevolent society. Within twenty years of the taking of this photograph an agrarian revolution had toppled the gentry from their dominance of rural society; but the beneficiaries of this revolution were the farmers and not the labourers. In 1885, after they had been enfranchised for the first time, rural labourers (at least those in the unionist community where there was a choice) would have no hesitation in voting for landlord candidates rather than representatives of the tenant farmers. All this illustrates that rural society was not divided simply into landlords on the one side and 'the people' on the other, but actually had many divisions. Most labourers had more reasons to resent farmers than landlords, with whom they would have had little contact. Those who were employed by landlords often enjoyed better houses and wages than those employed by farmers.

2   This photograph, taken in 1893, shows four generations of the McKinneys, a presbyterian farming family, at their home at Sentry Hill, Carnmoney, Co. Antrim. The figure in the chair in the doorway is Thomas George McKinney (1807-1893), whose father John (1750-1826) was reputedly the emissary who carried the order to rise to the United Irishmen at Roughfort in 1798 and whose uncle was killed at the Battle of Antrim.

The next generation is represented by William Fee McKinney (1832-1917), lying on the grass. Both father and son attended dinners in honour of their landlord in the 1850s but by the 1870s had become enthusiastic supporters of the tenant right movement and prominent local liberals. In 1886 William Fee McKinney attended the conference of Ulster liberals which determined to oppose Gladstone's proposals for home rule: twenty-six years later he signed the Ulster covenant to fight home rule. William Fee McKinney's son John (1862-1934) is standing to the right of the picture while his granddaughter Elsie (1893-1978) is in her mother's arms in front of the house.

Elsie's brother Tom, born the year after this photograph was taken, fought and died at the Battle of the Somme in July 1916. He was a member, not of the 36th Ulster Division as might have been expected, but of the public schools regiment, which he was entitled to join because he attended the Royal Belfast Academical Institution. The McKinneys shared fully in the rising prosperity of the Irish countryside in the second half of the nineteenth century and had the extra benefits of proximity to the Belfast area and its growing food demands. Their land holdings increased and their home at Sentry Hill was rebuilt in the 1880s.

3 This arch was constructed in 1885 in front of the Belfast White Linen Hall at the junction of Donegall Square and Donegall Place for a royal visit of the prince and princess of Wales. It was reported that the arch contained examples of everything made in Belfast from bales of linen under the arch to models of steam engines and ships. The slogans on the arch included 'Employment is nature's physician', 'Trade is the golden girdle of the globe', 'Temperance is a girdle of gold' and 'Man goeth forth unto his work and to his labour until the evening'. These quotations, which capture well the spirit of Victorian Belfast, are clearly inspired by Samuel Smiles, author of the popular book *Self help* and other such work. His son W. H. Smiles was managing director of the Belfast Rope Work Company, one of the largest of its kind in the world.

During the later nineteenth and early twentieth centuries Belfast's population grew at a colossal rate, which contrasted sharply with trends not only in the south and west of Ireland but also with other parts of Ulster. In 1841 Belfast's population of 70,447 was less than a half that of Co. Fermanagh and less than a quarter that of Co. Donegal. By 1911 Belfast, with a population of 386,947, was only 6,000 short of the total population of Cos Donegal, Fermanagh, Cavan and Monaghan, added together.

4 St Patrick's catholic cathedral, Armagh, c. 1890. The foundation stone of the
cathedral was laid in 1840 but the dedication service did not take place until 1873.
Designed by J. J. McCarthy in a grand gothic style, the cathedral symbolised the
spiritual revival and growing prosperity of the catholic church and people in the
nineteenth century.

5   Interior of the presbyterian assembly hall, Fisherwick Place, c. 1905, designed by the architects firm of Young and MacKenzie as a suitable debating chamber for the prosperous and confident presbyterian community.

6   St Patrick's church, Ballymacarrett, 1905, designed by Samuel P. Close, for the Church of Ireland in the late nineteenth century to cater for its numerous working class parishioners in East Belfast.

7 Members of the Ulster liberal party at the house of commons, 1882. Back row from left to right: John Givan (Co. Monaghan), Andrew Marshall Porter (Co. Londonderry), James Dickson (Dungannon), Thomas Lea (Co. Donegal). Front row from left to right: William Findlater (Co. Monaghan), Sir Thomas McClure (Co. Londonderry), Thomas Alexander Dickson (Co. Tyrone), James Nicholson Richardson (Co. Armagh). The photograph does not include Rev John Kinnear (Co. Donegal) and Edward Falconer Litton (Co. Monaghan).

8 The Ulster Reform Club, Royal Avenue, Belfast, 1891.

9 Conservative gathering at Sea Park, Carrickfergus, 5 October 1883, on the occasion of the visit of Sir Stafford Northcote. Back: Edward Shirley Finnigan (conservative party organiser), Edward MacNaghten M.P. (Co. Antrim), Thomas Greer M.P. (Carrickfergus), James Porter Corry M.P. (Belfast), Sir John Preston, Lord Claud Hamilton M.P. (Liverpool), Ian Trant Hamilton M.P. (Co. Dublin), William Ewart, M.P. (Belfast), John William Ellison-Macartney M.P. (Co. Tyrone). Middle row: John Monroe, Q.C., Sir Henry Hervey Bruce M.P. (Coleraine), Lord Arthur William Hill M.P. (Co. Down), Sir Thomas Bateson M.P. (Devizes), Marquess of Waterford, Sir James McGarel-Hogg M.P. (Truro), Earl of Yarmouth. Front: Viscountess of Crichton, Earl of Belmore, Lady Hill, Sir Stafford Northcote M.P. (North Devon), Duke of Abercorn, Countess of Yarmouth, Viscount Crichton M.P. (Co. Fermanagh). Identification of individuals by A. B. Cooke.

10 Interior of the Ulster Constitutional Club, May Street, Belfast, 1891.

11 Key to a print of the Irish nationalist party, 1886. Only the Ulster M.P.s have been identified.

7. Bernard Kelly (South Donegal).
12. Timothy Michael Healy (North Monaghan and South Londonderry).
18. Sir Joseph Neale McKenna (South Monaghan).
19. Alexander Blaine (South Armagh).
24. Joseph Gillis Biggar (West Cavan).
40. Matthew Joseph Kenny (Mid Tyrone).
44. John Francis Small (South Down).
49. Arthur O'Connor (East Donegal).

51. Justin Huntley McCarthy (Newry).
55. James Edward O'Doherty (North Donegal).
59. Patrick O'Hea (West Donegal).
60. William James Reynolds (East Tyrone).
64. William Hoey Kearney Redmond (North Fermanagh).
66. Henry Campbell (South Fermanagh).
79. William O'Brien (South Tyrone).
80. Thomas O'Hanlon (East Cavan).

Two other figures of special note are (63) Charles Stewart Parnell, party leader, and (65) Timothy Charles Harrington, chief party organiser.

league in October 1882. The main object of this new body was national self-government; further agrarian reform was a secondary aim. These developments caused the collapse of cooperation between the northern tenant right associations on the one side and the land league and national league on the other. The political repercussion of this split would be evident at ensuing by-elections.

On November 1881, shortly after the appointment of the rt hon. Hugh Law, M.P. for Co. Londonderry, as lord chancellor of Ireland, a meeting of the Derry liberal union took place in Coleraine.[48] After discussing several possibilities the members chose as the new liberal candidate A. M. Porter, Q.C., who was recommended by Law chiefly on the grounds that he would be the next attorney general, and indeed, on 7 November it was announced that he had succeeded to this post. On 11 November a meeting of land league representatives from Co. Londonderry was held in Derry city, under the chairmanship of Rev. Harold Rylett.[49] C. J. Dempsey, editor of the *Ulster Examiner*, was selected as a candidate on land league and nationalist principles. The same day, the *Belfast Newsletter* announced that Sir Samuel Wilson, an Ulsterman who had made his fortune in Australia and now lived in Hughenden Manor, formerly the home of Disraeli, had been asked to stand as a conservative and had consented. Wilson was presbyterian, Porter unitarian, and Dempsey catholic.

In his address Porter stated that he was a strenuous supporter of Gladstone and regarded the land act as the greatest legislative boon ever conferred upon Ireland.[50] He hoped that the good feeling that would result from the act would allow the government to dispose of its exceptional powers. Dempsey said his principles were 'land for the people' and the 'legislative independence' of Ireland.[51] He claimed that the land act was due to the efforts of Michael Davitt and C. S. Parnell, who were now in prison, and he urged the electors to support him as a protest against their imprisonment and the coercion laws. Wilson stated that he was an independent conservative.[52] He believed amendments to the land act should be introduced to give greater facilities to farmers to purchase their land, and regretted that the act failed to deal properly with leaseholders.

During the election campaign the candidates reiterated the points in their addresses. The question of confidence in Gladstone was clearly the main issue. Porter was assisted at his meetings by T. A. Dickson, other M.P.s, and a considerable number of presbyterian ministers.[53] A circular to liberal canvassers from R. H. Todd, Porter's conducting agent, emphasised the voluntary nature of Porter's organisation and the importance of Gladstone's policies in the election:

> Use every legitimate effort in your power to secure Mr Porter's return. Remember that the volunteer workers of the various districts won by their individual exertions many a hard fought battle, and on them and them alone depends the issue of the present contest. Buckle to your work. Take charge of a number of townlands, and be sure you bring to the poll every man in your district who will vote for Mr Porter. Remember, lastly, that the issue in the present contest is between Gladstone, with his policy of peace, justice, and progress on the one hand, and Salisbury, with his policy of class legislation and obstruction on the other.[54]

Wilson was assisted in his campaign by various conservative notables and E. S. Finnigan from the Ulster constitutional union, who acted as his election agent. Sir John Ross was present during the campaign and later gave an amusing description of some of Finnigan's activities in Co. Londonderry:

> He was an expert in all the methods of winning an election and was a most genial and amusing man. I learned for the first time the secret machinery of electioneering. For instance, we often wonder how the voices at the public meetings strike in so readily at the proper moment; the truth is they are nearly all supplied by the election agent. The following example will show how it is done:
> Sir Samuel: 'Gentlemen, as one interested in your great historic county and, as one who heartily desires your prosperity, I have come down . . .'
> Mr Finnigan (to the reporter of the tory paper): 'Long may you live and run up and down'. (Prolonged applause.)
> Sir Samuel: 'The statesman who now holds the office of prime minister, Mr Gladstone . . .'
> Mr Finnigan: (a voice) 'To hell with him!' (Loud, prolonged, and enthusiastic cheering).[55]

Dempsey in his campaign had aid from some home rule M.P.s such as W. A. Redmond and Edmund Leamy.[56] The whole contest took an unexpected turn, however, when on 28 November the Ulster papers reported a letter that had appeared in the London *Times* from F. H. O'Donnell, home rule M.P. for Dungarvan, saying that he had been instructed to proceed to Co. Londonderry to ask Parnell's supporters in the county to vote against the liberals as the conservatives now had the same policies on land as the liberals.[57] O'Donnell then arrived in the county. It now became clear that O'Donnell's instructions had come from Parnell, who was in jail and had decided that as a home ruler could not be elected the next best thing would be to defeat the liberal.[58] O'Donnell gave Parnell's assurance to Dempsey of a seat at a later date, and shortly after nomination on 5 December Dempsey withdrew, urging his supporters to vote against 'the salaried official of the worst coercion government that ever misgoverned your unfortunate country'.[59]

The result of the election was Porter 2,701, Wilson 2,054, and Dempsey 58 votes. It is difficult to say exactly how the different denominations cast their votes. The *Derry Journal* of 7 December claimed that most catholics, who numbered altogether around 1,200, had voted conservative, but two days later said that some catholics had voted liberal. The *Londonderry Sentinel* of 8 December stated that some catholics had supported the liberal, but did not try to place a number on them. We may observe that the percentage turn-out at the by-election was considerably lower than at the Tyrone by-election and the general election in Co. Londonderry. Quite possibly a large number of catholics abstained and the others were split between liberal and conservative. The liberal vote had slightly fallen from 1880 but not so significantly as to suggest a massive catholic withdrawal. Probably, as at the general election in the county, a majority of the protestants who voted backed the liberal. It is likely there was still a considerable presbyterian–catholic vote.

Co. Monaghan, 1883

The next by-election in Ulster came a year and a half later when John Givan, M.P. for Co. Monaghan, vacated his seat to become crown solicitor for Cos Kildare and Meath. By this stage the continued unrest on the land issue and the government's special measures against the land league and the national league had led to deteriorating relations in Co. Monaghan between the liberal M.P.s for the county and their liberal supporters who were predominantly catholic.[60] On 3 March 1883, for example, severe criticism against Givan appeared in the *People's Advocate* for his recent denunciation of the land league and his declaration of support for the government, claiming that many of his principal backers in 1880 had been land league enthusiasts, and attacking the government. Among protestants in the county, fears about the situation had been aroused by the recent Crossmaglen treason-felony trial, as well as the fenian explosions in England.[61]

Shortly after the announcement in early June of Givan's appointment, a letter was printed in the press from Parnell that said that T. M. Healy, home rule M.P. for Co. Wexford, would contest the vacant seat.[62] The Co. Monaghan liberal association called a representative county meeting at Castleblaney for 19 June. A day earlier a deputation of liberal tenant farmers, mainly although not entirely protestant, in company with T. A. Dickson, persuaded Henry Pringle, a Church of Ireland merchant from Clones, Co. Monaghan, to agree to stand as a liberal.[63] At the meeting on 19 June, held in Castleblaney catholic church, where a large number of catholic priests and lay delegates from the different country parishes were present, the names of Healy and Pringle were put forward for selection. Healy, a catholic journalist and M.P. for Co. Wexford, was chosen by an overwhelming majority.[64] Pringle, however, continued his candidature. Also on 19 June a meeting of conservatives in Monaghan chaired by a tenant farmer, Robert Wilson, chose John Monroe, a Church of Ireland queen's counsel, as conservative candidate.[65]

In his address Healy drew special attention to that clause of the land act that bore his name, and stated his belief that a peasant proprietorship was the final solution for the land problem. Indeed, Healy seems to have been selected partly because of this clause, which it was felt would give him a broad appeal.[66] Parnell, John Dillon, and Timothy Harrington assisted Healy. All emphasised the land issue, claimed that the nationalist party under Parnell were the best people to deal with it, and denounced the Ulster liberals. Besides these well known supporters, Healy also had the help of several of the former liberal organisers.[67] At the meetings the speakers called for the support of all denominations. Healy had the backing of the catholic bishop of Clogher, Dr James Donnelly, and the full organisational assistance of the catholic clergy. In a letter to Tobias Kirby, rector of the Irish College, Rome, about the election, Donnelly drew attention to both the strength and the limits of his electoral influence:

> Healy was unanimously selected as candidate by the Monaghan catholic convention. I demanded from him a public retraction of his remark concerning the Propaganda circular, which he gave, after some hesitation, at a public meeting, on 24 June. Without that, there might have been serious consequences had I opposed him. The catholic people of Clogher are loyal to Rome, but insist on their freedom of political agents.[68]

Pringle in his address said that he stood as an independent liberal and believed that the ultimate answer to the land problem was every farmer owning his land, but in the more immediate context the land act should be amended to include leaseholders. He was helped at his meetings by J. N. Richardson and T. A. Dickson. Richardson proclaimed that Pringle was 'supporting the true interests of the tenant farmers, the interests of law and order', while Dickson denied the conservatives were sincere in their advocacy of land reform.[69] In his address Monroe also advocated farmer ownership of land as the only solution to the land question.[70] He was aided in his campaign by E. S. Finnigan. In speeches Monroe emphasised that he was the tenant farmer candidate and claimed that throughout the campaign the landlords had no position on his platform. He declared that the object of Parnell was not simply the improvement of the farmers, as he claimed, but the establishment of an Irish republic.[71]

When the results were announced it was found that Healy had won with 2,376 votes, while Monroe received 2,011 and Pringle 274. The electoral register in Co. Monaghan was half catholic and half protestant.[72] According to several reports, the catholics, who in 1880 had polled almost solidly for the liberals, had voted nearly entirely for the home rule candidate.[73] A letter in the *People's Advocate* after the general election made the statement, which was probably fairly accurate, that since catholic and protestant electors were equal in number and as about 150 catholics abstained, the 265 majority for Healy must have meant that 415 protestants supported Healy.[74] Another letter in the *Northern Standard* admitted that protestants had voted for Healy, but claimed that they did so because of his views on the land and not through any belief in home rule.[75]

Co. Londonderry, 1884

Following the nationalist victory at Co. Monaghan in mid-1883 the national league spread to many parts of the north and the nationalists held a number of large public rallies that led to several well attended Orange demonstrations.[76] The next by-election occurred, however, in Co. Londonderry, where the liberals had strong presbyterian support and the national league and Orange order do not seem to have had as many adherents as elsewhere. When a seat in the county became vacant after Porter's appointment as master of the rolls in late December 1883, the conservatives decided not to contest the vacancy because, they said, a general election would be coming soon and they felt it inexpedient to involve the constituency in the turmoil of a contest.[77] The nationalists of the county decided that because of the restricted franchise they were without the power to make their opinions effective.[78]

These reasons for non-intervention in the election were no doubt fair ones, but at the same time both parties must have been well aware of the strength of liberal sympathies in the constituency. The Co. Derry liberal union met on 10 December and selected Samuel

Walker, a Church of Ireland queen's counsel and solicitor general.[79] The *Derry Journal* claimed that Walker had been chosen in preference to a catholic candidate because the presbyterian liberals would not support a catholic, while Thomas MacKnight stated that a catholic liberal candidate had not been picked because of the opposition there would have been to his candidature from the nationalists.[80] Which view was correct it is hard to say; probably there was a good deal of truth in both. At the nomination on 10 January 1884, which was uncontested, Walker's nomination papers were signed by catholics and protestants.[81]

Co. Down, 1884
The 1884 November by-election in Co. Down was caused by the succession of Viscount Castlereagh on 6 November to the marquisate of Londonderry. On 11 November a meeting of liberal delegates from the different polling districts in Co. Down took place in the rooms of the Ulster liberal society in Belfast and Arthur Sharman Crawford, another son of William Sharman Crawford, was selected.[82] In his address he declared his support for Gladstone, stated the view that the 1881 land act needed amendment, and backed extension of the franchise and local option.[83] On 14 November a general meeting of the Co. Down constitutional association was held in the Ulster constitutional club, at which a recommendation of the executive committee that R. W. B. Ker, a substantial county landowner, be the conservative candidate, was accepted. In his address Ker deplored the agricultural depression, which he believed arose from restrictive duties on home products abroad and free access to foreign goods at home.[84]

Although neither candidate made very pronounced statements on the land question in their addresses, both subsequently issued broader comments on the subject. In a letter to the papers dated 22 November Ker stated his support for the bill for land purchase that Lord Arthur Hill had introduced into parliament, and his sympathy for the position of glebe land owners.[85] Sharman Crawford also declared during the campaign his backing for peasant proprietorship, but in a rather dilatory manner, seeming first to want to limit it to Ulster and then agreeing it should be extended.[86] Some of his speakers, especially T. A. Dickson, were more outspoken on the matter.[87] Noticeably neither party made much reference to the nationalists or the national league. This lack of comment may well have been caused by the concern of both sides for the nationalist vote.

The catholic vote in Co. Down numbered between 2,000 and 2,500 electors.[88] Most had voted liberal in 1880 but since that time the nationalists had increased their influence among them. The situation was further complicated by certain ill feeling that had arisen, shortly before the election, between Co. Down catholic and protestant liberals over the appointment of a coroner in North Down.[89] At a meeting of nationalist delegates from the different polling districts in Castlewellan on 26 November it was decided to advise nationalist voters to abstain.[90] The conservative candidate was criticised for his conservatism and the liberal was attacked as being a supporter of the liberal government, which had imprisoned the Crossmaglen men after the treason-felony trial of 1883. Sharman Crawford was also criticised for his views on the land question.

The campaign was the first one fought in Ireland under the new corrupt and illegal practices act (1883), the major effect of which was to severely curtail candidates' expenses. Maximum expenditure for candidates was now limited to £200 for boroughs with less than 500 voters, with small additional sums for increased numbers of electors; in counties the maximum expenditure was £500 for counties with less than 2,000 electors, and small extra sums for bigger constituences.[91] At this election advertisements in the newspapers were few, compared with previously, and candidates now had to rely almost entirely on unpaid canvassers and helpers. The liberals set up in important centres committees that arranged a canvass and the provision of conveyances on polling day.[92] After the election, however, the liberals were criticised for lack of energy in these activities and the suggestion was made that local radical associations were required.[93]

The conservatives seem to have been much better organised. The Co. Down constitutional association proved of great assistance. A few months prior to the election, E. S. Finnigan, secretary of the association and also of the Ulster constitutional club, in company with Lord A. W. Hill, honorary secretary of the Ulster constitutional club, had gone round the county, called meetings, and initiated or reorganised committees for each polling district in preparation for the next election.[94] Finnigan acted as Ker's election agent and issued printed instructions to canvassers, committees, and polling agents. Special attention was drawn to the new conditions:

The chairman at the first meeting should point out the altered circumstances under which an election has now to be conducted; the absolute prohibition of any paid employment except what is allowed by the new act; the abolition of hired conveyances; the strict limitation of expenditure;

and the severe penalties which will follow a breach of the law.

He should impress upon those present that success can alone result from the well directed efforts of volunteers, while he should point out the responsibility which is now imposed upon all who take part in the election, and the absolute necessity, in their own interests as well as those of the candidate, that each should carry out faithfully the work allotted to him and that all should adhere rigidly to the provisions of the law.[95]

Local gentry and other supporters provided free transport.

The result of the polling was Ker 4,387 and Crawford 3,998 out of a total electorate of 12,412 votes. In part this outcome was the consequence of an efficient, widespread, conservative organisation and a rather weak liberal organisation which lacked permanent local political associations. In part also it may have been due, as several writers made the point, to Crawford's political inexperience and lack of radicalism on the land question.[96] What probably contributed equally to the liberal defeat was the withdrawal of much of the catholic vote. Thomas MacKnight later claimed that many catholics had polled for the conservative.[97] But figures subsequently produced by the *Morning News* strongly suggested that most catholics had abstained, a verdict accepted by Joseph Perry of the Co. Down tenants' association, who also said that of those catholics who did vote, the majority backed Ker.[98] Thus the liberals had clearly lost a lot of their catholic support, but still retained substantial protestant backing.

Co. Antrim, 1885

On 5 May 1885 the newspapers reported the death of James Chaine, M.P. for Co. Antrim. Within a short time the hon. R. T. O'Neill, second son of Lord O'Neill, announced his intention to stand for election.[99] No selection meeting was reported in the press, but at subsequent meetings of conservatives his candidature was approved; although there was a Co. Antrim constitutional association, it seems to have played no direct part in his selection. On 8 May a private meeting of the Co. Antrim central tenant right association was held in the liberal headquarters in Belfast.[100] It was agreed to request W. P. Sinclair, a native of Belfast but now a prominent Liverpool businessman, to contest the seat. Sinclair submitted an election address to a special committee set up on 8 May which accepted it, and on 13 May the *Northern Whig* reported that he was the official liberal candidate.

In their addresses both candidates made a point of declaring support for the union, a clear sign that this issue was coming to the fore.[101] They also called for amendment to the land act and advocated land purchase. Details are hard to come by concerning party organisation, but from the presence of well known tenant righters at Sinclair's meetings it is clear that he had the working support of the tenant right movement, while in O'Neill's case the presence of various notable conservative gentry at his meetings indicate he had their help.[102] Probably O'Neill was assisted by the Co. Antrim constitutional association; local groups such as the Lisburn conservative working men's club certainly aided him.[103] Neither party alluded much to the nationalists.

Nationalist organisation seems to have been less well developed in Antrim than Down. The main statement on the election from a local nationalist source came on 15 May at a meeting of the Ballycastle catholic and national registration association, when the following resolution was passed:

> As the friends of Messrs Sinclair and O'Neill have followed the time honoured custom of ignoring the catholic and nationalist voters in the selection of candidates for the representation of county Antrim, and as their published addresses are visibly uncatholic and unnational, resolved — that we withhold our support from both candidates during the coming election, and respectfully submit the adoption of a similar course to the consideration of the other catholic and nationalist voters of the county.[104]

Correspondents in the *Morning News* backed this view,[105] and at a meeting of the Irish national league on 19 May T. M. Healy urged the nationalists and catholics of the county not to return a supporter of the government, saying that the man who voted for a whig would be an 'abomination'.[106]

At the beginning of the election the two candidates had put forward rather similar policies. With the arrival of T. A. Dickson at the end of the first week of the campaign, however, Sinclair's programme took on a more radical look. In a speech on 17 May Dickson, to the embarrassment of the *Northern Whig*, attacked the liberal government for its contemplated renewal of the coercion laws and its abandonment of a land purchase scheme, which he upheld vigorously.[107] On 21 May the *Morning News* carried the report of a statement from Sinclair undertaking to oppose the coercion laws if elected. It was also reported on the same day that the government had promised a new land purchase bill.

The election occurred on 21 May. The result was Sinclair 3,971 and O'Neill 3,832 votes. Total electorate figures are not available, but assuming they were similar to 1880 the number who voted was slightly down on the general election. Several factors seem to have assisted Sinclair. First, his support of leaseholders' rights no doubt helped in a county where leaseholders were very numerous among the electors.[108] Secondly, O'Neill's advocacy of fair trade may have alienated voters in the Belfast area; in the Belfast polling district there was a very low turn-out.[109] Thirdly, the activities of Dickson probably aided Sinclair as almost certainly did the announcement of the government's backing for land purchase. Fourthly, reports from the different areas suggest that many catholics abstained but some did vote for Sinclair because of his views on coercion.[110]

Co. Down, 1885

On 26 June it was publicly announced that Lord A. W. Hill had been appointed comptroller of the household under the new conservative government. As a consequence Hill vacated his seat, but immediately announced his intention to recontest the seat. On 29 June a meeting of delegates of the Co. Down tenant farmers' association was held in the Ulster reform club and J. S. Brown, a Belfast presbyterian linen manufacturer and former liberal candidate for Belfast, was selected as liberal candidate for the seat.[111] Hill's address stated simply that he hoped his past conduct in parliament would be taken as a guarantee for future actions.[112] In his address Brown declared that the future progress of Ireland was bound up with the union.[113] In the election campaign Mathew Wylie acted as Brown's election agent and E. S. Finnigan as Hill's. Because of a more pronounced temperance position, Brown received criticism during the election from members of the licensed vintners' trade.[114] The glebeowners' association declared their support for Hill on account of his promise to protest against their exclusion from the 1881 land act.[115]

In the early stages of the election neither candidate referred to the nationalists, probably because both hoped for nationalist support. On 3 July a convention of delegates from the different branches of the national league in Co. Down was held in Downpatrick.[116] At this convention Hill was condemned for his part in opposing national league meetings in Co. Down in 1884 and nationalists were urged to back Brown; this nationalist support was not exactly enthusiastic, as we can see from the editorial of the *Morning News* on 7 July which stated that nationalists entered the election not to help the 'deceitful' whigs but to teach Hill a lesson. Shortly after this meeting, a personal letter was sent from Hill to all the protestant electors. It stated that the nationalist convention had

urged people to vote against him because of his defence of protestantism and loyalty, warned that his defeat would appear as a
home rule victory, and urged protestant liberals to support him in
defence of their religion and future liberties.[117]

The result of the election was Hill 5,097 and Brown 4,696 votes.
There were a number of reasons for this liberal defeat. First, in contrast to the situation in Antrim, the conservatives appear to have
been much better organised than the liberals. After the election the
liberal organisation was the subject of severe criticism in the press.[118]
It should also be noted that far fewer presbyterian ministers were
involved in the liberal organisation than before.[119] Secondly, publicans and members of the glebeowners' association appear to have
voted solidly against Brown.[120] Thirdly, while several reports suggest
that some catholics polled for Hill, many voted for Brown, but the
proclamation of nationalist and catholic support for Brown at
the nationalist convention and the call for protestant unity made
privately by Hill appears to have caused the loss of a certain number
of presbyterian liberal electors.[121]

At Westminster Ulster M.P.s had witnessed considerable change
since 1880 in their relations with the main parties. Local conservatives and the tory party leadership had divided sharply in 1881
over response to demands for land reform. The visit of Sir Stafford
Northcote to the province in October 1883, as Mr A. B. Cooke has
shown, failed to give Ulster conservatives their desired influence on
the party's policies towards Ireland.[122] Ulster conservatives opposed
the redistribution bill, which they feared would strengthen Parnell's
vote, but in spite of appeals to the party leadership they received
little backing. Disillusionment over this matter led to efforts in early
1885 by some Ulster tories to set up a separate Irish party at Westminster.[123] This did not happen in the end although Ulster conservatives continued to feel that their interests were ignored by the
conservative party and were concerned about the close relations
between some of the party leaders, especially Lord Randolph
Churchill, and Parnell.

For the Ulster liberals as well, relations with the party leadership
at Westminster had deteriorated by 1885. The 1881 land act had
been welcomed by the Ulster liberal M.P.s but subsequently
members felt that the government paid them little attention in
drawing up their policies for Ireland. In mid-1885 T. A. Dickson,
who had emerged as the leading Ulster liberal, had published a
pamphlet very critical of the government's policies, urging reforms
such as land purchase. But Dickson was sceptical of the Ulster

liberal M.P.s' impact on the government: 'so far as our influence is
concerned we might as well be members for Timbuctoo'.[124]

For the home rule party also, relations with the main parties at
Westminster had undergone important developments by 1885. The
strengthening of his position throughout the country indicated that
Parnell could well have a strong role in the next parliament. Some
English conservatives, in particular Lord Randolph Churchill, saw
the advantages that a close connection with Parnell could bring,
both in parliament as a whole and to their own position within the
conservative party.[125] For Parnell this gave him a new position of
influence and strength. Careful attention to conservative sensibilities
helped prevent opposition from that quarter to the franchise and
redistribution bills. With both main parties conscious of internal
division and keen to strengthen their position in parliament,
Parnell's role at Westminster had assumed new importance.

Thus, by late 1885 the parliamentary representation in Ulster had
changed little on the surface from 1880. The home rulers had gained
a place from the liberals and the liberals had won a seat from the
conservatives. The 1885 by-elections revealed that both liberals and
conservatives had strong backing among the protestant farmers.
But the liberals had lost much of their catholic support and the
home rule party had gained a strong position among catholics in
Ulster, although home rule organisation in the province was weak.
The two 1885 by-elections also showed that the land question was
becoming less important in election affairs. In the rest of the country
the home rule party had slightly increased its number of M.P.s at the
expense of the other parties, but more significantly the by-elections
strengthened Parnell and his group, which continued to grow in
importance in the party and the country.

In comparison with the situation before 1874 the political scene in
the province had been transformed. The issue of land reform had
played a vital part in changing political loyalties. The nature of the
franchise, with its strong farmer base, had been of great assistance
to the liberals who benefited from a largely catholic–presbyterian
vote. The conservatives had profited from the existence of the
borough seats, which by mid-1885 supplied over half of the Ulster
conservative M.P.s. The nationalists, dependent usually on at least
a good catholic vote, had not gained from the restricted system. To
meet the new opportunities the liberals had availed of the tenant
movement as well as assistance from the Ulster liberal society. The
conservatives had sought to adapt their organisation away from its

landlord base, but with only limited success. The nationalists had failed, except in a few places, to provide efficient organisation.

The situation that confronted the parties at the next general election would be very different from before. Not only had changes in the electoral system, introduced in 1883-5, transformed the setting for the political struggle, but the land question was now relegated to second place in importance behind the question of home rule. The size as well as the social and religious composition of the electorate were drastically altered. Party organisation, required on a scale not seen before to cope with the greatly expanded electorate and constituencies, was dependent very largely on voluntary aid. How the party electoral machines would cope with all this remained to be seen. Clearly, events in 1880-5 had brought new alignments among large sections of the population, and the key question was now raised about the ability of the parties and their leaders to adjust and face the new challenge.

IV NATIONALISTS AND UNIONISTS DIVIDE

CHAPTER 10 *The 1885 general election*

'It seems to us', declared the editorial of the *Witness*, 13 November 1885, 'that the great question before Irish, and especially Ulster, constituencies in the present electioneering contest is the maintenance of the legislative union between Great Britain and Ireland.' Throughout Ireland in 1885 the issue of home rule was undoubtedly the main political subject of the day, but another matter was also important to Ulster. The liberal and conservative parties were involved in keen electoral contests in many northern constituencies. The general election would settle this struggle between the different sides and subsequent events in the following year would consolidate the result. For both the nationalist and unionist movements the years 1885-6 were of crucial significance in deciding the form and spirit of their respective parties.

The single most noticeable feature in Irish party politics in 1885 was the growth and reorganisation of the home rule movement. By 1885 Parnell and his followers completely dominated the parliamentary party. In common parlance the term 'home ruler' had given way to 'nationalist'. The national league provided for the nationalist party an effective widespread organisation through its local branches. County conventions, composed mainly of national league delegates and catholic clergy, selected parliamentary candidates, under the supervision of representatives from the organising committee of the league, which was controlled by Parnell. A pledge was introduced to bind the M.P.s together into a tightly disciplined party. Thus, as Dr Conor Cruise O'Brien has remarked, the national league had turned the home rule movement from a loose grouping of independent elements into "a well knit political party of a modern type . . . effectively monopolising the political expression of national sentiment."[1]

In response to this nationalist reorganisation the Irish loyal and patriotic union was formed in Dublin in May 1885 by a number of southern businessmen, landowners, and academics.[2] It sought to organise opposition in the three southern provinces to the nationalists, and to unite liberals and conservatives on a common platform of maintenance of the union. The Irish loyal and patriotic

176

union also published pamphlets and leaflets which were widely circulated. In its aim of bringing together liberals and conservatives the I.L.P.U. was successful and in many cases candidates came forward in the election simply as 'loyalists'.[3] In Ulster, however, these appeals for unity between supporters of the union went largely unheeded and both parties continued to act independently.

For all the parties in Ulster as in the rest of Ireland, the new conditions brought about by the electoral legislation of 1883-5 presented great difficulties as well as opportunities. Thanks to the corrupt and illegal practices act, which severely limited electoral expenses, party organisation had to be largely voluntary. The franchise act changed very considerably the size and character of the electorate. Overall in Ulster the number of voters increased by nearly 180 per cent between 1884 and 1885; the percentage of labourers and catholics among the electors grew considerably. As a result of the redistribution act there were now 27 county and 6 borough electoral divisions in the province compared with 9 county and 10 borough constituencies previously. Contests were still held on one day but the polls for the different constituencies were held over a series of days.

Because of the greatly increased activity at the elections, due not only to the growth in the number of constituencies, electors and party organisation, but also the heightened interest in the issues, our study of this general election will be different from that in previous chapters. First, the three main parties and their approach to the contests are examined separately, area by area: then an analysis is carried out of the issues involved and the results of the polls, and finally comments are made about the outcome of the elections. Previous studies of these contests have concentrated on Fermanagh and North Armagh, where documentary evidence is plentiful, but as we shall see, these two areas were not in fact typical, and a detailed study of all the constituencies, relying on newspaper as well as documentary sources, allows a better, more accurate picture to emerge.

The parties in Ulster: (a) conservatives
During 1885 the Ulster conservatives reorganised at both central and local level. The principal centre of this activity was the Ulster constitutional club in Belfast. On 3 June 1885 at a meeting of the executive committee of the club a special committee was formed for the purpose of giving aid throughout the province in registration and general election work.[4] Lord Crichton was appointed chairman

and Lord Arthur Hill became honorary secretary. Closely connected with this committee was E. S. Finnigan, secretary of the club
and also of the Cos Down and Antrim constitutional associations.
During the year Hill and (especially) Finnigan played an important
role, particularly in north-east Ulster, where they helped to set up
new political associations, assisted with registration, and ironed out
differences between conservative supporters. The club was an
important centre for meetings and conferences.

Besides the Ulster constitutional club another central organisation
of the northern conservatives was the loyal Irish union, which was
inaugurated at a meeting of leading Ulster conservatives at Belvoir
Park outside Belfast on 8 August 1885.[5] The prime object of this
body was to provide a common meeting ground for all supporters of
the union between Great Britain and Ireland. The idea of an anti-
nationalist union had been discussed among conservatives as far
back as 1881,[6] but it only became widespread in the first half of 1885,
and the loyal Irish union was an attempt to form such a movement.
The impact of this group seems to have been rather limited, however, for it established only a couple of local branches,[7] did not dis-
place the existing conservative associations or the Ulster constitutional club, and attracted few liberals. As regards its aim of
promoting unity it was later accused by liberal sources of using the
idea to outmanoeuvre their party in some constituencies.[8] But many
conservatives remained anxious to promote cooperation among all
supporters of the union.

Conservative reorganisation at local level differed considerably
from area to area. As a result of the 1883 corrupt practices act
election management could no longer be left in the hands of
organisers paid by the candidates. In many of the constituencies
there were constitutional associations, but up to 1883 their organisational role had been rather a limited one. Now they assumed
entire responsibility for electoral matters, a situation further complicated by the redistribution and franchise changes. Their work
involved not only the setting up of associations for the recently
created divisions but also the building of new structures to involve
the greatly expanded electorate that sought a part in the conservative organisation.

This local reorganisation involved the important question of the
role of the Orange order in the conservative party. The franchise act
gave a special significance to Orangeism, since as a result of the act
the small farmers and many labourers, both in town and country,
were enfranchised, and the Orange lodges drew a lot of their

backing from these sections. For the conservatives, Orange support was important because, although the Orangemen were only a minority of the protestant voters, they were a well organised group which accounted for a large proportion of the new electorate, and whose support the conservatives needed against the liberals with their strong base among the farmers.

In the past the influence of the Orange order in the conservative organisation had generally been limited apart from some areas such as Cos Fermanagh and Armagh. At Orange meetings in early 1885 in various parts of Ulster, however, dissatisfaction was expressed that the conservative M.P.s were not properly representing the Orangemen and protestants of Ulster, and comment was also passed about the new political power that the franchise act would give to the Orangemen.[9] Therefore the conservatives in their reorganisation faced a problem of dealing with two matters that in many ways were contradictory — gaining liberal and Orange support.

Conservative reorganisation during 1885 was at its most efficient in Co. Down. At a meeting of the Co. Down constitutional association on 22 January 1885 a resolution was passed that the association should restructure its local committees to embrace all classes of believers in the union.[10] Lord Arthur Hill, honorary secretary of the association, and E. S. Finnigan, full-time secretary, were appointed to organise the new committees throughout the county. Speaking at the establishment of one such body at Ballynahinch on 7 May, Finnigan explained that

> It was proposed to form a large committee in each of the polling districts into which the county would be divided, this committee to be composed of the members of the present district committees, together with the representatives of the agricultural labouring class, and those who would have a vote as lodgers, employees, and servants. The Orange association would have a well defined position. The district master and district officers, together with the master of each of the lodges in the district, would be appointed, or other brethren nominated by them, upon each committee.[11]

Under the guidance of Hill and Finnigan, especially the latter, similar local committees were set up throughout the county.[12] Conventions of delegates from these bodies were then held to establish divisional associations and to select conservative candidates, great care being taken to prevent any group taking individual action on the matter and causing disunity. Lord Arthur Hill, an Orangeman and sitting M.P. for the county, was selected on 6 May for West

Down, Capt. R. W. B. Ker, the other M.P., was chosen for East Down on 19 September, and Col. Thomas Waring, an Orangeman and prominent landowner in Co. Down, was picked for North Down on 23 September. The local Bangor committee had tried to choose Col. Waring for North Down in May but he declined, saying a representative convention should first be held. In the case of South Down, however, there was difficulty in finding a candidate and only at the end of October was it decided to put forward W. H. Kisbey, Q.C..[13]

Conservative reorganisation in Co. Antrim proceeded on somewhat similar lines to that in Co. Down. The county constitutional association decided in early 1885 to widen its membership,[14] and the Orange order was given a special position in many of the new organisations. At a meeting of conservative electors at Glenarm in Mid Antrim on 6 August 1885, for example, E. S. Finnigan explained that in their election of delegates to a divisional convention to select a conservative candidate, half should be Orangemen.[15] This view was also expressed at a meeting of electors in Ballymoney to pick representatives for the North Antrim convention, the chairman stating that the Orangemen would choose their delegates independently of the other electors at the meeting.[16]

In Mid Antrim there appears to have been a certain amount of conflict between the Orangemen and the main conservative organiser in the constituency, John Young, and not until 24 October was a conference called of delegates from the different districts.[17] The Mid Antrim constitutional association was then formally established, with advice from E. S. Finnigan. Hon. R. T. O'Neill, who had been defeated at the 1885 Antrim by-election, was chosen as conservative candidate on this occasion. In the same month in Mid Antrim the Ahoghill conservative working men's club was opened.[18] In North Antrim on 1 October Edward Macnaghten, Q.C., sitting M.P. for the county, was selected as candidate for the division at a meeting of constituency delegates.[19]

In South Antrim the Lisburn conservative association played a leading role in setting up committees for the division.[20] Meetings of representatives took place in July and August. Sir Richard Wallace was suggested as candidate but he declined to stand because of ill-health and the rigours that he feared a modern election campaign would entail.[21] At a meeting of 150 delegates on 6 October at the Ulster constitutional club, a constitutional association, with low subscription rates to attract wide support, was inaugurated for the constituency and W. G. Ellison Macartney, a lawyer and son of

J. W. Ellison Macartney, was then selected as candidate.[22] In East Antrim delegates of the party in the division met in the constitutional club in mid-June and Capt J. M. McCalmont, an army officer originally from Belfast, was picked as their candidate. During the summer new associations were established in various parts of East Antrim.[23] In the establishment of this conservative organisation in the four Antrim divisions, former members of the Co. Antrim constitutional association, such as John Young and Wellington Young, played an important part, as did E. S. Finnigan.

At the beginning of 1885 no county conservative association existed in Co. Londonderry. In early January a local constitutional body was set up at Castledawson and other such organisations appeared eventually in the county. But activity by the conservatives had failed by midsummer to make any noticeable impact on the political scene in the two divisions, as several critics in the papers pointed out. On 3 September delegates from constitutional associations and groups in South Londonderry met and plans were drawn up to form an executive committee for the constituency; an invitation to stand was issued to Col. Hugh McCalmont, an army officer, which he accepted.[24] The liberals rejected invitations to join the conservatives and selected their own candidate.

In North Londonderry conservative organisations were even slower to appear. By late September no attempt had been made to form a divisional association or select a conservative candidate; this lack of action may partly have arisen from a desire among some Londonderry conservatives not to oppose the liberal candidate Samuel Walker, sitting M.P. for the county. But at the very end of September a meeting was held of protestant working men in Limavady to consider the representation of the division. Speakers on this occasion said that they did not want an agreement with the liberals, accused Walker of blindly supporting Gladstone who had concluded the 'Kilmainham treaty' with the nationalists in 1882, and declared that they wanted a man to represent the working men's interest as well as free education for their children and decent houses. It was resolved that the meeting, 'consisting chiefly of working men, now for the first time entitled to the franchise', should set up a committee to meet with other local bodies to select a candidate.[25]

At this meeting few of the local gentry were present, but three weeks later, when the committee reported back to another gathering in Limavady, many were. The committee revealed that it had approached an Ulster merchant, H. S. Cooke, working in London, who was known for his tendencies towards 'conservative democracy', but he was unable to accept due to ill health. Henry Mulholland, son of John Mulholland, M.P. for Downpatrick, was then selected as conservative candidate for the constituency.[26] An indication of the social tensions involved may be seen in the snide comment by the *Londonderry Standard*, 6 November, that Mulholland had been asked to come forward by the 'rag-tag and bob tail'. Mulholland, however, had no hesitation in appealing to the protestant labourers and in deploring their bad conditions.[27]

Nor did conservative reorganisation and selection of candidates go smoothly in Armagh. At a meeting of the Co. Armagh constitutional association on 25 February 1885[28] it was agreed that the conservative party in the county should be broadened; on 12 May another meeting was held at which, after an address from E. S. Finnigan on reorganisation, persons were appointed from each polling district to set up branch associations. Little difficulty arose with either Mid or South Armagh. In the former, bodies were established, such as the Richhill constitutional association with an annual subscription of one shilling per annum 'in order to enable every labourer to join'.[29] At a conference of delegates from these different groups on 6 October, the Mid Armagh constitutional association was formally inaugurated; T. G. Peel, the prominent local Orangeman and conservative organiser, took a leading role in the proceedings. On 13 October the association accepted a recommendation from a sub-committee to select Prof. John McKane, a professor of law from Queen's College, Belfast.[30] Although the Orange order does not appear to have been directly involved in the Mid Armagh organisation, many of the leading members of the main association were Orangemen and local lodges subsequently endorsed the choice of candidate.[31]

In South Armagh little conservative organisation occurred, chiefly because the nationalists had a large majority on the electoral register. About a week before nomination day, however, a Dr H. G. Grey published an address as a constitutionalist and meetings were held in his favour.[32] But just before nomination day he withdrew. Although Grey in his address had stated that he stood at the wishes of a number of South Armagh constituents, the reasons for his sudden candidature and then withdrawal would seem to lie elsewhere. The nationalists in Armagh had encountered difficulty over the selection of their South Armagh candidate. For fear that apathy or hostility on the part of their supporters would lose them an otherwise certain seat, it was privately agreed between T. G. Peel, on behalf of the conservatives, and T. M. Healy, for the nationalists, that the conservatives would not fight South Armagh if the nationalists agreed to contest Mid Armagh and so upset the plans of a liberal in that division.[33] Although a nationalist was very unlikely to win Mid Armagh, his candidature would spoil the liberals' chances; this in fact it did. Grey's campaign was clearly a part of these political manoeuvres and prevented the appearance of an independent nationalist in South Armagh.

Affairs were not arranged so easily in North Armagh, however, and events there illustrate well some of the tensions within the new conservative organisation. During early 1885 a number of local associations were set up in North Armagh. The guiding force in all this was J. B. Atkinson, a prominent Portadown solicitor and leading Armagh conservative, but not an Orangeman. Writing to another conservative in Loughgall on 18 May 1885 to urge him to set up a local association, he described the work that he and others had done in Portadown:

Portadown always had a constitutional association and what we have done is simply to enlarge it to admit the artisans. We have been working for months and have the greater part of the division organised . . . I hold no division can be worked without having several associations . . . I think we are to be commended for proceeding to organise, to be ready when required . . .[34]

Certain conflicts arose between these groups over the question of seniority,[35] but these seem to have been solved satisfactorily and in late June and early July conferences of delegates were held to select a candidate. By the first week of July John Monroe, Q.C. attorney general, had emerged as the conservative candidate with the unanimous backing of the Portadown, Lurgan, Lurgan working men's, and Clonmacte (but not Loughgall) conservative associations.[36]

Opposition to this choice soon appeared among conservative supporters, especially in the Orange ranks. The county grand Orange lodge on 18 June had requested conservative associations to consider candidates for the coming elections and submit their views to a gathering on 6 July.[37] The outcome of this meeting was not immediately reported in the papers, but it later emerged that Major E. J. Saunderson, former liberal M.P. for Co. Cavan and now a prominent Orangeman, was put forward as conservative candidate by Rev. Thomas Ellis, county chaplain, an active political figure at previous elections and friend of T. G. Peel's, and he was accepted by those present. By late July and early August meetings were being held in support of Saunderson, and several Orange lodges in the

North Armagh division announced their backing for him.[38] From this time until mid-October Monroe and Saunderson held rallies in North Armagh in opposition to each other.

The issues involved in this conflict were several. First, Rev. Thomas Ellis played an important part in Saunderson's candidature, which may have arisen because of resentment felt by Ellis at his diminished role in conservative affairs; as the pamphlet which he published shows, he believed that the Orange order, of which he was grand county chaplain, should be the main conservative organisation in the constituency.[39] Also, there was considerable personal enmity between Ellis and J. B. Atkinson.[40] Secondly, resentment was expressed on several occasions, especially from Orange platforms, against the conservative government's actions and there was opposition on some people's part to Monroe because he was in the government; Saunderson on the other hand was spoken of as a good Orangeman and an able speaker.[41]

Thirdly, and what was probably the most important of all, there was considerable concern among many of the North Armagh Orangemen that they did not have a sufficient say in the new conservative organisation. An example of this feeling can be seen in a letter of 22 July from Robert Courtney, district secretary of the Portadown Orangemen, to Rev. Thomas Ellis, enquiring whether Saunderson was going to be put forward for the seat.

> We, the Orangemen of Portadown, consider that he should be put for-ward by the grand lodge and that it should support us. There is no time to be lost and we do not know what to do. There is a very strong feeling amongst the Orangemen of this district, that owing to the manner that they have been treated by the conservative party here and the insults given to them saying there were only about 50 Orangemen [who] had votes in Portadown, a great many of them are of opinion that they will resign the Orange Institution altogether as they cannot see what use it is in this part if they can be made fools of the way they have been in this matter.[42]

Atkinson did not believe that the Orange order should have an influential role in the local conservative organisation, because they were not numerous in proportion to the whole electorate,[43] but the Orangemen felt that they were being ignored unjustly.

In the weeks that followed Saunderson issued an address and spoke at many Orange meetings. As several observers remarked, he sought especially the support of the Orange labourers and others who were newly enfranchised. An editorial in the *Ulster Gazette* on 22 August noted with alarm that he was deliberately seeking the labourers' vote by calling for a great increase in the number of labourers' cottages, a step that the paper believed would put an extra burden on the farmers' rates. It was also observed that he was very sympathetic to the weavers' needs, a subject particularly relevant in Lurgan and Portadown.⁴⁴ In his speeches, Saunderson, while backing the conservative party in a general manner, said that because of the recent close relations between some conservatives and the nationalists, loyalists must be prepared to fend for themselves. He also stated that the well-being and liberties of the loyalists of Ireland were seriously threatened by the nationalists, to whom he attributed the lawlessness and disorder of the previous five years.⁴⁵ Monroe in his speeches declared that he had the endorsement of all the associations except one, defended the government against criticism, and referred to the recent conservative land purchase act.⁴⁶

By the end of August Saunderson had obtained very wide and strong Orange support, beyond even what he and Ellis had expected. On 26 August Ellis wrote to Saunderson:

> I spent two hours yesterday with Locke and other leading Orangemen of Portadown trying to make a compromise about you and Monroe, but I might as well have talked to the wall. *They are determined to have you.* In fact now I am very doubtful whether your withdrawing would not do more [harm] than good for they claim that if you were withdrawn they would vote for a liberal. *The Orange* spirit is aroused, and now it is *victory or death* with them. They have gone beyond the power and control of leaders so you are in for it, for better or worse.⁴⁷

Efforts by leading conservatives such as Lord Arthur Hill and Sir Thomas Bateson during August to heal the split were useless.⁴⁸ Finally at the beginning of October, faced with this widespread opposition and concerned about the embarrassment that a contest between two conservatives would cause and about the possibility that a nationalist or liberal would win the seat due to a split conservative vote, Monroe resigned. His letter of resignation was accepted at a meeting of constitutional association representatives on 10 October.⁴⁹ For a time Monroe's supporters contemplated running another candidate against Saunderson, but finally decided against it.

If the conservatives' main problem in Co. Armagh was disunity, that in Co. Fermanagh was apathy.⁵⁰ At a meeting of the Enniskillen constitutional club on 13 February 1885 it was resolved to widen the scope of the club. But by October little had been done to set up an effective conservative organisation and registration had been seriously neglected. J. W. Dane, a local solicitor and secretary of the club, sought to organise their supporters but with negligible success; in spite of repeated appeals by him in midsummer for funds the response was very poor and by November 1885 there were only about ninety members altogether in the club.[51]

On 15 October, following a circular issued by E. M. Archdale in his capacity as secretary of the Fermanagh grand Orange lodge, a convention was held in Enniskillen of delegates from the different polling districts.[52] J. C. Bloomfield, a minor Fermanagh landlord and founder of the Belleek potteries, was chosen for North Fermanagh; £600 was raised for his campaign at the meeting but additional money proved difficult to find. On 1 November, at a meeting in Lisnaskea, Frank Brooke, a local land agent, was selected for South Fermanagh.[53] Under J. W. Dane's directions, committees were set up in both areas and an election campaign commenced, but there was little of the enthusiasm found in Cos Antrim, Down or Armagh.

In the counties examined so far the conservatives made little or no attempt to treat with the liberals. In Co. Tyrone, however, the question of conservative–liberal union assumed considerable importance because the numbers of catholics and protestants were roughly similar in the four new divisions. In April 1885 the Tyrone united club had been formed to bring together all constitutionalists.[54] In spite of this the Tyrone constitutional association at a meeting on 3 June appointed members to set up conservative bodies in the new divisions. This work was proceeded with, and local and divisional conservative associations were established with considerable efficiency.[55] But the idea of union had made an impact among many Tyrone conservatives, who viewed a united protestant movement as the best means to defeat the nationalists. Approaches were made by both the central Tyrone constitutional body and some local associations to the Tyrone liberals during the summer, but these received no positive response and the liberals proceeded with forming their own associations.[56]

While no formal link was made with the liberals, however, there were influential people in the liberals' ranks who favoured union.[57] Efforts were now made by the conservatives to win over liberal supporters. On 2 October the divisional constitutional association in East Tyrone changed its name to the united constitutional society of East Tyrone; at the same meeting, J. M. Stuart, a Scottish conservative who had issued an address as a conservative earlier in the year, was accepted as candidate.[58] In Mid-Tyrone in July the conservatives asked H. H. Moore, a local solicitor, to stand but he said he would not do so until he was certain of wide support, and not until late October did he finally consent.[59] In East Tyrone the liberals picked a candidate but he withdrew before nomination, while in Mid Tyrone they did not choose one at all.

In North Tyrone the conservatives selected as their candidate in early June the marquis of Hamilton, who made great efforts to win liberal support. He arranged for a conservative to back down before a liberal in East Donegal to obtain unity among constitutionalists there.[60] He was rewarded by the president of the Tyrone liberal association giving him his backing; when he became duke of Abercorn on the death of his father, his brother was selected for the seat on 13 November and the liberals also supported him.[61]

In South Tyrone, however, the conservatives clashed with T. A. Dickson. The South Tyrone conservative association on 7 September chose as their candidates John Ross, Q.C., a presbyterian conservative well liked in liberal circles,[62] but four days later Dickson declared his intention to stand as a liberal, claiming that this had been known for some time. A bitter feud broke out between Dickson and the conservatives and when Ross decided not to stand they chose on 11 November Capt. Somerset Maxwell, a Co. Cavan landowner and prominent Orangeman.[63] The Orange order does not seem to have had much direct say in these new Tyrone organisations, probably because of the conservatives' wish to win liberal support, but it can be observed that at a meeting of the county grand Orange lodge in early November resolutions were passed endorsing the conservative candidates.[64]

In Cos Donegal, Monaghan, and Cavan there was limited conservative activity. Lt-col. H. H. A. Stewart, a minor Donegal landlord, put forward his name for East Donegal but withdrew in favour of a liberal, thanks to the efforts of the duke of Abercorn to encourage liberal–conservative union.[65] The conservatives actively assisted the liberals in East Donegal. Stewart then stood for North Donegal and A. H. W. Foster, another conservative Co. Donegal landlord, contested South Donegal; neither had apparently much organisation. In Monaghan the county conservative association continued fairly actively in existence but with little change in structure. In late September Sir John Leslie, bt (M.P. for the county 1871-80) consented to stand for North Monaghan. At the end of November S. E. Shirley (M.P. for the county 1868-80) issued an address as a conservative for South Monaghan.[66] In Co. Cavan there was little conservative organisation. Only shortly before nomination did a conservative candidate, Samuel Saunderson, brother of Major E. J.

Saunderson, appear.[67]

In the boroughs the conservatives faced the same problems of reorganisation and of having to deal with their Orange supporters in some constituencies and the liberals in others. In common with conservative associations elsewhere, the Belfast conservative association in early 1885 reorganised into divisional bodies; these had executive and general committees and took on responsibility for selection of candidates. But on 14 March a letter appeared in the press from Samuel Hunter, on behalf of the executive committee of delegates from the Orange lodges of East Belfast, to protest about the conservative reorganisation.[68] He stated that whereas the constitutional associations of Antrim and Down had admitted the right of the Orange order to a say in the selection of candidates, this had not happened in Belfast. Hunter also said that, at a meeting of the grand Orange lodge of Belfast on 9 March, a resolution was passed that two of the Belfast M.P.s should be Orangemen. The Belfast association does not appear to have made any response to this protest and the divisional associations proceeded to choose candidates.

In North and West Belfast little difficulty arose over selection. In the former a meeting of the general committee on 16 April in the constitutional club picked William Ewart, one of the sitting Belfast M.P.s.[69] For the latter, J. H. Haslett, a local chemist and merchant, was recommended as a candidate by the executive committee of the divisional association on 25 April but the recommendation was not finally accepted by the general committee until 19 October, the delay being caused by hesitation on Haslett's part in accepting and by time spent in negotiations with the liberals over a suitable candidate.[70] Selection did not proceed so easily in the other two constituencies.

On 20 January at a meeting of delegates from East Belfast Orange lodges, E. W. S. de Cobain, borough cashier and former grand master of the Belfast Orangemen, was chosen as candidate for the constituency.[71] This choice and the protest on 14 March seem to have had no effect on the official conservative organisers of the division. On 14 April the executive and general committees of the East Belfast conservative association selected as their candidate J. P. Corry, the other Belfast M.P. who was not an Orangeman.[72] From April onwards meetings were held in support of both de Cobain and Corry.

In South Belfast the Orange and protestant working men's associations on 31 March chose for the division Robert Seeds, Q.C., who had stood unsuccessfully in 1880. At a meeting of Orangemen on 14 April William Johnston was put forward to contest the seat. Meetings of the executive committee of the South Belfast conservative association were held in late April and early May and the names of Seeds and Johnston were proposed along with that of Major E. J. Saunderson.[73] None of the candidates received the required two-thirds majority, although on each occasion Seeds received the most votes and the selection was deferred. Saunderson withdrew his name, and Johnston and Seeds held meetings throughout the summer in support of their candidature. In October the selection procedure started again. Eventually a meeting of the general committee on 30 October resulted in a tie between the two candidates and neither was formally adopted.[74] Both continued their campaigns to polling day.

In these intra-conservative struggles in East and South Belfast several issues seem to have been at stake. First, the Orangemen in Belfast demanded a say in the conservative organisation which they believed they were entitled to and had not received.[75] Speakers at de Cobain's and Johnston's meetings insisted that the Orangemen should have the right to select two candidates for Belfast. They stated that they needed Orange representatives to speak for the Orange electors. The Belfast conservative divisional associations resisted this demand and, while prepared to allow some accommodation, were determined to act as the main party organisation. Secondly, there was a certain amount of personal conflict. William Johnston was determined to return to politics and the Belfast conservative party did not want him, as in 1868.

In addition to these two issues there appears to have been a considerable degree of social conflict involved. Several Belfast Orange representatives in early 1885 had made speeches about the rights of the working men and, at the meetings of the joint committee of East Belfast Orange delegates, expression was given to the idea that protestant working men should have their own representatives. The point was made also that because of the change in electoral law concerning election expenses M.P.s no longer needed to be men of great wealth.[76] At de Cobain's meetings, speakers stated that Corry, as a leading industrialist, could not adequately look after the interests of the working men. Addressing a meeting in mid-June de Cobain accused Corry of voting in parliament against measures favourable to labour, and advocated support for the trade union movement and industrial reform.[77]

At the same time, however, as making these social comments, de Cobain and his followers expressed their concern for the defence of protestantism and also their belief that their present M.P.s had not been doing this adequately.[78] In South Belfast the social and purely 'Orange' aspects of the intra-conservative struggles were mixed. Seeds in his speeches dwelt largely on social issues, but Johnston (standing with the backing of a number of the Orange leaders), while giving some place to social matters in his speeches, attacked Seeds for not sufficiently declaring his support for protestantism and the Orange order. Johnston's main line of political argument was his intention to back both and to give Orangeism a strong representative.[79]

In Newry the committee of the local constitutional association called a meeting of conservative electors in early November to discuss selection of a candidate. Up to this point it had been assumed that Henry Thomson, the sitting M.P. for Newry, would allow his name to go forward. At the meeting on 9 November, however, Thomson said that he would not stand again.[80] Further meetings were held, but in the end no candidate was selected, although James Henderson, owner of the *Newry Telegraph* and the *Belfast Newsletter*, was considered. After the nomination, when a nationalist was put forward unopposed, Henderson wrote a public letter to say that a number of Newry conservatives, especially some Orangemen, had wanted him to stand, but the association had failed to ask him in time.[81] Newspaper reports suggested that the Newry association's inactivity was a result of divisions between members of the association and some Orangemen and also between liberals and conservatives in Newry.[82]

While these reasons for the non-appearance of a conservative candidate in Newry may have had some influence it is likely that certain broader political manoeuvring also played a part. In a private letter dated 12 November 1885 to the national league organiser in Ulster, Timothy Harrington, Michael McCartan, a Newry solicitor and nationalist, explained that he had just been approached by E. S. Finnigan to arrange a secret political deal. Finnigan claimed that he was keen to promote the conservative cause against the liberals. He offered that if the nationalists would remain neutral or support tory candidates in East and North Down and in Mid, South, and North Antrim, 'he thinks he could almost guarantee no opposition in Newry borough'.[83] Probably the non-appearance of a conservative or liberal in Newry was linked to this arrangement. The confusion over Henderson's selection may have been deliberate.

In Derry city the conservative agent, Samuel McDermott, former conservative party agent, continued to organise electoral matters for the local association. By 1885 there was a Derry working men's constitutional association which seems to have had good relations with the other conservatives.[84] On 24 September an election address appeared in the *Londonderry Sentinel* from the former member, C. E. Lewis. Whether or not a selection meeting took place is unclear, but his candidature proceeded without any problem and eventually with the support of the city's liberals.

Thus conservative reorganisation varied considerably between constituencies. Originating in most cases from earlier constitutional associations, new broad-based local conservative organisations were established. These new bodies often had close relations with the Orange order, sometimes on a formal basis. During the election campaign there were frequent calls from Orange lodges to members to assist the conservative candidates as best they could. This reorganisation was not without its difficulties as the disparate elements within the conservative ranks occasionally came into conflict, with important consequences for the conservatives. Of the party candidates, Haslett and Corry (Belfast), Lewis (Derry), McKane (Mid Armagh), and Stuart (East Tyrone) were presbyterian, de Cobain (East Belfast) was methodist, and the rest were members of the Church of Ireland.

Besides the selection of candidates these new associations were responsible for looking after registration of electors and taking charge of the election campaign. A study of the lengthy revision sessions of 1885 show that they carried out this former task well, particularly in the north-east of the province.[85] The work at these courts was done either by the older constitutional associations or the new divisional organisations that were formed during 1885. In most cases the conservatives were represented by solicitors, who had previously worked for tory interests, with the assistance of local agents. E. S. Finnigan played an important part in this registration drive, giving advice to various groups and helping at the revision sessions.

Restrictions imposed on party organisation by the 1883 corrupt practices act placed a heavy burden on the conservative election machinery but the new associations responded well in many areas to the challenge. Election workers now had to be almost all volunteers and considerable effort was required to establish an efficient election machinery for purposes of canvassing, attending polling booths, and arranging transport. Associations depended for election expenses nearly entirely on subscriptions from members. Landlords and their agents played a much less important role in conservative organisation than before and were regarded in some areas as a liability. In Co. Fermanagh, for example, the conservative agent warned a supporter about too many landlords on election platforms: 'the less landlords we have the better but we must have some.[86] Elsewhere, however, especially in the east among the new labourer voters, landlords as candidates or helpers were no disadvantage. Indeed, since the professional and merchant groups were largely liberal at this stage, the gentry were essential to provide conservative candidates.

The new conservative organisation was most effective in Belfast and Cos Antrim, Armagh, Down, and Tyrone, less effective in Derry city and Cos Monaghan, Londonderry, and Fermanagh, and largely non-existent in Newry and Cos Cavan and Donegal. In the cases of Londonderry and Fermanagh this weakness may partly be explained by the absence of constitutional associations in these counties and the complete domination of election affairs by the gentry before 1885. Several historians have written of 'parochialism and passivity' in conservative organisation before and during 1885, and the failure of the Co. Fermanagh conservatives (the best documented of the local associations) has been given as evidence of this.[87] But, as we have seen, conservative organisation was especially poor in Co. Fermanagh: elsewhere it was much more impressive.

The parties in Ulster: (b) liberals

For the Ulster liberals the changing political circumstances of 1885 brought their own particular problems of reorganisation. The year began well for them with the opening of the Ulster reform club on New Year's Day 1885. The building was formally opened by the marquis of Hartington ten months later at an impressive ceremony, after which a large public dinner was held, attended by representatives of local liberal groups from different parts of the province.[88] But in spite of this good start the reform club failed to provide the central organisation for the liberals that had been envisaged.

In early January 1885 a subcommittee was set up in the club to fix a meeting with the Ulster liberal society to organise united political action, but nothing came from this. In February another subcommittee was formed to arrange political debates and conferences at the club.[89] This project seems to have been more successful and a number of political meetings were held, including one addressed by James Bryce, M.P. In early April criticism was voiced against the reform club for not bringing representatives of tenant associations into its organisation, but such points went unheeded.[90]

On 30 September the club established a confidential political committee to collect information on the constituencies and on possible candidates. The committee was composed of all the Ulster liberal M.P.s and the officers and some members of the club. The first meeting was held on 16 October and thereafter every Tuesday. At these meetings, which were attended mainly by the club representatives and rarely by M.P.s, they discussed candidates for seats still unfilled. The outcome of these discussions is not clear. Prior to the general election a circular was sent out to all club members urging them to assist the liberals.[91]

The Ulster liberal society continued in existence under the presidency of Lord Waveney (until his death in February 1886) and the secretaryship of Mathew Wylie. Wylie gave some assistance to the liberals at registration sessions in 1885, but he seems to have done little in the way of setting up new associations. The lack of strong central liberal organisation was accompanied by differences over policy and over the question of relations with the other parties. Another problem for the liberals linked with these was the catholic–protestant tension within their ranks and the falling away of catholic support among the electorate.

From early in 1885 the question of liberal conservative union had been widely discussed in the liberal papers. H. de F. Montgomery, a reforming landlord with some liberal sympathies, frequently sent letters to the *Northern Whig* that called for the union of liberals and conservatives, saying that there were no real differences between them and that they must unite in the face of the common enemy, the nationalists. In August Montgomery wrote that while he regretted to have to express the struggle in religious terms he believed all catholics had become supporters of Parnell, a fact that liberals should realise and act upon.[92]

The strongest opposition to this policy came from T. A. Dickson, who had published his pamphlet *An Irish policy for a liberal government* (London) in mid-May 1885. In it he recommended the abandonment of the coercion acts, the passing of a land purchase act, the amendment of local government on a comprehensive scale, and an entirely new departure in the administration of Irish affairs. The aim of Dickson by these radical policies was clearly to give the liberals a distinctive advanced position that would prevent union with the conservatives and win back catholic support. On 28 May in a speech at a large liberal gathering in Belfast Dickson completely rejected such a union, stated that there were large differences between the two parties, and argued that a linkup would foster sectarian hatred by dividing the country into two hostile camps. He said that they would never show their catholic fellow countrymen that they had lost faith in their liberal principles: he anticipated the time 'when in Ireland they would have a loyal national liberal party — a liberal party composed of all creeds and classes, a party whose aim it would be to advance the best interests of our common country'.[93]

Although some press reports declared that Dickson's ideas had been accepted by the Ulster liberal party as their programme for the general election, there is no evidence that any representative meeting of Ulster liberals took place and adopted this policy, although some small liberal groups did support it.[94] The matter remained a controversial one, full of difficulties for the liberals. When James Bryce at the Ulster reform club on 14 April advocated that the liberals should seek to win catholic and home rule support,[95] one member of the audience wrote to him: 'The chief obstruction to raising a platform on reasonable lines will be the dread of sending anti-catholic liberals into the ranks of the tories.'[96] On the other hand, union with the conservatives threatened to lose the liberals their remaining catholic support. W. T. McGrath, a leading catholic liberal, wrote to the *Northern Whig* in August on this subject to argue that such a union would drive catholics out of the liberal ranks, partly as a result of the way people like Montgomery implied that all catholics were 'rebels' and that protestants faced great danger from a catholic majority.[97]

The Co. Antrim liberal victory in May had given encouragement to Dickson and his viewpoint, but the Co. Down defeat in July had the opposite effect. The growing importance of the national question from midsummer onwards, and the increasing awareness of the failure of the liberals at the revision courts, were further causes of discouragement to Dickson's policies. With no central view on the subject, the relations of the liberals with the other parties in the election campaign were to be determined entirely by local circumstances.

Another matter about which the liberals failed to develop a strong, effective policy was the land question. S. C. McElroy and other liberal tenant righters urged the liberals throughout 1885 to take a radical stand on this issue, but to no effect. In late September McElroy wrote a letter to the newspapers to express anxiety over the liberals' lack of an agrarian policy and to warn that the Ashbourne land purchase act, passed in August 1885 by the conservative government, threatened their support among the farmers.[98] Finally on 9 November a conference on the land question was held in the Ulster reform club under the auspices of the Ulster land committee, at which resolutions were passed demanding reforms in the 1881 land act and better housing for labourers.[99] Many prominent Ulster liberals were present and the liberal party was favourably spoken of, but there does not seem to have been any formal declaration of support by the Ulster liberal party for the resolutions.

For the liberals as well as for the conservatives the changes in electoral law relating to political organisation, the franchise, and the distribution of constituencies, required substantial reorganisation at the local level. The basis of liberal organisation at the beginning of 1885 lay very largely in the tenant right associations. From this basis new divisional bodies had to be formed to deal with an increased electorate that contained not only farmers but many labourers. Also there was the question of relations with the conservatives. The success of the liberals in facing these matters differed considerably between constituencies.

In Co. Londonderry, where the liberals with their strong tenant association backing had controlled the parliamentary representation of the county since 1874, the party organisation changed little in face of the challenges of 1885. At the beginning of the year the chief liberal body in the county was the Co. Derry liberal union, but apart from rejecting overtures for a joint programme from some conservatives the union failed to develop new policies or associations, perhaps because conservative opposition appeared weak and members were confident about the popularity of the two sitting liberal M.P.s. On 12 September, however, at a meeting of the executive of the liberal union McClure indicated that he would not stand again. Samuel Walker, the other sitting M.P., was duly chosen for the northern division but it was not until 5 October that William Findlater, M.P. for Co. Monaghan, was selected for South Londonderry at a gathering of liberal representatives for polling districts in the division. Subsequent to these selections, well attended local meetings, which included farmers and labourers, were held in the county, although no special effort was made to incorporate the latter in the liberal organisation.[100]

In North Antrim the Route reform association was formed in Ballymoney on 3 April 1885 by members of the tenant right associations in the district;[101] representatives from other tenant right groups in the division were later included in the new body. Among the aims of this organisation were preservation of the union with Great Britain, amendment of the land laws, and the improvement of the conditions of labourers. In late August a meeting of the association was held and W. P. Sinclair, the recently elected liberal M.P. for the county, was selected to stand for the divisional seat. On this occasion John Pinkerton, a local member of the association, was also suggested as a candidate, but he refused to allow his name to go before the meeting, which, he said, 'while it represented the presbyterian farmers, did not, in his opinion, adequately represent the Roman Catholics or the labourers'.[102] He subsequently stood as an independent for the division. A Route farmers' and labourers' association was formed, but not until after the election on 1 December.[103]

In East Antrim local committees were set up from June onwards in areas such as Ballyclare, Carrickfergus, and Larne, with assistance from Mathew Wylie as well as Carrickfergus liberals and tenant association workers. On 17 October a meeting of delegates from various polling districts in East Antrim was held in Belfast when it was decided that the liberals of the constituency should put forward a candidate.[104] M. R. Dalway, former independent conservative M.P. for Carrickfergus, was selected, although his candidature was not confirmed until the end of the month. In spite of warnings from the liberal leaders to local organisations, such as the Roughfort liberal association, to persuade labourers to join, there is little evidence of a strong effort in this direction.[105]

In Mid and South Antrim liberal reorganisation does not seem to have been so efficient as in the other two divisions. In mid October a meeting of delegates from different polling districts took place and a committee was set up to select a candidate, but only in the second week of November did J. D. Barbour, a prominent Lisburn manufacturer, emerge as the party nominee. In Mid Antrim a conference of liberal delegates in late October passed a resolution in support of T. A. Dickson as candidate. Dickson was still standing for a Tyrone seat at this stage and accepted the Antrim offer only about two weeks before nomination day.[106] In neither of these divisions does much local organisation seem to have occurred and tenant right associations were not even noticeably evident in assisting the liberal cause, probably because the new constituency divisions removed the dominant influence and leadership of the Route association, and because the land question was not the main issue.[107]

In Co. Down the liberal organisation was much less efficient. On

30 May 1885 a meeting of delegates representing different polling districts in North Down took place in Newtownards to set up a central committee and make plans for the selection of a candidate. In mid-October J. S. Brown, who had been defeated at the 1885 Down by-election, was chosen.[108] In East Down delegates from various districts met on 13 November and names of possible candidates were discussed but none picked.[109] In South and West Down there was little activity by the liberals and no candidates were selected. This apathy in Co. Down may partly have arisen from disillusionment caused by the by-election defeat.

In Co. Armagh by 1885 the county liberal association formed in 1881 had collapsed, but had been replaced by a new central liberal association. On 9 October a meeting of the association was held in Armagh at which representatives from all the polling districts of Mid Armagh were present. It was resolved to ask James Wylie, a land commissioner, to stand. Wylie agreed and for the next 6 weeks the liberals conducted a vigorous campaign in the constituency against the conservative candidate. But on the day of nomination a nationalist candidate came forward and Wylie withdrew, reckoning that the nationalist's candidature would mean the loss of his catholic support and so cause his defeat.[110] This appearance of the nationalist was the result of a secret conservative–nationalist pact. (See below p.206.) In North Armagh liberal organisation existed primarily in the shape of the Portadown liberal club. At a meeting in early November of the club and representatives from other local committees, Thomas Shillington, a Portadown businessman and prominent liberal, was selected.[111] There does not appear to have been any liberal organisation in South Armagh.

In Cos Fermanagh, Monaghan, and Cavan, and three of the four Co. Donegal divisions, there is no evidence of the liberals making any attempt at organisation during 1885. In the remaining county divisions the liberals did organise, but in these counties the question of union with the conservatives was an important one, whereas in Cos Down, Antrim and Armagh it had not had a direct influence on the liberal electoral machinery. In East Donegal liberals and conservatives cooperated in assisting the candidature of Thomas Lea, sitting liberal M.P. for the county, and a conservative candidate in the division withdrew for the sake of unity among constitutionalists.[112]

From early in the year, union between liberals and conservatives had been a subject of great controversy in Co. Tyrone. On 21 May the Tyrone liberal association discussed plans for reorganisation;

confidence was expressed in Dickson as leader of the Ulster liberals in the house of commons. Two days later Dickson met some of the leading Tyrone liberals, who gave their backing to his policies and his opposition to union with the conservatives.[113] Committees were now reported as being established in the various divisions to form liberal organisations. Approaches in mid-June by Tyrone conservatives to the Tyrone liberal association, seeking cooperation, came to nothing.[114] On 19 June an organising committee was set up for South Tyrone and it was stated in the papers that Dickson would be the liberal candidate for the division.[115]

But from this time on developments started to go against the position of Dickson and his followers. The national league continued to grow in strength in the county. Towards the end of June a Father Macartney, speaking at a national league meeting at Donoughmore, said that the change of mind of the Ulster liberals on coercion had come too late.[116] During July preparations got under way for the registration planned for September and it became apparent to many of the liberals that they could expect little support from the newly enfranchised labourers, either catholic or protestant. On 3 August E. T. Herdman, president of the Tyrone liberal association, wrote a letter to the press acknowledging differences between conservatives and liberals but saying they must join together in opposition to the nationalist party, which sought to make Ireland a distinct nation, separate from Great Britain.[117] These developments seem to have greatly harmed liberal support and organisation and at the revision courts in early September there were no liberal agents present, the conservatives taking it upon themselves to look after all 'loyalists'.

The situation developed differently in each division. In South Tyrone, four days after the conservatives announced that John Ross would be their candidate, T. A. Dickson declared his intention to stand on his original policy. A bitter feud now broke out between the conservatives and Dickson, with the latter saying that he had intended for some time to stand, while the former said Dickson had only recently come forward and would divide the unity of those opposed to the nationalists.[118] A private conference about the matter was held in the Belfast constitutional club, but this failed to provide an amicable solution.[119] Finally on 18 November Dickson withdrew, obviously aware that the conservative's candidature would spoil his chances. In a statement he blamed 'the persevering hostility . . . manifested by the landlord section of the tory party' for his withdrawal and urged the liberal tenant farmers in Co. Tyrone

to resent the 'arrogant pretensions' of the conservatives.[120] Several
local liberal committees in South Tyrone subsequently resolved to
abstain in the election. The conservative–liberal conflict in South
Tyrone seems to have been partly a result of bad feeling between
Dickson and local conservatives on personal grounds.

In the other divisions the liberals were less prepared to stand on
their own. In early September it had been rumoured that J. B.
Gunning Moore would come forward for a Tyrone division. On 16
October he issued an address for East Tyrone, but on 17 November
his committee decided that he should withdraw to avoid a split in the
loyalist vote. On 21 October at a meeting of the North Tyrone
liberal association, under the chairmanship of E. T. Herdman, president of the county liberal association, a pledge was taken to
support the conservative candidate for North Tyrone, the marquis
of Hamilton, if the conservatives did not contest South Tyrone; at
this point Ross had just retired from South Tyrone and an alternative conservative had not yet been picked for the division.
Although Somerset Maxwell was later chosen by the conservatives
in opposition to Dickson, the liberals continued to back Hamilton
and in the last weeks of the campaign Herdman spoke on
Hamilton's platform. In Mid Tyrone a meeting of local liberals on
24 October deferred selection of a candidate and no one was chosen
in the end.[121]

In the boroughs the liberals faced similar problems of reorganisation. In Belfast during late 1884 the revived liberal
association had considerably increased membership and at
its annual meeting in January 1885 the need for new divisional
organisations was emphasised.[122] In spite of certain religious and
social tensions[123] the association continued to grow and on 13 April
the Belfast liberal club was started under its auspices as a political
and social centre for Belfast liberals with a low subscription fee to
encourage wide membership. During August J. S. Brown, president of the Belfast liberal association, rejected union with the conservatives.[124] But the impetus was not maintained, perhaps because
of a growing awareness among the liberals of the success of the
other parties in relation to the new electors.

In East Belfast a local liberal club opened at Mountpottinger
during the first week of October. On 24 October at a meeting of the
general committee of liberal electors of East Belfast R. W. Murray,
a Belfast merchant, was chosen as candidate. Arrangements were
made for canvassing and organising his campaign. In South Belfast
at a gathering of liberal electors on 3 November John Workman,

another merchant, was selected as candidate and a committee was set up to organise his campaign. In West Belfast there does not seem to have been any liberal organisation and most of the liberals appear to have accepted the conservative candidate, who was chosen so as to appeal to as wide a range of non-nationalists as possible. In North Belfast no liberal organisation materialised. On 9 October, however, Alexander Bowman, secretary of the Belfast trades council, and a former Belfast liberal, was presented with a petition signed by between 400 and 500 electors asking him to come forward as the working men's candidate for North Belfast. He consented and a committee was formed to assist him.[125]

In Newry the liberal party seem to have collapsed altogether. In Derry some liberals survived, but did not put forward a candidate for the city. The question of whom they should support at the election, however, was an important one, as it became clear during August and September that the liberals held the balance between the conservatives and the nationalists. On 23 November at a meeting of Derry liberals a decision was taken to abstain in the election, partly as a consequence of the conservatives opposing the liberals in Co. Londonderry.[126] Just prior to the poll, however, pleas were made by a number of prominent Ulster liberals to the Derry liberals to vote for the conservative and save the city from the nationalists.[127] At a gathering of liberals in Derry on 25 November the decision to abstain was revoked and it was left to each to decide how to vote;[128] a proposed agreement with Parnell for them to support the nationalist candidate in return for the nationalist vote in North Londonderry was not accepted, which left the way open for the liberals to back the conservative candidate.

With the franchise and redistribution reforms of 1884-5 the problems of registration increased enormously for the liberals. From a study of the revision sessions it is clear that the liberals met this challenge less effectively than the other two parties.[129] They developed no new scheme of organisation to deal with the changed situation and continued to rely on the efforts of Mathew Wylie. In the circumstances of the greatly increased electorate Wylie could not cope alone, but rarely is there evidence of local associations helping with this work. Apart from Co. Londonderry and some of the Antrim divisions, the attendance of liberal agents at the revision courts was seldom regular or effective. After the general election, indeed, the *Witness* passed harsh comment on the liberal inactivity: 'with the exception of four or five county divisions in Ulster the liberals gave themselves no trouble about the register and suffered matters to tide on without any guidance and judgement, to go by default.'[130]

The liberal electoral organisation was strongest in Cos London-derry and Antrim, weak in Belfast and Cos Down, Armagh, and Tyrone, and largely non-existent elsewhere. Where liberal candidates stood, committees were organised, canvassing carried out, and public meetings held. There is far less evidence of participation of presbyterian ministers in the liberal organisation than before, and none of catholic clerical involvement. All the liberal candidates were presbyterian except J. D. Barbour, who belonged to the Church of Ireland. The two independent candidates, Pinkerton and Bowman, organised their own campaigns; Bowman refused on principle to canvass.

Viewing liberal reorganisation in general during 1885 it is apparent that the liberals found considerable difficulty in readjusting to the new circumstances brought about by the electoral reform acts of 1883-5. The fact that the liberals were traditionally based mainly on tenant right associations, and not party political organisations, no doubt contributed to this. Also it is clear that the changing political circumstances found them uncertain over policy and their relations with other parties. Thus the picture of the liberals that emerges at this time is one of inactivity and bad organisation, and not one of vitality and good organisation as suggested by an apologist of the liberals and several modern historians.[131]

The parties in Ulster: (c) nationalists
For the nationalists in Ulster the electoral changes of 1883-5 presented both considerable opportunities and difficulties. By 1885 it was clear that a significant proportion of the catholics in the province would support the nationalist party, and as catholics were a majority in many of the new divisions this meant that nationalists could expect to make a large inroad into the parliamentary representation of the north. At the same time, however, the nationalists faced two difficult problems: first, the construction of an effective political organisation to replace the original home rule associations, which had collapsed; secondly, the question of their relationship to protestants and to the other parties.

Although the nationalists at the start of 1885 did not have a proper organisation in Ulster, they had the beginnings of one in the national league, which had branches in many of the northern counties and towns. In late 1884 and early 1885 important developments occurred in the leadership in Ulster. During 1884, in the absence of much attention from the central committee of the national league in Dublin, the movement in the province had come under the leadership of the local council in Belfast. An important adjunct of this was that the Belfast body was sympathetic towards the person and policies of Michael Davitt, who was at odds with the Dublin leadership because of his support for land nationalisation. Steps were taken in the second half of 1884 and beginning of 1885 to reassert the authority of the central committee.

In July 1884 the headquarters in Dublin issued a circular to all the northern branches, insisting that they must adhere to its leadership. Nothing more happened until the end of the year when Timothy Harrington, M.P., secretary of the league, instructed the Belfast council to convene a meeting in December. This instruction was rejected and Harrington himself organised a meeting in Belfast on 29 December which was addressed by T. P. O'Connor, J. G. Biggar, and other nationalist M.P.s. Resolutions were passed, which expressed confidence in the Irish nationalist parliamentary party under the leadership of Parnell and recorded thanks to the central committee in Dublin for its work in the north.[132]

This meeting was a clear challenge to the local leaders of the national league in Belfast. Shortly afterwards, John Duddy, president of the Belfast council, wrote to the papers to complain that the Dublin committee sought to replace their organisation in Belfast with a more pliable body. He stated that the main reason for these actions was concern over Michael Davitt's connections with the Belfast body: 'The public know very well that it is our friendship for and our admiration of that stainless patriot that has drawn upon us the enmity of the national league'.[133]

Faced with this challenge, however, the national league organisation in Belfast collapsed and by 24 January 1885 only one branch out of a total of five remained.[134] In the last week in January a meeting was held in St Mary's Hall in Belfast to reorganise the national league in the town. J. G. Biggar, on behalf of the central committee, chaired the meeting and a provisional committee was established to set up new local branches.[135] These changes were followed by other steps to remove Davitt's influence. C. J. Dempsey, editor of the *Morning News*, retired early in 1885 from his post, largely it seems as a result of political pressure arising from this conflict. Writing to John Pinkerton, Dempsey remarked: 'I have ceased to have any connections with the *Morning News*. . . . I am too great a disciple of Davitt's . . . the M.P.s want me effaced from Ulster politics.'[136] These moves by the Dublin headquarters were completely successful and no effective opposition appeared.

Under the active direction of Harrington the national league now underwent considerable expansion in the north in several stages during 1885. Meetings were held of existing national league representatives and sympathisers in most of the Ulster counties in January and February to discuss redistribution. The opportunity was taken at these meetings by Harrington or his associates to urge upon all present the need for strong efforts to set up local branches. Then in May and early June conventions were held in the counties, often chaired by Harrington, and talks were given on the problems of organisation in preparation for registration and the general election. Throughout the summer meetings were held in the constituencies, at which addresses were given by leading nationalist M.P.s.

While these meetings took place to arouse nationalist support, organisation at the local level grew through national league branches, which were established throughout the province to act as the organisational framework of the nationalist party. Although the national league was primarily aimed at farmers, attempts were made to include labourers, and resolutions were often passed at national league meetings in favour of labourers' interests.[137] R. E. Beckerson of the chief secretary's office, in his report to Lord Carnarvon on national league activity over the period 1 Jan.–30 June 1885, commented: 'The most noteworthy feature is the progress that the league is making in Ulster, especially in Armagh, Down, Fermanagh, Tyrone and Monaghan; three new branches have even been started in Co. Antrim.'[138]

With the national league branches acting as local political organisations, county committees were established for the purpose of overall control of the nationalist movement in each county. Speaking on 1 June 1885 at a convention in Newry of delegates from national league branches in Cos Armagh and Down and Newry, Harrington urged that they should form county committees composed of the priests of the county as ex-officio members and delegates from the various national league and registration associations of the county.[139] This was also the basic structure of the county conventions called in October and November to select parliamentary candidates. The chairman of the selection conventions was usually a member of the nationalist parliamentary party and the organising committee of the national league, which were therefore able to exercise an important influence over affairs in the constituencies. T. P.

O'Connor, who himself presided at a convention, described what normally happened:

> These conventions were presided over by a member of the party; he came there with his written instructions, the first of which was to get the man through who had been chosen by the committee in Dublin. He had also in many cases a second or third name up his sleeve, so to speak. In some cases where the candidate was known as somewhat undesirable, the chairman was expected to take any and every measure to prevent his being chosen.[140]

In Ulster this procedure worked efficiently and with little sign of protest.

In speeches during the year, nationalist politicians often referred to the importance of uniting catholics and protestants in the nationalist movement.[141] At the same time the nationalist party was keen to retain the support and help of the catholic clergy. Acceptance by the party leadership in the middle of 1885 of catholic claims in educational matters won the approval of the catholic hierarchy, which had hitherto been suspicious of Parnell and his plans.[142] The national league throughout Ireland was based largely on the catholic parochial framework and in many instances local catholic clergy themselves set up branches of the league or were later invited to participate.[143] Nationalist politicians had recognised the organisational and leadership value of the catholic clergy by giving them a special place in the county conventions. Indeed their position in these selection conferences was strengthened by the intervention of Archbishop Walsh of Dublin: in late September he wrote to Tobias Kirby that he had got 'the position of the priests recognised *as priests* in the county conventions for the selection of M.P.s'.[144] The failure of the nationalists to make a significant appeal to the protestant electorate became even clearer in the last quarter of the year when the party decided to run candidates only in divisions with a catholic majority.

The extent of nationalist organisation varied considerably between constituencies. The first convention in Ulster to select candidates for the forthcoming elections was held in Co. Cavan where there had been a strong base of home rule support as far back as 1874. The convention took place on 19 October at St Patrick's College in Cavan town.[145] There were present around 32 clergy and 140 lay delegates from different national league branches throughout the county, along with two representatives from Dublin, Arthur O'Connor M.P. and Bernard Kelly M.P. After a private meeting, presided over by Rev. Dr Finnegan, P.P., Drumlane, it was announced that they had selected J. G. Biggar, the former county member, for West Cavan, and Thomas O'Hanlon, a licensed grocer from Derry, for East Cavan. Public speeches followed.

In the case of both Cos Monaghan and Donegal, there was not such a long tradition of nationalist organisation as in Cavan. T. M. Healy's success as a home rule candidate in the 1883 by-election in Monaghan had marked the beginning of a nationalist movement in the county. Growth in the number of national league branches, however, was especially noticeable in early 1885. This development had the approval of Bishop Donnelly who had earlier been suspicious of the land league,[146] and the bishop was at the railway station in Monaghan on 22 October to greet the two party representatives, T. M. Healy and T. P. O'Connor, on their arrival to attend the convention for the county.[147] At the subsequent meeting held in the Christian Brothers' school in the town, Healy was selected for the northern division and Sir J. N. McKenna, a lawyer from Youghal, for the southern.

In Co. Donegal the national league had made relatively little impact before 1885 but in that year it grew considerably with catholic clergy playing a leading part in setting up and leading local branches.[148] At the selection convention on 10 November, held in the national league hall in Letterkenny, 53 clergy and 176 lay representatives from 48 national league branches were present as well as representatives from the Dublin committee.[149] J. E. O'Doherty, a Derry solicitor, was selected for the northern division; Bernard Kelly, a Ballyshannon businessman, for the southern; Arthur O'Connor, M.P. for Queens Co., for the eastern; and Patrick O'Hea, a Cork solicitor, for the western. In Donegal, as in Cavan and Monaghan, public meetings were held throughout the year to arouse public support for the nationalist cause.

In Cos Tyrone, Fermanagh, and to a lesser extent Armagh, nationalist organisation was also widespread and efficient. In Tyrone there were already a number of national league branches at the beginning of 1885 but in the course of the year these expanded rapidly.[150] After a conference of national league delegates at Omagh on 22 May, secretaries were appointed for each of the four divisions in Tyrone to set up organising committees in each constituency and a central body was formed to supervise the whole county.[151] The convention to select parliamentary candidates was held on 29 October. The numbers at the meeting were so large that it had to be held in an Omagh shirt factory.[152] A total of 51 clergy, 175 lay representatives from 43 national league branches and 3 registration associations, and 10 guests attended. For North Tyrone they chose John Dillon, a Dublin-born doctor and former M.P. for Co. Tipperary, for Mid Tyrone M. J. Kenny, a lawyer from Co. Clare and former M.P. for Ennis, for East Tyrone, W. J. Reynolds, a Dungannon solicitor, and for South Tyrone William O'Brien, editor of *United Ireland* and former M.P. for Mallow.

During 1885 in Fermanagh considerable steps were taken to set up an effective nationalist organisation and to arouse sympathy for the nationalist cause. In May, June and July conferences were held in Enniskillen under national league auspices.[153] Advice was given on various electoral matters and money was raised to fund registration costs. Catholic clergy took a prominent part in these various meetings but so also did Jeremiah Jordan, an Enniskillen methodist and former liberal. On 20 October the selection convention for the county was held in the catholic literary society rooms in Enniskillen.[154] Jordan's name was put forward as candidate but he withdrew in favour of the two candidates chosen by the party representatives from Dublin — W. H. K. Redmond, former M.P. for Co. Wexford, who stood for North Fermanagh, and Henry Campbell, the private secretary of Parnell, who came forward for South Fermanagh. Jordan was selected later as nationalist candidate for West Clare.

In Co. Armagh there were only four national league branches in the county at the beginning of 1885,[155] but in the course of the year the organisation grew. A selection convention for the county was held in Armagh city on 19 November and Alexander Blain, a local tailor, was chosen for South Armagh, while it was also decided not to contest the other two divisions.[156] During the selection procedure, however, difficulties arose that later led to a nationalist candidate being nominated at the last moment for Mid Armagh. According to his memoirs T. M. Healy, who presided at the Armagh convention on behalf of the Dublin central committee, went to the meeting with instructions to oppose James Dempsey, former editor of the *Morning News*, who was one of those to be put forward as a potential candidate.[157] Although Parnell had earlier promised Dempsey a seat because of his cooperation at the Co. Londonderry by-election of 1881, he had turned against him on account of his sympathies for Michael Davitt. Healy proposed another candidate, a local man called Ivor McGuiness, but the clergy favoured Dempsey. Deadlock ensued and finally Healy put forward Blane, who knew nothing about it beforehand, as a compromise candidate, and he was selected.

There was concern, however, that an independent nationalist might stand for the seat and Blane would lose because, in Healy's words, 'nobody knew him and snobbery was rampant.' So private arrangements were made by Healy with the leading Armagh conservative organiser, T. G. Peel, that Blane would be unopposed in South Armagh and in return the nationalists would contest Mid Armagh to spoil the liberal's chances there. On nomination day for Mid Armagh, Edmund Leamy, also nationalist candidate for North-East Cork, was put forward for the division, although he had no chance of winning. A conservative candidate appeared briefly in South Armagh, which effectively scotched rumours of an independent nationalist standing for the seat, but he withdrew shortly before nomination, leaving the field clear for Blane.

Such deals of course, did have dangers if discovered and Healy described amusingly how he and Peel dispelled any suspicions of their followers:

> That night Peel came to me in the dark. His friends, he mourned, were suspicious because they had seen us talking together. Said he, 'You'll be speaking to-night to celebrate Blane's election, and I'd like you to give me a few "touches" just to show the nationalist hatred of me.' I gladly agreed, and before the meeting assembled I got "made wise" on Peel's seed, breed, and generation. I descanted, therefore, on his misdeeds, past, present, and to come, to the delight of the crowd.
>
> Next morning, on leaving Armagh, I found Peel at the railway station. Greeting me ruefully, he took me to the waiting-room and complained, 'Oh, sir, I asked you to give me a "few touches", but I didn't expect such a scourging!' 'Well,' I apologized, 'how could I gauge what would dispel the suspicions of your friends? Now they can't blame you for a little talk with me!'[158]

Although Healy's later account does not tie in exactly with the precise chronology of events in these Armagh constituencies, there is little doubt that he and Peel did come to such an agreement, which explains the otherwise largely inexplicable appearance of their candidates in the respective divisions.

In Cos Londonderry, Antrim, and Down nationalist organisation was effective in some areas but noticeably weak in others. In Londonderry national league activity was stronger in the southern part of the county than in the north. Catholic clergy do not seem to have been so prominent in the national league branches as elsewhere. Rev. John McCullagh, P.P., in fact, refused an invitation to attend the inaugural meeting of the Eglinton national league branch. In a letter read out at the meeting he said that he thought it

best to leave the branch in the hands of the local lay organisers so
that 'small farmers and working men of all creeds and denominations,
whose interests are to be promoted by the league, will more readily
join you when they see you know that you will have no sectarian
motives in mind'.[159] In contrast to most other nationalist selection
conventions in the province the meeting was held not in a catholic
hall but in the old court house at Magherafelt on 16 November.[160]
T. M. Healy was selected for South Londonderry. No one was
chosen for the northern division but it was agreed to back whomso-
ever Parnell recommended from the other parties.

In Co. Antrim there was only a small number of national league
branches. The county convention was held on 17 November at
Loughgiel, near Ballymoney.[161] It was agreed not to field any candidate of their own and to support only the persons endorsed by
Parnell. Delegates, both clerical and lay, were appointed to each
division to receive communications from the nationalist leader as to
whom their followers should vote for. The national league was weak
also in Co. Down. In the first week of November a convention was
held in Newry to select candidates for Co. Down, and J. F. Small, a
solicitor from Newry and M.P. for Co. Wexford, was picked for
South Down. No candidates were chosen for the other divisions and
the question of whom nationalists should support in these areas was
left to the party leadership.[162]

As regards the boroughs, here also the nationalist organisation
was based on the national league. In Belfast the newly constituted
national league held meetings and conventions from early in the
year, and in the press the intention of the nationalists to contest
West Belfast was frequently reported. Because of the death of
Bishop Dorrian the selection convention for Belfast was postponed
until mid-November. Thomas Sexton, a Dublin journalist and well
known former member for Co. Sligo, was chosen for West Belfast.
It was decided not to contest the other divisions.[163] In early
November J. H. McCarthy, journalist and former M.P. for
Athlone, was selected for Newry at an open-air convention held in
the town.[164] In Derry city it was rumoured for some time that
Thomas Sexton would be the nationalist candidate, but at the
selection convention for the city in the first week of November,
Justin McCarthy, author, journalist, and former M.P. for
Longford, was chosen.[165] There were delegates at the convention
from three national league branches in the city and a registration
association.

In face of the challenge and opportunity provided by the new franchise and redistribution laws, the nationalists in Ulster began 1885 in a weak position but in the end responded well, especially in mid and west Ulster. At the revision sessions the national league put forward professional agents, backed by local organisers.[166] Some of these registration agents were former workers for the liberals or catholic registration societies while a number were provided from southern constituencies by the central national league organisation. The nationalist efforts at the registration courts in Ulster in 1885 were later described graphically by A. M. Sullivan jun., who left his studies in Dublin to come to help the nationalist cause.

> The nationalists had perceived that it was in the revision courts that constituencies were to be lost or won, and upon the work of revision they concentrated all their force. They had at their disposal the services of a brilliant band of young solicitors, and recognising the value of the enthusiasm of youth, the national league trained an army of young men and boys, taught them the franchise act, instructed them in the mysteries of the 'inhabitant householder' and in technicalities of a lodger's claim, and sent them forth to find electors to be put upon the register. The quest was most successful.

Sullivan recalled the enthusiasm of his support for the cause.

> When the register was complete, no time was lost in preparations for the elections. Youth again was summoned to the political class room. Personally I was far better acquainted with the provisions of the ballot act and corrupt practices act than I was of the Gallic war, at a time when I was supposed to be studying the Gallic war and not the ballot act. Thus it happened that in the middle of my teens I found myself, at his request, taking part in Willie Redmond's campaign in North Fermanagh at the end of the autumn of '85.[167]

Viewing their position generally, the nationalists were well organised in Cos Cavan, Donegal, Monaghan, Tyrone, and Fermanagh, and in Newry and Derry; in a few of the other constituencies they also had a reasonable organisation. The national league provided the basis of their movement and the local branches, aided or led very often by catholic clergy, gave invaluable assistance in canvassing and organising affairs on election day. The strong central organisation of the league not only supplied important help in setting up local groups and arranging selection of candidates but also provided financial assistance for registration and election costs. Thus, from a position of weakness in early 1885, the nationalists had dramatically improved their position by the eve of the poll. All their candidates in Ulster were catholic.

Because the nationalists did not put forward candidates for every northern division, this left an uncommitted nationalist vote in some areas, which now became very important in the struggle between liberals and conservatives. In late October 1885 the possibility arose that Parnell would come to a private arrangement with the Ulster liberals over some of the constituencies not contested by nationalists. On 23 October 1885 Katherine O'Shea wrote to Lord Richard Grosvenor, the liberal chief whip, to say that her husband, Capt. W. H. O'Shea, had failed to win renomination for a Co. Clare division and, with Parnell's backing, she was anxious to find him a seat in Ulster as a liberal.

> Under the circumstances Mr Parnell promises that if Mr O'Shea is adopted as the liberal candidate for Mid Armagh, where the catholic votes are within 600 of the episcopalians and presbyterians combined, Mr Parnell will get him the whole of the former vote and will moreover give his votes for East Down, North Armagh, and North Derry to the liberal candidates. He will also secure the Irish vote in Wolverhampton to Mr Fowler. . . . The arrangement will certainly cause a gain of three seats to the liberal party, East Down, North Derry and Mid Armagh, which can only be won by such a combination.[168]

While it was known in liberal circles that Mrs O'Shea was Parnell's mistress, the reason given for this request to the liberals was the usefulness of Capt. O'Shea as an intermediary between Parnell and the liberals.[169]

Shortly after this letter was sent, Capt. O'Shea met Grosvenor, confirmed what his wife had said, and stated that T. A. Dickson had agreed to these arrangements but wished South Tyrone to be included.[170] Although Dickson's wish could not be granted because William O'Brien had already been chosen as nationalist candidate for the division,[171] O'Shea proceeded to Belfast where, in Dickson's company, he made enquiries about the possibility of this candidature. Grosvenor, in order to help matters, contacted the rt hon. Samuel Walker who was in Co. Londonderry to promote his own campaign. Walker agreed to assist, although fearful of the danger of losing liberal presbyterian votes if news of a compact with Parnell were disclosed.[172]

Apparently through Dickson, information that the liberals were dealing with Parnell did reach the papers around 29 October, but by this time the possibility of O'Shea standing as a liberal for Mid Armagh had largely faded. According to Walker, 'O'Shea went to Armagh to see the R.C. primate and some priests but they would not touch him as a candidate.'[173] Walker also said that he was satisfied that O'Shea, because he was a catholic, would lose protestant liberal support. These problems were mentioned by O'Shea a short time later when he reported to Grosvenor his withdrawal from the venture because he had found that 'Mr Parnell has (or had) exaggerated the number of his adherents and . . . it is impossible to rely upon the casting of a compensating number of presbyterian votes for a catholic. . . .'[174]

On 24 November Parnell wrote a public address to nationalists in Ulster in constituencies where there were no party candidates.[175] He advised that in North Londonderry the conservative should be supported, but if the Derry city liberals backed the nationalist then North Londonderry nationalists ought to vote for the liberal. In South and Mid Antrim he urged the nationalists to support the liberals, while in North Antrim he declared his preference for John Pinkerton. In North Down he declined to make a firm declaration for either candidate, but said that it should not be forgotten that J. S. Brown 'never lost an opportunity of making himself offensive to the nationalists', and recommended nationalists in North Down, as also in East Antrim and North Armagh, to support liberals only if they firmly opposed coercion. In Belfast he urged nationalists to back the liberals in the South and East divisions if liberal voters stayed away from the poll in the West, endorsed Bowman in North Belfast, and said that if liberals did not abstain in West Belfast then he recommended that they vote for de Cobain in the East division.

Number of contests and issues
In Ulster at the 1885 general election 27 out of 33 constituencies were contested. Altogether 6 candidates, 2 conservative and 4 nationalist, were elected unopposed. In 10 divisions conservatives fought liberals, in 14 conservatives stood against nationalists, in one a liberal ran against a nationalist, while in the remainder there were various combinations of parties involved. In the rest of Ireland 52 out of 68 constituencies were contested. For each division in the southern provinces, excluding Dublin University, there was one nationalist candidate selected by a nationalist convention under the supervision of the national league committee in Dublin, which was chaired by Parnell. Besides a couple of independent nationalists, the opposition to Parnell's nominees in the south came from conservative candidates and some liberals and 'loyalists', most of whom had rather similar policies of support for the union and other general reforms.

Such unity of approach to the issues of 1885 as witnessed in southern anti-nationalist candidates was not found among Ulster politicians. For the liberals and conservatives in the north the main issues in their election addresses were maintenance of the union, land reform, and better conditions for labourers. The two parties, however, tended to put different emphasis on these matters. The conservatives gave prime place in their addresses to support for the union between Great Britain and Ireland and for the integrity of the empire, both of which they now saw threatened by home rule. Most stated their belief that the union was necessary for the peace and prosperity of Ireland. Only in the addresses of William Johnston (South Belfast) and J. M. Stuart (East Tyrone) was home rule specifically opposed on the grounds that it threatened protestantism.[176] Some argued that home rule would bring social and economic revolution, while many wrote of their strong belief in the empire. H. L. Mulholland (North Londonderry) proclaimed:

> As an Irishman, my own interests are bound up with yours; and if favoured with your confidence and honoured by your choice it will be my earnest endeavour to uphold those principles of policy which tend to develop the resources and increase the strength of that great empire in whose prosperity Ireland must share so long as the union is maintained.[177]

The liberals were often accused of having mismanaged Ireland and the empire over the previous five years and of being weak willed against home rule.

After the question of the union the next most prominent issue in the conservatives' addresses was the condition of the labourers. Support was frequently declared for better housing for them. The farmers were reminded that the conservatives had introduced a land purchase act, and promises (usually rather vague ones) were made that whatever further reforms were needed the conservatives would back them. A number referred to the contemporary economic depression and some urged 'fair trade', while others said they awaited the outcome of the commission set up to investigate the reasons for the depression.

The independent conservative candidates differed little in policies from the other conservatives. All made strong declarations of support for the union and the empire. De Cobain (East Belfast) declared that he would consider it his 'special province . . . to watch over and defend the interests of the working classes' and said that he would seek amendments to the employers' liability act and an extension of the municipal franchise to the working classes.[178] Seeds (South Belfast) stated that he was the first parliamentary candidate in Belfast to advocate the employers' liability act and would advocate amendments.[179] Johnston made a general comment about supporting social reform and dealt at length with what he saw as the threat to the union and the empire. Several conservative candidates declared their backing for temperance reform. De Cobain and McKane endorsed female suffrage.[180]

Although tending not to deal with the matter to such length as the conservatives, the liberals in their election addresses all declared their support for the maintenance of the union between Great Britain and Ireland and the integrity of the empire. In most cases the stated reason for opposition to home rule was fear for the prosperity and safety of the country. Frequently the liberals expressed their backing for the empire. T. A. Dickson declared:

> I shall oppose any attempt to weaken the supremacy of the imperial parliament, or to disturb the union between Great Britain and Ireland, believing as I sincerely do that the effect would be disastrous to the best interests of our own country. No measures or proposals shall have my support which aim at separation, or which tend in any degree to impair the integrity of the empire.[181]

The liberal candidates frequently dealt at length with the land question. Among the reforms they advocated were a reduction of judicial rents, the amendment of the 1881 land act to include lease-holders, and an extension of the land purchase scheme. They also endorsed better housing for labourers, an extension of local government, and temperance reform. Many of the candidates mentioned their support for free trade. Thomas Shillington (North Armagh) and John Workman (South Belfast) were the only liberal candidates to endorse female suffrage.[182] Alexander Bowman, independent labour candidate for North Belfast, advocated free primary and technical education, free trade, reduction of hours of labour, and an extension of the vote to women householders.[183]

The nationalists did not have election addresses. Speaking at the first nationalist convention in Co. Wicklow in early October, Parnell repeated an earlier statement that in the new Westminster parliament the nationalist party platform would consist of a single plank — 'the plank of legislative independence'.[184] As regards the future of an Irish parliament he declared his belief that it was impossible to give guarantees, but if Ireland was treated fairly the desire for separation would not increase. He stated also that in any future settlement the Irish parliament must have the right to protect its industries. Several weeks later at the Galway convention he again emphasised the importance of legislative independence, saying the party believed that:

> without the right of making our own laws upon Irish soil all land acts, all

labourers acts, all extensions of the franchise are useless and . . . the desolation of our country must continue, its people diminish and its towns decay, until we have wrested from our English rulers the right of making for Ireland her laws in her own parliament.[185]

Other speakers at this Galway convention spoke of the 'national cause of Ireland', the struggles of Ireland over seven centuries, and English misgovernment in Ireland.

In their speeches the Ulster nationalist candidates reiterated these points. They declared enthusiastic support for the principle of Irish legislative self-government, and for Parnell and the nationalist party. At a meeting at Belleek, Co. Fermanagh, on 19 November W. H. K. Redmond proclaimed that they would be enemies of English power in Ireland 'so long as England refused them their parliament, which God ordained they should have'.[186] Frequently the union was declared to have been a failure. In a speech in Belfast in November 1885 Thomas Sexton stated: 'We look back to the year of the union, along that level plain of years to see the shameful, the miserable results of English ruin in Ireland . . . The population of Ireland was greater than now, the comfort of the people was greater. . . .'.[187] He then asserted that the policy of England in Ireland had been to ruin her manufacturing industries and her agriculture. Speakers often referred to past sufferings of the Irish people and claimed that a new future now lay ahead, thanks to the franchise changes and the nationalist party. William O'Brien, at a rally at Glenties, Co. Donegal, on 18 September, remarked:

> This Celtic race of yours will neither die nor go to America. This Celtic race of ours is looking up in the world. . . . You have the weapon of popular organisation in the national league, and you have the weapon of the new franchise. For centuries the enemies of Ireland have had it all their own way. Here in Donegal you and your fathers before you lived in perpetual terror of your lives, terror of eviction, terror of starvation. . . . You had no body to speak for you, no body to fight for you. . . . Well, these days are gone — thank God for it, and the day of the peoples' power has come.[188]

Great emphasis was placed in northern nationalist speeches on the call for the end of landlordism. In his speech at Belleek in November W. H. K. Redmond urged the people to help the nationalist party to drive the landlords out:

> What had landlordism done for them in the past that they should trust it in the future? Let them listen to the cry of those who suffered in the past, saying to them in the name of God to take this opportunity that had been given to them to drive these men from the face of the country, and

secure for themselves, their children and the Irish race, the right to live in peace on the soil that God had given them.[189]

On various occasions speakers denied that the nationalist party was hostile to protestants, and appeals were made to protestant and catholic farmers to unite against the landlords, who, it was claimed, were deliberately keeping them apart.[190] Support was often declared for the interests of the labourers.

Results of the poll in Ulster

In Newry, South Armagh, East Cavan, and West Donegal nationalist candidates were elected unopposed, while in East and West Down conservative candidates were returned without a contest. Results in the remaining constituencies are best studied in the order in which they occurred, because the outcome of the earlier elections was important to the later ones. On 26 November the polls for Belfast and Derry city took place. In East Belfast E. S. W. de Cobain, independent conservative, received 3,033 votes against 2,929 for the conservative Sir J. P. Corry, bt, and 870 for the liberal R. W. Murray. In North Belfast 3,915 votes were cast for William Ewart, conservative, and 1,330 for Alexander Bowman, independent. The South Belfast result was William Johnston, independent conservative, 3,610; John Workman, liberal, 990; and Robert Seeds, independent conservative, 871. Several newspaper reports suggested that the catholic vote went to de Cobain in East Belfast and William Johnston in South Belfast;[191] in view of Parnell's letter it is likely that in North Belfast catholics backed Bowman.

In West Belfast and Derry the results were very close. In the former J. H. Haslett, conservative, received 3,780 votes and Thomas Sexton, nationalist, 3,743, while in the latter C. E. Lewis, conservative, obtained 1,824 votes and Justin McCarthy, nationalist, 1,792. The turn-out in both constituencies was just over 93 per cent, higher than anywhere else in Ireland. From press accounts it is clear that the two nationalists received the vast majority of the catholic votes, and the two conservatives the vast majority of the protestant votes, including those of the protestant liberals, which, given the closeness of the two denominations in the two divisions, was of crucial importance;[192] this was in spite of urging in the *Northern Whig* before the election of 26 November that liberals should abstain because of conservative action in South Tyrone and South Londonderry. This protestant liberal support for the conservatives was now to have consequences in other elections. On 28 November the editorial in the *Morning News* declared that after the way the liberals had acted in Derry and West Belfast, catholics in North Londonderry and Mid Antrim should be ashamed of themselves if they backed the liberals there.

On 28 November the North Tyrone and North Antrim elections occurred. The result in North Tyrone was Lord E. W. Hamilton, conservative, 3,345 votes, and John Dillon, nationalist, 2,922. Again it seems that nearly all catholics supported the nationalist and nearly all protestants, including the presbyterian liberals, backed the conservative. In an angry speech after the result was announced Dillon declared that since the liberal votes in the division were largely given against the nationalist then the catholic votes in North Londonderry and Mid Antrim should be cast against the liberal.[193] This advice was to cost the liberals dearly. In North Antrim the conservative Edward Macnaghten, Q.C., received 3,233 votes, less than half the total cast, but won the contest because his opponents divided the other votes almost equally, with W. P. Sinclair, liberal, obtaining 2,149 votes and John Pinkerton, independent, 1,915. Pinkerton appears to have won most of the nationalist vote but not much else. Rev. J. Nolan, C.C., from Ballycastle, wrote to Pinkerton:

> I feel you did not get the support you counted on from the liberal party. Had you followed the plan I suggested of canvassing the liberal farmers and labourers' vote and let the nationalist vote be given for you at the last moment it seems to me it would have been more prudent. . . . [Many] said that as soon as the tendency of the nationalist vote was made manifest it was their duty to go to the opposite side.[194]

Two days later the elections took place for North Armagh, West Cavan, North Londonderry, and North Monaghan. In North Londonderry the outcome was H. L. Mulholland, conservative, 5,180 votes and the rt hon. Samuel Walker, Q.C., liberal 3,017. In this contest the catholic vote, which numbered around 2,850 according to one source,[195] was of vital importance and from several reports it is clear that, in revenge for how liberals voted in Derry city and North Tyrone, it was cast for the conservative.[196] The liberals had actually improved their position since 1880 in Co. Londonderry because their vote for this one division was similar to what it had been at the previous general election for the whole county, but with the catholic vote cast for the conservative they were unable to win. In North Armagh Major E. J. Saunderson, conservative, received 4,192 votes against 2,373 for Thomas Shillington, liberal, and here again it is possible, although there is no press comment on the subject, that the catholic vote was an important element in

Saunderson's victory.

In North Monaghan T. M. Healy, nationalist, polled 4,055 votes and Sir John Leslie, bt, conservative 2,685. Writing after the election to Lord Salisbury, Lady Leslie recorded:

> Monaghan is now a thing of the past and the man who fought for it snuffed out. My dear good Sir John made a gallant fight. Of course he never expected to win. He fought to call the muster roll of the loyalist protestants and well did they respond — so well that we almost can name the few absent ones. 750 good catholics stayed away for the sake of the family.[197]

The West Cavan result was J. G. Biggar, nationalist, 6,425, and Samuel Saunderson, conservative, 1,779. It is very likely that the voting took place on denominational grounds but before the election there was discontent among some protestant farmers against the landlords and this may have rebounded against Saunderson.[198]

In Fermanagh there seems also to have been some unrest among protestant farmers about landlord presence in the conservative ranks, although the conservative organisers had tried to minimise this. The result of the polling in North Fermanagh on 1 December was W. H. K. Redmond, nationalist, 3,255, and J. C. Bloomfield, conservative, 2,822. Besides attributing the conservative defeat to poor organisation, press reports suggested that some protestants may have abstained on account of the feeling against landlords.[199] Shortly before the election Bloomfield's agent had written: 'If the protestants can be got to vote I think we should still win but between ourselves they are excessively apathetic and anything but favourable to Bloomfield or anyone connected with the landlords.'[200]

On 1 December there were elections in North Donegal, North Down, and Mid Tyrone. In the first of these J. E. O'Doherty, nationalist, secured 4,597 votes and Lt-col. H. H. A. Stewart, loyalist, obtained 952. In the second Col. Thomas Waring, conservative, won 4,315 votes, while J. S. Brown, liberal, received 2,841. Again the catholic vote may have been of considerable help to Col. Waring in North Down, although we can note that a large number of people abstained in the election. In the third M. J. Kenny, nationalist, secured 4,299 votes, while H. H. Moore, conservative, won 2,657. Kenny later stated his belief that he only received five protestant votes.[201]

In the ensuing elections the pattern of voting which had emerged over the previous week continued. Where a liberal fought a conservative the catholic vote assisted the conservative.[202] The liberals actually increased their supporters, especially among the farmers; the conservatives also boosted theirs, chiefly among labourers, but in addition they enjoyed vital catholic support.[203] In Mid Antrim the hon. R. T. O'Neill, conservative, with 3,832 votes defeated T. A. Dickson, liberal, with 2,713. A report put the catholic vote at 2,300 and it was suggested that the majority supported O'Neill.[204] In East Antrim Capt. J. M. McCalmont, conservative, received 4,180 votes against 2,105 for M. R. Dalway, liberal. Again it was reported that most of the catholics, who numbered around 1,000, voted for the conservative.[205] In South Antrim W. G. E. Macartney, conservative, with 5,047 votes won against J. D. Barbour, liberal, with 3,680. Reports varied on how catholics polled in South Antrim but it is likely they backed the conservative. In the Antrim by-election of 1885, before the county was split into four divisions, the victorious liberal received 3,971 votes, while at the general election the four liberal candidates secured a total of 10,647 votes but won no seats, mainly because catholic support went to the conservatives or an independent.

In the remaining constituencies where a nationalist faced a conservative or liberal or both, most catholics voted nationalist and most protestants either conservative or liberal. In Mid Armagh Prof. John McKane, conservative, obtained 4,178 votes, while Edmund Leamy, nationalist, won 2,667. In East Tyrone a nationalist, W. J. Reynolds, received 3,919 votes and a conservative, J. M. Stuart, 3,361. In South Tyrone William O'Brien, nationalist, gained 3,435 votes and Capt. S. H. Maxwell, conservative, 3,382. M. J. Kenny, M.P. for Mid Tyrone, later claimed Reynolds polled about 100 protestant votes, by virtue of his being a local man.[206] William O'Brien stated that he himself had secured between 40 and 50 protestant votes and also that 70-80 catholics had deserted him.[207] A local report also suggested that quite a large number of protestant liberals had abstained from the election because of the row over Dickson.[208]

In South Down J. F. Small, nationalist, with 4,995 votes defeated W. H. Kisbey, Q.C., conservative, with 3,743. Although Small was nominated by a protestant and Kisbey by a catholic, voting seems to have been along denominational divisions.[209] In south Monaghan the nationalist Sir J. N. McKenna obtained 4,735 votes against the conservative S. E. Shirley's 963. In South Fermanagh Henry Campbell, nationalist, received 3,574 votes while Frank Brooke, conservative, won 3,181. The one contest where a liberal faced a nationalist, East Donegal, ended in victory for the nationalist

Arthur O'Connor, who obtained 4,089 votes gainst 2,992 for the liberal Thomas Lea, in spite of the conservative electors having fully backed Lea.

Finally in South Londonderry T. M. Healy, nationalist, received 4,723 votes, Col. Hugh McCalmont, conservative, 2,341, and William Findlater, liberal, 1,816. In this one case, however, there is some evidence that protestants supported the nationalist. Healy and a local agent, Louis Smith, claimed that around 500 presbyterians voted for him.[210] Given the denominational figures for the division and the result of the voting it is possible that a considerable number did back him, although 500 may be too high a figure. Healy also claimed that covenanters abstained at the election.[211]

In North Londonderry and Mid Antrim the liberals probably enjoyed a considerable majority of the presbyterian vote and could have won easily with catholic support. In North and East Antrim and North Down they secured more than 50 per cent of the presbyterian vote and could also have won with catholic backing. In Mid Armagh and East and West Down a liberal alliance of over 50 per cent of presbyterians and most catholics could possibly have brought liberal victories.

Summary of results
With the conclusion of the general election it was clear that very significant changes had occurred in the parliamentary representation of Ulster. A total of 16 conservative and 17 nationalist M.P.s had been returned for the province. This contrasted strongly with 1880 when 18 conservative, 9 liberal, and 2 home rule M.P.s were returned.[212] In 1880 the northern M.P.s had consisted of 14 landowners and the rest merchants, manufacturers, or members of the upper professions: apart from 7 presbyterians and 2 catholics, all belonged to the Church of Ireland. In 1885, however, conservatives numbered 5 of the 6 borough M.P.s and comprised a linen manufacturer, a merchant, a solicitor, a former borough cashier and a minor landowner. The 11 conservatives from county divisions included 7 who were prominent landowners or related to important landed families, usually in the divisions which they represented. Of the remaining conservatives, 2 were barristers, 1 an army officer and 1 a professor of law: the 2 barristers, it may be noted, were related to major landowners in their divisions. Conservatives schooled in Ulster numbered 5, while the others were educated privately or at English public schools, and 6 went to university, half to Trinity College, Dublin, and half to Oxford or Cambridge. All

except C. E. Lewis (Derry city) had family connections with Ulster. Only 3 M.P.s were presbyterian, 1 was methodist, and the other 12 were members of the Church of Ireland. About 9 out of the 16 were Orangemen.

The background of the nationalist M.P.s differed considerably from that of the conservatives. Of the nationalist M.P.s, 7 belonged to the legal profession, 2 were merchants, 3 were journalists, 1 was a shopkeeper, 1 a tailor, 1 a private secretary, and 1 a rentier.[213] One of the barristers, Sir J. N. McKenna, South Monaghan, had a small landed estate in Co. Cork. Only 1 nationalist was educated at an English public school and the others attended Irish schools, including Clongowes and Christian Brothers' schools, while 4 seem to have received only a primary education: 2 went to queen's colleges, 1 to University College, London, 1 to Trinity College, Dublin, 1 to the catholic university and 1 to Maynooth College. Of the Ulster nationalist M.P.s, only 8 had family connections with the province. All the nationalists were catholic. Most, if not all, were members of the national league. This divergence between the two parties in the social background of M.P.s is accounted for partly by the differing availability of candidates on each side due to social variations and is also due to the fact that the nationalist party provided a salary for its M.P.s while the conservative party did not.

The significance of the changes that had taken place in 1885 in the parliamentary representation of Ulster can be clearly seen in a comparison of 1885 and earlier results. M.P.s from a landed background numbered 25 in 1868, 19 in 1874, 15 in 1880, and 8 in 1885. Members who were merchants, came from the professions, or were shop-keepers or wage-earners, totalled 4 in 1868 and 24 in 1885. All the M.P.s belonged to the Church of Ireland except for 2 in 1868, 8 in 1874, 11 in 1880 and 21 in 1885. In 1885 presbyterians M.P.s numbered 3 compared with 2 in 1868 and 7 in 1874 and 1880. There were no catholic M.P.s in 1868, 2 in 1874 and 16 in 1885. Whereas in 1868 all the Ulster M.P.s except 4 were educated privately or at English public school, by 1885 the number had fallen to 12; the number with university education also declined.

Party organisation in Ulster in 1885 had changed greatly from that at previous general elections, owing, to a considerable extent, to the 1883 corrupt practices act and the franchise and redistribution acts. This transformation was also partly a result of the growing demand among the population for a larger say in political organisation and affairs. The conservative party had witnessed a marked acceleration in its development away from structures controlled by powerful landed families to broadly based conservative associations that selected candidates and ran the campaigns. The Orange order had an influential place in this modern political framework. For the nationalist party a new organisation was created based largely on national league branches and an important structure was established for choosing candidates and assisting their elections. The catholic clergy had a prominent role in this scheme. The liberal organisation witnessed comparatively little change and in the counties remained based largely on tenant right associations. All three parties had central bodies with different degrees of control over local associations and groups.

In the rest of Ireland 68 nationalists and 2 conservatives were elected. Thus the total number of Irish M.P.s was 18 conservatives, and 85 nationalists.[214] The 2 southern conservatives, elected for Dublin University, were queen's counsels: both were members of the Church of Ireland. The southern nationalists consisted of 5 landowners, 6 rentiers, 5 merchants or industrialists, 15 belonging to the upper professions such as solicitors or barristers, 12 from the lower professions such as journalists and teachers, 20 farmers, shopkeepers, or wage earners, and 3 of undefined occupation. Of the southern nationalists all were catholic except 5. As regards their educational background, only a few had been educated privately or at English public school, while about a third had just received a primary schooling and 27 attended university, mainly Trinity, the queen's colleges or the catholic university. The nationalist party's effective organisation lay in the national league.

In Ulster the election had clearly brought about a very significant transformation in the political representation of the province and in the alignment of sections within the electorate. Perhaps the most startling change was the complete failure of the liberal party. There seem to be several reasons for their collapse. First, they had poor organisation. Their original political party structure, based on the tenant right societies, had not been reorganised sufficiently in face of the new demands caused by the changes in the electoral system, particularly the growth in the electorate and the number of divisions. Secondly they were outmanoeuvred on several occasions by the conservative and nationalist parties, which combined against them. In perhaps as many as six constituencies liberals could have defeated tories if only they had enjoyed extensive catholic support.

Finally, the liberals lacked determined leadership and their policies failed to appeal to a wide enough section of the electors. Shortly after the election Thomas MacKnight wrote to Gladstone about the liberal defeat:

> The low franchise has given electoral power to all the agricultural
> labourers, who in Ulster are, among the catholics, firm nationalists, and,
> among the protestants, Orangemen. When both of these parties com-
> bined against us we were almost necessarily and inevitably beaten.
> Under the old franchise we could have carried nearly all Ulster. The
> tenant farmers generally increase in intelligence and liberality and are
> grateful for what you have done for them, and for old Ireland.[215]

Although MacKnight was too optimistic in his account of liberal
support among the tenant farmers, as the evidence of the 1885 by-
elections indicated, it is clear that the failure of the liberals to win
over the new voters was of considerable importance to the outcome
of the elections. In the changed political circumstances of the time
the liberals, with their policies of land reform, temperate support of
the union, and an appeal to catholic and protestant electors, were
not regarded as relevant by the majority of the voters.

The conservatives had now emerged as the sole elected representatives of non-nationalist opinion in Ulster. In part their success
over the liberals was due to superior organisation. From a narrow
base of county and borough constitutional associations that had
played a limited role in electoral affairs, they had evolved efficient
election machinery in many parts of the province. In addition they
had played the tactics game against the liberals in an effective
manner; in a number of areas the catholic vote was vital for the
conservatives. One individual in particular played a key role in the
conservative reorganisation and tactics. As T. M. Healy, in some
comments about the conservative victory over the liberals,
remarked, 'The man to whose generalship I think most of the
success is due, by which the tories got everything and the whigs
nothing, is E. S. Finnigan. . . . '[216] Besides all this the Ulster conservative party had ably adjusted to the new concerns of the electorate.

A prominent Ulster conservative, Lord Deramore (formerly Sir
Thomas Bateson), later gave an interesting account of the new
political situation in the province:

> The protestant working men are masters of the situation. Under the
> existing franchise the labourers and artisans control the representation
> of all the non-nationalist seats in Ulster. The farmers are really nowhere.
> In 1885, under the lead of the resident gentlemen, the labourers and
> artisans swept every so-called liberal from the different hustings in
> Ulster, and sent 16 members to support your government, the bulk of the
> farmers going for the Gladstone candidates in hope of securing more
> plunder. . . .

It is not the farmers who hold Ulster for the queen, but the labourers and artisans, officered by the landlords.[217]

In this letter Deramore was deliberately attempting to down-grade the importance of the farmers in the electorate, but his comments contain a good deal of truth. The number of gentry among the Ulster conservative M.Ps was lower proportionately than in 1868, but, considering developments in the intervening years, it was surprising how they had survived so well. The conditions of their political role, however, were very different from what they had been before. Their wealth and prestige gave them certain advantages, especially in coping with the expense of living in London, but they were dependent on their political associations and on a broad acceptance of their policies among the protestant electorate, especially the labourers.

There would seem to be several reasons why the conservatives won the approval of the protestant labourers. During the election the conservatives had made a more distinct appeal to the labourers than the liberals, who primarily sought the farmers' support; probably to some degree the labourers backed the conservatives as a protest against the farmers. The conservatives were quite efficient in expanding their organisation to bring in labourers and small farmers, through new structured links with the Orange order in many divisions. Orangeism was still a minority movement among Ulster protestants but it was especially strong in parts of Belfast and among the newly enfranchised agricultural labourers.

Important generally for the conservatives was the fact that they were strongly identified with the defence of the union, the empire, and protestantism, which was now regarded as the main issue. This greatly assisted their cause among protestant voters of all social classes, in county and town. Through their links with the Orange order, which brought great organisational benefit, they consciously wooed the 'protestant' vote, even though this obviously undermined their chances of real support from liberal protestants or catholics (although in 1885 catholic votes were given for the conservatives as a nationalist electoral tactic). Clearly the gentry and the Orange order played a more important role in the new conservative organisation than some historians have allowed.[218]

For the nationalists the general election brought seventeen seats in contrast to the three that they had held before the general election. Their electoral success can be attributed considerably to the effectiveness of the party electoral machinery. In his memoirs A. M. Sullivan jun. described later the smooth running of their new political organisation in Fermanagh and elsewhere.

> The nationalist organisation was being tried for the first time. It proved
> surprisingly efficient. Very little change was ever made in it, and it won
> the tribute of imitation by its foes. The work of bringing voters to the poll
> became so perfect that in the last three elections for North Tyrone in
> which I took part ninety-eight per cent of the living electors recorded
> their votes.[219]

In addition the party leadership had successfully played the tactics
game not only against opponents but also to prevent internal splits.
The nationalist support came almost entirely from catholic electors,
many of whom had previously backed the liberals. In part this
catholic rejection of the liberals seems to have stemmed from a
feeling among catholics that they did not have a sufficient say in the
liberal organisation and also that the liberals were not prepared to
change their policies to meet catholic needs, especially over education. After the election an editorial in the *Weekly Examiner*
welcomed the collapse of the liberals and stated: 'One of the
principal tenets of their political doctrine was a stubborn denial of
catholic claims for denominational education.'[220] But what was also
important for the liberal failure among northern catholics was the
appeal that the objects of the nationalist party now had for them.

The nationalist party with its policy of home rule appeared to
offer a better future. It provided expression to the consciousness
aroused by the land league and national league and allowed catholics
a clear political place.[221] They would soon have, declared J. H.
McCarthy after his election for Newry, "a parliament suited for a
free, catholic country".[222] The party gave promise of change and
improvement in a whole range of social, economic and religious
fields. In addition the success of the nationalists among catholics in
the southern provinces, together with the group identity that clearly
now existed among catholics in Ireland, may also partly account for
the success of the nationalists in the north. In March 1886 Dr Patrick
MacAllister, the new bishop of Down and Connor, expressed his
satisfaction at 'seeing the catholics of Belfast working in harmony
with the rest of Ireland in the cause of nationality.'[223] Through its
links with the catholic clergy, which brought great organisational
benefits, and its efforts to achieve catholic unity, the party had set
out to win the whole catholic vote as a priority, even though this
obviously weakened its appeal to protestants.

In spite of objections from various quarters it was clear that
politics were polarising sharply along protestant–catholic lines. The
editorial in the *Impartial Reporter* of 17 December protested

strongly:

> For our own part we heartily condemn any attempt from any side to sow religious opposition among the people. The boundaries of religion and politics are not coterminous; and we will resolutely oppose to hold that the sacred of religion, where God is omnipotent, shall be dragged down to the level and strife of party politics.

But the outcome of the election was that both unionism and nationalism had become very largely identified with religious division and all the social, sectarian, and sectional interests associated with the two religious groups. But the two camps were not yet completely segregated. Protestants were strongly divided within the pro-union camps. There had not yet been a clear-cut fight over home rule. Even if only for short-term tactical reasons, catholics had voted for the conservative candidates in some areas. The liberals were still a major force, in the countryside if not among the parliamentary representation. In the past political fortunes had changed rapidly and it was possible that this could happen again.

CHAPTER 11 *By-elections, 1885-6*

Between the last contest in the general election of 1885 and the first return of the next general election in the following year less than seven months elapsed. By the end of this brief period, however, the political world had undergone 'an utter change of scene', as Thomas MacKnight called it.[1] The cause of this greatly altered picture was the announcement on 8 April 1886 by Gladstone of a home rule bill for Ireland and the consequent realignment of party groupings in both Ulster and Great Britain in reaction to this. Only two by-elections (both held in February) occurred during these months. Before dealing with these contests, attention will first focus on political developments up to 8 April. The two by-elections will then be studied, and lastly the debate over the home rule bill will be looked at.

The final outcome of the 1885 general election in both Ireland and Great Britain left the political future very uncertain for all the parties in Ulster. Apart from the two Dublin university members, the Ulster conservative M.P.s were now the only non-nationalist parliamentary representatives in the whole country. There was still a conservative ministry in parliament but it was a minority government and in recent years the Ulster conservatives had felt little faith in its good intentions. The nationalist party controlled 85 seats in Ulster and elsewhere, which not only gave it great standing in Ireland but also considerable power at Westminster where it held the balance of seats between the two main parties. However, neither party had yet shown itself as willing to back home rule. The liberals in Ulster now had no seats but the liberal party was the largest in parliament.

Within a short time of the close of the 1885 general election the various political groupings in the province sought to strengthen their positions. On 8 January 1886 a meeting of the executive of the Ulster constitutional club established the loyalist campaign committee to organise public opinion on the home rule question in Ulster and Great Britain.[2] Although this new body was meant to be a broad one for all non-nationalists, it was composed very largely of conservatives. The committee organised an extensive campaign of public meetings in Ulster to protest against home rule, provided speakers to address pro-union meetings in Great Britain, and

226

worked along with the Irish Loyal and Patriotic Union to spread information on the unionist cause.[3]

An important event in this campaign was a mass rally arranged by the committee on 22 February in the Ulster Hall in Belfast and attended by most of the leading conservatives in the north.[4] Lord Randolph Churchill addressed the meeting. His speech, however, contained little that was not already being said at local political gatherings, and besides encouraging some of the loyalist leaders,[5] his presence was of no real importance in the Ulster scene, in spite of his earlier comment about using the 'Orange card'. Approaches were made to the Ulster reform club in mid-January to assist in the campaign, but these were rejected.[6] Efforts to encourage co-operation at constituency level between liberals and conservatives came to nothing in the east of the province but elsewhere the north-west loyalist registration and electoral organisation was set up to unite all non-nationalists, particularly in Tyrone.[7]

At Westminster, because of their suspicions about the intentions of the conservative government, a number of Ulster conservative M.P.s took steps in mid-January 1886 to organise their own independent group. William Johnston recorded in his diary on 14 January: 'At 3, seven Ulster M.P.s met in St Stephen's Club. I was moved to the chair. We unanimously decided on action.'[8] Within a short time it was decided to form a broad-based group including supporters from constituencies outside Ulster. By 23 January there were as many as twenty-six M.P.s working together as a pro-union Irish party.[9] This new organisation gave the sixteen Ulster conservatives a much stronger position than in the previous year and the minority conservative government was now obliged to take their viewpoint seriously into consideration in Irish affairs. The chairmanship of the new party was rotated at meetings between members, probably because of personal rivalries,[10] but Col. E. J. Saunderson soon emerged as the dominant figure, although some members still regarded him with suspicion.[11]

For the nationalist party in Ulster the results of the 1885 general election brought great elation. Public meetings were held throughout the province under the auspices of the national league in support of home rule; new branches of the league were formed.[12] Suggestions that home rule would be resisted by force and a civil war take place were rejected as nonsense. On 6 March the *Ulster Examiner* commented: 'There is no more danger of civil war with Kane, Hanna, and Johnston for its triumvirate, than there was of the queen's crown being kicked into the Boyne when the alien church was disestablished.'[13] At meetings appeals were frequently made to protestants to join the national league, although catholic clergy continued to play a leading role in the organisation of the movement.[14]

The first formal meeting of the nationalist parliamentary party took place in Dublin in the second week of January.[15] Nearly all the Ulster M.P.s were present, Parnell was unanimously elected as chairman, and two resolutions were passed. The first declared that as representatives of the Irish nation they reaffirmed the inalienable right of the Irish people to legislate for themselves; the second announced satisfaction that nationalists were a majority of the Ulster representation, and gave assurances that in a native parliament the rights of all fellow countrymen would be respected. The Irish nationalist parliamentary party was now in a very strong position at Westminster. All members were pledge-bound to support the party under the leadership of Parnell. The nationalist party held the balance between the two major parties in the house of commons.

Although badly defeated at the 1885 general election, the Ulster liberal party survived. The relative silence of the liberals in the first three months after the general election seems to have been a result of their faith in Gladstone and a desire not to get involved in the conservatives' campaign of protest against home rule. While talk of union with the conservatives was rejected firmly by the party leadership, steps were taken in this direction in the north-west of the province. E. T. Herdman, president of Tyrone liberal association, and the duke of Abercorn were the main organisers behind the north-west loyalist registration and electoral association, established on 9 January 1886 to provide a central organisation with local branches for all anti-nationalists.[16] At the annual meeting of the Tyrone liberal association, however, on 20 January Herdman was replaced as chairman by T. A. Dickson, who denounced the scheme.[17] Nonetheless in some areas, such as Mid Tyrone, branches of the N.L.R.E.A. were formed with both former liberals and conservatives.[18] Elsewhere, liberals seem to have made little effort to improve their organisation, although the Route farmers and labourers association was formed on 1 December 1885 and the South Derry liberal union was established in the middle of December.[19]

Efforts to persuade the Ulster reform club or the Ulster liberal society to organise a public meeting of liberal representatives to discuss the future were turned down, partly because of T. A. Dickson's opposition, as premature before Gladstone had made his plans for

Ireland known.[20] Finally, in response to a request from Gladstone to hear views on the future government of Ireland, a representative meeting of Ulster liberals was organised: nearly 600 liberal delegates met in the Ulster Hall on 19 March 1886.[21] Two resolutions, disapproving any exceptional coercive legislation for the country and calling for new measures on the land question, were passed with little opposition.

The third major resolution before the conference, however, created a sharp division of opinion. It expressed confidence in Gladstone, called for greater local government, but strongly opposed the establishment of a separate Irish government. The majority of speakers supported this motion and declared their opposition to home rule for various social, economic, and religious reasons. A minority of speakers, led by T. A. Dickson, opposed the measure on the grounds that they must have confidence in Gladstone on account of his past record and that it would be wrong to close the options open to him. Among other points it was argued that people could live peacefully under a home rule government. An amendment to the resolution proposed by Dickson and his friends was rejected and this third resolution was carried by a large majority.[22] These resolutions were then communicated by a liberal deputation to Gladstone.

Mid Armagh, 1886

The death of the M.P. for Mid Armagh, Professor McKane, occurred suddenly on 11 January 1886. Shortly after, the selection committee of the divisional constitutional association met and extended an invitation to Sir J. P. Corry, defeated conservative candidate in Belfast in 1885 and former M.P. for the town, to stand for Mid Armagh. He accepted and his candidature was approved at a general meeting of the association.[23] The other parties were not so swift to make arrangements about the vacancy.

After the death of McKane the liberal press had suggested that if the conservatives were sincere in their idea of conservative and liberal union they should let the liberals have Mid Armagh, but this suggestion had no effect. Rumours that a liberal might contest the seat were widespread in the period immediately after the seat became vacant, the most likely candidate being James Wylie, who had contested the seat in 1885 but withdrew before nomination. By the end of the second week, the Armagh city branch of the national league had met and decided to back Wylie, but this did not meet with Parnell's approval.[24] T. A. Dickson was now approached by some leading liberals in the division and finally on 27 January he agreed to stand; the local nationalists apparently backed his candidature.[25]

In a brief election address Corry referred to his past parliamentary experience and, in the only specific point of policy, declared that he was opposed to home rule, which he believed would inevitably lead to the separation of Great Britain and Ireland and the break-up of the empire. Dickson's address was much broader and more detailed. He said that his views on the connection between the two countries were well known: he was opposed to separation, and he favoured maintaining the integrity of the empire. Then he stated that the great question of the day was the land question, and he urged the compulsory sale of land. He declared his support for Gladstone.[26]

The poll occurred on 1 February. The result of the voting was Corry 3,930 and Dickson 2,974. In view of the votes cast for the nationalist candidate in 1885 and reports after the by-election, it seems that Dickson received around 300 protestant votes and all of the catholic vote.[27] Dickson's failure was clearly in part due to his late candidature, but also it is apparent that by this time the question of defence of the union had taken a predominant place in the minds of the protestant electors. The conservative with his firm declaration of support for the union appeared a safer candidate; conservative accusations of a liberal–nationalist alliance aided the conservative.[28] Dickson's brother-in-law, Robert MacGeagh, described the situation to James Bryce:

> Mid Armagh election this week emphasises the fact that the liberal party here has, for the time, disappeared as a factor in Ulster politics. While most of the leaders and the more intelligent followers remain true to the party, the great masses of the rank and file, especially in rural districts, have gone over to the tories; or rather forgetting old differences in face of what they consider the common danger, the masses of the two parties have amalgamated as unionists, sinking for the moment all minor questions.
>
>   Hence Dickson was left high and dry and Corry swept in on the tide of 'loyal union'. Altho' the enclosed record of Corry's votes on the land bill was circulated, broadcast among the farmers, and that he publicly admitted its accuracy, and said he could justify it if he had time, it did not lose him a vote. In fact, I believe, if he had told the agricultural constituency he would try to have the act repealed, it would have made little difference, so throughly were the electors alarmed by the charges brought against Dickson of being in the nationalist interest. The home rule scare carried the election, and every other consideration will be regarded as of secondary importance in every protestant homestead in

Ulster until this bogey is laid. The people here are getting more and more determined to oppose an Irish parliament in any form, and I believe the fiat of such an assembly will never run in this province till the strong arm of might enforces it.

MacGeagh stated then that Dickson's friends regretted that he was out of parliament at this time: 'He was the only one of the Ulster liberal members who was looked on with any tolerance by the nationalist lot, as they knew his sympathy with them was much stronger and his views far in advance of his Ulster colleagues.'[29]

North Monaghan, 1886

The North Monaghan by-election arose over T. M. Healy's decision to take his seat for Co. Londonderry rather than Monaghan. At the county convention before the general election, a committee had been appointed to select another candidate for the division in the event of Healy winning in both constituencies and deciding to take his seat in parliament for Londonderry. A meeting was held in early January of the committee, which consisted of four catholic clergymen and three laymen, and it was resolved to ask Parnell to recommend a candidate in place of Healy. In early February it was announced that Patrick O'Brien, a catholic merchant from Liverpool had been selected.[30] O'Brien did not put out an election address, but was assisted in his campaign by a number of nationalist M.P.s.

Shortly before the close of the nominations, J. C. Hall, protestant medical officer for Monaghan union, came forward as a constitutionalist. In his address he declared himself in favour of maintaining the integrity of the empire, stated that he was opposed to handing over the country to 'the mercies' of the national league, and called for a proper settlement of the land question. Hall does not appear to have had the assistance of the Co. Monaghan constitutional association, but there were several clergymen on his platform at meetings, and as he was an Orangeman he undoubtedly had Orange support.[31] The result of the election was O'Brien 4,015 and Hall 2,551. There was no evidence of denominational intervoting. Party differences, however, were now given an entirely new aspect with the announcement of Gladstone's proposals for Ireland on 8 April 1886.

Since returning to power in February 1886 Gladstone had been keenly considering various proposals for the future of Ireland. Different public bodies in Ulster and elsewhere responded well to his request to hear views on the government of the country.[32]

Through James Bryce, the Belfast-born presbyterian M.P.
for South Aberdeen, Gladstone received private reports on the
attitudes of the Ulster liberals, which stressed that they were
strongly opposed to a new legislative body for Ireland.[33] In reaction
to Bryce's comments Charles Russell, a Co. Down catholic who had
become M.P. for South Hackney, advised that the Ulster liberals
had unjustified fears about home rule and would eventually accept
such a measure if there were guarantees of religious freedom and a
generous land act.[34] Whether or not these views from Ulster mattered
in any way to the liberal leader is unclear but in the end, influenced
in part by the strength of the Irish nationalist party in parliament
and divisions within his own party, Gladstone decided to endorse
home rule.[35]

On 8 April 1886 Gladstone sought leave in the commons to introduce a home rule bill for Ireland and a week later promised to bring
in an extensive land purchase act. Before proceeding to give details
of the new proposals, Gladstone mentioned that he had considered
the question of the protestant minority in Ireland and Ulster:
various suggestions for the special treatment of Ulster had been put
to him but he found none satisfactory, although he believed that
there were a number of possibilities that could be discussed later.[36]
Then he outlined his plans for a legislative body that would sit in
Dublin, and would legislate for Ireland as well as control the
country's administration. Defence and foreign relations would still
be controlled by Westminster, and the Irish legislature would be
subject to all the prerogatives of the crown. He stated the belief that
they stood face to face with Irish nationality and that his solution
was the best one for the future of Ireland and the British Isles.

Many hours of debate followed Gladstone's first speech on the
government's home rule proposals before the vote for its second
reading on 7 June. In the first nationalist speech in the house Parnell
welcomed the home rule bill, although he voiced some criticisms of
parts of it. In subsequent speeches he rejected any idea of not
including Ulster in the arrangement: 'we cannot give up a single
Irishman.'[37] Other nationalists repeated and developed these points.
The bill was welcomed as an end to the strife between England and
Ireland. The union was described as a failure, and a parliament in
Dublin was welcomed as the best means to govern the country.
Ireland's position in the empire was upheld. Reference was also
made to fears of protestants and opposition in Ulster. It was
denied that there was catholic intolerance or that the nationalist
party was sectarian. Landlords and English conservatives were

accused of inflaming protestant fears.[38]

Many of the Ulster conservatives spoke against the bill.[39] They did not attempt to argue for the exclusion of Ulster from the bill but opposed it in its entirety. Several stated that they would not desert their fellow loyalists and protestants in the rest of Ireland. Their grounds for opposing home rule were several. First, they believed that it would only be the first concession towards complete separation. Secondly, they objected to being put under a Dublin parliament controlled by the nationalist party and the national league. Thirdly, they believed that the social, economic, and religious interest of Ulster and of protestants would suffer under a home rule parliament. Finally, speakers denounced home rule as a threat to the crown, the empire, and the constitution, to which they expressed their firm attachment.

In their opposition to the home rule bill, the Ulster conservatives were fully backed by the conservative party at Westminster.[40] Equally importantly, a section of the liberal party under the marquis of Hartington also opposed Gladstone's measures. Hartington argued that this new proposed system would be regarded in Ireland as only a first step towards separation, and warned of the threat this would be to the unity of the British Isles and to the empire. Joseph Chamberlain suggested the exclusion of Ulster from the bill. Finally on 8 June the vote for the second reading of the bill took place. It was defeated with 341 votes against the measure and 311 votes in support; crucial to the government's defeat was the defection of a sizeable number of liberals.[41] On 25 June the session was brought to a close and a general election was called.

CHAPTER 12 *The 1886 general election*

The year 1886, as T. W. Moody has commented, was a landmark in Anglo–Irish relations.[1] The commitment of Gladstone and the majority of his parliamentary party to bring about home rule for Ireland placed this issue firmly to the fore and altered fundamentally the conditions of Irish and British politics. Irish self-government now became a real possibility for the first time. For parties in Ulster 1886 was also a time of great significance. These months saw the final stages in a realignment of political forces that had begun in 1885. The divisions that finally emerged in 1886 in Ulster would prove of fundamental and lasting significance in the political development of the province.

In the brief period between Gladstone's introduction of his government of Ireland bill on 8 April 1886 and the dissolution of parliament at the end of June, the various political forces in both the north and the rest of Ireland organised to rally their supporters. Outside of Ulster the principal efforts of Irish opponents of home rule were concentrated in the work of the Irish loyal and patriotic union. The union brought together all those opposed to home rule in Ireland, but its main attention focussed on an extensive campaign of meetings and the distribution of leaflets in Great Britain.[2] Supporters of home rule in Ireland greeted Gladstone's bill with acclaim, although occasionally with some reservations. In the southern provinces numerous resolutions were passed by national league branches, town commissioners, and conferences of catholic clergy, in support of the measure.[3] Outside Ulster, however, the main efforts of the nationalist movement were directed towards meetings and influencing public opinion in Great Britain.

In Ulster nationalist supporters had acknowledged Gladstone's bill with the same enthusiasm as elsewhere. The hopes engendered were well expressed in a speech by Andrew McErlean, a prominent Belfast nationalist, not long after Gladstone's announcement of his support for home rule. According to the *Weekly Examiner*, he stated that:

> National prospects never looked brighter than now, and the Irish people were receiving the reward of their undying energies for the cause of their native land by witnessing that the great intellectual power of the civilised

234

world was moved on their behalf, and that the head of the government of England had proclaimed himself in favour of home rule.[4]

A number of public meetings in support of Gladstone were held under the auspices of the national league. Local branches of the national league declared their support for the home rule bill, as did various groups of catholic clergy.[5] Within Ulster, however, the most noticeable response to Gladstone's bill came from those opposed to it. Organisations such as the Belfast chamber of commerce, local presbyterian presbyteries, and Church of Ireland vestries declared their opposition to the bill.[6] The loyalist campaign committee (with a new name, the Ulster loyalist anti-repeal union) continued to organise public meetings throughout the province and to send speakers to Great Britain to address anti-home rule meetings.[7]

Resolutions strongly condemning Gladstone's proposed measures were passed at numerous local Orange lodge meetings and the Orange order organised a series of pro-union demonstrations, although friction arose between some of the leading Orangemen, such as William Johnston and Lord Arthur Hill, and the loyalist anti-repeal union over the question of the leadership of the unionist movement.[8] In early April Johnston stated that the Orangemen would fight to resist home rule but had not yet made any effort to arm, as it was unlikely that home rule would be granted.[9] Gladstone's speech on 8 April, however, altered things and by the end of the month a provisional Orange committee was set up 'to take such steps as may be necessary to maintain the union . . . and the security of the protestant faith'.[10] Newspapers now reported Orangemen drilling in different parts of the north, and efforts appear to have been made to obtain firearms for them.[11] How far such armed organisation developed is unclear, but shortly after the defeat of the home rule bill this line of resistance was ended. William Johnston, in a comment in his diary on a meeting of the provisional committee on 11 June, remarked simply: 'We decided to stop drilling for the present.'[12]

The parties in Ulster: (a) liberals
Of the three political groupings in Ulster the liberals were most affected by the changed political circumstances brought about by Gladstone's measures on 8 April. Less than a week later several of the most prominent Belfast liberals joined with conservatives in a well attended meeting in Belfast in protest against the bill.[13] On 30 April a large demonstration of Ulster liberals opposed to Gladstone's actions was held in the Ulster Hall in Belfast. Resolutions

were passed that protested against the home rule bill as 'fraught with danger to the industrial, social, and moral welfare of the country' and stated that Ireland was an integral part of the United Kingdom.[14] From this time on, the liberals opposed to the government of Ireland bill were usually called liberal unionists, and the conservatives simply unionists.

In June a permanent organisation was formed to promote the united action of all Ulster liberals who were against home rule; this new body was first called the Ulster liberal unionist committee and then, after the general election, the Ulster liberal unionist association.[15] An executive committee was established with Thomas Sinclair as chairman and Mathew Wylie, former secretary of the Ulster liberal society, as one of the secretaries.[16] A sub-committee was also created to confer with Ulster conservatives on united action in the union interest at the general election. Speakers were sent to Great Britain to put forward the Ulster liberal unionist position.

From the names of those who attended the Belfast meeting at the end of May and of the members of the liberal unionist executive committee, it is clear that the vast majority of the leading liberals in Ulster opposed the home rule bill. On 28 May, however, a gathering took place in Belfast of a small number of liberals who declared themselves supporters of the proposed measure.[17] The leading figure on this occasion was Thomas Shillington, the prominent Portadown liberal. A letter of support was read out from T. A. Dickson. At the meeting the Irish protestant home rule association was established to promote national self-government for Ireland, which was described as a right and necessary objective. The formation of a specifically protestant party was seen as justified because of protestant fears. An executive committee and general council were formed, with Thomas Shillington as president. A main branch of the association was set up in Dublin and a number of smaller branches were established in the southern provinces. During the general election, speakers were sent to England and Scotland to address public meetings.[18]

In the Ulster constituencies the liberals were divided, although it is clear that the great majority became liberal unionists. The role that these former liberals played in the new unionist movement differed greatly between divisions. Where their strength in a constituency was significant in the balance between unionists and nationalists, they were given an important role, but otherwise their position was discounted. In Cos Antrim and Down most of the liberals appear to have become liberal unionists, but there is little evidence of formal links between them and the unionists in regard to party organisation, although it was reported that former liberals attended meetings in support of unionist candidates.[19] Control of political affairs in this area lay firmly under the control of the former conservatives and their organisation. In South Down, however, liberal unionists and unionists met on 1 July and selected R. S. Corbitt, from Rathfriland, as liberal unionist candidate.[20] Some liberals in both counties did support Gladstone. At a meeting in North Antrim of the Route tenants' defence association in late May, confidence was expressed in Gladstone, and at the beginning of July it was announced that S. C. McElroy, secretary of the association and the Ulster land committee, at the request of colleagues in the land movement, had consented to stand for the division as a Gladstonian liberal.[21] In Mid Antrim on nomination day J. H. McKelvey, a farmer from Co. Tyrone, was put forward as a Gladstonian liberal candidate.

In the third week of May the South Derry liberal union forwarded resolutions to Gladstone opposing his home rule measure. Contact was made between liberals and conservatives with the latter agreeing to accept a liberal unionist candidate if the South Derry liberals used their influence with their liberal friends in Derry city.[22] On 14 June a joint committee of liberals and conservatives selected Thomas Lea, former liberal M.P. for Donegal, as a liberal unionist candidate for the division. In North Derry the liberal union declared its support for Gladstone, but failed to put forward a local candidate.[23]

In North Tyrone the divisional liberal association, led by E. T. Herdman, came out in opposition to Gladstone, and, under the auspices of the North-west loyal registration and electoral association, supported the unionist Lord E. W. Hamilton against J. O. Wylie, a barrister and former land commissioner, who stood as a Gladstonian liberal with nationalist backing.[24] In East Tyrone liberal unionists joined with conservatives to form a local branch of the N.L.R.E.A. in Dungannon in early June, and on 19 June at a joint meeting of liberal unionists and conservatives, Mathew Megaw, a Belfast businessman resident in London, was selected as liberal unionist candidate.[25] In Dungannon a local branch of the Irish protestant home rule association was also established.[26]

Meetings of liberal unionist and conservative delegates were held in Mid Tyrone in late June to pick a candidate, but only on 29 June was it announced that H. H. Moore, unsuccessful conservative

candidate in 1885, would be standing again.[27] In contrast, arrangements were made much sooner in South Tyrone. At a meeting on 9
June liberal unionist and conservative delegates from each polling
district, under the auspices of the N.L.R.E.A., T. W. Russell, a
well known temperance reformer, originally from Scotland but
brought up in Co. Tyrone, was chosen as the liberal unionist candidate.[28] In East Donegal liberals seemed to have cooperated with the
conservatives in selecting Capt. T. B. Storey, a retired army officer
from Raphoe, as conservative candidate.[29]

In Co. Armagh the liberal organisation had almost entirely
collapsed by the general election. On 23 April the Portadown liberal
club, under the chairmanship of Thomas Shillington, declared its
support for Gladstone's home rule bill.[30] But the numbers present at
this meeting appear to have been no more than about twenty, and
the bulk of the former liberals in the county were clearly opposed
to the bill, although they lacked any new type of organisation.
Newspaper reports, however, tell of former liberals attending
unionist meetings.[31] Two members of the Irish protestant home rule
association stood as nationalist candidates for Armagh constituencies — James Williamson, an Armagh solicitor, for North
Armagh, and R. R. Gardner, an Armagh engineer and iron-
founder, for Mid Armagh.

In the remaining county constituencies the liberals were entirely
absorbed into the other parties. This appears to have happened in
Newry, although a liberal unionist candidate, R. C. Saunders, a
barrister, was selected. In Belfast the only division where the liberal
unionists remained a distinct and decisive force was West Belfast.
Both former liberals and conservatives were on the pro-union
executive committee and general council in West Belfast, and J. H.
Haslett, conservative member for the seat, had their mutual
backing.[32] Meetings of the Irish protestant home rule association
were held in the division, and support declared for the nationalist.[33]
In East Belfast Robert McCalmont, an agricultural chemist and a
member of the association, stood as a Gladstonian liberal. In Derry
the leading liberals backed C. E. Lewis, conservative M.P. for the
city, although there was a small number of Gladstone's supporters
among the liberals.

During the election campaign the liberal unionists in the Tyrone,
Londonderry, East Donegal, West Belfast, and Derry city divisions
ran joint meetings and fully cooperated in organisation for polling
with the conservatives; in the north-west divisions this cooperation
took place under the auspices of the N.L.R.E.A.[34] In Cos Antrim,

Down, and Armagh (apart from South Down) the liberal unionists do not seem to have retained district organisations or cooperated with the conservatives in a formal manner during the campaign, although they were often present at conservative meetings. Reports show that presbyterian ministers gave some assistance to the liberal unionist campaign.[35] The Ulster reform club does not seem to have played any organisational part in the election.[36]

The organisation of the Gladstonian liberals, who clearly represented a minority of the liberal movement, differed considerably between areas. In North Antrim McElroy probably had the assistance of the Route tenants' defence association, but elsewhere, as for example in North Tyrone, the Gladstonian liberals seem to have relied on assistance from the nationalist organisation.[37] Likewise where members of the Irish protestant home rule association stood as nationalists they had the support of the nationalist organisation. In a number of constituencies, especially West Belfast, the association organised meetings and helped non-unionist candidates.[38] T. A. Dickson, we may note, stood for a Scottish seat as a Gladstonian liberal. Of the liberal unionist candidates, T. W. Russell and J. O. Megaw were presbyterians as was at least one Gladstonian liberal, S. C. McElroy; the others seem to have been members of the Church of Ireland.

The parties in Ulster: (b) conservatives
Gladstone's announcement of his home rule bill spurred the conservatives to further activity in protest. Local constitutional associations arranged public meetings to voice opposition to the bill and prominent conservatives continued to take a leading part in the demonstrations and meetings organised by the Orange order and the Ulster loyalist anti-repeal union. In the preparations for the general election the conservative organisations that had come into being in 1885 operated in much the same manner as previously except that in certain areas the conservatives cooperated with the liberal unionists. The Orange order appears to have been integrated into the conservative organisation in many of the constituencies in the same way as at the preceding general election.

In Co. Antrim delegates from local branches in each polling district in a division assembled at meetings of the divisional constitutional associations and chose their candidates; the four Co. Antrim conservative M.P.s were reselected. As before, the Orange order picked a number of the delegates. In East Antrim some friction did arise from the feeling of Orangemen in one district that they were being excluded from the central organisation and selection body of the divisional association, but this appears to have been satisfactorily dealt with.[39] In North, Mid, and East Down the selection procedure and organisation for the selection was conducted by the conservatives in a similar fashion. The conservative divisional associations held meetings of delegates and the three M.P.s were reselected; reports tell of Orange lodge grand masters attending these meetings. In the months prior to the general election new local conservative registration and electoral associations were established, as in Banbridge on 21 May. In South Down conservative delegates met liberal delegates on 1 July and agreed to select a liberal unionist candidate.[40]

In Co. Armagh the divisions that had appeared in the conservative and Orange ranks in 1885 had disappeared entirely in face of the new challenge of home rule. In North Armagh Col. E. J. Saunderson returned to the constituency on 21 June to begin his campaign, and at the meeting in Portadown on that day to welcome him back many of his former opponents were present. Appreciation was expressed at the meeting about his forthright speaking in parliament, which was undoubtedly a factor to help remove any lingering ill-feeling about his selection the previous year. The local constitutional associations gave their backing to him.[41] In Mid Armagh a meeting of delegates on 14 June expressed confidence in Sir J. P. Corry, the newly elected M.P., who began his campaign soon after.[42] South Armagh was ignored by the conservatives.

In Co. Fermanagh conservative organisation in 1885 had been poor, and attempts were made early in the next year to remedy this. Although a number of local committees were formed by June 1886, proposed divisional associations and procedures for calling selection conventions had still not been established. In the second week of June W. H. Archdale (M.P. for the county 1874-85) issued an address as a conservative candidate for North Fermanagh. On 15 June a meeting was held of leading conservatives in the division, summoned by a circular issued by J. W. Dane, principal party organiser in the constituency in 1885, and some others.[43] Objections were raised over the peremptory way Archdale had put himself forward, but those present eventually accepted him. In South Fermanagh a meeting of conservatives in Lisnaskea at the end of June selected as their candidate Frank Brooke, who had contested the seat in 1885.[44] The Orange order does not seem to have had a fixed place in the Fermanagh conservative organisation, but many of the conservatives at these selection conferences were prominent

Orangemen.

In Co. Monaghan on 25 June a meeting of the county constitutional association took place in the Orange Hall, Monaghan, and it was resolved to contest the northern division.[45] Sir John Leslie, bt, defeated conservative candidate for the division in 1885, was selected eventually. It appeared for a time that South Monaghan would be uncontested by the conservatives, but shortly before nomination the hon. P. C. Westenra, brother of Lord Rossmore, issued an address.[46]

Neither of the Co. Cavan seats was contested by the conservatives. In Co. Donegal Capt. T. B. Storey, a retired army officer from Raphoe, was chosen as conservative candidate at a joint meeting of liberals and conservatives on 3 July.[47] The two other conservative candidates, A. H. W. Foster in South Donegal and Lt-col. H. H. A. Stewart in North Donegal, seem to have simply put themselves forward. Only in East Donegal was there a proper conservative organisation.

In Cos Tyrone and Londonderry there was much greater co-operation between conservatives and liberal unionists. In Tyrone new branches of the north-west loyal registration and electoral association continued to be formed with both conservatives and liberals, and conservative organisations such as the East Tyrone united constitutional association agreed to join it.[48] Joint meetings of liberals and conservatives, usually under the auspices of the N.L.R.E.A., were held to select candidates.[49] Liberal unionists were selected for East and South Tyrone while for North Tyrone Lord E. W. Hamilton, conservative M.P. for the seat, was reselected and for Mid Tyrone H. H. Moore, unsuccessful candidate in 1885, was chosen.

In April the conservative association of South Londonderry offered to join the N.L.R.E.A. if the liberal unionists did also, and said that they would accept a liberal unionist candidate for the division from a choice of three names selected by the liberal unionists, if the latter tried to persuade the liberal unionists in Derry city to support the conservative. An agreement was reached eventually on this, and a liberal unionist was asked by the united liberal unionist and conservative committees of the division on 14 June to contest the seat.[50] In South Londonderry H. L. Mulholland, conservative M.P. for the division, was reselected; details are not available as to how exactly this happened, but his candidature clearly had the support of the liberal unionists and conservatives in the division.

In Belfast efforts were made from several sides to heal the split in the conservative and Orange ranks in 1885. At a meeting of the grand Orange lodge in Belfast at the end of December 1885 resolutions were passed declaring that Orangemen were anxious to cooperate with other constitutional bodies. At the annual meeting of the Belfast constitutional association on 16 April 1886 in the Ulster constitutional club, William Johnston and E. S. W. de Cobain were selected as vice-presidents of the association, and confidence was expressed in the four borough M.P.s. In East Belfast a joint meeting of representatives from the Orange lodges in the division and the East Belfast constitutional association took place on 7 May and confidence was expressed in de Cobain, the sitting M.P. This statement of confidence was repeated in both the Orange lodges and the constitutional association in the division in late May and early June, and de Cobain was duly nominated. In South Belfast the divisional constitutional association unanimously chose William Johnston as their candidate. Conservatives cooperated with liberal unionists in West Belfast and J. H. Haslett, unsuccessful candidate for the division in 1885, was reselected.[51]

Selection did not proceed so smoothly in North Belfast.[52] On 25 June it was reported that William Ewart, M.P., had been chosen again as candidate for the constituency by the executive and general committee of the divisional constitutional association. But Col. E. J. Saunderson now sought to replace him by a friend and neighbour, Somerset Maxwell, defeated conservative candidate in South Tyrone in 1885, on the grounds of Ewart's age and ill health. Saunderson wrote to Lord Randolph Churchill in support of Maxwell but got no encouragement. Meetings were arranged in North Belfast in sympathy with Maxwell. A requisition from over 500 Orange working men was presented to Maxwell asking him to stand because he was a friend of Saunderson and would stand up more forcefully to the Parnellities than Ewart. The duke of Abercorn asked Lord Salisbury to intervene against Maxwell. Finally, however, Maxwell decided to retire because (he said) he feared a contest might cause disunion and endanger the seat. Probably this controversy reflected a conflict between Saunderson and other leading conservatives.

In Derry city the sitting conservative M.P., C. E. Lewis, came forward for reelection in mid June. How precisely he was selected is not clear as the newspapers carry no report of a formal selection and the first indication that he would stand again came on 15 June when his election address appeared in the *Londonderry Sentinel*.

He may have been selected at a private meeting of the city conservative society, but there was no protest among conservatives over his standing for reelection. In Newry a number of conservative electors approached James Henderson of the *Belfast Newsletter* in the early part of June and asked him to stand. He refused and not until the beginning of July did a liberal unionist candidate, R. C. Saunders, emerge.[53]

In the election campaign the conservatives cooperated with the liberal unionists in the north-west of the province and West Belfast. Apart from areas where conservatives were organised together with liberal unionists in branches of the N.L.R.E.A., the conservatives had local committees and organisations in the different polling districts that handled canvassing, the arrangement of meetings, and organisation for polling day. E. S. Finnigan was an important figure in the conservative organisation, but the local bodies seem to have been more able to function on their own by this stage. There were also presbyterian and Church of Ireland clergy present at the conservative meetings. It can be noted that landlords were once more in evidence on conservative platforms; the social tensions that had arisen in 1885 over the question of their place in the conservative ranks in some places seem to have largely disappeared.[54] All the conservative candidates were members of the Church of Ireland, except for Sir J. P. Corry, bt, C. E. Lewis, and J. H. Haslett, who were presbyterian.

The parties in Ulster: (c) nationalists
Throughout the first half of 1886 the national league continued to grow in Ulster. In his report to the lord lieutenant on the progress of the league over the period 1 Jan. – 30 June 1886, R. E. Beckerson noted the spreading influence of the movement in Ulster:

> In the northern division I notice that some branches — not those in towns — are stated to number over 1000 members — for instance Corry branch, Co. Mon., has 1000 members. . . . Again Omagh branch collected £335 during past quarter principally for election purposes — there are 285 in the branch, therefore more than £1 a head was subscribed.[55]

As regards the number of national league branches in this period, Beckerson recorded the following number for each county on 30 June 1886: Antrim 13, Armagh 20, Donegal 44, Down 27, Fermanagh 26, Londonderry 21, Monaghan 19, and Tyrone 35 (Cavan was not included in this report). He also reported 1 branch for Belfast.

In the general election of 1886 the national league provided the organisation for the nationalist party, as had happened in 1885. In those constituencies where nationalist M.P.s had been returned in 1885, no formal selection of candidates took place and the former members simply came forward again. W. S. Blunt in his diary reported hearing from Michael Davitt that it was intended to replace the four nationalist M.P.s who announced their intention not to stand again, including one from Ulster, with protestant home rulers 'so as to give an answer to the "no-popery" cry'.[56] This did not happen, but the nationalists do seem to have attempted to win protestant support by putting forward protestant nationalists, backing protestant Gladstonian liberals, and deliberately seeking the protestant vote in a number of Ulster divisions.

The only vacancy in the northern nationalist seats occurred in South Down where J. F. Small gave up his place because of ill health. On 30 June a convention of national league representatives was held at Hilltown under the presidency of a local priest, Rev. D. Mooney.[57] No representative from the Irish parliamentary party was present, but the meeting obviously had the approval of the party. Michael McCartan, a Belfast solicitor brought up in South Down, was chosen. Two other nationalist candidates came forward for Co. Down. On 21 June it was reported in the press that the nationalists in East Down were planning to run a candidate for the election, but not until early July did one appear, in the person of Henry McGrath, a poor law guardian from Portaferry.[58] In North Down Richard McNabb, a local farmer, put his name forward as a nationalist candidate shortly before nomination. Likewise in West Down J. B. McHugh, a barrister, appeared as a nationalist candidate just before nomination. Only in South Down did a selection convention meet.

In South Antrim a nationalist candidate, John Duddy, appeared on nomination day, but his nomination papers were filled in incorrectly and so they were rejected.[59] No other nationalists came forward in Co. Antrim, but the nationalists gave their support to the two Gladstonian liberals standing in the county. In Armagh Alexander Blane stood again for the southern division, while James Williamson and R. R. Gardner, both members of the Irish protestant home rule association, were nominated for North and Mid Armagh, respectively, as nationalists.[60] No public conventions seem to have been held to select them.

In Co. Tyrone the three nationalist M.P.s stood again, while the field was left clear in North Tyrone for a Gladstonian liberal to take on the sitting conservative member. In Cos Cavan, Monaghan, and

Donegal the nationalist M.P.s all recontested their seats. In Co. Londonderry T. M. Healy came forward once more for the southern division but the northern division was left uncontested. In Newry J. H. McCarthy stood for reelection, while in Derry city Justin McCarthy, unsuccessful nationalist candidate in 1885, was nominated a second time for the seat.

In Belfast Thomas Sexton contested the western division where he had been narrowly defeated at the previous general election. Sexton's position was strengthened after a meeting in late June of members of the former central council of the Belfast national league (which had been dissolved in early 1885), when a letter was read out from Michael Davitt urging them to give all possible support to Sexton, which they agreed to do.[61] In North Belfast C. J. Dempsey, a licensed vintner, came forward as a nationalist, while in South Belfast Andrew McErlean, a solicitor and prominent national league member, stood for the party. In neither McErlean's nor Dempsey's case does a formal selection convention seem to have taken place.

In their election campaign the nationalists were assisted by members of the Irish protestant home rule association. This was especially so in West Belfast, where the association held meetings in support of Sexton.[62] In a number of constituencies, such as South Tyrone, the nationalist candidates made a point of having protestants on their nomination papers and, whenever possible, as chairman of their meetings.[63] At the same time they relied on the national league and the catholic clergy for electoral organisation. These different aspects of nationalist politics can be seen in the case of W. J. Reynolds, party candidate for East Tyrone.

Reynolds' election correspondence shows him writing to various prominent protestants to ask them to appear with him on his platform.[64] He contacted the secretary of the national league in Dublin to request leaflets suitable for distribution among the protestant electors.[65] He also wrote to catholic clergy in the division to ask them to attend his meetings,[66] to seek information on absentee voters, and to urge them to support his cause among their parishioners: 'I think it would be well to give a few hints to the people on Sunday how to mark their votes.'[67] A. M. Sullivan jun. in his memoirs amusingly recorded a sermon in a South Donegal chapel during the general election in favour of the local nationalist candidate.[68] An incident involving the national league in South Tyrone may also be noted. James Brown, a supporter of T. W. Russell, received the following letter from the vice-president of Donaghmore national league branch:

> We are directed by the local branch of the N. League to communicate the following resolution of 67 branches of the league in Ulster sent round expressing their indignation at your nomination of so unworthy a candidate in opposition to William O'Brien. . . .
>
> We view with dissatisfaction the conduct of Mr James Brown (head of the firm of D. Browne & Son) in nominating T. W. Russell for South Tyrone in opposition to Mr William O'Brien the popular candidate and hereby resolve if any further support be given that gentleman we will terminate all further business relations with the firm —
>
> Now therefore choose between Russell in parliament and your old customers in trade.[69]

All the nationalist candidates were catholic except for James Williamson and R. R. Gardner, who were protestant (probably members of the Church of Ireland); they both belonged to the Irish protestant home rule association. Richard McNabb may also have been protestant.

Number of contests and issues
In 1886 only 33 constituencies in Ireland were contested compared with 79 in 1885; outside Ulster, a mere 7 divisions out of 68 witnessed contests. In the three southern provinces there were 6 conservative and 2 liberal unionist candidates. A nationalist candidate stood for each seat in the southern provinces, making a total of 70 nationalist candidates, of whom 62 were returned unopposed. In Ulster 26 of the 33 constituencies were contested, compared with 27 in the previous general election. In the province there were 24 conservatives, 5 liberal unionists, 4 Gladstonian liberals and 26 nationalists. In all, 7 candidates were elected unopposed; this consisted of 3 conservatives and 4 nationalists. In 17 divisions conservatives faced nationalists, in 5 liberal unionists fought nationalists and in 5 Gladstonian liberals opposed conservatives.

In the addresses of the few southern conservatives and liberal unionists prime place was given to declarations of opposition to home rule. The conservatives and liberal unionists in Ulster also placed support for the union first and foremost in their addresses.[70] Various reasons were given by the conservatives for their opposition to home rule. On the one hand, home rule was seen as the first step towards separation: it threatened both the union between Great Britain and Ireland, and the integrity of the empire. In addition to viewing home rule as a danger to religious liberties and the economic well-being of the country several candidates also referred to their opposition to being governed by a parliament that would be dominated by Parnell and his national league followers, whom they believed guilty of outrage, oppression, and hatred of England. On the other hand, conservatives supported the union because they believed that they had full representation in the Westminster parliament, which had removed most of the country's grievances, and they were part of a worldwide empire that brought great benefit to Ireland. Rarely were other matters apart from the home rule question discussed in conservative manifestoes.

In the addresses of the liberal unionists the question of home rule was likewise the main issue and the views given by them were similar to those stated by the conservatives. Thomas Lea declared that any measure to weaken the union 'will be disastrous to the interests of Ireland, injurious to England and Scotland, and very damaging to the empire'.[71] The liberal unionists frequently said they were supporters of Lord Hartington. Most called for further land reforms, in particular advocating schemes to enable tenants to buy their land on fair terms. Only two Gladstonian liberals, S. C. McElroy and Robert McCalmont, appear to have issued election addresses.[72] Both declared themselves ardent followers of Gladstone. McElroy urged compulsory sale of land. He also supported cottages and plots of land for labourers and free education for their children. The Irish protestant home rule association issued an address to the protestants of Ireland.[73] It rejected the idea that the liberties of protestants would be taken away by an Irish parliament. It stated that the foremost statesman of the century had undertaken the task of creating a responsible Irish government; against him were selfish territorial and class interests. The address finally declared: 'Fellow protestants, our interests are bound up with those of our native land. Let us unite with our fellow countrymen in a spirit of tolerance and trust.'

The nationalists did not issue election addresses. In his speeches in England, where he addressed meetings in support of liberal candidates, Parnell dwelt at length on two objections to the home rule bill, first, that it would lead to separation, and secondly, that it would bring about oppression of protestants. As regards the first point, Parnell stated that such an idea was preposterous and referred to Canada and Australia as examples of contented colonies with self-government within the British empire.[74] The second objection he also dismissed entirely. Speaking at Plymouth on 26 June, he said that the alarm raised about the safety of the protestant minority came not from the protestants of Ireland as a whole, but from a few fanatical Orangemen in the north.[75]

The nationalists in the north dwelt on a number of subjects in their speeches. Speaking at Fintona on 22 June at the opening of the nationalist election campaign, William O'Brien, stated that home rule was now a certainty, that protestants had nothing to fear for their homes or religion, and that it was the landlords who were the main threat.[76] These points were frequently repeated and elaborated by other speakers. No power on earth, John Dillon proclaimed, would stand between the people of Ireland and home rule.[77] Thomas Sexton spoke of the 'natural claim of Ireland'.[78] Others stated that the union had failed to bring benefits. It was pointed out that the liberal land purchase bill that went with the home rule bill was much better than anything the conservatives had given. Protestants and catholics were urged to unite behind home rule.[79]

Results of the poll in Ulster
The general election of 1886 was fought on the same electoral register as the 1885 general election, but the alterations in party fortunes and alliances that had occurred between the two occasions were to bring about certain significant changes in the results. In South Armagh, West and East Cavan, and West Donegal nationalist candidates were nominated unopposed, while in East and South Antrim and North Londonderry conservative candidates were returned without a contest. Again the contested polls were held over a period of about two weeks. Before long it became clear the conservatives had held all their protestant votes of 1885 and added many of the former liberal votes. The nationalists continued to win the catholic vote and also some protestant supporters. An important question remained of just how many protestant votes the nationalists would win. Also it was not clear if there would be many liberal abstentions.

The first poll of the general election in Ulster was in Derry city. The result was C. E. Lewis, conservative, 1,781 votes, and Justin McCarthy, nationalist, 1,778; thus Lewis's majority of 29 in 1885 was reduced to 3. From newspaper reports of the polling it is clear that all the catholic voters supported McCarthy, plus nearly 30 presbyterian liberal voters, while all the protestant voters except these 30 backed Lewis.[80] One account claimed that Gladstone had written a personal letter to some 20 liberals in Derry asking them to vote for McCarthy.[81] Subsequently on petition Lewis was unseated and McCarthy declared elected. At the election petition trial a small number of Lewis's votes were found on scrutiny to be improper and so his majority disappeared; it was revealed that Lewis's agent had paid the travelling expenses of a voter.[82]

In West Belfast the comparative position of the two candidates, both of whom had stood in 1885, altered slightly but significantly. Thomas Sexton, nationalist, received 3,832 votes and J. H. Haslett, conservative, 3,729; compared with 1885, Haslett's vote had dropped by 51 and Sexton's had increased by 89. This new state of affairs seems to have been due to the complete unity now prevailing in the nationalist ranks, with the former members of the national league council in Belfast backing Sexton,[83] and the support of some protestants for Sexton due to the influence of the Irish protestant home rule association. After the election Sexton declared: 'Let us not forget how much we are indebted to our protestant friends for our victory.'[84]

Clearly, however, the protestant nationalist vote was a very small one. The *Belfast Newsletter* put it at 6 which is obviously too low,[85] but even the president of the Belfast national league, Rev. Patrick Convery, could only claim that around 60 protestants had voted for Sexton.[86] At a subsequent election petition trial it was proved that some 13 cases of personation had taken place in West Belfast and at least 5 personators had cast their vote for Sexton, but as there was no proof that Sexton knew of it, the election was allowed.[87] In Newry 1,183 votes were cast for the nationalist J. H. McCarthy, while 761 were polled for the liberal unionist R. C. Saunders.

In East Belfast the conservative E. W. S. de Cobain received 5,055 votes and Robert McCalmont, Gladstonian liberal, obtained 1,239. In South Belfast William Johnston, conservative, won 4,542 votes and Andrew McErlean, nationalist, 657. In North Belfast the conservative William Ewart had 4,522 votes, while the nationalist C. J. Dempsey received 732. Compared with the 1885 results the conservatives had consolidated their position in South and North Belfast, winning all the conservative and some of the liberal and independent vote, while in East Belfast they failed to poll the total conservative vote and may have lost slightly to the Gladstonian liberal. The nationalists and the Gladstonian liberal fared badly and probably received little more than the catholic vote, although the Gladstonian liberal in East Belfast may have won some protestant votes.

The picture that emerged in the first borough contests would now be repeated elsewhere. In North Antrim Edward Macnaghten, conservative, won 4,429 votes compared with S. C. McElroy, Gladstonian liberal, who polled 1,910. In contrast to the earlier result it seems that Macnaghten added around half the 2,149 liberal votes of 1885 to his own 1885 conservative support, while McElroy had some of the remaining liberal votes plus many of the 1,915 catholic and nationalist voters who had previously backed the independent, John Pinkerton. It is probable that many liberals abstained. The total number of votes cast fell by 958 compared with the previous election. In Mid Antrim the conservative, the hon. R. T. O'Neill, obtained 4,631 votes, while the Gladstonian liberal J. H. McKelvey won 933; these figures, viewed comparatively with the 1885 result, suggest that a considerable number of liberals supported O'Neill while many abstained.

Neither East nor West Down was contested in 1885, but in 1886 both were. In the former division the result was Capt. R. W. B. Ker, conservative, 5,093 and Henry McGrath, nationalist, 2,561; in the latter division the outcome was Lord Arthur Hill, conservative, 6,589, and J. B. McHugh, nationalist, 2,561. In South Down Michael McCartan, nationalist, won 4,786 votes, while R. S. Corbitt, liberal unionist, polled 3,816; this represented a small increase in the unionist vote and a slight fall in the nationalist backing, compared with 1885. In North Down Col. Thomas Waring, conservative, gained 4,959 votes, while Richard McNabb, nationalist, obtained 969. These figures suggest that Waring had won some of the liberal vote, although many seem to have abstained.

In North Armagh the conservative Col. E. J. Saunderson received 4,570 votes and James Williamson, nationalist, 1,677. In Mid Armagh Sir J. P. Porter, bt, conservative, with 4,160 votes, defeated his nationalist opponent, R. R. Gardner, with 2,522. Compared with the 1885 general election result in North Armagh and the by-election result in Mid Armagh, these figures again suggest that the conservatives won liberal votes but other liberals abstained. There is no evidence of significant numbers of protestants backing the nationalist in either Armagh or Down, and it is clear that the vast bulk of catholics were voting nationalist and nearly all the pro-testants conservative or liberal unionist.

In Cos Monaghan, Fermanagh and three divisions of Co. Donegal, where conservatives faced nationalists as they had in the previous year, the pattern of voting was almost identical to that in 1885. In North Fermanagh the nationalist W. H. K. Redmond polled 3,128 votes, while the conservative W. H. Archdale obtained 2,862. In South Fermanagh Henry Campbell, nationalist, won 3,553 votes and Frank Brooke, conservative, 2,320. In both the Fermanagh elections the conservatives improved on their 1885 figures, which was probably evidence of better organisation and the decline of anti-landlord feelings among supporters. The result in North Monaghan was Patrick O'Brien, nationalist, 3,962, and Sir John Leslie, bt, conservative, 2,491; and in South Monaghan Sir J. N. McKenna, nationalist, 4,715, and the hon. P. C. Westenra, conservative, 1,009.

In North Donegal J. E. O'Doherty, nationalist, won 4,263 votes and Lt-col. H. H. A. Stewart, conservative, 914. In South Donegal Bernard Kelly, nationalist, received 4,905 votes and A. H. W. Foster, conservative, 1,399. All these candidates had stood at the previous general election and the results in 1886 were no different from those seven months earlier. In East Donegal, where in 1885 a nationalist had faced a liberal, a nationalist, Arthur O'Connor, obtained 3,972 votes against the conservative Capt. T. B. Storey's 2,551. After the election O'Connor claimed that 250 presbyterians had supported him, although there is no other evidence to back this claim.[88]

In South Londonderry the sitting nationalist member, T. M. Healy, received 4,626 votes, which was only 3 fewer than what he won in 1885, but Thomas Lea obtained the larger number of 4,737, which was 580 more than the combined liberal and conservative vote in the previous year. A later report in the *Derry Journal* stated that as catholics were in a minority of 400 in the electorate and Healy had only 111 votes fewer than Lea, a significant number of presbyterians must have supported Healy; this would put the presbyterian nationalist vote in the division at around 300, which is probably a fair figure.[89] As regards Lea's increase in the anti-nationalist vote, we may note Healy's later claim that in 1885 covenanters in the division had abstained on principle but after the introduction of the home rule bill they decided to vote against him.[90] In Mid Tyrone M. J. Kenny, nationalist, won 4,145 votes and H. H. Moore, conservative, 2,475; both candidates had received similar numbers of votes in 1885. Lord E. W. Hamilton in North Tyrone, who had beaten a nationalist in 1885, defeated a Gladstonian liberal, J. O. Wylie, winning 3,219 votes while Wylie polled 2,867; viewed in comparison with the 1885 result, the appearance of a Gladstonian liberal had failed to increase the anti-unionist vote.

Viewed overall it is clear that most catholic voters supported nationalist candidates and most protestant voters backed unionist candidates. Some protestants did vote for nationalists, although it is difficult to put a precise figure on their numbers. Thomas Shillington, a member of the Irish protestant home rule association from

Armagh, put the total of protestant home rule votes at over 2,500 in the six constituencies where protestant home rulers had stood.[91] This estimate covers the three divisions contested by Gladstonian liberals and the other three divisions in which members of the I.P.H.R.A. had come forward as nationalists. A figure of another 400-500 can be added to this to include protestant home rule votes in West Belfast, Derry city, South Londonderry, and South Tyrone. Probably it is fair to say that around 3,000 protestants (former liberals) had voted for home rule candidates. Clearly the bulk of former liberals now backed the unionist movement, although it is apparent that a fair number did not vote at all, usually in divisions with a large pro-union majority.

Summary of results

The outcome of the 1886 general election was not very different from that of the previous general election.[92] For Ulster 16 nationalists, 15 unionists, and 2 liberal unionists were returned, compared with 17 nationalists and 16 conservatives in 1885. Subsequently a unionist, C. E. Lewis, was unseated on petition and his place taken by Justin McCarthy, nationalist. The unionists consisted of 8 landowners, an army officer, 3 solicitors or barristers, 2 from a manufacturing or merchant background, and a former borough cashier. The liberal unionists comprised a merchant and a temperance official with commercial background. Of the liberal unionists, 1 was congregationalist and the other presbyterian, as were 2 unionists, while the remaining 13 unionists, apart from 1 methodist, were members of the Church of Ireland. The Ulster nationalists consisted of 1 rentier, 3 merchants, 7 from the upper professions, 2 from the lower professions, a shopkeeper, a tailor, and 1 in an undefined category.[93] All were catholic.

In the rest of Ireland 2 unionists and 68 nationalists were elected. The social, educational and religious background of these M.P.s was almost exactly the same as in 1885. Of the nationalist M.P.s all were catholic except for 7, of whom 6 were members of the Irish protestant home rule association.[94] But the association seems to have had only a very minor success among southern protestants in general, and most protestant electors appear to have been unionist and most catholic voters nationalist.[95] Although around 10 per cent of the population in the three southern provinces, protestants were thinly distributed over the country and so unable to return unionist M.P.s, except for Dublin University which was an exceptional case because of its graduate electorate.

In Ulster political organisation was much the same as in 1885. However, within liberal ranks, which were now depleted, there were the new liberal unionist and Gladstonian liberal groups. Clearly the liberal unionists were by far the stronger of the two sections, although they survived as a separate organisation in only a few constituencies; elsewhere members were absorbed into the conservative organisation. Nationalist organisation in Ulster remained the same as at the previous general election, but it now had the assistance of the Irish protestant home rule association. In the other provinces there was little unionist activity outside Dublin and Cork, southern unionist activities being directed towards the campaign in Great Britain. The nationalist party had an almost complete monopoly of political power in the southern provinces.

Thus the 1886 general election in Ulster saw an important consolidation of the outcome of 1885. The final position left the parliamentary representation for the province looking very different from the previous period. While there had been 2 home rule, 9 liberal, and 21 conservative M.P.s elected in 1880, the return for the province six years later was markedly different: now there were 16 nationalists, 15 unionists, and 2 liberal unionists. The social and religious backgrounds of these M.P.s had also altered dramatically. While most of the M.P.s in 1880 had been landowners, merchants, or members of the upper professions, six years later less than a third owned land, while nearly half were merchants or came from the upper professions and the remainder belonged to the lower professions or other groups. In 1880 there were only 2 catholic M.P.s but now catholic M.P.s numbered 16.

Changes in the franchise and the distribution of seats as well as the rules for election expenditure had helped create this new picture. The increase in the number of catholic voters as well as the enfranchisement of many labourers considerably affected the fortunes of the parties: both factors aided the nationalists, while the second also helped the conservatives. Changes in the electoral system imposed new difficulties for the parties because clearly the organisational structures that had worked under the old conditions were not sufficient to cope with the altered circumstances. In addition an increasingly politicised electorate now demanded an effective role in the party machines.

In their reorganisation the conservatives and nationalists had responded well to the challenges of 1885-6 but the liberals had reacted poorly. While the former two bodies developed effective local and central organisations, the liberals failed to respond similarly. Thanks partly to strong leadership at the top and a well structured response at local level, the nationalist party created a strong nationalist movement throughout Ireland, including Ulster. The conservatives, with able organisers such as E. S. Finnigan, successfully restructured their political framework, particularly at grass roots level, and strengthened their position. In contrast to both parties the liberal leadership and organisation did not develop so effectively and its main liberal unionist wing was consequently reduced to a minor position in the unionist movement.

The land issue was now relegated to the background and the question of the union had emerged as the matter of foremost importance in the minds of the people of Ulster. Over this subject there had emerged a clear division on denominational grounds among the electorate. On the one side almost all protestant electors, former liberals and conservatives alike, were in one political grouping, the unionist movement, which was dominated by the conservatives. In spite of various social divisions, they had come together in face of what they regarded as a threat to their well-being. With even greater unanimity, nearly all catholic voters, former liberals and home rulers alike, were now in another political grouping, the nationalist movement. The catholic community, in pursuit of what it saw as its best interest, had given its wholehearted support to the nationalist party.

The overall outcome of the general election was that the conservative party under Lord Salisbury emerged as the new government at Westminster and the proposed home rule legislation for Ireland was dropped. But in Ulster the forces of unionism and nationalism, based on clearly defined religious divisions, had now emerged as the main political forces. This state of affairs has proved to be of enormous durability. Over the next three-and-a-half decades some mixed denominational voting still took place, for parties such as the liberal unionists or the Gladstonian liberals. Divisions also occurred within the ranks of the unionist movement on a few occasions, as in the first decade of the new century, over surviving agrarian tensions and other social conflicts. Fundamental alignments, however, had been established which would lead to partition in 1921 and which have remained basically to this day.

CONCLUSION

Ten years after the 1886 general election, Thomas MacKnight published his memoirs which were concerned primarily with the years covered in this study of Ulster elections. In the opening page MacKnight commented that a 'social and political revolution' had occurred, although, he added, 'it may yet be far from complete'.[1] As we have seen, not only did unionist-nationalist rivalry emerge clearly for the first time in Ulster politics but the population split on a firmly denominational basis over this matter. Subsequently the revolution was completed and it took place largely, although not entirely, along the lines laid down in these critical years. Nationalists achieved self-government, but only for twenty-six Irish counties, while unionists won a separate arrangement, but just for six Ulster counties. Within the newly established Northern Ireland, politics continued to be divided largely between unionist and nationalist and this division was still based on religious differences.

This in-depth study of all Ulster elections during this formative period has helped establish a more accurate picture of developments than previous works which have been based on case studies of particular areas or on general evidence from declarations of party aims. For example, writers have often been influenced by the fact that Irish nationalism in the 1880s was led by Parnell, who was a protestant and who often made appeals to the nation as a whole, but as we have seen from what happened on the ground in the Ulster constituencies in 1885 the nationalist appeal was in practice directed to only the catholic section of the population. Again, it has been argued that the Orange order and the gentry played little part in the new unionist political machinery that emerged in 1885-6, but we have seen that this was far from the case. At the same time while the strategic value of the Orange vote and organisation must be emphasised, the responsibility for this lay not with English politicians such as Randolph Churchill with talk of an 'Orange card', but in fact with E. S. Finnigan, an individual who has been mentioned in almost no historical surveys of the period.[2]

The political confrontation which emerged in 1886, and which proved so lasting, assumed the form it did during the developments of the previous eighteen years. No doubt there were links of sorts with the past which protagonists, later emphasized to justify their contemporary positions, but it was the conditions and changes of the period, 1868-86, that led to politics in Ulster, and indeed in the rest of Ireland, taking the specific form that they did by 1886. Past developments made it likely that religious divisions would be influential and also that nationalist politics would become important. What occurred during these decades, however, determined how significant such matters would become and what their relationship would be to each other and to other aspects of Ulster and Irish society.

In the early part of this period, as the election results clearly show, politics did not centre round the national question in Ulster (or indeed in the rest of Ireland), and instead liberals and conservatives dominated the political scene. As Dr R. V. Comerford has also argued in his recent study of the fenians and mid-Victorian politics and society,[3] it was by no means inevitable that nationalism should emerge as the principal force in Irish politics. Both at the level of parliamentary representation and among the electorate, politics were not yet divided entirely along denominational lines. During these years, however, the political picture changed dramatically. Within Ulster, a unionist movement emerged, of former liberals and conservatives, to face the new nationalist movement which had appeared throughout Ireland. The religious division between protestant and catholic became the single most important social feature of the new political scene.

It is remarkable how strong the correlation between the denominational divide and nationalist-unionist politics became at this time and how the significance of the outcome of the 1885-6 general elections has survived. Despite some exceptions, by 1886 most protestants were unionist and most catholics were nationalist. This was most noticeable on the unionist side where spokesmen, particularly former conservatives, often identified protestantism with unionism. The strong connection between religion and politics was also true on the nationalist side but it was perhaps less immediately obvious because their leader was a protestant and efforts were made in 1886, particularly through the Irish protestant home rule association, to attract protestants; Parnell however, was very much an exception to his group and the association had little success. Overall, the nationalist movement made a direct appeal to catholics and was probably even more successful than the unionist cause in identifying its political aims with the vast bulk of its immediate religious group.

From this period, with its climax in 1885-6, a political scene emerged which proved of lasting significance. Events of 1912-23 determined territorial and constitutional structures but did not basically alter the political scene that evolved at this time. In Ulster, and later in Northern Ireland, the nationalist-unionist conflict and its corresponding religious divisions are still evident. Today's official unionist party alone can trace its roots directly back to 1886, but the other parties, with the exception of the Alliance party, lie within the basic framework of the political and sectarian divisions of this period. In the rest of Ireland, including the Ulster counties of Monaghan, Cavan and Donegal, these years were also very important. The constitutional question emerged as the main issue, displacing other social and regional conflicts on the political agenda. Although the old nationalist party has disappeared, the origins of the principal Irish parties lie in the conflict over the constitutional question, particularly as experienced in the civil war of 1922-3.[4] The inheritors of the nationalist movement and party in the Irish Free State, and later the Republic, continued to be based largely in the catholic community. Southern protestants, especially in Donegal, Cavan and Monaghan, by and large retained a separate political identity up to the late 1930s, electing independent T.D.s but, following constituency boundary changes and a fall in protestant numbers, they ceased to have any real relevance in the political scene.[5]

This period, therefore, saw the emergence of nationalist and unionist politics and the polarisation of society on religious grounds. But the special features of these new developments and their relationship to the contemporary situation must be stressed. The new unionist movement was concerned with defending the union but because of events of the previous two decades it represented only protestants. The failure of the Ulster liberals to hold catholic support meant that the new combination of former liberals and conservatives represented just one part of the Ulster population. This new unionist movement, furthermore, was dominated by the conservative, Orange-backed element in Ulster society, with the gentry still prominent, at the expense of the more radical, liberal section. All this had great implications for the character of the future unionist movement. The new nationalist movement, on the other hand, which also emerged, represented only catholics. The old home rule movement had made little headway among Ulster protestants and the new nationalist movement of the mid-1880's was one based firmly in the catholic community: it was strongly rooted in the needs of catholics and backed fully by the catholic clergy. As a result of this, unionism and nationalism in Ulster assumed their particular forms at this time.

Clearly the period under study is of great importance. By 1886 the political scene in Ulster had been transformed to assume its modern form. The character of the parliamentary representation, the issues involved, and the behaviour of the electorate irrevocably and dramatically changed between 1868 and 1886. The reasons for these changes are complex, but there were a number of important factors and developments. To understand the political changes of this period it is necessary to look first at the electoral system, secondly at the nature of society and the key developments that occurred in it, and finally at the role of the parties, their organisational structures and leadership.

The nature of the electoral system helped to shape these developments. The composition of the electorate, which vitally affected the outcome of elections, resulted from the effect of the franchise laws together with geographical differences in religious distribution and disparities in the social position of the denominations. The increase in the number of catholic and labourers' votes brought about by the franchise changes of 1884 was of special significance. The ballot act probably gave rise to some changes in voting patterns, although it did not ensure complete secrecy in voting because of the widespread adoption of the tally-card system. Coercion was not a serious matter before 1872, and when electors turned against landlord M.P.s in the early 1870s, it was primarily because of the new climate of political opinion. The corrupt practices act of 1883, by limiting election expenditure, was a relevant factor in the emergence in 1885 of the new, voluntary political organisations with their broad social basis. To some small extent, however, the political events of the 1870s had already caused a move in this direction, even among the conservatives.

The significance of the extension of the franchise to the population at large due to the 1884 act must be stressed. The importance of the 1918 franchise act in broadening political participation to new groups has been emphasised but it can be argued that the earlier act was in fact more significant. Between 1884 and 1885 the number of electors in Ulster increased by nearly 180 per cent. Only adult male householders had the vote but this meant that most families of all social and religious sections were now enfranchised. The 1918 act gave the vote to other adult males and some women (those aged 30 or over who were ratepayers), but for families in Ulster, as in the rest of Ireland it was the 1884 act that gave most the vote for the first time. This period then was crucial for the establishment of first time voting preferences for families which habit and tradition would maintain.

The nature of society and the changes that occurred at this time were also important for these new political developments. The dominance of the gentry at the beginning of the period reflected their pre-eminent economic and social role which was accepted generally. The growing unrest over the land question, which eventually upset their position, had some roots in underlying landlord-tenant problems. But what caused the new and eventually successful challenge to their role in the 1870s and the 1880s was, first, the misguided land act of 1870 which unduly raised hopes of change and then, in fact, gave additional complications to landlord-tenant relations. The second factor was the new land movement which effectively harnessed the growing protest and received a vital extra impetus because of the depression in agriculture, 1878-80. Growing confidence among prosperous members of the farming community as well as the expanding professional and business groups explains where the leadership of this land movement came from.

The rise of unionism and nationalism was also strongly affected by social and economic factors. Although parts of Ulster witnessed a population decline similar to most other parts of Ireland, and Ulster farmers were just as keen as others to obtain extra rights, there was greater industrialisation, more secure land tenure and so better overall prosperity in Ulster than elsewhere in Ireland: population fell by only 33 per cent in the former compared with 50 per cent in the latter.[6] Because of this, northern unionists had much less reason to question the benefits of the union than did southern nationalists, and so home rule was less attractive to the former than to the latter. However, such a major regional, social and economic division could have led to a straightforward split between a totally unionist Ulster and the rest of Ireland which was entirely nationalist. To understand why this did not happen it is necessary to look at the religious factor in society.

In the years following 1868 an important undercurrent of religious conflict can be detected. The new political leaders in Ulster in the 1860s and 1870s tended to be presbyterians who challenged the dominance of the Church of Ireland gentry, while in the 1880s a new group of catholic politicians emerged. Rural protest was strongest among presbyterian and catholic farmers. Clearly then, in the protest movement of the 1860s, 1870s and 1880s against the old system of landlord dominated politics, there were religious tensions, but not simply between protestant and catholic. In the 1880s, however, with the rise of the unionist and nationalist movements the religious factor emerged in an even more important and, this time, more sharply polarised form, which had a strong sectarian effect on unionism and nationalism.

For catholics and protestants in late nineteenth century Ireland both religious conflict and the strength of denominational bonds had an important impact on their political positions. Although most specifically religious issues were settled by the 1880s, this whole area still coloured people's views on broader political matters, including the question of the link with Great Britain. Various religious controversies, such as that over education, had caused catholic disillusionment with the connection, a feeling not experienced by protestants, who saw the possibility of a majority catholic, home rule parliament as a threat. The strengthening of denominational ties and identities during the nineteenth century meant that for most people in Ireland, the links with their respective religious groups were very important.

By 1885-6 nearly all Ulster catholics, of every social rank, strongly identified with the political aspirations of their co-religionists elsewhere in Ireland, who saw their best future in a Dublin parliament and so voted nationalist. Because of their different experiences in all these areas, Ulster protestants voted unionist, a political stance shared with their co-religionists in other parts of Ireland. Religious division was important not only within Irish society but between nationalist Ireland and Britain. The distinct identities of both protestant and catholic which had been strengthened by religious trends during the second half of the nineteenth century helped to overcome potentially significant divisions of class and region.

The importance of the religious element in Irish nationalist opinion has been stressed elsewhere, particularly by Dr R. V. Comerford for the mid-Victorian period and by Dr Tom Garvin for the 1890s and early 1900s.[7] Frank Wright has similarly identified its importance for Ulster unionism in the late nineteenth and early twentieth centuries.[8] Without this religious element in our period it is possible that either Irish nationalism would not have arisen in an effective form or it would have been identified solely with social and economic grievances, without any denominational division. On the other hand, it is difficult to see how the religious element could have been eliminated, not least because many other societies in Western Europe in the late nineteenth and early twentieth centuries also saw parties develop along denominational lines.[9] The fact remains, however, that nationalism and unionism did emerge, religious divisions remained important, and the shape of politics took on a particular form in the special relationship of the two divisions which has proved to be remarkably durable.

Economic and social tensions between protestant and catholic in Ulster probably played some part in the rise of the opposing camps of unionist and nationalist, but their importance should not be exaggerated, chiefly because the other main divisions and conflicts in society did not correlate to a simple protestant catholic divide. Members of the Church of Ireland owned most of the land and dominated official positions, at the expense not just of catholics but also of presbyterians. Catholics were over-represented among unskilled labourers and small farmers while presbyterians dominated the skilled jobs and larger farm sector, but most ordinary members of the Church of Ireland had little or no special advantage in these latter areas. After, and not before, the events of 1885-6, when a strong community identity emerged between protestants of all denominations on the one side, and between all catholics on the other, these tensions assumed more significance.

In all the changes of this period, the organisational structures and leadership of the parties, and how they responded to contemporary issues, were of great importance. The liberals, directed by the Ulster liberal society, drew valuable assistance from the tenant right movement in the general elections of 1874 and 1880. The liberal response to the land question brought them considerable support from both catholic and protestant farmers. Over reliance on the tenant right associations in 1885, however, when new groups and new issues had altered the political scene, proved disadvantageous for the liberals in the general election of that year. Poor strategy and weak leadership also damaged their performance in 1885. Their defeat in the general election of that year was critical because in the new unionist movement which emerged the following year the liberals, as a result of this defeat, were relegated to second place in relation to the conservatives, both at local and central level. Subsequently, they did represent some marginal unionist divisions and they influenced government policy in the 1890s through their party connections in England,[10] but their role continued to diminish until 1912 when the liberal unionist group in Ulster ceased to have any sort of separate party identity.

The conservative party of the late 1860s with its landowning M.P.s and its heavy reliance on landlords, their agents and finance, was incapable of meeting adequately the rising tenant farmer challenge of the 1870s. The growth of new associations from the mid 1870s onwards, and a willingness of Ulster conservative M.P.s to back agrarian reform, had only limited success. These associations, however, provided the basis for the new divisional conservative associations that emerged in 1885 and, backed by the Orange order, proved to be very effective in the general election of that year. Energetic leadership and good tactics, combined with this new organisation, provided the conservatives with remarkable success but only among the protestant electorate.

The conservative victory of 1885 meant that when the new unionist movement of former liberals and conservatives emerged in 1886, effective control of the protestant political community, at both local and parliamentary level, lay not with liberals, who were willing to co-operate politically with catholics, but with conservatives who were unlikely to do so. The conservative divisional associations in the north-east of the province continued as the new unionist local organisations. The conservative and Orange tradition rather than the radical, liberal tradition had gained the upper hand in protestantism and unionism, which were now closely identified. Ironically, the nationalist leadership decision to give catholic support to the conservatives in 1885 in Ulster was vital for this crucial development in the balance of power in the unionist movement. The 1885 result also served to restore the gentry to a prominent place in Ulster politics and in the new unionist movement contrary to trends at previous elections. Subsequently, the gentry shared the leadership of the unionist party with other social groups.[11] Nonetheless, events of 1885-6 gave them back a role in northern politics which survived into the twentieth-century.

The original home rule organisation was inappropriate and ineffective in Ulster. It had neither the strong central support system of the liberals nor the local, individually based party machinery of the conservatives in this early period. The new nationalist movement of the mid 1880s, however, had an excellent organisation based on the central body and the branches of the national league and supported by the catholic clergy. These new structures were vital for the nationalist success of 1885 in Ulster, as were the energetic leadership and tactical manoeuvrings of the leadership. The whole approach of the party, however, both in its organisation and in the decisions it made, such as to contest only catholic majority constituencies, and to follow the catholic line on education, guaranteed its achievements at the polls in 1885, but only among catholics.

In 1886 the nationalist party, through the Irish protestant home rule association, did try to broaden its base. But the main features of the party had already been established in 1885 and it would be neither willing nor able to really change them, as Dr James Loughlin has recently pointed out.[12] Clerical involvement continued to be a major feature of nationalist party politics and in Ulster in the late nineteenth century, it seems to have been greater than elsewhere in Ireland:[13] catholic clergy retained a prominent place in northern nationalism until well into the twentieth century.[14] Although the catholic community had previously reflected a variety of political views, events of 1885-6 resulted in the vast bulk of the community identifying with the nationalist movement. Subsequently, divisions emerged within this movement but a basic political identity for the catholic population was established during these years.

Additional comment can be made on the role at this time of the catholic clergy in nationalist politics and the Orange order and the gentry in unionist politics. Contemporary partisan commentators often gave these groups a dominant position in their opponents' organisations. Some protestant critics saw the catholic clergy as actually leading their people into the nationalist movement.[15] Such a view is clearly exaggerated as various other factors were important for the rise of nationalism such as social and economic issues. It is probable that the catholic electors were led by their clergy only when it suited them but undoubtedly the catholic clergy were a key factor in the new nationalist organisation of 1885.[16] Perhaps more importantly, the overwhelmingly broad and public declaration of support by so many clergy was important for ensuring near unanimity among the catholic population at this key period. Various political and social tensions within the large number of people who now made up the nationalist community were overcome by the avowedly official catholic endorsement of the movement.

Catholic and nationalist commentators often saw a malign influence in the role of the Orange order and of the gentry in the unionist movement, arguing that without these two elements protestants would have been much more willing to accept nationalism.[17] Such an argument had many weaknesses and ignored the reasons why protestants rejected nationalism. It also failed to take account of the fact that the protestant electors, like their catholic counterparts, would not be led by these groups when it did not suit them as, for example, in 1885 when the Orange and gentry leadership was obliged to pay attention to electors' demands. But undoubtedly the

Orange order played a key role in winning the strategically important labourers' vote and the willingness of the gentry to support the
new local associations was important. Later the order widened its
membership from a minority to a majority of protestant electors
and so provided a valuable vehicle to contain various social and
religious divisions, by stressing a common protestant identity, and to
confront a now united catholic movement.[18]

The years 1885-6 were the climax to a period of great political
change and popular mobilisation in the whole country. The extension
of the franchise and changes in the laws of party expenditure, as well
as the high degree of popular excitement over the issues that now
held the public attention, meant entirely new demands were placed
on the party organisations. The nationalists and conservatives in
Ulster established widespread, broad-based party branches to
incorporate the new political demands and to organise the population effectively. The liberals failed to meet this challenge. The
structure and spirit of the new party organisations had a very
important bearing on the type of politics and society to emerge in
Ulster at this time. These parties reflected certain divisions in society
and particular important elements had key roles in the new party
structures. The decisions by both the nationalist and conservative
party leadership to adapt their organisations in the way they did
(important no doubt to meet the challenges of 1885-6 and to win
the elections) had a far-reaching influence on the new political and
social confrontations to materialise at these elections.

Clearly the years 1868-86 were of great importance. What is not
so clear is why those decades in particular should have been so
influential. Other decades in the nineteenth century had witnessed
significant events but none had such obvious lasting relevance.
Various political movements had successfully courted public
opinions previously but none had achieved such permanence as the
new unionist and nationalist groupings. Part of the answer to this
question lies in the nature of some of the broader changes that
occurred. This was the era when for the first time the vast majority
of the people could read and write. Key social and economic
developments, in particular the main resolution of the land
question, the enormous growth of Belfast and the strengthening of
religious identities, all of which set the scene for modern Ulster,
occurred in this period. The other part of the answer lies in the very
significant extension of the franchise and the rise of modern political
parties, that took place in these years of mass political mobilisation
and electoral change.

The importance of such developments has been noted elsewhere by political scientists. In many parts of Europe the particular divisions that emerged as important at the end of the nineteenth and the beginning of the twentieth centuries have remained significant.[19] Party systems have continued remarkably true to the traditions and shape of the politics established at this point where broad based modern parties, with a wide franchise, came into being for the first time. People have then simply voted for the same parties as their parents. Even when particular parties have collapsed and new ones have arisen, they have often remained within the basic framework of the party system established at this earlier stage.[20]

The nationalist and unionist movements that emerged between 1868-86 were clearly a result of the specific conditions of the period. Had political developments been otherwise the outcome of these years may well have been very different. This could have affected not only the initial appearance of these movements but also the particular shape that they eventually assumed. Possibly a more sensitive and effective government reaction to the situation in Ireland in the early 1870s could have undermined home rule and nationalist demands. A liberal-conservative, and eventually labour-conservative split, might have been the basic divide in Ulster and Irish politics, as happened in nineteenth and early twentieth century Scotland and Wales, where nationalism failed to win wide support.[20] A better organised and more responsive liberal movement in the north could perhaps have kept a joint catholic/presbyterian vote and a straightforward north/south split could have emerged. A nationalist party that was not so anxious to win the entire catholic vote, by whatever means were necessary, might have won over a significant number of protestants.

Such outcomes are hypothetical, but other consequences of these years are more concrete. The nationalist and unionist movements that emerged were firmly based in denominational divisions. There was no room for a third party, such as the liberals, based on inter-denominational or secular support, as in Holland,[21] which could have prevented the dominance of a majority party, either in Ulster or the rest of Ireland. Within the unionist camp, the former conservatives, with strong gentry and Orange involvement, emerged as the leading group in the protestant community at the expense of the former liberals. This had important social and political consequences for the emerging new unionist movement. The catholic community was now united on an all-Ireland basis behind the nationalist party. The events of this period meant Irish nationalism emerged as a catholic movement with strong clerical involvement, unlike Italian nationalism which was anti-clerical. The beginnings of a tradition of catholic-protestant political cooperation were destroyed and this made it very difficult to subsequently establish joint political and governmental cooperation. The special features of these new nationalist and unionist movements were clearly a result of the developments of these years.

Neither the polarisation of politics along denominational lines nor the emergence of nationalism are unique to the province or to Ireland but have strong parallels in contemporary Europe. Although it was no longer a major factor in politics in Great Britain by this stage, religious conflict remained important in other parts of Western Europe. In Germany, Switzerland and Holland there were significant divisions between protestant and catholic parties.[22] Various European countries, such as Norway and Italy also experienced the rise of nationalist politics.[23] The situation in Ulster, however, differed from the situation in these countries in that, besides religious differences, there was also a split over the national question and, because of the changes we have witnessed, each division powerfully reinforced the other. The developments of the years 1868-86 saw the emergence in Ulster of two distinct political movements, based firmly on particular religious groups, with strongly opposed views on the nature of the nation and state, and, in effect, on the crucial issue of sovereignty. This situation has survived and is the basic source of the 'Northern Ireland problem' today.

The divisions of this early period have remained of fundamental importance but this is not because they are inevitably rooted in past conflict or simply reflect a fundamental, inescapable division. The political, social and religious divisions that are so influential in twentieth-century Ulster only emerged in their contemporary form between 1868-86 resulting from the particular events and developments of those years although, of course, they did have some roots in the past. Their survival to the present may seem surprising but the reasons for this can be found by examining political developments elsewhere. In many European countries the political systems that emerged at the end of the nineteenth century and the beginning of the twentieth century, when states had modernised, the mass of people had been educated and the franchise had been extended, have proved lasting and important.[24] In Northern Ireland modern politics reflect the party system and divisions which appeared at this significant point in history when similar fundamental changes occurred: events of 1912-20 determined the size and constitution of the new state but the basic nature of its politics were established at this period. What *is* surprising is the absence of tranquil, gradual change in recent decades and the emergence of the 'troubles' with their community strife and death toll.

Some present-day commentators, both in Ulster and from outside, have attributed the rise and continuance of this community strife to irrational, prejudiced behaviour. Such an analysis, however, ignores the reality of the conflict that emerged from the political crisis of these formative years and which has survived ever since, with only certain modifications due to the new conditions of the twentieth century. Two sources of conflict — religion and nationalism — emerged as key elements in the political scene of this period, around which new party groupings and organisations were formed. Conflict over either of these issues (which have caused deep problems in other countries) could well have diminished in time, as has happened elsewhere, and the parties could have modified their positions. But in Ulster and then in Northern Ireland each issue has continued to reinforce the other, and the parties have not been able, or willing, to change adequately, partly because of their structures and ethos which emerged at this time. It is the convergence of both sources of conflict in the particular political form which took shape in the late nineteenth century that has created the severe and continuing polarisation of the community.

One other reason for the lack of effective, peaceful change in recent times is surely the belief that these religious and political divisions are fundamental and so cannot be changed. The association of particular divisions with certain political views has been regarded as inescapable and 'natural' and the conflict in Northern Ireland has been seen as inevitable and inexorable. However, the particular state of Ulster politics which emerged in the period 1868-86, and which has remained so influential to the present, was the result of the political and social developments of the time. In these formative years, party leaders, organisers and supporters, influenced and aided by the social, economic and religious developments of their age, created a new order of politics where the religious and national divisions were firmly inter-related in a form that is still basically evident today. Knowledge of our history, of how and why all this happened when it did, may enlighten us; it may also help us cope with the *real* burden of our past.

ABBREVIATIONS

Some short titles other than those listed below are used in the notes. In these cases the full title and the date of publication are given in the first citation.

A.G.	*Armagh Guardian*
A.Std.	*Armagh Standard*
Amer.Hist.Assoc.	*American Historical Association*
B.L., Add. MS	British Library, Additional MS
B.M.N.	*Belfast Morning News*
B.N.L.	*Belfast News Letter*
C.N.	*Cavan News*
C.Chron.	*Coleraine Chronicle*
C.Const.	*Coleraine Constitution*
D.I.	*Down Independent*
D.J.	*Derry Journal*
D.R.	*Derry Recorder*
E.A.	*Enniskillen Advertiser*
F.J.	*Freeman's Journal*
F.M.	*Fermanagh Mail*
F.T.	*Fermanagh Times*
Healy, *Letters*	T.M. Healy, *Letter and leaders of my day* (2 vols, London, 1928).
I.H.S.	*Irish Historical Studies*
I.R.	*Impartial Reporter*
L.G.	*Londonderry Guardian*
L.J.	*Londonderry Journal*
L.Sent.	*Londonderry Sentinel*
L.S.	*Londonderry Standard*
Livingstone, *Fermanagh*	Peadar Livingstone, *The Fermanagh story* (Enniskillen, 1969).
Livingstone, *Monaghan*	Peadar Livingstone, *The Monaghan story* (Enniskillen, 1980).
McElroy, *Route land crusade*	S. C. McElroy, The Route land crusade . . . (Coleraine, n.d.).
McKeown, 'Land in South Antrim'	Paschal McKeown, 'The land question and elections in South Antrim, 1870-1910'. M.S.Sc. thesis, Queen's University of Belfast, 1981.

MacKnight, *Ulster as it is*	Thomas MacKnight, *Ulster as it is, or twenty eight years experience as an Irish editor* (2 vols, London, 1896).
Murphy, *Derry and modern Ulster*	Desmond Murphy, *Derry, Donegal and modern Ulster, 1870-1921* (Derry, 1981).
N.L.I.	National Library of Ireland
N.R.	*Newry Reporter*
N.Star	*Northern Star*
N.S.	*Northern Standard*
N.T.	*Newry Telegraph*
N.W.	*Northern Whig*
O'Brien, 'The Irish party'	Conor Cruise O'Brien, 'The Irish parliamentary party, 1880-90' (Ph.D. thesis, University of Dublin, 1954)
O'Brien, *Parnell and his party*	Conor Cruise O'Brien, *Parnell and his party, 1880-90* (London, 1957; corrected ed., 1964).
P.A.	*People's Advocate*
P.R.O.	Public Record Office [of Great Britain]
P.R.O.N.I.	Public Record Office of Northern Ireland
Rev.Pol.	*Review of Politics*
S.P.O.	State Paper Office of Ireland, Dublin Castle
Savage, *Origins of the unionists*	D. C. Savage, 'The origins of the Ulster unionist party, 1885-6', *I.H.S.,* xii, no. 47 (Mar. 1961), pp 185-208.
T.Const.	*Tyrone Constitution*
T.Cour.	*Tyrone Courier*
Thornley, *Isaac Butt*	David Thornley, *Isaac Butt and home rule* (London, 1964).
Ulster census, 1871	*Census of Ireland, 1871 (province of Ulster,* [C964-1-X], H.C. 1874, lxxiv, pt 1.
Ulster census, 1881	*Census of Ireland, 1881 (province of Ulster),* [C3204], H.C. 1882, lxxviii.
Ulster census, 1891	*Census of Ireland, 1891 (province of Ulster),* [C6626-IX], H.C. 1892, xcii.
U.E.	*Ulster Examiner*
U.G.	*Ulster Gazette*
U.T.	*Ulster Times*

Vaughan, 'Landlord-tenant relations'	W. E. Vaughan, 'A study in landlord and tenant relations in Ireland between the famine and the land war' (Ph.D. thesis, University of Dublin, 1973).
Vaughan and Fitzpatrick *Population*	W. E. Vaughan and A. J. Fitzpatrick (ed.), *Irish historical statistics: population, 1821-1971 (Dublin, 1978).*
W.E.	*Weekly Examiner*
W.N.	*Weekly News*
W.W.	*Weekly Whig*
Walker, 'Irish electorate'	B. M. Walker, 'The Irish electorate, 1868-1915', in *I.H.S.,* xviii, no. 71 (Mar. 1973), pp 359-406.
Walker, 'Party organisation in Ulster'	B. M. Walker, 'Party organisation in Ulster, 1865-92: registration agents and their activities in Peter Roebuck (ed.), *Plantation to partition: essays in honour of J. L. McCracken* (Belfast, 1981), pp 191-209.

NOTES

INTRODUCTION

1 A. M. Sullivan, *New Ireland* (2 vols, London, 1877), ii, 411.
2 K. T. Hoppen, *Elections, politics, and society in Ireland, 1832-1885* (Oxford, 1984).
3 Peter Gibbon, *The origins of Ulster unionism: the formation of popular protestant politics and ideology in nineteenth-century Ireland* (Manchester, 1975); P. J. Buckland (ed.), *Irish unionism, 1885-1923: a documentary history* (Belfast, 1973); Desmond Murphy, *Derry, Donegal and modern Ulster, 1870-1921* (Derry, 1981; hereafter cited as Murphy, *Derry and modern Ulster*): John Magee 'The Monaghan election of 1883 and the "invasion of Ulster"' in *Clogher Record*, viii (1974), pp 147-66; Paul Bew and Frank Wright, 'The agrarian opposition in Ulster politics, 1848-87' in Samuel Clark and J. S. Donnelly (ed.) *Irish peasants: violence and political unrest, 1780-1914* (Wisconsin, 1983), pp 192-229.
4 Thomas MacKnight, *Ulster as it is, or twenty-eight years experience as an Irish editor* (2 vols, London, 1896), i, 7-10.
5 Paschal Grousset, *Ireland's disease: the English in Ireland* (London, 1887; Belfast reprint, 1986).

I ULSTER SOCIETY, 1861-91

CHAPTER 1 *Country and town*

1 J. B. Doyle, *Tours in Ulster: a handbook to the antiquities and scenery of the north of Ireland* (Dublin, 1854), pp 1-2.
2 W. E. Vaughan and A. J. Fitzpatrick, *Irish historical statistics: population, 1821-1971* (Dublin, 1978), p. 27 (hereafter cited as Vaughan and Fitzpatrick, *Population*).
3 *N.W.*, 26 Apr. 1859.
4 Paschal McKeown, 'The land question and elections in South Antrim, 1870-1910' (M.S.Sc. thesis, The Queen's University of Belfast, 1981), p. 71.
5 B. M. Walker, *Sentry Hill: an Ulster farm and family* (Belfast, 1981), pp 69, 124.
6 J. H. Whyte, *The tenant league and Irish politics in the eighteen-fifties* (Dundalk, 1966), pp 6-9.
7 Below, p. 37.
8 Vaughan and Fitzpatrick, *Population*, p. 27.
9 *Summary of the returns of owners or land in Ireland, showing with respect to each county, the number of owners below an acre, and in classes up to 100,000 acres, and upwards, with the aggregate acreage and valuation of each class*, pp 21, 25, H.C. 1876 (422), lxxx, 55, 59.
10 *Agricultural statistics of Ireland for the year 1876*, p. 7 [C1749], H.C. 1877, lxxxv, 535 (hereafter cited as *Agricultural statistics, 1876*).
11 *Returns showing the number of agricultural holdings in Ireland and the tenure by which they are held by the occupiers*, p. 1 [C32], H.C. 1870, lvi, 737 (hereafter cited as *Return of holdings, 1870*).
12 W. E. Vaughan, 'An assessment of the economic performance of Irish landlords, 1851-81' in F. S. L. Lyons and R. A. J. Hawkins (ed.), *Ireland under the union: varieties of tension. Essays in honour of T. W. Moody* (Oxford, 1980), pp 180-81.

13 Information on size of landholdings from *Return of owners of land of one acre and upwards in the several counties, counties of cities and counties of towns in Ireland* [c. 1492], H.C. 1876, xxx, 61-394 (later cited as *Irish landowners*). Details of Hertford estate from *N.W.*, 19, 20 Dec. 1872. Hamilton's rental from *Report of her majesty's commissioners of enquiry into the working of the landlord and tenant (Ireland) act, 1870*, p. 481 [C2779-1], H.C. 1881, xviii, 699.

14 See Lord Ernest Hamilton, *Forty years on* (London, 1922), pp 71-93.

15 *Ballywalter Park* (Belfast, 1985).

16 *C. Const.*, 20 Mar. 1880.

17 W. E. Vaughan, 'A study in landlord and tenant relations in Ireland between the famine and the land war' (Ph.D. thesis, University of Dublin, 1973), p. 320 (hereafter cited as Vaughan, 'Landlord-tenant relations'); W. E. Vaughan, *Landlords and tenants in Ireland, 1848-1904*, (Dublin, 1984).

18 S. C. McElroy, *The Route land crusade; being an authentic account of the efforts made to advance land reform by the Route tenants' defence association, the Antrim central tenant-right association and the Ulster land committee* (Coleraine n.d.) p. 30 (hereafter cited as McElroy, *Route land crusade*).

19 Vaughan 'Landlord-tenant relations', p. 320.

20 *Agricultural statistics, 1876*, p. 7; *Return of holdings*, pp 16-17.

21 *Census of Ireland for 1861. Part V. General report*, p. liii, H.C. 1863 (3204-IV), lxi, 53.

22 MacKnight, *Ulster as it is*, i, 79-82, 110.

23 See David Steele, *Irish land and British politics: tenant-right and nationality, 1865-1870* (Cambridge, 1974), p. 314.

24 James McKnight to Gladstone, 2 April 1870 (B.L. Gladstone papers, Add. MS 44426/68).

25 McElroy, *Route land crusade*, p. 30.

26 Ibid., p. 31; circular from W. J. Moore, secretary of Down farmers' union, May 1872 (P.R.O.N.I., Moore papers, D877/27A).

27 *L.S.*, 15 Oct. 1873.

28 *N.W.*, 21, 22 Jan. 1874.

29 McElroy, *Route land crusade*, p. 31.

30 Circular from W. J. Moore, secretary of Down farmers' union, May 1873 (P.R.O.N.I., Moore papers, D877/27A). For Co. Monaghan see Peadar Livingstone, *The Monaghan story* (Enniskillen, 1980), p. 334 (hereafter cited as Livingstone, *Monaghan*). For southern tenants' associations, see James O'Shea, *Priests, politics and society in post-famine Ireland: a study of County Tipperary, 1850-1891* (Dublin, 1984), p. 72.

31 Livingstone, *Monaghan*, p. 334.

32 McElroy, *Route land crusade*, p. 61.

33 *T.Const.*, 5 Mar. 1880; *I.R.*, 11 Mar. 1880.

34 See editorial of *N.W.*, 15 Mar. 1880.

35 See R. W. Kirkpatrick, 'Origins and development of the land war in mid-Ulster' in F. S. L. Lyons and R. A. J. Hawkins (ed.), *Ireland under the union: varieties of tension. Essays in honour of T. W. Moody* (Oxford, 1980), pp 213-18.

36 J. L. McCracken, 'The consequences of the land war', in T. W. Moody and J. C. Beckett (ed.), *Ulster since 1800, first series: a political and economic survey* (London, 1955), p. 62.

37 Sir Thomas Bateson to marquis of Salisbury, 30 Dec. 1880 (Hatfield House, Salisbury papers).

38 See, for example, C. S. Parnell in Co. Fermanagh, *Ulster Ex.*, 11 Nov. 1880, and Michael Davitt and John Dillon in Co. Down, *B.N.L.*, 24 Dec. 1880.

39 *U.E.*, 2 Nov., 10 Dec. 1880.

40 *U.E.*, 11 Nov. 1880; *L. Sent.*, 10 Nov. 1881.
41 Rev. D. C. Abbot to H. de F. Montgomery, 18 Dec. 1880 (P.R.O.N.I., Montgomery papers, D627/428/7).
42 Francis Thompson 'Attitudes to reform: political parties in Ulster and the Irish land bill of 1881' in *I.H.S.*, xxiv, no. 95 (May 1985), pp 327-40.
43 The *Londonderry Standard,* however, we may note, had urged peasant proprietorship from the 1850s. For an account of the views of its best-known editor, James McKnight, see Paul Bew and Frank Wright 'The agrarian opposition in Ulster, 1848-87' in Samuel Clark and James Donnelly (ed.), *Irish peasants: violence and political unrest, 1780-1914* (Wisconsin, 1983), pp 194-7.
44 MacKnight, *Ulster as it is,* i, 398-9.
45 *F.J.*, 18 Oct. 1882.
46 See *I.R.*, 20, 27 Oct., 29 Dec. 1881.
47 *L.S.*, 27 Jan. 1883.
48 *B.N.L.*, 6 Feb. 1886.
49 *D.J.*, 4 Nov. 1886.
50 H. H. McNeile to Lord Cairns, 4 Feb. 1882 (P.R.O., Cairns papers, 30/51/16f/102).
51 See Peadar Livingstone, *The Fermanagh story* (Enniskillen, 1969; hereafter cited as Livingstone, *Fermanagh*), pp 258-64, and J. C. Rutherford, *An Ards farmer; or an account of the life of James Shanks, Ballyfounder, Portaferry* (Belfast, 1913), pp 62-5.
52 Olive Robinson, 'The economic significance of the London companies as landlords in Ireland during the period 1800-70' (Ph.D. thesis, The Queen's University of Belfast, 1957), pp 289-301.
53 *Report from the select committee on the Irish Society and the London companies (Irish estates),* pp 5, 257, H.C. 1890 (322), xiv, 5, 257.
54 See account of protest meeting, *L.S.*, 24 Aug. 1872.
55 *Census of Ireland, 1871 (province of Ulster),* pp 991-7 [C964-1-x], H.C. 1874, lxxiv, pt 1, (hereafter cited as *Ulster census, 1871*), 991-7.
56 *Census of Ireland, 1891 (province of Ulster),* pp 976-81 [C6626-ix], H.C. 1892, xcii, (hereafter cited as *Ulster census, 1891*), 1000-5.
57 J. W. Boyle, 'A marginal figure: the Irish rural labourer' in Samuel Clark and J. S. Donnelly (ed.), *Irish peasants: violence and political unrest, 1780-1914* (Wisconsin, 1983), pp 331-5.
58 See *Royal commission on labour: the agricultural labourer, vol. iv, Ireland, pt iv,* [C6892-xviii], pp 9-11, H.C. 1893-4, xxvii, pt 1, 9-11.
59 W. M. Thackeray, *The Paris sketch book and Irish sketch book,* (London, 1877), p. 508.
60 Leslie Clarkson, 'The city and the country', in J. C. Beckett and others, *Belfast: the making of the city* (Belfast, 1982), p. 159. Population figures from Vaughan and Fitzpatrick, *Population,* pp 36-7.
61 E. E. Evans and B. S. Turner, *Ireland's eye: the photographs of R. J. Welch* (Belfast, 1977), p. 22.
62 *Ulster Census, 1881,* p. 144.
63 See C. F. Smith, *J. N. Richardson of Bessbrook* (London, 1925).
64 See Henry Patterson, 'Industrial labour and the labour movement, 1820-1914' in Liam Kennedy and Philip Ollerenshaw (ed.), *An economic history of Ulster, 1820-1914* (Manchester, 1984), p. 176.
65 J. L. McCracken, 'The later nineteenth century' in T. W. Moody and J. C. Beckett (ed.), *Ulster since 1800, second series: a social survey* (London, 1957), p. 50.
66 E. R. R. Green, 'Business organisation' in Moody and Beckett, ibid., p. 115.
67 R. D. C. Black, 'The progress of industrialisation' in T. W. Moody and J. C. Beckett (ed.), *Ulster since 1800, first series: a political and economic survey* (London, 1955), p. 50.

⁶⁸ K. H. McConnell, 'Population trends' in ibid., pp 77-8.
⁶⁹ See Vaughan and Fitzpatrick, *Population*, pp 5-16.
⁷⁰ Ibid., pp 27-41.
⁷¹ J. C. Beckett, 'Belfast — a general survey' in J. C. Beckett and R. E. Glasscock (ed.), *Belfast: the origin and growth of an industrial city* (London, 1967), p. 189.
⁷² *Thom's directory, 1865.*
⁷³ *Local government and taxation of towns inquiry commission (Ireland): part I. Report and evidence with appendices*, pp 281-2 [C1696], H.C. 1877, xxxix, 281-2, (hereafter cited as *Local government inquiry, part I*).
⁷⁴ *Local government and taxation of towns inquiry commission (Ireland): part III. Report and evidence with appendices*, p. 127 [C1787], H.C. 1877, xl, 357.
⁷⁵ *Local government inquiry, part I*, p. 21; G. H. Bassett, *Book of Antrim* (Dublin, 1888), pp 209-17.
⁷⁶ Samuel McSkimin, *The history and antiquities of the county of the town of Carrickfergus* (Belfast, 1849; new ed., with notes and appendix by E. J. McCrum, 1906), pp 106-18; *Local government inquiry, part I*, pp 9-10 and 244-6.

CHAPTER 2 *Religion*

¹ W.M. Thackeray, *The Paris sketch book and Irish sketch book* (London, 1877), p. 509.
² All the above figures are from Vaughan and Fitzpatrick, *Population*, pp 51-62.
³ *Ulster Census, 1871*, tables xxxi and xxxii from each county report.
⁴ *General census report, 1871*, p. 116.
⁵ *Ulster census, 1871*, pp 989-98.
⁶ Including those called general labourers, most of whom can be assumed to be agricultural labourers.
⁷ *General census report, 1871*, pp 84-5.
⁸ J. I. D. Johnston, 'The Clogher valley as a social and economic region in the eighteenth and nineteenth centuries' (M. Litt thesis, University of Dublin, 1974), pp 151-62, (hereafter cited as Johnston, 'Clogher valley').
⁹ See T. W. Freeman, *Ireland* (London, 1950), p. 173.
¹⁰ Stephen Gwynn, *Experiences of a literary man* (London, 1926), p. 19.
¹¹ *Return of holdings, 1870*, pp 12-17; *Ulster census, 1871*, p. 914.
¹² See Johnston, 'Clogher valley', pp 160-62.
¹³ See below, pp 66-7, and *Ulster Census, 1881*, pp 127.
¹⁴ See Livingstone, *Monaghan*, pp 241, 287; *Fermanagh*, p. 182.
¹⁵ In the case of Co. Antrim see Paschal McKeown, 'The land question and elections in South Antrim, 1870-1910' M.S.Sc. thesis, Queen's University, Belfast, 1981), p. 70 (hereafter cited as McKeown, 'Land in south Antrim'), and Richard McMinn, 'The myth of "Route" liberalism in County Antrim, 1869-1900' in *Éire-Ireland*, xvii, no. 1 (spring 1982), p. 142.
¹⁶ E.g. report of meeting in Ballyridley, Co. Down, 10 Feb. 1881 in J. C. Rutherford, *An Ards farmer: or an account of the life of James Shanks, Ballyfounder, Portaferry* (Belfast, 1913), pp 58-9; see also An Irish presbyterian, *Ulster and home rule* (Belfast, 1886), p. 11.
¹⁷ See valuable comments by Richard McMinn, 'Presbyterianism and politics in Ulster, 1871-1906' in *Studia Hibernica*, xxi (1981), p. 131.
¹⁸ Minutes of meeting, 20 Nov. 1879, minute book of Co. Fermanagh grand Orange lodge (P.R.O.N.I., D1402/1).
¹⁹ Daniel McLaughlin, *A short history of the parish church of St John the evangelist, Killowen, Coleraine* (Coleraine, 1900), pp 12-15.

20 See Rutherford, *An Ards farmer: or an account of the life of James Shanks, Bally-founder, Portaferry* (Belfast, 1913), pp 55-9.
21 Livingstone, *Monaghan*, pp 334-5.
22 J. L. McCracken, 'The consequences of the land war', in T. W. Moody and J. C. Beckett (ed.), *Ulster since 1800, first series: a political and economic survey* (London, 1955), p. 61.
23 Person unknown to Francis O'Neill, 19 Jan. 1882 (P.R.O.N.I., O'Neill papers, D1481). See T. W. Moody, *Davitt and Irish revolution 1846-82* (Oxford, 1981), pp 445-8, (hereafter cited as Moody, Davitt).
24 Quoted in Livingstone, *Fermanagh*, p. 260.
25 Aiken McClelland, 'The later Orange order' in T. D. Williams (ed.), *Secret societies in Ireland* (Dublin, 1973), p. 130 (hereafter cited as McClelland, 'The later Orange order').
26 Rev. D. C. Abbot to H. de F. Montgomery, 18 Dec. 1880 (P.R.O.N.I., Montgomery papers, D627/428/7).
27 James Crossle to A. R. Jackson, 25 Nov. 1880 (P.R.O.N.I., copy letter book of James and Henry Crossle, Verner papers, D236/488/1-5); Lord de Ros to Lord Beaconsfield, 7 Jan. 1881 (Hughenden, Disraeli papers, B/xxxi/x/236); H. de F. Montgomery to Gladstone, 30 Nov. 1880 (B.L., Gladstone papers, Add. MS 44467/78).
28 Livingstone, *Fermanagh*, p. 261.
29 Sir Thomas Bateson to marquis of Salisbury, 27 June 1882 (Hatfield House, Salisbury papers).
30 *N.W.*, 26 June 1883; MacKnight, *Ulster as it is*, ii, 17; *L.S.*, 3 July 1883.
31 See John Magee, 'The Monaghan election of 1883 and the "invasion of Ulster"' in *Clogher Record*, viii, no. 2 (1974), pp 147-66; Livingstone, *Monaghan*, pp 334-44.
32 See *W.E.*, 13 Feb. 1886.
33 Sir Thomas Bateson to Lord Salisbury, 16 Jan. 1886, enclosing letter from Major W. J. Hall to Bateson, 14 Jan. 1886 (Hatfield House, Salisbury papers).
34 *Ulster census, 1891*, p. 974.
35 *Return . . . of the names of the persons holding the commission of the peace . . . and, number of such persons that are protestant, number Roman Catholics, and number that are members of other persuasions*, pp 1-117, H.C. 1884 (13), lxiii, 333-449 (hereafter cited as *Return of J.P.s*).
36 For criticism from presbyterians see Edward Macnaghten to Lord Ashbourne, 22 Sept. 1891, in A. B. Cooke and A. P. W. Malcomson (ed.), *The Ashbourne papers, 1869-1913* (Belfast, 1974), p. 150; for criticism from catholics see John Harbison to Isaac Butt, 17 Mar. 1875 (N.L.I., Butt papers, MS 8698 (7)).
37 Thomas O'Hagan to James McKnight, 21 Oct. 1870 (P.R.O.N.I., O'Hagan papers, D2777/9/81/1/1).
38 Thomas O'Hagan to John Harbison, 25 Apr. 1869 (P.R.O.N.I., O'Hagan papers, D2777/9/50/3).
39 *Ulster census, 1871*.
40 *Return of J.P.s*.
41 *Ulster census, 1871*, pp 311, 425, 641.
42 See Neilson Hancock, 'Ireland' in *Fortnightly Review*, clvii (Jan. 1880), p. 6.
43 Livingston, *Fermanagh*, pp 399-400.
44 For a reference to catholic feelings on the matter in Armagh see meeting of catholic electors in Armagh, *U.G.*, 2 Oct. 1875; see also *B.N.L.*, 17 Dec. 1875.
45 *Ulster census, 1871*, p. 47; *Ulster census, 1891*, pp 146,150.
46 *Ulster census, 1871*, p. 152.
47 A. C. Hepburn, 'Work, class and religion in Belfast, 1871-1911' in *Irish Economic and Social History*, x (1983), p. 50.

48 Ibid., p. 49.
49 *General census report, 1871,* pp 110-16.
50 A. J. Megahey, 'The Irish protestant churches and political issues, 1870-1914' (Ph.D. thesis, The Queen's University of Belfast, 1969), p. 44 (hereafter cited as Megahey, 'The Irish protestant churches').
51 See T. W. Freeman, *Ireland* (London, 1950), p. 173.
52 C. J. Woods, 'The catholic church and Irish politics, 1879-92' (Ph.D. thesis, Nottingham University, 1968), pp 3-9 (hereafter cited as Woods, 'The catholic church, 1879-92').
53 See Megahey, 'The Irish protestant churches', pp 21-2.
54 David Kennedy, 'The catholic church' in T. W. Moody and J. C. Beckett (ed.), *Ulster since 1800: second series: a social survey* (London, 1957), pp 170-81.
55 See Emmet Larkin, 'The devotional revolution in Ireland, 1850-75' in *Amer. Hist. Assoc.,* lxxvii, no. 3 (June 1972), pp 625-52, (hereafter cited as Larkin, 'Devotional revolution').
56 E. R. Norman, *The catholic church and Ireland in the age of rebellion, 1859-73* (London, 1965), pp 15-18, 412-14 (hereafter cited as Norman, *The catholic church, 1859-73*).
57 See Larkin, 'Devotional revolution', p. 649.
58 *Anglo-Celt,* 18 July 1868; *W.E.,* 6 Mar. 1886.
59 *M.N.,* 14 July 1885; *F.T.,* 23 July 1885.
60 See Norman, *The catholic church, 1859-73,* pp 20-22.
61 Woods, 'The catholic church, 1879-92', pp 6-12; *W.E.,* 13 Mar. 1886.
62 See pp 39-40.
63 Norman, *The catholic church, 1859-73,* p. 404.
64 Ibid., pp 34-9, 408, 414-15.
65 R. V. Comerford, *The fenians in context: Irish politics and society 1843-82* (Dublin, 1985), pp 183-4.
66 Bishop Dorrian to Lord Dufferin, 27 Sept. 1871 (P.R.O.N.I., Dufferin and Ava papers, D1071H/B/F).
67 Dr James Donnelly to Tobias Kirby, 1 July 1883, in P. J. Corish (ed.), 'Kirby papers: Irish College, Rome. Guide to material of public and political interest, 1862-1883' in *Archivium Hibernicum,* xxx (1972), p. 114 (hereafter cited as 'Kirby papers 1').
68 For the reaction of an Irish catholic M.P. to this, see Albert Barry, *Life of Count Arthur Moore* (Dublin, 1905), p. 230.
69 Rev. Ambrose Macaulay, *Patrick Dorrian, Bishop of Down and Connor, 1865-85* (Dublin, 1987).
70 *M.N.,* 7 Nov. 1885.
71 See J. C. Beckett, 'Ulster protestantism' in T. W. Moody and J. C. Beckett (ed.), *Ulster since 1800, second series: a social survey* (London, 1957), pp 159-69; also G. C. Daly, 'Church renewal: 1869-77' in Michael Hurley (ed.), *Irish Anglicanism, 1869-1969* (Dublin, 1970), pp 23-38; and R. F. G. Holmes, *Henry Cooke* (Belfast, 1918), pp 201-9.
72 See R. F. G. Holmes, 'Ulster presbyterianism and Irish nationalism', in S. Mews (ed.), *Religion and national identity: Studies in Church History,* 18, (Oxford, 1982), pp 541-2.
73 See Ian Budge and Cornelius O'Leary, *Belfast: approach to crisis. A study of Belfast politics, 1813-1970* (London, 1973), pp 78-9.
74 See Norman, *The catholic church, 1859-73,* pp 283-6; for a discussion of this in the specifically Irish context, see K. B. Nowlan, 'Disestablishment: 1800-1869' in Michael Hurley (ed.), *Irish Anglicanism, 1869-1969* (Dublin, 1970), pp 1-22.
75 See Norman, *The catholic church, 1859-73,* p. 284.
76 Ibid., pp 346-7, 400-07.

77 Ibid., p. 458.
78 Ibid., p. 17; *L.S.,* 8 Feb., 27 May 1868; 18, 25 Oct. 1873.
79 *B.N.L.,* 26 July 1870.
80 See ibid., 12 July 1870.
81 *U.E.,* 22 Sept. 1868.
82 See Norman, *The catholic church, 1859-73,* pp 416-25, and *L.Sent.,* 29 Sept., 1 Oct., 24 Nov., 8 Dec. 1885.
83 For example, see 'An Irish presbyterian', *Ulster and home rule* (Belfast, 1886), p. 17; C. F. Smith, *J. N. Richardson of Bessbrook* (London, 1925), pp 17-18; W. S. Armour, *Armour of Ballymoney* (London, 1934), p. 60.
84 For an interesting study of extreme protestantism and politics in Ulster, see Frank Wright, 'Protestant ideology and politics in Ulster' in *European Journal of Sociology,* xiv (1973), pp 213-80 (hereafter cited as Wright, 'Protestant ideology').
85 *B.N.L.,* 23 Jan. 1874.
86 *L.J.,* 8 Aug. 1868.
87 In Co. Fermanagh the gentry played an important role in the Order throughout this period (Livingstone, *Fermanagh,* p. 256).
88 McClelland, 'The later Orange order', p. 131.
89 See Richard McMinn, 'Presbyterianism and politics in Ulster, 1871-1906' in *Studia Hibernica,* xxi (1981) (hereafter cited as McMinn, 'Presbyterianism'), pp 127-46.
90 B. M. Walker, *Sentry Hill: an Ulster farm and family* (Belfast, 1981), p. 54.
91 Quote is from Megahey, 'The Irish protestant churches', cited in McMinn, 'Presbyterianism', p. 131.
92 From McMinn, 'Presbyterianism', p. 140.
93 *D.R.,* 4 July 1868.
94 J. A. Rentoul, *Stray thoughts and memories* (Dublin, 1921), pp 32-5.
95 A. M. Sullivan, *Old Ireland: reminiscences of an Irish K.C.* (London, 1927), p. 37.
96 B. M. Walker, *Sentry Hill: an Ulster farm and family* (Belfast, 1981), p. 67.
97 *Ulster census, 1871,* pp 1045-59; *General census report, 1891,* pp 474-6; *Ulster census, 1891,* p. 996.
98 *Ulster census, 1871,* p. 1058.
99 See W. S. Armour, *Armour of Ballymoney* (London, 1934), pp 11-12.
100 *General census report, 1871,* pp 166, 174.
101 *U.E., 2 Feb. 1874.*
102 See T. W. Moody, 'The Irish university question of the nineteenth century' in *History,* xliii (1958), pp 90-109.
103 Norman, *The catholic church, 1859-73,* p. 254.
104 *The newspaper gazetteer and guide to advertisers . . . for 1860* (London, 1861); *Newspaper press directory . . . 1884* (London, 1884); *Newspaper press directory . . . 1895* (London, 1895); useful information on Ulster newspapers also came from J. M. Barkley, 'Belfast newspapers, v: 1850-70' in *Pace,* vii, no. i (spring 1975), pp 8-10, and 'Belfast newspapers, vi: 1860-74' in *Pace,* vii, nos. 2/3 (summer/autumn 1975), pp 15-17.
105 *U.E.,* 14 Mar. 1868.
106 R. G. F. Holmes, 'Henry Cooke, 1788-1868' (M.Litt. thesis, University of Dublin, 1970), p. 479.
107 *F.T.,* 4 Mar. 1880.
108 *B.N.L.,* 18 Feb. 1874.
109 *Nation,* 29 July 1865.
110 A. M. Sullivan, *New Ireland* (2 vols, London, 1877), ii, 410-14.

CHAPTER 3 *The voters and the constituencies*

[1] Quoted in Neal Blewett, 'The franchise in the United Kingdom, 1885-1918', in *Past & Present*, no. 32 (Dec. 1965), p. 39.

[2] For a detailed study of this question, see B. M. Walker, 'The Irish electorate, 1868-1915', in *I.H.S.*, xviii, no. 71 (Mar. 1973), pp 359-406 (hereafter cited as Walker, 'Irish electorate').

[3] Information on the operation of this legislation as it affected both counties and boroughs comes from the above article except where stated.

[4] Quoted in K. T. Hoppen, *Elections, politics and society in Ireland, 1832-1885* (Oxford, 1984), p. 28.

[5] *B.N.L.*, 6 Apr. 1880.

[6] *C. Chron.*, 21 Nov. 1868.

[7] Information on the operation of this legislation as it affected both counties and boroughs comes from Walker, 'Irish electorate'.

[8] See *General census report, 1871*, p. 116.

[9] See above, pp 18-19.

[10] See above, pp 15-16.

[11] From report in *B.M.N.*, 3 Apr. 1880, of Dungannon election.

[12] From report in *A.G.*, 6 Oct. 1876, of revision sessions.

[13] Private estimate of C. H. Brett, 1880 (P.R.O.N.I., L'Estrange and Brett papers, D1905/2/257/6).

[14] *Newry election: an alphabetically arranged list of electors who voted, and those who did not, at the election held in Newry on the 20th of November, 1868* (Newry, 1868), p. 18; *State of the poll at the general election held for the city of Londonderry, 20 Nov. 1868* (Derry, 1868).

[15] *B.N.L.*, 11 Oct. 1864; private estimate of C. H. Brett, liberal agent, 1868 (P.R.O.N.I., L'Estrange and Brett, D1905/2/78/1); private estimate of C. H. Brett, 1880 (P.R.O.N.I., L'Estrange and Brett, D1905/2/247/6).

[16] For Donegal and Monaghan, see *U.E.*, 29 Jan. 1874; *P.A.*, 7 July 1883. For Cavan see *C.W.N.*, 9 Apr. 1880.

[17] For Down see *B.M.N.*, 4 Mar. 1880. For Antrim see *N.W.*, 1 Apr. 1880; *Witness*, 15 May 1885. For Londonderry see *B.M.N.*, 9 Sept. 1881.

[18] *A.G.*, 9 Sept. 1881; *B.M.N.*, 9 Sept. 1881.

[19] See Walker, 'Irish electorate', p. 397.

[20] *Return showing the religious denominations of the population, according to the census of 1881, in each constituency formed in Ulster by the redistribution of seats act, 1885*, p. 1, H.C. 1884-5 (335), lxii, 339.

[21] See Walker, 'Irish electorate', p. 364.

[22] In 1868, 277 persons voted in Bandon, Co. Cork, out of a total of 295 electors. Of these 277, 59 per cent were protestant although protestants were only 32 per cent of the population (D. J. O'Donoghue, *History of Bandon* (Cork, 1970), p. 27).

[23] See *U.E.*, 26 Mar. 1874; *W.W.*, 3 Oct. 1885.

[24] For a detailed treatment of this subject, see B. M. Walker, 'Party organisation in Ulster, 1865-92: registration agents and their activities' in Peter Roebuck (ed.), *Plantation to partition: essays in Ulster history in honour of J. L. McCracken* (Belfast, 1981), pp 191-209.

[25] Ibid., p. 193.

[26] *Report from the select committee on registration of parliamentary voters (Ireland); together with the proceedings of the committee, minutes of evidence appendix and index*, H.C. 1874 (26), xi, p. 78.

[27] Healy, *Letters*, i, 230.

II TORIES SUPREME

CHAPTER 4 *The 1868 general election*

1 Sir John Ross, *The years of my pilgrimage* (London, 1924), p. 11.
2 See K. T. Hoppen, 'Landlords, society and electoral politics in mid-nineteenth century Ireland' in *Past & Present*, no. 75 (1977), pp 62-93; *Elections, politics and society in Ireland, 1832-88*, (Oxford, 1984).
3 See P. J. Jupp, 'Irish parliamentary representation and the catholic vote, 1801-20' in *Hist. Jn.*, x, no. 2 (1967), pp 183-96; and B. M. Walker (ed.), *Parliamentary election results in Ireland, 1801-1922* (Dublin, 1978).
4 Sir Charles Gavan Duffy, *My life in two hemispheres* (2 vols, London, 1898; reprint, Shannon 1968, with introduction by J. H. Whyte), i, 62.
5 J. H. Whyte, *The tenant league and Irish politics in the eighteen-fifties* (Dublin, 1966), pp 4-5.
6 K. T. Hoppen, *Elections, politics and society in Ireland, 1832-85* (Oxford, 1984), p. 238.
7 Whyte, op. cit., pp 4-5.
8 *B.N.L.*, 28 Sept. 1868.
9 *Banner*, 19 Nov. 1868.
10 *U.E.*, 21 Mar. 1868.
11 *F.J.*, 12 Nov. 1868.
12 For northern reaction to the fenians see *L.J.*, 11 Jan. 1868, *B.N.L.*, 11 Jan. 1868.
13 *L.S.*, 3 Oct. 1868.
14 See below, pp 51-71, for information on particular Ulster addresses; see David Thornley, *Isaac Butt and home rule* (London, 1964; hereafter cited as Thornley, *Isaac Butt*), pp 27-37, for information on southern addresses.
15 See Thornley, op. cit., pp 27-37.
16 See Cornelius O'Leary, *The elimination of corrupt practices in British elections, 1868-1911* (Oxford, 1963).
17 *N.W.*, 19-30 Dec. 1872.
18 Except where stated otherwise information on M.P.s' landowning has come from *Return of owners, 1876*.
19 Captain Henry Meynell, R.N., to Sir G. F. Seymour, 4 Apr. 1858 (P.R.O.N.I., Hertford papers, Mic.257/29).
20 *B.N.L.*, 10, 12, 24 Nov. 1868.
21 Lord Londonderry to D. S. Ker, 7 Feb. 1852 (P.R.O.N.I., Martin and Henderson papers, D2223/21/7.)
22 *B.N.L.*, 2 and 25 Nov. 1868.
23 *B.N.L.*, 9 Sept. 1868.
24 See Murphy, *Derry and modern Ulster*, pp 148-52.
25 *B.N.L.*, 11, 23 Nov. 1868.
26 *B.N.L.*, 14, 25 Nov. 1868.
27 *I.R.*, 12 Nov. 1868; *E.A.*, 26 Nov. 1868.
28 *I.R.*, 17 Sept., 29 Oct. 1868.
29 *B.N.L.*, 10 Oct. 1868.
30 *A.G.*, 25 Sept. 1868.
31 J. A. Rentoul, *Stray thoughts and memories* (Dublin, 1921), p. 24; *L.J.*, 12 Sept. 1868.
32 *B.N.L.*, 26 Nov. 1868.
33 *L.S.*, 26, 30 Sept. 1868.
34 *L.J.*, 17 Oct. 1868.
35 *Thom's directory, 1869*, p. 268.

36	*Anglo-Celt,* 8 Oct. 1868.
37	*Anglo-Celt,* 18 July, 3 Oct. 1868.
38	*N.S.,* 18 July 1868.
39	Ibid., 15 Aug. 1868.
40	*N.S.,* 8, 15, 22 Aug., 5, 28 Sept. 1868.
41	Ibid., 10 Oct. 1868.
42	Ibid., 10 Oct. 1868; *N.Star,* 10 Oct. 1868.
43	*N.Star,* 24 Oct. 1868; *N.S.,* 14 Nov. 1868.
44	*N.Star,* 31 Oct. 1868.
45	*N.S.,* 5 Dec. 1868.
46	*N.Star,* 24 Nov. 1868.
47	See reports in press, 10 Sept. – 7 Oct. 1868.
48	Ulster liberal society papers, 1865-9 (P.R.O.N.I., Dufferin and Ava papers, D1071H/B/F).
49	See reports of revision sessions in press, 10 Sept. – 7 Oct. 1868.
50	List of annual subscribers to the Ulster liberal society from 1 Aug. 1865; list of committee of management of the Ulster liberal society, 1865 (P.R.O.N.I., Ulster liberal society papers, 1865-9, Dufferin and Ava papers, D1071H/B/F).
51	W. A. Maguire, *Living like a lord: the second marquis of Donegall, 1764-1844* (Belfast, 1984), pp 91-2, 97.
52	See Ian Budge and Cornelius O'Leary, *Belfast: approach to crisis. A study of Belfast politics, 1813-1970* (London, 1973), pp 41-95.
53	*N.W.,* 13 Sept. 1867.
54	MacKnight, *Ulster as it is,* i, 150-51; *B.M.N.,* 6 Mar. 1868.
55	*N.W.,* 14 Oct. 1868.
56	Ibid., 5 Nov. 1868.
57	*B.N.L.,* 2 Oct. 1868.
58	Ibid., 20 Aug., 10 Sept. 1868.
59	Ibid., 10 Sept. 1868.
60	Notebook of C. H. Brett, agent for Thomas McClure (P.R.O.N.I., L'Estrange and Brett papers, D1905/2/78/1).
61	*N.W.,* 13 Nov. 1868.
62	*B.N.L.,* 2 Oct. 1868.
63	*N.W.,* 2 Dec. 1868.
64	*List of the electors of the borough of Belfast who voted at the general election, 1868* (Belfast, 1868).
65	Wright, 'Protestant ideology', pp 254-5.
66	See Murphy, *Derry and modern Ulster,* pp 110-15.
67	*L.S.,* 23 May 1868.
68	*L. Sent.,* 24 Nov. 1868.
69	Ross, *The years of my pilgrimage* (London, 1924), p. 14.
70	*L.Sent.,* 9 Feb. 1869.
71	Ibid., 29 Jan – 12 Feb. 1869.
72	*B.N.L.,* 10 Nov. 1868. See *Londonderry working men's protestant defence association: report: inaugural meeting etc., held on Friday 17 April 1868* (Derry, 1868). *Minutes of evidence taken before the commissioners . . . for the purpose of making inquiry into the evidence of corrupt practices amongst the freemen electors of the city of Dublin,* p. 660 [C93.1] H.C. 1870, xxxiii, 693.
73	*State of Derry poll* (Derry, 1868).
74	The term 'non-conformist' is used in the poll book to mean non-subscribing presbyterians, methodists, and independents.
75	*N.T.,* 28 July 1868.
76	Ibid., 1 Aug. 1868.

[77] Ibid., 4 Aug. 1868.

[78] Ibid., 19 Nov. 1868.

[79] *List of electors at Newry, 1868* (Newry, 1868). Those with valuation between 14 and 18 are given in brackets.

[80] *Union of Newry (part of). Valuation of the several tenements comprised in the portion of the above named union situated in the county of Down* (Dublin, 1864), pp 195-6.

[81] *Directory and handbook for Newry, Warrenpoint, Rostrevor . . .* (Newry, 1868).

[82] *B.N.L.*, 11 Oct. 1868.

[83] Ibid., 13 Oct. 1868.

[84] See above, pp 22-3.

[85] *B.N.L.*, 26 Nov. 1868.

[86] *N.W.*, 21 Nov. 1868.

[87] *B.N.L.*, 25 Jan. 1868.

[88] *N.W.*, 22-7 Jan. 1869.

[89] Earl of Belmore, *Parliamentary memoirs of Fermanagh, county and borough, from 1613 to 1885* (Dublin, 1885), pp 2-3.

[90] Above, pp 21-2.

[91] *I.R.*, 13 Aug. 1868.

[92] *E.A.*, 15 Oct. 1868.

[93] Ibid., 15 Oct. 1868.

[94] Ibid.

[95] Ibid., 26 Nov. 1868.

[96] *I.R.*, 26 Nov. 1868.

[97] Lord Mayo to Lord Abercorn, 5 Feb. 1868 (P.R.O.N.I., Abercorn viceregal papers, T2541/V.R.85/37).

[98] Lt-col. rt hon. T. W. Taylor to Lord Abercorn, 5 Feb. 1868 (P.R.O.N.I., Abercorn viceregal papers, T2541/V.R.85/37).

[99] Rt hon. H. T. Lowry Corry to Lord Abercorn, 7 Feb. 1868 (P.R.O.N.I., Abercorn viceregal papers, T2541/V.R.197).

[100] See Belmore, *Parliamentary memoirs*, p. 119.

[101] *B.N.L.*, 12 Nov. 1868.

[102] *T.Const.*, 25 Sept. 1868; bills for registration work from Henry Kelly to Lord Ranfurly (P.R.O.N.I., Dungannon borough revision papers, D847/8).

[103] *N.W.*, 19 Nov. 1868.

[104] *B.N.L.*, 18 Nov. 1868.

[105] See Murphy, *Derry and modern Ulster*, pp 87-8.

[106] *B.N.L.*, 10 Nov. 1868.

[107] Ibid., 18 Nov. 1868.

[108] *Col. Chron.*, 22, 29 Aug. 1868.

[109] *L.Sent.*, 1 Oct. 1872.

[110] *D.R.*, 21 Nov. 1868.

[111] Ibid., 12 Sept. 1868.

[112] *U.T.*, 5 Oct. 1837; *A.G.*, 28 Oct. 1864; *B.N.L.*, 13 Oct. 1866.

[113] *B.N.L.*, 10 Nov. 1868.

[114] Frank McKee to Rev. Henry McKee, 11 Nov. 1868 (P.R.O.N.I., McKee papers, D1821/1/8).

[115] *B.N.L.*, 18 Nov. 1868.

[116] Ulster liberal society papers 1865-9 (P.R.O.N.I., Dufferin and Ava papers, D1071/H/B/F).

[117] David Thornley, 'Isaac Butt and the creation of an Irish parliamentary party, 1868-79' (Ph.D. thesis, University of Dublin, 1959), p. 595.

[118] *L.J.*, 11 Nov. 1868.

CHAPTER 5 *By-elections, 1868-74*

1 *N.W.*, 20 Dec. 1872.

2 See Bernard Falk, *Old Q's daughter: the history of a strange family* (London, 1937).

3 As later described by F. H. Seymour to W. T. Stannus, 17 Sept. 1860 (P.R.O.N.I., Mic. 257/33.).

4 J. W. Stannus to marquis of Hertford, 27 July 1869 (P.R.O.N.I., Hertford papers, Mic. 257/33).

5 These actions were described by Sir G. F. Seymour to Lt-gen. F. H. Seymour, 3 Aug. 1869 (P.R.O.N.I., Hertford papers, Mic. 257/33).

6 *B.N.L.*, 3 Aug. 1869.

7 *B.N.L.*, 4 Aug. 1869.

8 Lt-gen. F. H. Seymour to Sir G. F. Seymour, 14 Aug. 1869 (P.R.O.N.I., Hertford papers, Mic. 257/33).

9 *B.N.L.*, 17 Aug. 1869.

10 MacKnight, *Ulster as it is*, i, 211.

11 McElroy, *Route land crusade*, p. 54.

12 *N.W.*, 19-30 Dec. 1872.

13 *B.N.L.*, 13 Aug. 1869.

14 *N.W.*, 28 Dec. 1872.

15 See below, p. 89.

16 List of expenses paid on behalf of Capt. Seymour, 1869 (P.R.O.N.I., Hertford papers, Mic. 257/43).

17 Bernard Falk, *Old Q's daughter: the history of a strange family* (London, 1937), pp 301-24.

18 W. T. Stannus to Sir G. F. Seymour, 4 Nov. 1869 (P.R.O.N.I., Hertford papers, Mic. 257/33).

19 *L.Sent.*, 15 Feb. 1870.

20 Ibid.

21 *L.G.*, 24 Feb. 1870.

22 *Names of the voters at the election held in Londonderry on Thursday, 17 Feb. 1870* (Derry, 1870).

23 *Hansard 3*, cxcix, 1553.

24 Sir F. W. Heygate to Disraeli, 9 Feb. 1870 (Hughenden, Disraeli papers, B/xxi/H/564).

25 *Hansard 3*, cxcix, 1853-54.

26 *B.N.L.*, 31 Dec. 1870.

27 Ibid., 3 Jan. 1871.

28 See Thornley, *Isaac Butt*, pp 83-110.

29 *N.S.*, 8 July 1871.

30 See above, pp 89-91.

31 *Dublin Evening Mail*, 8 July 1871.

32 Cardinal Cullen to Dr James Donnelly, 15 July 1871 (P.R.O.N.I., Clogher diocesan papers, Dio. RC1/11/A/32).

33 *F.J.*, 20 July 1871.

34 *F.J.*, 21 July 1871.

35 *N.S.*, 22 July 1871.

36 John Ferguson to Isaac Butt, 14 Aug. 1872 (N.L.I., Butt papers, MS 8694(8)).

37 *L.Sent.*, 27 Aug. 1872.

38 Ibid., 14 Sept. 1872.

39 *L.Sent.*, 22 Oct. 1872; *L.S.*, 28 Aug. 1872.

40 *L.Sent.*, 6 Aug. 1872.

41 Ibid., 24 Sept., 10 Oct. 1872.

42 Ibid., 23 Nov. 1872.
43 Ibid., 10 Aug. 1872.
44 Richard Dowse to Lord Hartington, 7 Oct. 1872 (Chatsworth House, Hartington papers, 340/510).
45 *L.Sent.*, 29 Oct. 1872; *L.S.*, 6 Nov. 1872.
46 V. T. H. Delany, *Christopher Palles: his life and times* (Dublin, 1960), pp 67-74.
47 *L.S.*, 6 Nov. 1872.
48 John Ferguson to Isaac Butt, 14 Nov. 1872 (N.L.I., Butt papers, MS 8694(20)).
49 *L.Sent.*, 14 Nov. 1872.
50 John Ferguson to Isaac Butt, 25 Nov. 1872 (N.L.I., Butt papers, MS 8694(22)).
51 Sir John Ross, *The years of my pilgrimage* (London, 1924), p. 16; *L.Sent.*, 3 Dec. 1872; MacKnight, *Ulster as it is*, i, 269.
52 *B.N.L.*, 22 Jan. 1873.
53 *B.N.L.*, 24 Jan. 1873.
54 MacKnight, *Ulster as it is*, i, 212; *B.N.L.*, 21 Dec. 1870.
55 *B.N.L.*, 31 Jan. 1873.
56 *N.W.*, 18 Feb. 1873.
57 *B.N.L.*, 18 Feb. 1873.
58 *B.N.L.*, 14 Mar. 1873.
59 James Greer to earl of Belmore, 14 Mar. 1873 (P.R.O.N.I., Belmore papers, D3007/P/20).
60 *T.Const.*, 14 Mar. 1873.
61 R. C. Brush to earl of Belmore, 14 Mar. 1873 (P.R.O.N.I., Belmore papers, D3007/p/19).
62 *T.Const.*, 21 Mar. 1873.
63 Col. hon. W. S. Knox to earl of Belmore, 15 Mar. 1873 (P.R.O.N.I., Belmore papers, D3007/P/27A); 18 Mar. 1873, ibid., D3007/P/45).
64 Francis Ellis to earl of Belmore, 21 Mar. 1873 (P.R.O.N.I., Belmore papers, D3007/P/57); *B.N.L.*, 25 Mar. 1873.
65 Printed handbill, 18 Mar. 1873 (P.R.O.N.I., Belmore papers, D3007/P/63).
66 *B.N.L.*, 25, 27 Mar. 1873.
67 Printed circular from T. C. Dickie, 31 Mar. 1873 (P.R.O.N.I., Carleton, Atkinson and Sloan papers, D1252/42/2).
68 Draft copy of instructions for agents, n.d. (P.R.O.N.I., Carleton, Atkinson and Sloan papers, D1252/42/2).
69 Mervyn Stewart to earl of Belmore, 17 Mar. 1873 (P.R.O.N.I., Belmore papers, D3007/P/37), earl of Enniskillen to earl of Belmore, 24 Mar. 1873 (P.R.O.N.I., Belmore papers, D3007/P/72).
70 Col. hon. W. S. Knox to earl of Belmore, 25 Mar. 1873 (P.R.O.N.I., Belmore papers, D3007/P/74); Earl of Enniskillen to earl of Belmore, 30 Mar. 1873 (P.R.O.N.I., Belmore papers, D3007/P/91); G. V. Stewart to earl of Belmore, 26 Mar. 1873 (P.R.O.N.I., Belmore papers, D3007/P/78).
71 Y. H. Burges to earl of Belmore, 28 Mar. 1873 (P.R.O.N.I., Belmore papers, D3007/P/83).
72 J. F. Lowry to earl of Belmore, 22 Mar. 1873 (P.R.O.N.I., Belmore papers, D3007/P/65).
73 S. Auchinleck to earl of Belmore, 24 Mar. 1873 (P.R.O.N.I., Belmore papers, D3007/P/71).
74 R. C. Brush to earl of Belmore, 5 Apr. 1873 (P.R.O.N.I., Belmore papers, D3007/P/106).
75 Sir Thomas Bateson to earl of Belmore, 19 Apr. 1873 (P.R.O.N.I., Belmore papers, D3007/P/126).

[76] James Greer to earl of Belmore, 9 Apr. 1873 (P.R.O.N.I., Belmore papers, D3007/P/117).

[77] Cecil Moore to Isaac Butt, 2 June 1873 (N.L.I., Butt papers, MS 8695(22)).

[78] *Hansard 3,* ccxiv, 1864-8.

[79] Thornley, *Isaac Butt,* p. 152.

III LIBERALS ADVANCE

CHAPTER 6 *The 1874 general election*

[1] *U.E.,* 31 Jan. 1874.

[2] See McElroy, *Route land crusade,* p. 25.

[3] See Thornley, *Isaac Butt,* pp 110-60; see also L. J. McCaffrey, 'Isaac Butt and the home rule movement: a study in conservative nationalism' in *Rev. Pol.,* xxii, no. 1 (Jan. 1960), p. 86.

[4] See Thornley, *Isaac Butt,* pp 176-204, for their role in the 1874 general election.

[5] *B.N.L.,* 17 Apr. 1872; *N.W.,* 14 Sept. 1872; *U.E.,* 1 Oct. 1873.

[6] W. J. O'Neill to Thomas Barry, 7 July 1873 (P.R.O.N.I., outletter book of the home government association and the home rule league, D213/P.30).

[7] Hugh Heinrick to Isaac Butt, 7 Mar., 13 Apr. 1873 (N.L.I., Butt papers, MS 8695(42)).

[8] *Proceedings of the home rule conference held at the Rotunda . . . 1873* (Dublin, 1873).

[9] Information on addresses has come from contemporary newspapers. Only where specific quotes are made are sources indicated.

[10] *B.N.L.,* 28 Jan. 1874.

[11] *B.N.L.,* 3 Feb. 1874.

[12] *U.E.,* 29 Jan. 1874.

[13] McElroy, *Route land crusade,* p. 31; *N.W.,* 10 Oct. 1873.

[14] Ibid., pp 24-7; *N.W.,* 12 Sept. 1873.

[15] *B.N.L.,* 29 Jan. 1874; *N.W.,* 31 Jan. 1874.

[16] *L.Sent.,* 29 Jan. 1874; ibid., 5 Feb. 1874.

[17] *N.W.,* 31 Jan. 1874.

[18] *N.W.,* 31 Jan. 1874; *L.S.,* 3 Feb. 1874.

[19] Election correspondence of C. H. Brett, 1874 (P.R.O.N.I., L'Estrange and Brett papers, D1905/2/17A/5).

[20] *N.W.,* 5 Feb. 1874.

[21] *B.N.L.,* 3 Feb. 1874.

[22] Ibid., 18 Feb. 1874.

[23] Thomas Bateson to Montague Corry, 24 Nov. 1874 (Hughenden, Disraeli papers, B/xxi/J/83).

[24] D. S. Ker to tenants, 1874 (P.R.O.N.I., L'Estrange and Brett papers, D1905/2/3).

[25] *N.W.,* 16 Feb. 1874.

[26] McElroy, *Route land crusade,* pp 23-8.

[27] H. H. McNeile to Lord Cairns, 10 Feb. 1874 (P.R.O., Cairns papers, 30/51/16f 94).

[28] *B.N.L.,* 5 Feb. 1874.

[29] H. H. McNeile to Lord Cairns, 10 Feb. 1874 (P.R.O., Cairns papers, 30/51/16f 94).

[30] *L.Sent.,* 17 Feb. 1874.

[31] Ibid., 17 Feb. 1874.

[32] *L.J.,* 13 Feb. 1874.

[33] *N.W.,* 11 Feb. 1874.

[34] Hugh Law to Gladstone, 15 Feb. 1874 (B.L., Gladstone papers, Add. MS 4442/260).

[35] *N.W.*, 27 Jan. 1874.

[36] Ibid., 31 Jan. 1874.

[37] Earl of Belmore to Disraeli, 31 Jan. 1874 (Hughenden, Disraeli papers, B/xxi/B/308a).

[38] Disraeli to earl of Belmore, 28 Jan. 1874 (P.R.O.N.I., Belmore papers, D3007/P/137).

[39] Earl of Belmore to Disraeli, 31 Jan. 1874 (Hughenden, Disraeli papers, D/xxi/B/308a).

[40] Capt. hon. H. W. L. Corry to earl of Belmore, 3 Feb. 1874 (P.R.O.N.I., Belmore papers, D3007/P/151).

[41] *U.E.*, 29 Jan. 1874.

[42] *B.N.L.*, 2, 4 Feb. 1874.

[43] *N.W.*, 6 Feb. 1874.

[44] *T.Const.*, 6 Feb., 26 June 1874; *B.N.L.*, 18 Feb. 1874.

[45] *E.A.*, 15 Jan. 1874; *B.N.L.*, 30 Jan. 1874.

[46] *B.N.L.*, 5 Feb. 1874.

[47] *E.A.*, 6 Feb. 1874.

[48] *E.A.*, 6 Feb. 1874.

[49] Ibid., 19 Feb. 1874.

[50] *A.G.*, 30 Jan. 1874.

[51] See above, p. 135.

[52] *N.W.*, 3 Feb. 1874.

[53] *A.G.*, 30 Jan. 1874.

[54] *B.N.L.*, 7 Feb. 1874.

[55] Ibid., 3 Mar. 1874.

[56] *N.W.*, 12 Feb. 1874.

[57] *C.N.*, 30 Jan. 1874.

[58] Ibid.

[59] Ibid., 13 Feb. 1874.

[60] Reginald Lucas, *Colonel Saunderson, M.P.* (London, 1908), p. 59.

[61] *C.N.*, 13, 20 Feb. 1874.

[62] Ibid., 20 Feb. 1874; as quoted in ibid., 27 Feb. 1874.

[63] *Hansard 3*, cxciv, 960-62.

[64] *N.S.*, 31 Jan. 1874.

[65] Ibid., 7 Feb. 1874.

[66] See below, pp 178-9.

[67] *N.S.*, 3 Apr. 1880.

[68] John Madden to Isaac Butt, 23 Feb. 1874 (N.L.I. Butt papers, MS 831).

[69] *N.S.*, 14 Feb. 1874.

[70] *L.S.*, 28 Jan. – 4 Feb. 1874.

[71] *L.Sent.*, 3 Feb. 1874; *L.S.*, 4 Feb. 1874.

[72] *N.W.*, 31 Jan. 1874; *L.S.*, 4 Feb. 1874.

[73] *B.N.L.*, 25 Feb. 1874; *N.W.*, 25 Feb. 1874; *B.M.N.*, 4 Mar. 1874.

[74] *B.M.N.*, 4 Mar. 1880.

[75] *N.W.*, 10 Feb. 1874.

[76] *C.N.*, 20 Feb., 13 Mar. 1874; John Madden to Isaac Butt, 23 Feb. 1874 (N.L.I., Butt papers, MS 831).

[77] See reports of revision sessions in press, 18 Sept. – 18 Oct. 1873.

[78] *N.W.*, 27 Jan. 1874.

[79] Ibid., 16 Sept. 1874.

[80] Ibid., 16 Sept. 1873.

81 Ibid., 13 Oct. 1873.
82 *B.N.L.*, 1 Feb. 1874.
83 *Col. Chron.*, 31 Jan. 1874.
84 Ibid.
85 Ibid.
86 *N.W.*, 7 Feb. 1874.
87 Ibid., 7 Feb. 1874.
88 Ibid., 30 Jan. 1874; *T.Const.*, 30 Jan. 1874.
89 *N.W.*, 27 Jan. 1874.
90 *T.Const.*, 13 Feb. 1874.
91 *N.W.*, 7 Feb. 1874.
92 *N.T.*, 29, 31 Jan. 1874.
93 *B.N.L.*, 2 Feb. 1874.
94 *N.W.*, 16 Feb. 1874.
95 *B.N.L.*, 2 Feb. 1874.
96 See above, p. 22.
97 *B.N.L.*, 2 Feb. 1874; *E.A.*, 29 Jan. 1874.
98 *I.R.*, 19 Feb. 1874.
99 *B.N.L.*, 2 Feb. 1874.
100 *A.G.*, 30 Jan. 1874.
101 *B.N.L.*, 19 Feb. 1873; *N.W.*, 23 Mar. 1880.
102 *B.N.L.*, 24 Jan. 1874.
103 *B.N.L.*, 30, 31 Jan. 1874.
104 Ibid.
105 *N.W.*, 28 Jan. 1874; ibid., 31 Jan. 1874; *U.E.*, 2 Feb. 1874.
106 *N.W.*, 31 Jan. 1874.
107 *U.E.*, 1 Jan. 1874.
108 Ibid., 31 Jan. 1874.
109 *B.N.L.*, 26 Jan. 1874.
110 Thomas McClure to Gladstone, 6 Mar. 1874 (B.L., Gladstone papers, Add. MS 44442/172).
111 Thomas McKnight to Gladstone, 11 Mar. 1874 (B.L., Gladstone papers, Add. MS 44443/89).
112 *N.W.*, 6 Feb. 1874.
113 R. J. Bryce to James Bryce, 4 Mar. 1874 (Bodleian, Bryce papers, F1 (6); ibid., *U.E.*, 7 Feb. 1874.
114 *L.J.*, 4 Feb. 1874; *L.Sent.*, 5 Feb. 1874.
115 *L.Sent.*, 27 Jan. 1874.
116 *L.S.*, 28 Feb. 1874.
117 Ibid., 31 Jan. 1874.
118 *L.Sent.*, 7 Feb. 1874.
119 The information on the social backgrounds of M.P.s has come from Thornley's *Isaac Butt*, pp 205-11, and his thesis, pp 600-03; *Return of owners; Thom's directory*.
120 *U.E.*, 29 Jan. 1874.
121 *Witness*, 20 Feb. 1874.
122 These figures on the social background of M.P.s count Philip Callan (elected for Co. Louth and Dundalk) only once, although he is included twice in the total number of home rule M.P.s.
123 Thornley, *Isaac Butt*, pp 176-94.
124 Ibid., p. 178.
125 Anonymous correspondent to J. S. Galbraith, C1875 (P.R.O.N.I., Belmore papers, D3007/P/168).

126 This can be seen in Armagh city where the catholics voted for the liberal candidate against the conservative John Vance. Subsequently we may note a catholic meeting in Armagh protesting against the protestant control of the city council. *U.G.*, 2 Oct. 1875; also that in parliament Vance was a strong opposer of changes in the municipal franchise (*Hansard 3*, ccxviii, 777-84).
127 H. de F. Montgomery to Thompson, 28 Jan. 1875 (P.R.O.N.I., Montgomery papers, D1121/4).

CHAPTER 7 *By-elections, 1874-80*

1 MacKnight, *Ulster as it is*, i, 296.
2 *B.N.L.*, 29 Mar. 1878; William Johnston to Montague Corry, 12 Feb. 1879 (Hughenden, Disraeli papers, B/xx1/J/107).
3 *N.S.*, 21 Feb. 1874.
4 *B.N.L.*, 5 Mar., 20 July 1874.
5 Ibid., 8 July 1874.
6 Ibid., 18 Feb. 1874.
7 *L.S.*, 28 Feb. 1874.
8 *D.R.*, 13 June 1874; *B.N.L.*, 11 Mar. 1874.
9 McElroy, *Route land crusade*, p. 61.
10 John Martin to M. H. Drury, 15 May 1874 (P.R.O.N.I., outletter book of the home government association and the home rule league D213/P.87).
11 John Martin to person unknown, 15 Jan. 1875 (P.R.O.N.I., outletter book of the home government association and the home rule league D213/pp 105-8).
12 *B.N.L.*, 4 Aug. 1874; *Nation*, 24 Apr. 1875.
13 James McAleese to Isaac Butt, 20 Sept. 1876 (N.L.I., Butt papers, MS 8698(41)).
14 *U.E.*, 24 Nov. 1877.
15 *A.G.*, 2 and 23 Oct. 1875; ibid., 6 Oct. 1876. In the early 1880s agents of other local catholic registration societies appeared in Derry city and Newry (*D.J.*, 6 Oct. 1880, *A.G.*, 10 Oct. 1884).
16 *U.G.*, 2 Oct. 1875.
17 Ibid., 2 Oct. 1875.
18 *U.E.*, 19 Oct. 1875.
19 *U.G.*, 23 Oct. 1875.
20 *B.N.L.*, 17 Dec. – 3 Jan. 1875.
21 *E.A.*, 10 Feb. 1876.
22 Marquis of Hamilton to Montague Corry, 23 June 1874 (Hughenden, Disraeli papers, B/xx1/H/38).
23 *U.E.*, 14 Aug. 1876; *L.S.*, 26 Nov. 1879.
24 *U.E.*, 19 Aug. 1876.
25 *B.N.L.*, 16 Aug. 1876; *U.E.*, 19 Aug. 1876.
26 *L.S.*, 23 Aug. 1876,
27 Ibid., 26 Aug. 1876.
28 Lord Enniskillen to earl of Belmore, 29 Aug. 1876 (P.R.O.N.I., Belmore papers, D3007/P/177).
29 *B.N.L.*, 28 Aug. 1876; *U.E.*, 26 Aug. 1876.
30 *B.N.L.*, 22 Aug. 1876.
31 *U.E.*, 18 Aug. 1876.
32 *B.N.L.*, 22 Mar. 1876.
33 William Johnston to Disraeli, 23 Apr. 1874; Lord Cairns to Disraeli, 29 Dec. 1875 (Hughenden, Disraeli papers, B/xxi/J/81 and 939).
34 *B.N.L.*, 23 Mar. 1876; *U.E.*, 23 Mar. 1876; *B.N.L.*, 27 Mar. 1876.

35 Ibid., *U.E.*, 28 Mar. 1878.
36 *N.W.*, 30 Mar. 1878.
37 *B.N.L.*, 1 Apr. 1875; *U.E.*, 30 Mar. 1878.
38 *B.N.L.*, 30 Mar., 1, 2 Apr. 1878.
39 Ibid., 30 Mar. 1878.
40 *N.W.*, 2 Apr. 1878.
41 *B.N.L.*, 3 Apr. 1878; *U.E.*, 2 Apr. 1878.
42 *N.W.*, 3 Apr. 1878.
43 Ibid., 3 May 1878.
44 Ibid., 4 May 1878.
45 Ibid.
46 Ibid., 8, 13 May 1878.
47 *B.N.L.*, 4 May 1878.
48 Ibid.
49 *N.W.*, 15 May 1878.
50 *B.N.L.*, 9 May 1878.
51 *B.N.L.*, 31 June 1878.
52 *B.M.N.*, 30 Mar. 1880; *N.W.*, 15 May 1878.
53 *N.W.*, 20-22 May 1878.
54 *L.Sent.*, 7 Dec. 1878.
55 Ibid.
56 *L.Sent.*, 10 Dec. 1878.
57 Ibid.
58 *L.Sent.*, 19 Dec. 1878; *L.S.*, 18 Dec. 1878.
59 *L.Sent.*, 17 Dec. 1878.
60 *L.S.*, 14 Dec. 1878.
61 *B.N.L.*, 16 Dec. 1878.
62 Mathew Wylie to Lord Waveney, 24 Dec. 1878 (P.R.O.N.I., Adair papers, D929/HA 12/F4/14).
63 *L.S.*, 15, 19 Nov. 1879.
64 Ibid., 15 Nov. 1879.
65 *L.Sent.*, 4 Dec. 1879.
66 *L.S.*, 3 Dec. 1879.
67 Charles Russell to Gladstone, 3 Apr. 1880 (B.L., Gladstone papers, Add. MS 44463/38).
68 *L.S.*, 10 Dec. 1879.
69 Ibid.
70 Ibid.
71 Ibid.
72 *L.Sent.*, 18 Dec. 1879.
73 Marquis of Hamilton to Montague Corry, 13 Jan. 1880 (Hughenden, Disraeli papers, B/xxi/H/42).
74 Thomas MacKnight to Gladstone, 5 Jan. 1880 (B.L., Gladstone papers, Add. MS 44462/21).
75 A. M. Sullivan, *New Ireland* (2 vols, London, 1877), i, 411.

CHAPTER 8 *The 1880 general election*

1 *F.T.*, 11 Mar. 1880.
2 Marquis of Hamilton to Montague Corry, 13 Jan. 1880 (Hughenden, Disraeli papers, B/xxi/H/42).

3 *B.N.L.*, 20 Sept. 1879; *N.W.*, 17 Sept., 13 Oct. 1879.
4 *L.Sent.*, 9 Oct. 1879; *N.S.*, 18 Oct. 1880.
5 *B.N.L.*, 2 Oct. 1879; *N.W.* 13 Oct. 1879; *N.S.*, 18 Oct. 1879.
6 Marquis of Hamilton to Montague Corry, 13 Jan. 1880 (Hughenden, Disraeli papers, B/xxi/H/42).
7 Sir Stafford Northcote, bt, to marquis of Hamilton, 18 Mar. 1880; (A. B. Cooke and A. P. W. Malcomson (ed.), *The Ashbourne papers, 1869-1913* (Belfast, 1974), p. 115).
8 Marquis of Hamilton to Montague Corry, 13 Jan. 1880 (Hughenden, Disraeli papers, B/xxi/H/42).
9 T. G. Hamilton to marquis of Hamilton, 8 Jan. 1880 (Hughenden, Disraeli papers, B/xxi/H/42a).
10 *L.J.*, 29 Mar. 1880.
11 Ibid., 15 Mar. 1880.
12 *D.J.*, 5 Apr. 1880.
13 Ibid., 31 Mar. 1880; *N.W.*, 10 Apr. 1880; *D.J.*, 5, 7 Apr. 1880.
14 Marquis of Hamilton to Disraeli, 4 Jan. 1880 (Hughenden, Disraeli papers, B/xxi/H/41).
15 *P.A.*, 10 Jan. 1880.
16 Ibid., 14 Feb. 1880.
17 Ibid., 20 Mar. 1880.
18 Charles Russell, Q.C., to Gladstone, 17 Mar. 1886 (B.L., Gladstone papers, Add. MS 56447).
19 *N.S.*, 17 Jan. 1880.
20 *P.A.*, 20 Mar. 1880; *N.S.*, 20, 31 Jan., 20 Mar. 1880.
21 *P.A.*, 7 Feb. 1880.
22 *F.J.*, 30 Mar. 1880; *C.N.*, 2 Apr. 1880.
23 Major E. J. Saunderson to his wife, 25 Mar. 1880 (P.R.O.N.I., Saunderson papers, T2996/1/36).
24 *F.J.*, 30 Mar. 1880; *C.N.*, 2 Apr. 1880.
25 *B.N.L.*, 15 Apr. 1880; *C.N.*, 9 Apr. 1880.
26 *B.N.L.*, 17, 18, 22 Mar. 1880.
27 *A.G.*, 20 Feb., 9 Apr., 19 Mar. 1880.
28 *U.G.*, 17 Apr. 1880; *N.R.*, 1 Apr. 1880.
29 *N.W.*, 16 Mar. 1880.
30 Ibid., 3 Apr. 1880; *N.R.*, 1 Apr. 1880.
31 *A.G.*, 8 Oct. 1880.
32 J. A. Pomeroy to H. de F. Montgomery, 3 Apr. 1880 (P.R.O.N.I., Montgomery papers, D627/294).
33 *N.W.*, 20 Mar. 1880.
34 John Harbison to Lord O'Hagan, 25 Apr. 1880 (P.R.O.N.I., O'Hagan papers, D2777/9/50/4).
35 *T.Cour.*, 3 Apr. 1880.
36 *B.M.N.*, 30 Mar. 1880.
37 *T.Const.*, 2 Apr. 1880.
38 *I.R.*, 11, 18 Mar. 1880.
39 *F.M.*, 8 Apr. 1880.
40 *F.T.*, 1 Apr. 1880; *F.M.*, 8 Apr. 1880.
41 *B.N.L.*, 27 Mar. 1880.
42 *B.M.N.*, 12 Apr. 1880.
43 *N.W.*, 9, 15 Mar. 1880.
44 *B.N.L.*, 22 Mar. 1880.
45 *D.J.*, 5 Apr. 1880.

46 *N.W.*, 23 April 1880.

47 John Harbison to Lord O'Hagan, 25 Apr. 1880 (P.R.O.N.I., O'Hagan papers, D2777/9/50/4).

48 *N.W.*, 9, 15 Mar. 1880.

49 McElroy, *Route land crusade,* pp 60-65.

50 S. C. McElroy to Lord Waveney, 5 Feb. 1879 (P.R.O.N.I., Adair papers, D929/HA/12/F4/14).

51 McElroy, *Route land crusade,* p. 66.

52 *B.N.L.*, 13 Mar. 1880.

53 H. H. McNeile to Lord Cairns, 3 Mar. 1880 (P.R.O., Cairns papers, 30/51/16/98); *B.N.L.*, 18 Mar. 1880.

54 *B.M.N.*, 30 Mar. 1880; *Witness*, 2 Apr. 1880.

55 *B.M.N.*, 27 Mar. 1880.

56 Election correspondence of Sir C. H. Brett, Co. Down liberal agent 1880 (P.R.O.N.I., L'Estrange and Brett papers, D1905/2/247/3).

57 *B.N.L.*, 29 Mar. 1880; *Witness*, 26 Mar. 1880.

58 *Copy of the shorthand writer's notes of the judgment and evidence on the trial of the Down county election petition*, p. 1, H.C. 1880 (260-sess. 2), lvii, 567.

59 Ibid., pp 42, 630.

60 Ibid., pp 163-73, 751-62.

61 Ibid., pp xix, 585.

62 Ibid., pp xi, 577.

63 This point was made by one of the judges at the election petition trial, ibid., pp xix, 585.

64 *N.W.*, 12 Apr. 1880; *B.M.N.*, 8 Apr. 1880.

65 Paschal McKeown, 'The land question and elections in South Antrim, 1870-1910' (M.S.Sc. thesis, Queen's University, Belfast, 1981), p. 69. Richard McMinn, 'The myth of "Route" liberalism in County Antrim, 1869-1900' in *Eire-Ireland*, xvii, no. 1 (spring issue), p. 142 (cf. p. 263 n. 4).

66 *N.W.*, 15 Apr. 1880; *B.M.N.*, 8 Apr. 1880.

67 *Return of charges made by candidates at the last elections by returning officers . . . also the total expenses of each candidate*, pp 36-43, H.C. 1880 (382-sess. 2), lvii, 36-43.

68 *Report of her majesty's commissioners of enquiry into the working of the Landlord and Tenant (Ireland) Act, 1870*, [C2779-1], H.C. 1881, xviii,

69 *Witness*, 12 Mar. 1880.

70 *B.M.N.*, 27 Mar. 1880; *N.W.*, 12 Apr. 1880; *D.J.*, 12 Apr. 1880; *P.A.*, 17 Apr. 1880.

71 *N.W.*, 11, 18 Sept., 5 Oct. 1879; *Col. Chron.*, 25 Oct. 1879; *L.Sent.*, 7 Oct. 1879; *B.N.L.*, 7, 8 Oct. 1879; *N.T.*, 22 Sept. 1879; *A.G.*, 24 Oct. 1879; *I.R.*, 16 Oct. 1879.

72 *B.N.L.*, 26 Mar. 1880.

73 Ibid., 24 Oct. 1874.

74 *Col. Const.*, 13 Mar. 1880.

75 Ibid., 10, 20 Mar. 1880.

76 Ibid., 7 Feb. 1880.

77 *N.W.*, 17 Apr., 20 July 1880; *Col. Const.*, 10 Apr. 1880.

78 *N.R.*, 13 Mar. 1880.

79 Ibid., 16 Mar. 1880.

80 *N.W.*, 5 Apr. 1880.

81 Ibid., 6 Apr. 1880.

82 See above, p. 23.

83 *N.W.*, 4 June 1880.

84 *B.N.L.*, 12 Mar. 1880.

85 Ibid., 20 Mar. 1880.

86 *N.W.*, 8 June 1880.
87 Election address of Col. the hon. W. S. Knox, 1880 (P.R.O.N.I., Dungannon borough revision papers, D847/8).
88 *N.W.*, 31 Mar. 1880.
89 *B.M.N.*, 5 Apr. 1880.
90 *T.Cour.*, 10 Apr. 1880.
91 *T.Cour.*, 11 June 1880.
92 *N.W.*, 15, 17 Mar. 1880.
93 *D.R.*, 23 Mar. 1880; *B.N.L.*, 15 Mar. 1880.
94 Henry Johnston to C. H. Brett, 4 Apr. 1880, election correspondence of C. H. Brett, Co. Down liberal agent, 1880 (P.R.O.N.I., L'Estrange and Brett papers, D1905/2/247/2).
95 *D.I.*, 10 Apr. 1880.
96 *B.M.N.*, 18 Mar. 1880.
97 *F.T.*, 25 Mar. 1880; *I.R.*, 18, 25 Mar. 1880.
98 *N.W.*, 20 Mar. 1880.
99 *L.Sent.*, 25 and 30 Mar. 1880.
100 *N.W.*, 12 Apr. 1880.
101 *D.J.*, 19 Apr. 1880; *B.M.N.*, 2 Apr. 1880.
102 *B.N.L.*, 11 Mar. 1880.
103 *N.W.*, 24 Mar. 1880.
104 *B.N.L.*, 13, 25, 31 Mar. 1880.
105 *N.W.*, 25, 26 Mar. 1880.
106 Ibid., 20, 27 Mar. 1880; *B.N.L.*, 13 Mar. 1880.
107 *B.N.L.*, 3 Apr. 1880.
108 The main sources used for social classification of M.P.s were *Dod's parliamentary companion, 1881; Irish catholic directory, 1881; Thom's directory, 1881; Return of owners*; and O'Brien, *Parnell and his party*, pp 11-35. C. C. O'Brien, 'The Irish parliamentary party, 1880-90' (Ph.D. thesis, University of Dublin, 1954) (hereafter cited as O'Brien 'The Irish party') was also consulted.
109 The number of Parnellites and the total home rule party includes Parnell's 3 seats won in 1880 but Parnell is included only once in the social and religion statistics.
110 I have accepted here Dr O'Brien's classification of rentier as a person of affluence whose source of income is unknown: I have not included relatives of landowners in this section as he does, but among landowners. O'Brien, 'The Irish party', pp 399-403.
111 O'Brien, *Parnell and his party*, pp 125-6.
112 Ibid.; Woods, 'The catholic church, 1879-92', pp 59-74.
113 Earl of Charlemont to Hugh Boyle, 7 Apr. 1880 (P.R.O.N.I., Charlemont papers, D266/367/21 A).
114 M. J. Craig, *The volunteer earl* (London, 1948), p. 249.
115 See *U.E.*, 2 Apr. 1880.
116 John Harbison to Lord O'Hagan, 25 Apr. 1880 (P.R.O.N.I., O'Hagan papers, D2777/9/50/4).

CHAPTER 9 *By-elections, 1880-85*

1 James Crossle to Sir William Verner, bt, 8 Sept. 1881 (P.R.O.N.I., Verner papers, out-letter books of James Crossle, D236/488/p. 232).
2 *N.W.*, 17 Apr. 1880; *B.M.N.*, 13 Apr. 1880.
3 Memorandum of the preliminary meetings in connection with the proposed reform club; 14 May – 22 Oct. 1880 (Ulster reform club, minute book of club, 4 May 1880 – 18 Mar. 1892).

[4] Copy of circular from Lord Waveney, 16 Feb. 1881 (Ulster reform club, minute book of club, 4 May 1880 – 18 Mar. 1892).

[5] Club minutes, 13 June 1884 – 1 Jan. 1885 (Ulster reform club, minute book of club, 4 May 1880 – 18 Mar. 1892).

[6] *B.N.L.*, 23 Dec. 1880.

[7] *N.W.*, 14 Sept. 1881.

[8] *U.E.*, 30 Sept. 1880.

[9] *A.G.*, 8 Oct. 1880.

[10] *B.N.L.*, 14 Apr., 25 Dec. 1880.

[11] Col. Burges to Henry Kelly, 26, 28 Dec. 1880 (P.R.O.N.I., Dungannon borough revision papers, D847/8).

[12] E. S. Finnigan to Henry Kelly, 13 Oct. 1881 (P.R.O.N.I., Dungannon borough revision papers, D847/8).

[13] *T.Cour.*, 10 Apr. 1880.

[14] *A.G.*, 7 Jan. 1881.

[15] See *W.N.*, 3 Jan. 1885.

[16] *B.N.L.*, 9 Sept. 1881.

[17] Extract from minutes, as enclosed in letter from Lord A. W. Hill to Lord Salisbury, 19 Aug. 1882 (Hatfield House, Salisbury papers).

[18] Letter from Lord A. W. Hill to Lord Salisbury, 24 Sept. 1882 (Hatfield House, Salisbury papers).

[19] *B.N.L.*, 9 Sept. 1882.

[20] A. B. Cooke, 'A conservative party leader in Ulster: Sir Stafford Northcote's diary of a visit to the province, October 1883' in *R.I.A. Proc.*, lxxv, sect. C, no. 75 (Sept. 1975), pp 61-84.

[21] *B.N.L.*, 4 Oct. 1883.

[22] *U.E.*, 5 Oct. 1880.

[23] *D.J.*, 6 Oct. 1880; *N.T.*, 2 Oct. 1884.

[24] *F.J.*, 18 Oct. 1882.

[25] *I.T.*, 16 Dec. 1882.

[26] Magee, 'Monaghan election', pp 156-66.

[27] *N.W.*, 12 June 1880; *U.E.*, 26 June 1880.

[28] *U.E.*, 26 June 1880.

[29] *Hansard 3*, cclii, 292.

[30] Ibid., cclxi, 928-32.

[31] See Francis Thompson, 'Attitudes to reform: political parties in Ulster and the Irish land bill of 1881' in *I.H.S.*, xxiv, no. 95 (May 1985), pp 327-40.

[32] See advice of Shaw Lefevre to Gladstone, Dec. 1880 in D. W. R. Ballman (ed.), *The diary of Sir Edward Walter Hamilton* (2 vols, Oxford, 1972), i, 93-4, 98; T. W. Moody, *Davitt and Irish revolution, 1846-82* (Oxford, 1981), p. 455.

[33] Sir Stafford Northcote to Edward Gibson, 29 Aug. 1881 (A. B. Cooke and A. P. W. Malcomson (ed.), *The Ashbourne papers, 1869-1913* (Belfast, 1974), p. 124).

[34] *B.M.N.*, 5, 6 Aug. 1881.

[35] Ibid., 15 Aug. 1881.

[36] *B.N.L.*, 22 Aug. 1881.

[37] Ibid., 23 Aug. 1881.

[38] *N.W.*, 22 Aug. 1881.

[39] *B.M.N.*, 26 Aug. 1881.

[40] *N.W.*, 25 Aug.; *B.M.N.*, 27 Aug. 1881.

[41] T. P. O'Connor, *Memoirs of an old parliamentarian* (2 vols, London, 1929), i, 236.

[42] *B.N.L.*, 19 Aug. 1881; election leaflet, Co. Tyrone by-election 1881 (P.R.O.N.I., Greer papers, T2642/8/22).

43 *N.W.*, 24 Aug., 1 Sept. 1881.
44 *B.M.N.*, 31 Aug. 1881; *U.E.*, 1 Sept. 1881.
45 *B.M.N.*, 29 Aug. 1881. It was later disclosed in a letter from Patrick Egan to Patrick Ford, proprietor of the *Irish World*, that £500 was spent out of land league funds to assist Rylett (*L.S.*, 6 Jan. 1883).
46 *N.W.*, 9 Sept. 1881; *U.E.*, 10 Sept. 1881; *U.E.*, 10 Sept. 1881.
47 James Crossle to Sir William Verner, bt, 8 Sept. 1881 (P.R.O.N.I., Verner papers, outletter books of James Crossle, D236/488/2/p. 232).
48 *B.M.N.*, 7 Nov. 1881.
49 Ibid., 12 Nov. 1881.
50 *N.W.*, 12 Nov. 1881.
51 *B.M.N.*, 7 Nov. 1881.
52 *L.Sent.*, 17 Nov. 1881.
53 *N.W.*, 18 Nov. 1881.
54 Printed circular from R. H. Todd, 21 Nov. 1881 (P.R.O.N.I., Drennan papers, D1513/3/3).
55 Sir John Ross, *The years of my pilgrimage* (London, 1924), p. 42.
56 *B.M.N.*, 17 Nov. 1881.
57 Ibid., 28 Nov. 1881.
58 See F. H. O'Donnell, *History of the Irish parliamentary party* (2 vols, London, 1910), i, 45.
59 *B.M.N.*, 6 Dec. 1881; the land league subscribed £550 to Dempsey's election funds as was later disclosed in a letter from Patrick Egan to Patrick Ford (*L.S.*, 6 Jan. 1883).
60 MacKnight, *Ulster as it is*, i, 35.
61 John Magee, 'The Monaghan election of 1883 and the "Invasion of Ulster"' in *Clogher Record*, viii, no. 2 (1974), p. 151 (hereafter cited as Magee, 'Monaghan election').
62 *N.W.*, 16 June 1883.
63 *P.A.*, 23 June 1883.
64 Magee, 'Monaghan election', pp 152-3.
65 Ibid.
66 *P.A.*, 23 June 1883; Magee, 'Monaghan election', pp 153-5.
67 *P.A.*, 30 June 1883.
68 Dr James Donnelly to Tobias Kirby, 1 July 1883 ('Kirby papers I; p. 144).
69 *P.A.*, 30 June 1883; *N.W.*, 26 June 1883; ibid., 28 June 1883.
70 *N.S.*, 23 June 1883.
71 Ibid., 23, 30 June 1883.
72 See p. 129.
73 *N.S.*, 7 July 1883; *P.A.*, 7 July 1883.
74 *P.A.*, 7 July 1883.
75 *N.S.*, 7 July 1883.
76 See Magee, 'Monaghan election', pp 156-66.
77 *L.Sent.*, 1 Jan. 1884.
78 *D.J.*, 9 Jan. 1884.
79 *L.S.*, 11 Dec. 1883.
80 *D.J.*, 11 Jan. 1884; MacKnight, *Ulster as it is*, ii, 47.
81 *D.J.*, 11 Jan. 1884.
82 *N.W.*, 12 Nov. 1884.
83 Ibid., 14 Nov. 1884.
84 *B.N.L.*, 15 Nov. 1884.
85 Ibid., 24 Nov. 1884.
86 *N.W.*, 21 Nov. 1884.

87 Ibid., 25 Nov. 1884.
88 *M.N.*, 29 Nov. 1884.
89 *B.M.N.*, 29 Nov. 1884.
90 Ibid., 10 Nov. 1884.
91 Cornelius O'Leary, *The elimination of corrupt practices in British elections, 1868-1911* (Oxford, 1962), p. 175.
92 *B.M.N.*, 26 Nov. 1884.
93 *N.W.*, 17, 22 Nov. and 2 Dec. 1884.
94 *B.N.L.*, 7 Nov. 1884; See for example, *Co. Down constitutional association: election organisation for the polling district of Gilford* (Downpatrick, 1884) (P.R.O.N.I., Carleton, Atkinson and Sloan papers, D1252/42/9).
95 *Co. Down election, Nov. 1884: instructions for canvassers, district committees and polling agents* (Belfast, 1884), (P.R.O.N.I., Carleton, Atkinson and Sloan papers, D1252/42/9).
96 *N.W.*, 1 Dec. 1884.
97 MacKnight, *Ulster as it is*, ii, 75.
98 *M.N.*, 28, 29 Nov. 1884, 13 July 1885.
99 *B.N.L.*, 9 May 1885.
100 McElroy, *Route land crusade*, p. 72.
101 *B.N.L.*, 9 May 1885; *N.W.*, 14 May 1885.
102 *N.W.*, 14 May 1885; *B.N.L.*, 20 May 1885.
103 *N.W.*, 14 May 1885.
104 *B.M.N.*, 16 May 1885.
105 Ibid.
106 *N.W.*, 19 May 1885.
107 *B.M.N.*, 18 May 1885.
108 *N.W.*, 2 June 1885.
109 *B.N.L.*, 23 May 1885.
110 *B.M.N.*, 23 May 1885.
111 Ibid., 30 June 1885.
112 *B.N.L.*, 29 June 1885.
113 *N.W.*, 30 June 1885.
114 *B.M.N.*, 2 July 1885.
115 *B.N.L.*, 7 July 1885.
116 *B.M.N.*, 4 July 1885.
117 See *N.W.*, 8 July 1885; *B.N.L.*, 10 July 1885.
118 *N.W.*, 9 July 1885; *B.M.N.*, 9 July 1885.
119 *N.W.*, 6 July 1885.
120 *B.M.N.*, 10 July 1885.
121 Ibid., 13 July 1885; *B.N.L.*, 10 July 1885; *M.N.*, 13 July 1885; *N.W.*, 10 July 1885.
122 See A. B. Cooke, 'A conservative party leader in Ulster: Sir Stafford Northcote's diary of a visit to the province, October 1883' in *R.I.A. Proc.*, lxxv, sect. C, no. 74 (Sept. 1975), pp 61-84.
123 Major E. J. Saunderson to his wife, 21 Feb. 1885 (P.R.O.N.I., Saunderson papers, T2996/2/B/259).
124 T. A. Dickson to Joseph Chamberlain, May 1885 (Chamberlain papers, JC8/6/3D/3).
125 See R. F. Foster, 'Lord Randolph Churchill and the prelude to the Orange card' in F. S. L. Lyons and R. A. J. Hawkins (ed.), *Ireland under the union: varieties of tension. Essays in honour of T. W. Moody* (Oxford, 1980), pp 257-63.

IV NATIONALISTS AND UNIONISTS DIVIDE

CHAPTER 10 *The 1885 general election*

1 O'Brien, *Parnell and his party*, p. 133.
2 P. J. Buckland (ed.), *Irish unionism, 1885-1923: a documentary history* (Belfast, 1973), pp 95-9.
3 Savage, *Origins of the unionists*, p. 194.
4 *B.N.L.*, 4 June 1885.
5 Ibid., 10 Aug. 1885.
6 Dunbar Barton to W. H. Smith, 2 Oct. 1881 (Strand House, W. H. Smith papers, PS7/9).
7 *Weekly News*, 5 Sept., 10 Oct. 1885.
8 *Weekly Whig*, 24 Oct. 1885; *N.W.*, 17 Oct. 1885.
9 *L.Sent.*, 10 Jan. 1885; *W.N.*, 28 Mar. 1885.
10 *W.N.*, 21 Feb. 1885.
11 Ibid., 9 May 1885.
12 See ibid., 21, 29 Feb. 1885; *B.M.N.*, 19 May 1885.
13 *W.N.*, 9 May, 26 Sept. 1885; *W.W.*, 7 Nov. 1885; *B.M.N.*, 19 May 1885.
14 *W.E.*, 14 March 1885.
15 *W.N.*, 8 Aug. 1885.
16 Ibid., 22 Aug. 1885.
17 Major E. J. Saunderson to his wife, 14 Aug. 1885 (P.R.O.N.I., Saunderson papers, T2996/2/B/273); *W.N.*, 3 Oct. 1885.
18 Ibid., 24 Oct. 1885.
19 Ibid., 3 Oct. 1885.
20 Ibid., 27 June 1885.
21 Sir Richard Wallace, bt, to Lord Salisbury, 17 Aug. 1885 (Hatfield House, Salisbury papers).
22 McKeown 'South Antrim politics', p. 37.
23 *W.N.*, 20 June 1885; *Belfast Telegraph*, 25 July 1885.
24 *L.Sent.*, 10 Jan., 28 July, 5 Sept. 1885.
25 Ibid., 1 Oct. 1885.
26 Ibid., 24 Oct. 1885.
27 *L.S.*, 6 Nov. 1885.
28 *U.G.*, 28 Feb. 1885; *Arm. Stand.*, 15 May 1885.
29 *U.G.*, 30 May 1885.
30 *W.N.*, 10, 17 Oct. 1885.
31 *A.S.*, 13 Nov. 1885.
32 Ibid., 27 Nov. 1885.
33 T. M. Healy, *Letters and leaders of my day*, (2 vols, London, 1928), (hereafter cited as Healy, *Letters*), i, 231-2.
34 Draft letter from J. B. Atkinson to James Atkinson, 18 May 1885 (P.R.O.N.I., Carleton, Atkinson and Sloan papers, D1252/42/3/22).
35 Draft letter from J. B. Atkinson to James Atkinson, 21 May 1885 (P.R.O.N.I., Carleton, Atkinson and Sloan papers, D1252/42/3/23).
36 *W.N.*, 18 July 1885; draft reply by J. B. Atkinson to Thomas Ellis's pamphlet, *The action of the grand Orange lodge of the county of Armagh on the 6th July 1885 by the Reverend Thomas Ellis, chairman upon the occasion, by whom this statement is represented to the conservatives and Orangemen of North and Mid-Armagh* (Armagh, 1885) (P.R.O.N.I., Carleton, Atkinson and Sloan papers, D1252/42/3/47) (hereafter cited as Atkinson, *Draft reply to Ellis*) (Ellis's pamphlet, which is also catalogued under this number, is hereafter cited as Ellis, *The action of the grand Orange lodge*).

[37] *W.N.*, 27 June 1885.

[38] Ellis, *The action of the grand orange lodge*, p. 6; *W.N.*, 12 Sept. 1885; *Portadown and Lurgan News*, 1, 8, 15 Aug. 1885.

[39] Ellis, *The action of the grand Orange lodge*, p. 4.

[40] Ibid.; Atkinson, *Draft reply to Ellis*.

[41] *W.N.*, 29 Aug. 1885; ibid., 12 Sept. 1885.

[42] Robert Courtney to Rev. Thomas Ellis, 22 July 1885 (P.R.O.N.I., Saunderson papers, T2996/4/2).

[43] Atkinson, *Draft reply to Ellis*.

[44] William White to Gladstone, 13 May 1885 (B.L., Gladstone papers, Add. MS 44497-215).

[45] *W.N.*, 22 Aug. 1885.

[46] Ibid., 22, 29 Aug. 1885.

[47] Rev. Thomas Ellis to Major E. J. Saunderson, 26 Aug. 1885 (P.R.O.N.I., Saunderson papers, T2996/4/4).

[48] See John Monroe to J. B. Atkinson, 18 Sept. 1885 (P.R.O.N.I., Carleton, Atkinson and Sloan papers, D1252/42/3/86); Sir Thomas Bateson, bt, to J. B. Atkinson, 20 Aug. 1885 (P.R.O.N.I., Carleton, Atkinson and Sloan papers, D1252/42/3/31).

[49] John Monroe to J. B. Atkinson, 8 Oct. 1885 (P.R.O.N.I., Carleton, Atkinson and Sloan papers, D1252/42/3/44); Account by J. B. Atkinson of meeting in Imperial Hotel, Portadown, on 10 Oct. 1885 (P.R.O.N.I., Carleton, Atkinson and Sloan papers, D1252/42/3/42).

[50] Bottomley, *The North Fermanagh elections*, pp 167-79.

[51] *F.T.*, 19 Feb. 1885; J. W. Dane to Col J. M. Richardson, 12 Nov. 1885 (P.R.O.N.I., Falls and Hanna papers, outletter book of J. W. Dane, D1390/26/7/p111).

[52] *F.T.*, 22 Oct. 1885; *W.W.*, 17 Oct. 1885.

[53] *F.T.*, 5 Nov. 1885.

[54] *W.E.*, 18 Apr. 1885; *W.N.*, 6 June 1885.

[55] See for example the establishment of the S. Tyrone constitutional association (ibid., 20 June 1885).

[56] See letter of William Ellison Macartney (*W.N.*, 3 Oct. 1885).

[57] See below, pp 193-201.

[58] *W.N.*, 3 Oct. 1885.

[59] *W.E.*, 18 July 1885; *T.Cour.*, 31 Oct. 1885.

[60] Duke of Abercorn to marquis of Hartington, 15 Nov. 1885 (Chatsworth House, Hartington papers, 340, 1832).

[61] *W.W.*, 21 Oct., 21, 28 Nov. 1885.

[62] *W.N.*, 12 Sept. 1885.

[63] *N.W.*, 12 Nov. 1885.

[64] *W.N.*, 7 Nov. 1885.

[65] Duke of Abercorn to marquis of Hartington, 15 Nov. 1885 (Chatsworth House, Hartington papers, 340, 1832).

[66] *N.S.*, 19 Sept., 27 Nov. 1885.

[67] *C.N.*, 4 Dec. 1885.

[68] *W.E.*, 14 Mar. 1885.

[69] *W.N.*, 18 Apr. 1885.

[70] Ibid., 25 Apr., 24 Oct. 1885.

[71] Ibid., 24 Jan. 1885.

[72] Ibid., 18 Apr. 1885.

[73] *W.E.*, 4 Apr. 1885; *W.N.*, 18 Apr. 1885; *N.W.*, 9 May 1885; *M.N.*, 6 May 1885.

[74] *W.N.*, 31 Oct. 1885.

75 Ibid., 11 Apr. 1885.

76 *W.N.*, 6 June 1885; *W.E.*, 24 Jan., 28 Feb. 1885.

77 *B.M.N.*, 25 June 1885.

78 *W.N.*, 6 June 1885; *N.W.*, 12 and 16 Nov. 1885.

79 *W.N.*, 31 Oct. 1885; *N.W.*, 23 Nov. 1885.

80 *W.W.*, 14 Nov. 1885.

81 *W.N.*, 28 Nov. 1885.

82 Ibid., *N.T.*, 28 Nov. 1885; *N.W.*, 25 Nov. 1885.

83 Michael McCartan to Timothy Harrington, 14 Nov. 1885 (McCartan papers, University College, Dublin, archives, P11/B).

84 *L.Sent.*, 29 Sept. 1885.

85 See Walker 'Party organisation', pp 198-200.

86 See Bottomley, *The North Fermanagh elections*, p. 175.

87 Savage, *Origins of the Ulster unionists*, pp 185-6; P. J. Buckland (ed.), *Irish unionism, 1885-1923: a documentary history*, pp 99-100, 106-10; P. M. Bottomley, *The North Fermanagh elections*, pp 169-72.

88 *N.W.*, 6 Nov. 1885.

89 Club minutes, 6 Jan., 6 Feb., 1885 (Ulster reform club, minute book of club, 4 May 1880 – 18 Mar. 1892).

90 *W.W.*, 4 Apr. 1885.

91 Club minutes, 30 Sept. – 20 Nov. 1885 (Ulster reform club, minute book of club, 4 May 1880 – 18 Mar. 1892).

92 See *N.W.*, 12 May, 22 July, 25 Aug. 1885.

93 *N.W.*, 29 May 1885.

94 *B.M.N.*, 25 May 1885; *N.W.*, 25 May 1885.

95 Bryce later claimed that he warned the Ulster liberals that home rule was coming; see letter in *N.W.*, 12 Apr. 1893. But there is no evidence of this at the time. See letter of John Rogers, *N.W.*, 13 Apr. 1893.

96 Robert Jamieson to James Bryce, 16 Apr. 1885 (Bodleian, Bryce papers, J1/9).

97 *N.W.*, 15 Aug. 1885.

98 See *W.W.*, 15 Aug., 3 Oct. 1885.

99 Ibid., 14 Nov. 1885.

100 *L.Sent.*, 5 Sept. 1885; *L.S.*, 14 Sept. 1885; *W.N.*, 10 Oct. 1885.

101 McElroy, *Route land crusade*, p. 56.

102 *W.W.*, 28 Aug. 1885.

103 McElroy, *Route land crusade*, p. 56.

104 *W.W.*, 27 June, 17 Oct. 1885.

105 Samuel Black to W. F. McKinney, 8 June 1885 (McKinney archives, Sentry Hill).

106 *W.W.*, 24, 31 Oct., 14, 21 Nov. 1885.

107 McKeown, 'Land in South Antrim', pp 38-41.

108 *M.N.*, 1 June 1885; *W.W.*, 17 Oct. 1885.

109 Ibid., 21 Nov. 1885.

110 *A.Std.*, 4 Dec. 1885.

111 *W.W.*, 7 Nov. 1885.

112 Ibid.

113 *B.M.N.*, 22 May 1885; *N.W.*, 25 May 1885.

114 See letter of W. E. Macartney, *W.N.*, 3 Oct. 1885.

115 *B.M.N.*, 20 June 1885.

116 *T.Cour.*, 27 June 1885.

117 Ibid., 8 Aug. 1885.

118 *W.W.*, 3 Oct. 1885; *T.Cour.*, 3 Oct. 1885.

119 *W.W.*, 21 Nov. 1885.

120 *N.W.*, 20 Nov. 1885.

121 *N.W.*, 19 Nov. 1885; *W.W.*, 24 Oct., 28 Nov. 1885.
122 *N.W.*, 29 Jan. 1885.
123 See report of annual meeting and also subsequent correspondence in *N.W.;* ibid., 29 Jan., 31 Jan., 4 Feb. 1885.
124 *N.W.*, 15 Aug. 1885.
125 *W.W.*, 10 Oct., 17 Oct., 31 Oct., 5 Nov. 1885.
126 *L.S.*, 23 Nov. 1885.
127 In particular E. T. Herdman, *L.Sent.*, 26 Nov. 1885.
128 Ibid.
129 See Walker, 'Party organisation', pp 202-3.
130 *Witness*, 18 Dec. 1885.
131 *The Ulster Liberal Unionist Association: a sketch of its history*, with introduction by J. R. Fisher (Belfast, 1913), p. 10; for example of modern histories see John F. Harbinson, *The Ulster unionist party, 1882-1973: its development and organisation* (Belfast, 1973), pp 7-8.
132 *W.E.*, 3 Jan. 1885.
133 Ibid.
134 Ibid., 24 Jan. 1885.
135 Ibid., 31 Jan. 1885.
136 C. J. Dempsey to John Pinkerton, 7 Feb. 1885 (P.R.O.N.I., Pinkerton papers, D1078/P/13).
137 *D.J.*, 30 Oct. 1885.
138 R. E. Beckerson to Lord Carnarvon, report on the progress of the Irish National League 1 Jan. – 30 June 1885. (S.P.O.I., C.S.O., carton 6).
139 *B.M.N.*, 2 June 1885.
140 T. P. O'Connor.
141 See, for example, speeches made in Newry on 1 June, *B.M.N.*, 2 June 1885.
142 See address from catholic bishops, *D.J.*, 9 Oct. 1885.
143 See *B.M.N.*, 2 June 1885; *A.Std.*, 30 June 1885.
144 Archbishop Walsh to Tobias Kirby, 26 Sept. 1885; P. J. Corish (ed.), 'Irish College, Rome: Kirby papers, part 3' in *Archivium Hibernicum*, xxii (1974), p. 4.
145 *B.M.N.*, 20 Oct. 1885.
146 See Magee, 'The Monaghan election', pp 149-50.
147 *B.M.N.*, 23 Oct. 1885.
148 Murphy, *Derry and modern Ulster*, pp 146-8.
149 *D.J.*, 11 Nov. 1885.
150 R. E. Beckerson to Lord Carnarvon, report of the progress of the Irish National League, 1 Jan. – 30 June 1885 (S.P.O.I., C.S.O., carton 6).
151 *W.E.*, 21 May 1885.
152 *D.J.*, 30 Oct. 1885.
153 *B.M.N.*, 28 May, 18 June, 11 July 1885.
154 *D.J.*, 21 Oct. 1885.
155 *W.E.*, 10 Jan. 1885.
156 Ibid., 21 Nov. 1885.
157 Healy, *Letters*, i, 231-3.
158 Ibid., pp 231-3.
159 *D.J.*, 7 Oct. 1885.
160 *L.Sent.*, 17 Nov. 1885.
161 *B.M.N.*, 18 Nov. 1885.
162 Ibid., 4 Nov. 1885.
163 *W.E.*, 14 Nov. 1885.
164 *N.R.*, 6 Nov. 1885.
165 *D.J.*, 9 Nov. 1885.

166 See Walker, 'Party organisation', pp 204-6.
167 A. M. Sullivan, *Old Ireland: recollections of an Irish K.C.* (London, 1927), pp 31-2.
168 Mrs Katherine O'Shea to Lord Richard Grosvenor, 28 Oct. 1885 (B.L., Gladstone papers, Add. MS 44316/63).
169 O'Brien, *Parnell and his party*, pp 166-70.
170 Capt. W. H. O'Shea to Lord Richard Grosvenor, 25 Oct. 1885 (B.L., Gladstone papers, Add. MS 44316/70).
171 T. P. O'Connor claimed that O'Brien's candidature was hurried on mainly by T. M. Healy, to spoil the plan of getting O'Shea a seat (O'Connor, *Memoirs of an old parliamentarian* (2 vols, London, 1929), ii, 6).
172 Rt. hon. Samuel Walker to Lord Richard Grosvenor, 29 Oct. 1885 (B.L., Gladstone papers, Add. MS 44316/80).
173 Rt. hon. Samuel Walker to Lord Richard Grosvenor, 31 Oct. 1885 (B.L., Gladstone papers, Add. MS 44316/82).
174 Capt. W. H. O'Shea to Lord Richard Grosvenor, n.d. (B.L., Gladstone papers, Add. MS 44316/79).
175 *W.W.*, 28 Nov. 1885.
176 *N.W.*, 24 Oct. 1885; *W.N.*, 7 Nov. 1885.
177 Ibid., 31 Oct. 1885.
178 *N.W.*, 16 Nov. 1885.
179 Ibid., 29 Oct. 1885.
180 Ibid., 14 Nov. 1885.
181 Ibid., 21 Nov. 1885.
182 Ibid., 25 Nov., 6 Nov. 1885
183 Ibid., 19 Nov. 1885.
184 *B.M.N.*, 10 Oct. 1885.
185 *F.J.*, 27 Oct. 1885.
186 *B.M.N.*, 20 Nov. 1885.
187 Ibid., 10 Nov. 1885.
188 *D.J.*, 21 Sept. 1885.
189 *B.M.N.*, 20 Nov. 1885.
190 Ibid., 23, 26, 27 Nov. 1885.
191 *W.W.*, 5 Dec. 1885; *W.N.*, 5 Dec. 1885.
192 *B.M.N.*, 28 Nov. 1885.
193 *W.E.*, 5 Dec. 1885.
194 Rev. J. Nolan to John Pinkerton, 30 Nov. 1885 (P.R.O.N.I., Pinkerton papers, D1078/P/14).
195 *W.W.*, 5 Dec. 1885.
196 *W.E.*, 12 Dec. 1885.
197 Quoted in Savage, *Origin of the Ulster unionists*, p. 186.
198 *C.N.*, 30 Oct. 1885.
199 *I.R.*, 3 Dec. 1885.
200 J. W. Dane to Major Thomas Auchinleck, 27 Nov. 1885 (P.R.O.N.I., Falls and Hanna papers, outletter book of J. W. Dane, D1390/26/7/p. 206).
201 *W.E.*, 12 Dec. 1885.
202 *United Ireland*, 5 Dec. 1885; *W.W.*, 12 Dec. 1885.
203 *W.W.*, 5 Dec. 1885; Thomas MacKnight to W. E. Gladstone, 17 Dec., 1885 (B.L., Gladstone papers, Add. MS 56446).
204 *W.W.*, 12 Dec. 1885.
205 *W.E.*, 12 Dec. 1885.
206 Ibid., 12 Dec. 1885.
207 Ibid.

208 *T.Cour.*, 12 Dec. 1885.

209 *W.W.*, 5 Dec. 1885.

210 *P.A.*, 12 Dec. 1885; *W.E.*, 12 Dec.

211 Healy, *Letters*, i, 259.

212 The main sources used for social classification of M.P.s were *Dod's parliamentary companion, 1886; Irish catholic directory, 1886; Thom's directory, 1886;* and O'Brien's *Parnell and his party*, pp 150-58, and 'The Irish party', pp 414-20.

213 T. M. Healy, elected for two Ulster seats, has been included twice in the total number of M.P.s but only once in the social statistics.

214 Second seats won by Arthur O'Connor and E. D. Gray have not been included in the social statistics but they are included in the total number of nationalists. T. P. O'Connor has been counted only once in both the social and overall figures for his Galway but not his Liverpool seat. Source of social and religious background of M.P.s was O'Brien, *Parnell and his party*, pp 150-51.

215 Thomas MacKnight to Gladstone, 17 Dec. 1885 (B.L., Gladstone papers, Add. MS 56446).

216 *W.E.*, 19 Dec. 1885.

217 Lord Deramore to marquis of Salisbury, 29 Apr. 1887 (Hatfield House, Salisbury papers).

218 Peter Gibbon, *The origins of Ulster unionism: the formation of popular protestant politics and ideology in nineteenth century Ireland* (Manchester, 1975), pp 112-40.

219 *B.M.N.*, 9, 10 Oct. 1885.

220 *W.E.*, 12 Dec. 1885.

221 *B.M.N.*, 9, 10 Oct., 4 Nov. 1885.

222 *N.R.*, 26 Nov. 85. Also see speech by Rev. Charles Quinn, P.P. at Camlough, *N.R.*, 28 Nov. 1885 and of Rev. Rooney in Newry, *N.R.*, 10 Dec. 1885.

223 *W.E.*, 13 Mar. 1886.

CHAPTER 11 *By-elections, 1885-6*

1 MacKnight, *Ulster as it is*, i, 156.

2 Savage, *Origins of the unionists*, p. 195.

3 Ibid, p. 196.

4 *B.N.L.*, 23 Feb. 1886.

5 Lord Rossmore to Lord Randolph Churchill, 25 Feb. 1886 (Churchill College, Cambridge, Randolph Churchill papers, 1/12/1392).

6 *N.W.*, 18 Jan. 1886.

7 See below, p. 384.

8 Diary of William Johnston, 14 Jan. 1886 (P.R.O.N.I., Johnston papers, D880/2/38).

9 Col. E. J. Saunderson to his wife, 23 Jan. 1886 (P.R.O.N.I., Saunderson papers, T2996/1/66).

10 Diary of William Johnston, 20 Jan. 1886 (P.R.O.N.I., Johnston papers, D880/2/38).

11 Lord Deramore to marquis of Salisbury, 26 June 1886 (Hatfield, Salisbury papers).

12 *W.E.*, 23 Jan.; *D.J.*, 8 Jan. 1886.

13 *W.E.*, 6 Mar. 1886.

14 Ibid., 23 Jan. 1886.

15 *N.W.*, 12 Jan. 1886.

16 Savage, *Origins of the Ulster unionists*, p. 199.

17 *B.N.L.*, 21 Jan. 1886.

18 *L.S.*, 18 Dec. 1885.

[19] *N.W.*, 15 Feb. 1886; McElroy, *Route land crusade*, p. 56.

[20] Club minutes, 23 Dec. 1885 – 26 Feb. 1886 (Ulster reform club, minute book of club, 4 May 1880 – 18 Mar. 1892).

[21] *N.W.*, 20 Mar. 1886.

[22] Differing reports emerged as to the number of votes cast for and against the resolution. A subsequent letter in the press from Finlay McCance, chairman of the convention, stated that it was passed by a substantial and undoubted majority (*N.W.*, 1 Apr. 1886).

[23] *B.N.L.*, 16 Jan. 1886.

[24] Ibid., 27 Jan. 1886.

[25] *N.W.*, 28 Jan. 1886.

[26] *B.N.L.*, 16 Jan. 1886; *N.W.*, 28 Jan. 1886.

[27] *W.E.*, 6 Feb. 1886.

[28] *N.W.*, 5 Feb. 1886; *Weekly Ex.*, 6 Feb. 1886.

[29] Robert MacGeagh to James Bryce, 5 Feb. 1886 (Bodleian, Bryce papers, J1/3).

[30] *W.E.*, 16 Jan. 1886; *B.N.L.*, 3 Feb. 1886.

[31] *B.N.L.*, 9 Feb. 1886.

[32] *Selection from the representations made to the first lord of the treasury by public bodies, in response to the invitation for the free communication of views on Ireland, contained in a letter addressed by the first lord of the treasury to Viscount de Vesci on 12th February 1886*, pp 3-4, H.C. 1886 (117-sess 1), lii, 775-6.

[33] James Bryce to Gladstone, 1 Dec. 1885 (Bodleian, Bryce papers, MS 10/92; James Bryce to Gladstone, 12 Mar. 1886 (B.L., Gladstone papers, Add. MS 56446).

[34] Charles Russell to Gladstone, 17 Mar. 1886 (B.L., Gladstone papers, Add. MS 56446).

[35] See A. B. Cooke and John Vincent, *The governing passion: cabinet government and party politics in Britain, 1885-86* (Brighton, 1974).

[36] *Hansard 3*, cciv, 1036-85.

[37] O'Brien, *Parnell and his party*, pp 138-92.

[38] See *Hansard 3*, cccv, 631, 659-60, 964, 1207, 1244, 1667-8.

[39] See ibid., 673-7, 1767-8; ibid., cciv, 1226-34, 1381-96.

[40] *Annual Register, 1886*, pp 106-10, 172-5.

[41] See W. C. Lubenow, *Parliamentary politics and the home rule crisis, the British house of commons in 1886* (Oxford, 1988).

CHAPTER 12 *The 1886 general election*

[1] T. W. Moody, 'Fenianism, home rule and the land war (1850-91)' in T. W. Moody and F. X. Martin (ed.), *The course of Irish history* (Cork, 1967), p. 291.

[2] *I.L.P.U. annual report 1886*, pp 3-13.

[3] *F.J.*, 1 June 1886; *M.N.*, 15 June 1886.

[4] *W.E.*, 24 Apr. 1886.

[5] *W.E.*, 17 Apr. 1886; *M.N.*, 21 June 1886.

[6] *B.N.L.*, 15, 23 and 28 Apr. 1886.

[7] Savage, *Origins of the unionists*, pp 200-01.

[8] *B.N.L.*, 17 May 1886; Savage, *Origins of the unionists*, pp 201-02.

[9] *B.N.L.*, 6 Apr. 1886.

[10] Savage, *Origins of the unionists*, p. 203.

[11] Ibid., pp 201-4.

[12] Diary of William Johnston, 11 June 1886 (P.R.O.N.I., Johnston papers, D880/2/38).

[13] *N.W.*, 14 Apr. 1886.

[14] *N.W.*, 1 May 1886.

15 In *History of the liberal unionists,* p. 20, it is stated that the Ulster liberal unionist committee was founded on 4 June but according to a report in *N.W.,* 15 June, it was not formed until 14 June.

16 See *History of the liberal unionists,* pp 20-21.

17 *W.E.,* 29 May 1886.

18 P. J. O. McCann, 'The protestant home rule movement, 1886-95' (M.A. thesis, N.U.I. (U.C.D.), 1972) (hereafter cited as McCann, 'Protestant home rulers'), pp 28-43.

19 *B.N.L.,* 8 July 1886.

20 *B.M.N.,* 2 July 1886.

21 *N.W.,* 28 May, 2 July 1886.

22 *N.W.,* 19 May 1886; *L.Sent.,* 15 June 1886.

23 *N.W.,* 15 June 1886; McCann, 'Protestant home rulers', p. 42.

24 *N.W.,* 7 July 1886.

25 Ibid., 7 June 1886; *B.N.L.,* 21 June 1886.

26 McCann, 'Protestant home rulers', p. 42.

27 *N.W.,* 28 June 1886; *B.N.L.,* 29 June 1886.

28 *N.W.,* 10 June 1886.

29 Ibid., 3 July 1886.

30 Ibid., 26, 28 Apr. 1886.

31 *N.W.,* 15 May 1886.

32 *B.N.L.,* 18 June 1886.

33 *B.M.N.,* 3 July 1886.

34 See reports of meetings in north-west of province and also W. Belfast, *N.W.,* 18 June – 12 July 1886.

35 See ibid., 29 June 1886.

36 Club minutes, 20 Apr. – 22 July 1886 (Ulster reform club, minute book of club, 4 May 1880 – 18 Mar. 1892).

37 *L.S.,* 12 July 1886.

38 *B.M.N.,* 3 July, 1886; *W.E.,* 10 July 1886.

39 See, for example, report of selection of N. Antrim delegates to convention, *B.N.L.,* 23 June 1886; ibid., 23 June 1886.

40 *B.N.L.,* 3 July 1886; ibid., 24 May 1886; *B.M.N.,* 2 July 1886.

41 Ibid., 22, 25 June 1886.

42 *N.W.,* 15 June 1886.

43 *B.N.L.,* 29 Jan. 1886; *F.T.,* 17 June 1886.

44 *B.N.L.,* 29 June 1886.

45 Ibid., 28 June 1886.

46 *B.N.L.,* 10 July 1886.

47 *N.W.,* 3 July 1886.

48 Ibid., 21 May 1886.

49 Above, pp 237-8.

50 *B.N.L.,* 7 Apr. 1886; *N.W.,* 15 June 1886.

51 *B.N.L.,* 1 Jan. 1886; *N.W.,* 17 Apr. 1886; *B.N.L.,* 18 May 1886; *N.W.,* 1, 16 June 1886; *B.N.L.,* 11, 21 June 1886.

52 Ibid., 25 June, 1886. Col. E. J. Saunderson to his wife, 25 June 1886 (P.R.O.N.I., Saunderson papers, T2996/1/81); Lord Randolph Churchill to Col. E. J. Saunderson, 28 June 1886 (P.R.O.N.I., Saunderson papers, T2996/3/18); *B.N.L.,* 29 June 1886; Savage, *Origins of Ulster unionists,* p. 205; *B.N.L.,* 1 July 1886.

53 *B.N.L.,* 26 June 1886.

54 For example, in Co. Fermanagh see reports of meetings, *N.W.,* 16 June; *N.W.,* 1 July 1886.

55 R. E. Beckerson to Lord Aberdeen, report on progress of the Irish National League, Jan.-June 1886 (S.P.O.I., C.S.O., carton 6).
56 W. S. Blunt, *The land war in Ireland* (London, 1912), p. 153.
57 *N.W.*, 1 July 1886.
58 *B.M.N.*, 21 June 1886.
59 *B.N.L.*, 8 July 1886.
60 See report of Armagh national league branch meeting, *W.E.*, 3 July 1886.
61 *W.E.*, 3 July 1886.
62 See *B.M.N.*, 30 June, 3 July 1886.
63 *W.E.*, 5, 17 July 1886.
64 W. J. Reynolds to James Dickson, 25 June 1886; W. J. Reynolds to Thomas Shillington, 25 June 1886 (P.R.O.N.I., Donnelly and Duffy papers, outletter book of W. J. Reynolds, 1885-6, D1813/1/2).
65 W. J. Reynolds to secretary of national league, 2 July 1886 (P.R.O.N.I., Donnelly and Duffy papers, outletter book of W. J. Reynolds, 1885-6, D1813/1/2).
66 W. J. Reynolds to Father Montague (Ardboe), 2 July 1886 (P.R.O.N.I., Donnelly and Duffy papers, outletter book of W. J. Reynolds, 1885-6, D1813/1/2).
67 For example, W. J. Reynolds to Rev. McAleavey (Rock), 9 July, 1886 (P.R.O.N.I., Donnelly and Duffy papers, outletter book of W. J. Reynolds, 1885-6, D1813/1/2).
68 A. M. Sullivan, *Old Ireland: reminiscences of an Irish K.C.* (London, 1927), pp 34-5.
69 D. Harte to James Browne, *c.* 1886 (P.R.O.N.I., Browne papers, T2279/5).
70 See *B.N.L.*, 16 June – 10 July 1886.
71 *B.N.L.*, 6 July 1886.
72 *N.W.*, 3 July 1886; *B.N.L.*, 3 July 1886.
73 *D.J.*, 9 July 1886.
74 *B.M.N.*, 30 June 1886.
75 Ibid., 28 June 1886.
76 Ibid., 23 June 1886.
77 Ibid.
78 Ibid., 3 July 1886.
79 Ibid.; ibid., 23 June 1886; ibid., 3 July 1886.
80 *W.E.*, 10 July; *L.Sent.*, 8 July 1886.
81 *N.W.*, 7 July 1886.
82 *B.N.L.*, 21-6 Oct. 1886.
83 Ibid., 8 July 1886.
84 *W.E.*, 10 July 1886.
85 *B.N.L.*, 7 July 1886.
86 *B.M.N.*, 10 July 1886.
87 *B.N.L.*, 4 Nov. 1886.
88 *D.J.*, 9 July 1886.
89 Ibid., 12 July 1886.
90 Healy, *Letters*, i, 259.
91 As quoted in James Loughlin, 'The Irish protestant home rule association and nationalist politics, 1886-93' in *I.H.S.*, xxiv, no. 95 (May 1985), p. 349; also McCann, 'Protestant home rulers', p. 44.
92 Sources for the social backgrounds of M.P.s were *Dod's parliamentary companion, 1887; Irish catholic directory, 1887; Thom's directory, 1886;* and O'Brien's 'The Irish party', pp 414-20. (Subsequently a unionist, C. E. Lewis, was unseated on petition and his place was taken by Justin McCarthy, nationalist.)
93 The member for W. Belfast, Thomas Sexton, is classified in this manner by

O'Brien although Sexton was sometimes a journalist (O'Brien, 'The Irish party', pp 399-402).
[94] McCann, 'Protestant home rulers', p. 60. These were William Abraham, Sir T. H. G. Esmonde, Jeremiah Jordan, Pierce Mahony, John Pinkerton, and C. K. D. Tanner. Apart from Pinkerton and Mahony elected in the 1886 general election, they were elected in 1885.
[95] See Ian d'Alton, 'Southern Irish unionism: a study of Cork unionists, 1884-1914' in *R. Hist. Soc. Trans.*, 5th ser., xxiii (1973), pp 71-88.

CONCLUSION

[1] Thomas MacKnight, *Ulster as it is*, i, p. 1.
[2] Born at Thomastown, Co. Kilkenny, 1840, Finnigan was a full time party organiser in Ulster, 1874-98.
[3] R. V. Comerford, *The fenians in context: Irish politics and society, 1848-82* (Dublin, 1985), p. 247.
[4] Basil Chubb, *Government and politics of Ireland* (1st edition, London, 1970) pp 70-96; Tom Garvin, *The evolution of Irish nationalist politics* (Dublin, 1981), pp 135-8.
[5] P. M. Sacks, *The Donegal Mafia: an Irish political machine* (New Haven, 1976), pp 53-4; Peadar Livingstone, *The Monaghan story* (Enniskillen, 1980), pp 419-23, 446-52. Kurt Bowen, *Protestants in a catholic state: Ireland's privileged minority* (Dublin, 1983), pp 47-77.
[6] W. E. Vaughan and A. J. Fitzpatrick (eds), *Irish historical statistics: population, 1821-1971* (Dublin, 1978), pp 15 and 16.
[7] R. V. Comerford, *The fenians in context: Irish politics and society, 1848-82* (Dublin, 1985), especially pp 30-32, 194 and 197. Tom Garvin, 'Priests and patriots: Irish separatism and the fear of the modern, 1890-1914', in *I.H.S.*, xxv, no. 97 (May, 1986), pp 67-81.
[8] Frank Wright, 'Protestant ideology and politics in Ulster', in *European Journal of Sociology*, xiv (1973), pp 213-80.
[9] Gordon Smith, *Politics in Western Europe* (London, 1972; 4th edition, London, 1983), pp 18-26.
[10] Catherine Shannon, 'The Ulster liberal unionists and local government reform, 1885-1898' in *I.H.S.*, xviii, no. 71 (March, 1973), pp 407-23.
[11] Alvin Jackson, *The Ulster party: Irish unionists in the house of commons, 1884-1911* (Oxford, 1989).
[12] James Loughlin, *Gladstone, home rule and the Ulster question, 1882-93* (Dublin, 1986), pp 220-50.
[13] Ibid., pp 245-6; see also Desmond Murphy, *Derry, Donegal and modern Ulster, 1790-1921* (Derry, 1981), p. 238.
[14] For example see Fermanagh in Peadar Livingstone, *The Fermanagh story* (Enniskillen, 1969) pp 227 and 330-4.
[15] See for example *Londonderry Sentinel* Sept. 29, 1885.
[16] Sean Connolly, *Religion and society in nineteenth century Ireland* (Dundalk, 1985), 'The influence of the catholic church on elections in nineteenth century Ireland', in *E.H.R.*, lxxv, pp 37-9; J. H. Whyte, (1960), pp 235-59.
[17] See James Loughlin, *Gladstone, home rule and the Ulster question* (Dublin, 1986), pp 125-131.
[18] For role of Orange order in the unionist party in the twentieth century see J. F. Harbinson, *The Ulster unionist party, 1882-1973*, (Belfast, 1973), pp 86-96.

[19] S. M. Lipset and Stein Rokkan, 'Cleavage structures, party systems and vote alignment: an introduction' in S. M. Lipset and Stein Rokkan, *Party systems and vote alignment* (New York, 1967), pp 50-6.

[20] Ibid. Gordon Smith, *Politics in western Europe* (London, 1972; 4th edition, London, 1983), pp 12-14, 44-6; A. R. Ball, *Modern politics and government* (London, 1988), pp 82-4.

[21] See Arend Lijphart, *The politics of accommodation: pluralism and democracy in the Netherlands.* (2nd ed., Berkeley, 1975).

[22] Gordon Smith, *Politics in western Europe* (London, 1972; 4th edition, London, 1983), pp 18-26; Jan Erik Lane and S. O. Ersson, *Politics and society in western Europe* (London, 1987), pp 56-64, 97-9; J. H. Whyte, *Catholics in western democracies* (Dublin, 1981), pp 47-75.

[23] See Alf Kaartvedt, 'The economic basis of Norwegian nationalism in the nineteenth century in Rosalind Mitchison (ed), *The roots of nationalism: studies in northern Europe* (Edinburgh, 1980), pp 11-19; Gordon Smith, *Politics in western Europe* (London, 1972; 4th edition, 1983), pp 297-302, 308-10; see relevant chapters in Richard Rose (ed.) *Electoral behaviour: a comparative handbook* (London, 1974).

[24] For information on the interesting debate on the significance of this period for southern Irish politics see J. H. Whyte, 'Ireland: politics without social bases' in Richard Rose (ed.) *Electoral behaviour: a comparative handbook* (London, 1974), pp 619-51; Peter Mair, 'Interpretation of the Irish party system' in *European Journal of Political Research*, 12 (1984), pp 289-307; Michael Gallagher, *Political parties in the republic of Ireland* (Dublin, 1985); Peter Mair, *The changing Irish party system* (London, 1987); Tom Garvin, *The evolution of Irish nationalist politics* (Dublin, 1981).

BIBLIOGRAPHY

I   Manuscript sources

Belfast

Public Record Office of Northern Ireland

Abercorn papers, T2541.
Adair papers, D929.
Belmore papers, D3007.
Browne papers, T2279.
Carleton, Atkinson and Sloan solicitors' papers, D1252.
Charlemont papers, D266.
Clogher diocesan papers, Dio. R.C.I.
J. W. Dane, solicitor's outletter book, D1390.
Donnelly and Duffy solicitor's papers, D1813.
Drennan papers, D1513.
Dufferin and Ava papers (including Ulster Liberal Society papers), D1071.
Dungannon borough revision papers, D847.
Fermanagh county grand Orange lodge minute book, D1402/1.
Hertford papers, Mic. 257 (originals in Warwick county record office, CR114A).
Home government association and the home rule league letter book, D213.
William Johnston papers, D880.
L'Estrange and Brett solicitors' papers, D1905.
McKee papers, D1821.
Martin and Henderson solicitors' papers, D2223.
Montgomery papers, D627.
Moore papers, D877/27A.
O'Hagan papers, D2777.
O'Neill papers, D1481.
Pinkerton papers, D1078.
Saunderson papers, T2996.
Verner papers. Outletter book of James Crossle, D236.

Ulster Reform Club

Memorandum of the preliminary meetings in connection with the proposed reform club. Minute book of club, 4 May 1880-18 Mar. 1892.

Cambridge

Churchill College, Randolph Churchill papers.

Carnmoney, Co. Antrim

Sentry Hill. McKinney archives.

Chatsworth House, Derbyshire

Hartington papers.

Hatfield House, Hertfordshire

Salisbury papers.

Dublin

National Library of Ireland
Butt papers, MS 8694.

State Paper Office of Ireland
C.S.O. Carton 6.

University College, Dublin, archives
McCartan papers.

London

British Library
Gladstone papers, Add. 56446.

Public Record Office
Cairns papers 30/51-16F-102.

Strand House.
W. H. Smith papers.

Oxford

Bodleian Library
Bryce papers, J1.
Disraeli papers, BXXXI (formerly housed at Hughenden).

II   Printed records

1   Parliamentary papers and records

(a)   Population reports

Census of Ireland for the year 1861. Part V: *General report,* [3204-IV],
  H.C. 1863, lxi.
Census of Ireland for the year 1871. Part I: vol. iii, *Ulster,* [C964- I to X],
  H.C. 1874, lxxiv, pt i. Part III: *General report* [C1377], H.C. 1876, lxxxi.
Census of Ireland for the year 1881. Part I: vol. iii, *Ulster,* [C3204], H.C.
  1882, lxxviii. Part II: *General report* [C3365], H.C. 1882, lxxvi, 385-851.
Census of Ireland for the year 1891. Part I: vol. iii, *Ulster,* [C6626] H.C.
  1892, xci. Part II: *General report* [C6780], H.C. 1892, xc.

(b)   Other reports and returns

Minutes of evidence taken before the commissioners . . . for the purpose of making inquiry into the evidence of corrupt practices amongst the freemen electors of the city of Dublin, [C-93.1], H.C. 1870, xxxiii.

Returns showing the number of agricultural holdings in Ireland and the tenure by which they are held by the occupiers, [C32], H.C. 1870, lvi, 737-56.

Report from the select committee on registration of parliamentary voters (Ireland): together with the proceedings of the committee, minutes of evidence, appendix, and index, H.C. 1874 (261), xi, 167-314.

Summary of the returns of owners of land in Ireland, showing with respect to each county, the number of owners below an acre, and in classes up to 100,000 acres, and upwards, with the aggregate acreage and valuation of each class, H.C. 1876 (422), lxxx, 35-59.

Return of owners of land of one acre and upwards in the several counties, counties of cities and counties of towns in Ireland [C.1492], H.C. 1876, xxx, 61-394.

Local government and taxation of towns inquiry commission (Ireland): part I. Report and evidence with appendices, [C1696], H.C. 1877, xxxix.

Local government and taxation of towns inquiry commission (Ireland): part III. Report and evidence with appendices, [C1787], H.C. 1877, xl.

Agricultural statistics of Ireland for the year 1876, [C1749], H.C. 1877, lxxxv, 529-600.

Return of charges made by candidates at the last election by returning officers . . . also the total expenses of each candidate, H.C. 1880 (382 - sess. 2), lvii, 36-43.

Copy of the shorthand writer's notes of the judgement and evidence on the trial of the Down county election petition, H.C. 1880 (260 - sess. 2), lvii, · 567-829.

Report of her majesty's commissioners of inquiry into the working of the landlord and tenant (Ireland) act, 1870, [C2779-1], H.C. 1881, xviii.

Return . . . of the names of the persons holding the commission of the peace . . . and, number of such persons that are protestant, number Roman Catholics, and number that are members of other persuasions, H.C. 1884 (13), lxiii, 331-449.

Return showing the religious denominations of the population, according to the census of 1881, in each constituency formed in Ulster by the redistribution of seats act, 1885, H.C. 1884-5 (335), lxii, 339-41.

Report from the select committee on the Irish society and the London companies (Irish estates), H.C. 1890 (322), xiv.

Royal commission on labour: the agricultural labourer, vol. iv, Ireland pt v, [C6894-xviii], H.C. 1893-4, xxvii, pt 1.

(c)   Records of parliament

Hansard's parliamentary debates, third series, vols 194-307. London, 1868-86.

III   Printed contemporary works

1   Reports and lists

Directory and handbook for Newry, Warrenpoint, Rostrevor . . . Newry, 1868.
List of the electors of the borough of Belfast who voted at the general election, 1868. Belfast, 1868.
List of electors at Newry, 1868. Newry, 1868.
Londonderry working men's protestant defence association: report: inaugural meeting etc., held on Friday 17 April 1868. Derry, 1868.
Newry election: an alphabetically arranged list of electors who voted, and those who did not, at the election held in Newry on the 20th of November, 1868. Newry, 1868.
Names of the voters at the election held in Londonderry on Thursday, 17 Feb. 1870. Derry, 1870.
Proceedings of the home rule conference held at the Rotunds . . . 1873. Dublin, 1873.
State of the poll at the general election held for the city of Londonderry, 20 Nov. 1868. Derry, 1868.
Union of Newry (part of). Valuation of the several tenements comprised in the portion of the above named union situated in the county of Down. Dublin, 1864.

2   Contemporary works of reference

Annual Register: a review of public events at home and abroad, for the year 1863 [etc]. New series, London, 1864 — (annual).
Bassett, G. H., *Book of Antrim.* Dublin, 1888. Reprinted Belfast, 1989.
  Book of Armagh. Dublin, 1886. Reprinted Belfast, 1989.
  Book of Down. Dublin, 1887. Reprinted Belfast, 1988.
Belfast and province of Ulster post office directory and official guide. Belfast, 1870 — (annual).
De Burgh, U. H. Hussey, *The landowners of Ireland: an alphabetical list of owners of estates of 500 acres or £500 valuation and upwards, in Ireland.* Dublin, 1978.
Dod's parliamentary companion. London, 1865 — (annual).
Irish catholic directory, almanac and registry. New series, Dublin, 1870 — (annual).
The newspaper gazetteer and guide to advertisers . . . for 1860. London, 1861 — (annual).
Thom's Irish almanac and official directory of the United Kingdom of Great Britain and Ireland, for the year 1861 [etc]. Dublin, 1861 — (annual). Title altered in 1881 to *Thom's Official Directory . . .*
Who's who: an annual biographical dictionary . . . London, 1898 — (annual).
Who was who, 1897-1916. London, 1920.

3 Newspapers

Anglo-Celt
Armagh Guardian
Banner of Ulster
Belfast Morning News
Belfast Newsletter
Belfast Telegraph
Cavan Weekly News
Coleraine Chronicle
Coleraine Constitution
Derry Journal (pre 1880 *Londonderry Journal*)
Down Recorder
Enniskillen Advertiser
Fermanagh Mail
Fermanagh Times
Freeman's Journal
Impartial Reporter
Londonderry Journal (post 1880 *Derry Journal*)
Londonderry Sentinel
Londonderry Standard
Nation
Newry Telegraph
Northern Standard
Northern Star
Northern Whig
People's Advocate
Tyrone Constitution
Tyrone Courier
Ulster Examiner
Ulster Gazette
Ulster Times
Weekly News
Weekly Whig
Weekly Examiner
Witness

4 Writings by contemporaries

Belmore, Earl of. *Parliamentary memoirs of Fermanagh, county and borough, from 1613 to 1885.* Dublin, 1885.

Dickson, T. A. *An Irish policy for a liberal government.* London, 1885.

Doyle, J. B. *Towns in Ulster: a handbook to the antiquities and scenery of the north of Ireland.* Dublin, 1854.

Grousset, Paschal. *Ireland's disease: The English in Ireland, 1887.* London, 1887; Belfast reprint, 1986.

Sullivan, A.M. *New Ireland.* 2 vols. London, 1877.

An Ulster presbyterian. *Ulster and home rule.* Belfast, 1886.
Thackeray, W. M. *The Paris sketch book and Irish sketch book.* London, 1877.

5   Later writings by contemporaries

Blunt, W. S. *The land war in Ireland.* London, 1912.
Gavan Duffy, Sir Charles. *My life in two hemispheres.* 2 vols. London, 1898; reprint, Shannon, 1968, with introduction by J. H. Whyte.
Gwynn, Stephen. *Experiences of a literary man.* London, 1926.
Hamilton, Lord Ernest. *Forty years on.* London, 1922.
Healy, T. M. *Letters and leaders of my day.* 2 vols. London, 1928.
McElroy, S. C. *The Route land crusade: being an authentic account of the efforts made to advance land reform by the Route tenants' defence association, the Antrim central tenant-right association and the Ulster land committee.* Coleraine, n.d.
MacKnight, Thomas. *Ulster as it is, or twenty-eight years experience as an Irish editor.* 2 vols. London, 1896.
O'Connor, T.P. *Memoirs of an old parliamentarian.* 2 vols. London, 1929.
O'Donnell, F. H. *History of the Irish parliamentary party.* 2 vols. London, 1910.
Rentoul, J. A. *Stray thoughts and memories.* Dublin, 1921.
Ross, Sir John. *The years of my pilgrimage.* London, 1924.
Sullivan, A. M. *Old Ireland: reminiscences of an Irish K.C.* London, 1927.

IV   Historical works

Armour, W. S. *Armour of Ballymoney.* London, 1934.
Ballman, D. W. R. (ed.). *The diary of Sir Edward Walter Hamilton.* 2 vols. Oxford, 1972.
Barkley, J. M. Belfast newspapers, v: 1850-70. In *Pace*, vii, no. 1 (spring, 1975), pp 8-10. Belfast newspapers, vi: 1860-74. In *Pace*, vii, nos. 2/3 (summer, autumn 1975), pp 15-17.
Barry, Albert. *Life of Count Arthur Moore.* Dublin, 1905.
Beckett, J. C. Ulster protestantism. In T. W. Moody and J. C. Beckett (eds.), *Ulster since 1800, second series: a social survey* (London, 1957), pp 154-67.
Beckett, J. C. and Glasscock (eds.), *Belfast: the origin and growth of an industrial city* (London, 1967).
Bew, Paul and Wright, Frank. The agrarian opposition in Ulster politics, 1848-87. In *Irish peasants: violence and political unrest, 1780-1914* (eds.), Samuel Clark and J. S. Donnelly. (Wisconsin, 1983), pp 192-229.
Bew, Paul. *Land and the national question in Ireland 1858-82.* Dublin, 1978.
Black, R. D. C. The progress of industrialisation. In T. W. Moody and J. C. Beckett (eds.), *Ulster since 1800: first series: a political and economic survey* (London, 1955), pp 50-9.

Blewett, Neal. The franchise in the United Kingdom, 1885-1918. In *Past and Present,* no. 32 (Dec. 1965), pp 27-56.

Bottomley, P. M. The North Fermanagh elections of 1885 and 1886. In *Clogher Record,* viii (1974), pp 167-81.

Boyce, D. George. *Nationalism in Ireland.* London, 1982.

Boyle, J. W. A marginal figure: the Irish rural labourer. In Samuel Clark and J. S. Donnelly (eds.), *Irish peasants: violence and political unrest, 1780-1914* (Wisconsin, 1983), pp 311-38.

Buckland, P. J. (ed.), *Irish unionism, 1885-1923: a documentary history.* Belfast, 1973.

Budge, Ian and O'Leary, Cornelius. *Belfast: approach to crisis. A study of Belfast politics, 1813-1970.* London, 1973.

Chubb, Basil. *Government and politics of Ireland.* London, first edition, 1970.

Clarksón, Leslie. The city and the country. In J. C. Beckett and others, *Belfast: the making of the city* (Belfast, 1982), pp 153-66.

Comerford, R. V. *The Fenians in context: Irish politics and society, 1848-82.* Dublin, 1985.

Connell, K. H. Population trends. In T. W. Moody and J. C. Beckett (eds.), *Ulster since 1800: first series: a political and economic survey.* (London, 1955), pp 70-8.

Connolly, Sean. *Religion and society in nineteenth century Ireland.* Dundalk, 1985.

Cooke, A. B. and Malcolmson, A. P. W. (eds.), *The Ashbourne papers, 1869-1913.* Belfast, 1974.

Cooke, A. B. and Vincent, John. *The governing passion: cabinet government and party politics in Britain, 1885-86.* Brighton, 1974.

Cooke, A. B. A conservative party leader in Ulster: Sir Stafford Northcote's diary of a visit to the province, October 1883. In *Proceedings of the Royal Irish Academy,* lxxv, section C (Sept.) 1975.

Corish, P. J. (ed.). Kirby papers: Irish College, Rome. Guide to material of public and political interest, 1862-1883. In *Archivium Hibernicum* XXX (1972), pp 29-115.

Craig, M. J. *The volunteer earl.* London, 1948.

D'Alton, Ian. Southern trade unionism: a study of Cork unionists, 1884-1914. In *Royal Historical Society Transactions,* 5th series, xxiii (1973), pp 71-88.

Daly, G. C. Church renewal: 1869-77. In Michael Hurley (ed.), *Irish Anglicanism, 1869-1969* (Dublin, 1970), pp 23-38.

Delany, V. T. H. *Christopher Palles: his life and times.* Dublin, 1960.

Falk, Bernard. *Old Q's daughter: the history of a strange family.* London, 1937.

Foster, R. F. Lord Randolph Churchill and the prelude to the Orange card. In F. S. L. Lyons and R. A. J. Hawkins (eds.), *Ireland under the union: varieties of tension. Essays in honour of T. W. Moody.* (Oxford, 1980), pp 257-68.

Freeman, T. W. *Ireland* London, 1950.

Garvin, Tom. Priests and patriots: Irish separatism and the fear of the modern, 1890-1914. In *Irish Historical Studies*, XXV, no. 97 (May, 1986), pp 67-81.

Garvin, Tom. *The evolution of Irish nationalist politics*. Dublin, 1981.

Gibbon, Peter. *The origins of Ulster unionism: the formation of popular protestant politics and ideology in nineteenth-century Ireland*. Manchester, 1975.

Green, E. R. R. Business organisation. In T. W. Moody and J. C. Beckett (eds.), *Ulster since 1800: second series: a social survey* (London, 1957), pp 110-18.

Harbinson, J. F. *The Ulster unionist party, 1882-1973: its development and organisation*. Belfast, 1973.

Hepburn, A. C. Work, class and religion in Belfast, 1871-1911. In *Irish Economic and Social History*, x (1983), pp 33-50.

Holmes, R. F. G. *Henry Cooke*. Belfast, 1981.

Holmes, R. F. G. Ulster presbyterianism and Irish nationalism in S. Mews (ed.), *Religion and national identity: studies in Church History*, 18 (Oxford, 1982), pp 535-48.

Hoppen, K. T. Landlords, society and electoral politics. In *Past and Present*, no. 75 (1977), pp 62-93.

Hoppen, K. T. *Elections, politics and society in Ireland, 1832-1885*. Oxford, 1984.

Jackson, Alvin. *The Ulster party: Irish unionists in the house of commons, 1884-1911*. Oxford, 1989.

Jupp, P. J. Irish parliamentary representation and the catholic vote, 1801-20. In *Historical Journal*, X, no. 2 (1967, pp 183-96.

Kennedy, David. The catholic church. In T. W. Moody and J. C. Beckett (eds.), *Ulster since 1800: second series: a social survey* (London, 1957), pp 170-81.

Kirkpatrick, R. W. Origins and development of the land war in mid-Ulster. In *Ireland under the union: varieties of tension. Essays in honour of T. W. Moody*, eds. F. S. L. Lyons and R. A. J. Hawkins. (Oxford, 1980), pp 201-35.

Love, E. L. and Ersson, S. O. *Politics and society in western Europe*. London, 1987.

Larkin, Emmet. The devotional revolution in Ireland, 1850-75. In *American Historical Association*, lxxvii, no. 3 (June, 1972), pp 625-52.

Lijphart, Arend. *The politics of accommodation: pluralism and democracy in the Netherlands*. Berkeley, second edition, 1975.

Livingstone, Peadar. *The Fermanagh story*. Enniskillen, 1969.

Livingstone, Peadar. *The Monaghan story*. Enniskillen, 1980.

Loughlin, James. The Irish protestant home rule association and nationalist politics, 1886-93. In *Irish Historical Studies*, xxiv, no. 95 (May, 1985), pp 341-60.

Loughlin, James. *Gladstone, home rule and the Ulster question 1882-93*. Dublin, 1986.

Lubenow, W. C. *Parliamentary politics and the home rule crisis. The British house of commons in 1886*. Oxford, 1988.

Ulster politics, 1868-86

Lucas, Reginald. *Colonel Saunderson, M.P.* London, 1908.

Magee, John. The Monaghan election of 1883 and the "invasion of Ulster". In *Clogher Record,* viii (1974), pp 147-66.

Maguire, W. A. *Living like a lord: the second marquis of Donegall, 1764-1844.* Belfast, 1984.

Mair, Peter. *The Irish party system.* Manchester, 1987.

Mitchison, Rosalind (ed.). *The roots of nationalism: studies in northern Europe.* Edinburgh, 1980.

Moody, T. W. The Irish university question of the nineteenth century. In *History,* xliii, no. 148, June, 1958, pp 90-109.

Moody, T. W. Fenianism, home-rule and the land war (1850-91). In T. W. Moody and F. X. Martin (cds.), *The course of Irish history.* Cork, 1967, pp 303-33.

Moody, T. W. *Davitt and Irish revolution 1846-82.* Oxford, 1981.

Murphy, Desmond. *Derry, Donegal and modern Ulster, 1870-1921.* Derry, 1981.

Macaulay, Rev. Ambrose. *Patrick Dorrian, Bishop of Down and Connor, 1865-85.* Dublin, 1987.

McCaffrey, L. J. Isaac Butt and the home rule movement: a study in conservative nationalism. In *Review of Politics,* xxii, no. 1 (Jan. 1960), pp 72-95.

McClelland, Aiken. The later Orange Order. In T. D. Williams (ed.), *Secret society in Ireland* (Dublin, 1973), pp 126-37.

McCracken, J. L. The consequences of the land war. In T. W. Moody and J. C. Beckett (ed.), *Ulster since 1800, first series: a political and economic survey* (London, 1955), pp 60-9.

McCracken, J. L. The later nineteenth century. In T. W. Moody and J. C. Beckett (eds.), *Ulster since 1800, second series: a social survey* (London, 1957), pp 44-53.

McLaughlin, Daniel. *A short history of the parish church of St John the evangelist, Killowen, Coleraine.* Coleraine, 1900.

McMinn, Richard. Presbyterianism and politics in Ulster, 1871-1906. In *Studia-Hibernica,* XX (1981), pp 127-46.

McMinn, Richard. The myth of 'Route' liberalism in County Antrim, 1869-1900. In *Eire-Ireland,* xvii, no. 1 (spring, 1982), pp 137-49.

McSkimin, Samuel. *The history and antiquities of the county of the town of Carrickfergus.* Belfast, 1849; new edition with notes and appendix by E. J. McCrum, Belfast, 1906.

Norman, E. R. *The catholic church and Ireland in the age of rebellion, 1859-73.* London, 1965.

Nowlan, K. B. Disestablishment: 1800-1869. In Michael Hurley (ed.), *Irish Anglicanism, 1869-1969,* (Dublin, 1970), pp 1-22.

O'Brien, Conor Cruise. *Parnell and his party, 1880-90.* Oxford, 1957; corrected impression, 1964.

O'Donoghue, D. J. *History of Bandon.* Cork, 1970.

O'Leary, Cornelius. *The elimination of corrupt practices in British elections, 1868-1911.* Oxford, 1963.

O'Shea, James. *Priests, politics and society in post-famine Ireland: a study*

of County Tipperary, 1850-1891. Dublin, 1984.
Patterson, Henry. Industrial labour and the labour movement, 1820-1914. In Liam Kennedy and Philip Ollerenshaw (eds.), *An economic history of Ulster, 1820-1914* (Manchester, 1984), pp 33-50.
Rokkan, Stein and Lipset, S. M. 'Cleavage structures, party system and voter alignment: an introduction' in Lipset and Rokkan (eds.), *Party systems and voter alignment*. New York, 1967.
Rutherford, J. C. *An Ards farmer: or an account of the life of James Shanks, Ballyfounder, Portaferry*. Belfast, 1913.
Savage, D. C. The origins of the Ulster Unionist Party. In *Irish Historical Studies*, xii (1961), pp 185-208.
Shannon, Catherine. The Ulster liberal and local government reform, 1885-1898. In *Irish Historical Studies*, xviii, no. 71 (March, 1873), pp 407-23.
Smith, C. F. *J. N. Richardson of Bessbrook*. London, 1925.
Smith, Gordon. *Politics in Western Europe*. London, 1972; 4th edition, London, 1983.
Solow, B. L. *The land question in the Irish economy, 1870-1903*. Cambridge, Mass., 1971.
Steele, David. *Irish land and British politics: tenant-right and nationality, 1865-1870*. Cambridge, 1974.
Thompson, Francis. Attitudes to reform: political parties in Ulster and the Irish land bill of 1881. In *Irish Historical Studies*, xxiv, no. 95 (May 1985), pp 327-40.
Thornley, David. *Isaac Butt and home rule*. London, 1964.
The Ulster Liberal Unionist Association: a sketch of its history, with introduction by J. R. Fisher, Belfast, 1913.
Vaughan, W. E. Landlord and tenant relations in Ireland between the famine and the land war, 1850-1878. In L. M. Cullen and T. C. Smout (eds.), *Comparative aspects of Scottish and Irish economic and social history, 1600-1900* (Edinburgh, 1977), pp 216-26.
Vaughan, W. E. and Fitzpatrick, A. J. *Irish historical statistics: population, 1921-1971*. Dublin, 1978.
Vaughan, W. E. An assessment of the economic performance of Irish landlords, 1851-81. In *Ireland under the union: varieties of tension. Essays in honour of T. W. Moody*, eds. F. S. L. Lyons and R. A. J. Hawkins. (Oxford, 1980), pp 173-99.
Vaughan, W. E. *Landlords and tenants in Ireland, 1848-1904*. Dublin, 1984.
Walker, B. M. The Irish electorate, 1868-1915. In *I.H.S.*, xviii, no. 71 (Mar. 1973), pp 359-406.
Walker, B. M. *Parliamentary election results in Ireland, 1801-1922*. Dublin, 1978.
Walker, B. M. *Sentry Hill: an Ulster farm and family*. Belfast, 1981.
Walker, B. M. Party organisation in Ulster, 1865-92: registration agents and their activities. In Peter Roebuck (ed.), *Plantation to partition: essays in Ulster history in honour of J. L. McCracken* (Belfast, 1981), pp 191-209.

Whyte, J. H. The influence of the catholic church on elections in nineteenth century Ireland. In *English Historical Review,* LXXV (1960), pp 235-59.

Whyte, J. H. Landlord influence at elections in Ireland, 1760-1885. In *English Historical Review,* LXXX (1965), pp 740-60.

Whyte, J. H. *The tenant league and Irish politics in the eighteen fifties.* Dublin, 1966.

Whyte, J. H. *Catholics in western democracies.* Dublin, 1981.

Wright, Frank. Protestant ideology and politics in Ulster. In *European Journal of Sociology,* xiv (1973), pp 213-80.

V Theses

Holmes, R. G. F. Henry Cooke, 1788-1868. M. Litt. thesis, University of Dublin, 1970.

Johnston, J. I. D. The Clogher valley as a social and economic region in the eighteenth and nineteenth centuries. M.Litt. thesis, University of Dublin, 1974.

Megahey, A. J. The Irish protestant churches and political issues, 1870-1914. Ph.D. thesis, The Queen's University of Belfast, 1969.

McCann, P. J.O. The protestant home rule movement, 1886-95. M.A. thesis, National University of Ireland, (U.C.D.).

McKeown, Paschal. The land question and elections in South Antrim, 1870-1910. M.S.Sc. thesis, The Queen's University of Belfast, 1981.

O'Brien, Conor Cruise. The Irish Parliamentary party, 1880-90. Ph.D. thesis, University of Dublin, 1954.

Thornley, David. Isaac Butt and the creation of an Irish parliamentary party, 1868-79. Ph.D. thesis, University of Dublin, 1959.

Vaughan, W. E. A study in landlord and tenant relations in Ireland between the famine and the land war. Ph.D. thesis, University of Dublin, 1973.

Woods, C. J. The catholic church and Irish politics, 1879-92. Ph.D. thesis, Nottingham University, 1969.

INDEX

Abercorn family, 3, 53, 55
Abercorn, first duke of, 3, 53, 55, 68
Abercorn, second duke of, see Hamilton, marquis of
Adair, Sir R. S. (later Lord Waveney), 75, 118, 138, 155, 193
Ahoghill conservative working men's club, 180
Alexander, S. M., 125, 137-8
Alexander, R. J., 95-7
Alliance party, 257
Andrews, W. D., 123-5
Anglo-Celt, 37, 56
Annesley, Lt col, the hon. Hugh, 56, 102
Antrim county: electorate 39-42; 1868 general election, 51-2; 1869 by-election, 74-8; 1874 general election, 94-7, 105; 1880 general election, 138-43; 1885 by-election, 170-2
Antrim, East: 1885 general election, 181, 196, 208, 211, 218-9; 1886 general election, 239, 248
Antrim, Mid: 1885 general election, 180, 196, 208, 211, 216, 218-9; 1886 general election, 237, 239, 250
Antrim, North: 1885 general election, 180, 196, 208, 211, 216, 219; 1886 general election, 237, 239, 249
Antrim, South: 1885 general election, 180-1, 196, 208, 211, 218; 1886 general election, 239, 244, 248
Antrim central tenant right association, 6, 9, 118, 138, 170
Antrim county constitutional association, 117-8, 139-42, 157, 170-1, 178-80, 188
Antrim county divisional conservative associations (1885), 179-81
Antrim South constitutional association, 180
Archdale, Capt. M. E., 53-4
Archdale, W. H., 99-100, 137, 240, 250
Argus, 37
Armagh: electorate, 40-2; 1868 general election, 70-1; 1874 general election,

108-9; 1875 by-election, 119-20; 1880 general election, 144
Armagh, county: electorate, 39-42; 1868 general election, 51, 54-5; 1873 by-election, 83-4; 1874 general election, 98-101; 1880 general election, 134-5
Armagh, North: 1885 general election, 183-5, 206, 211, 216; 1886 general election, 238, 240, 244, 250
Armagh, Mid: 1885 general election, 182-3, 206, 218-9; 1886 by-election, 229-30; 1886 general election, 238, 240, 244, 250
Armagh, South: 1885 general election, 182-3, 206-7; 1886 general election, 240, 244, 248
Armagh borough conservative association, 70, 101, 144, 157
Armagh central liberal association, 197
Armagh county conservative association, 55, 72, 101, 156-7, 182
Armagh county constitutional divisional associations, 182-5
Armagh county liberal registration association, 155, 197
Armagh county farmers' club, 101
Armagh Guardian, 36
Armagh Herald, 36
Armagh Mid constitutional association, 182, 229
Ashbourne act, of 1885, 9
Atkinson, J. B., 183-4

Ballot act, 46, 83, 87, 141, 258
Ballycastle catholic and national registration association, 171
Ballymena, 11
Ballyshannon Herald, 37
Ballyshannon home rule association, 118
Banner of Ulster, 36, 48
Barbour, J. D., 196, 201, 218
Barton, Capt. C. R., 100
Bateson, Sir Thomas (later Lord Deramore), 7, 21, 22, 88, 185, 222-3

317

Ederney tenants' association, 137

Education of M.P.s, 71, 113, 150, 220, 252

Education question, 24, 33-4, 80, 82-3, 91, 93, 102-3, 107, 130, 204, 224, 260

Educational standards, 24, 33-4, 37

Eglinton national league branch, 207

Electorate: qualifications, 39, 43; numbers enfranchised, 40-41, 43; denominational composition, 41-3; exclusion of women, 44, 258

Ellis, Rev. Thomas, 135

Ellison Macartney, J. W., 85-9, 92, 98-9, 113, 115, 131, 135-6, 140, 149, 159, 181

Ellison Macartney, W. G., 180, 218

Enniskillen: electorate, 40-2; 1868 general election, 66-8; 1874 general election, 108-9; 1876 by-election, 120; 1880 general election, 147

Enniskillen Advertiser, 36, 67

Enniskillen conservative association, 156-7, 185

Enniskillen, Earl of, 13, 66-7, 87, 121

Ewart, William, 122-3, 148-9, 188, 191, 215, 242, 249

Farney tenants' defence association, 6, 133

Farnham family, 56

Farnham, Lord, 134

Fay, C. J., 93, 102, 113, 118, 133-4, 159

Fay, P. McC., 102

Fenians, 49, 80, 115, 165, 256

Ferguson, John, 81

Ferguson, Sir R. A., 62

Fermanagh county: electorate 39-42; 1868 general election, 53-4; 1874 general election, 98-100, 105; 1880 general election, 136-7

Fermanagh, North: 1885 general election, 186, 206, 217; 1886 general election, 240, 250

Fermanagh, South: 1885 general election, 186, 206, 218; 1886 general election, 240, 250

Fermanagh farmers' association, 8

Fermanagh Times, 36, 129

Findlater, William, 133, 195, 219

Finnegan, Rev. Dr, 204

Finnigan, B., 99

Finnigan, E. S., 117, 125, 131, 140-2, 156, 164, 167, 169, 172, 178-81, 190-1, 222, 243, 254

Forde, Lt col. W. B., 52, 96, 104

Forster family, Co. Monaghan, 57

Forster, W. E., 135

Foster, A. H. W., 187, 191, 241

Frazer, Alexander, 147

Freeman's Journal, 35, 102

Gage, Conolly, 53

Gardner, Edward, 13, 96, 118

Gardner, R. R., 238, 244, 246, 250

Garvin, Tom, 260

Germany, 266

Getty, S. G., 59

Gibson, Edward, 160

Gifford, Lord, 128

Givan, John, 132-3, 165

Gladstone, W. E., 5, 7, 9, 79, 82, 117, 164, 168, 181, 221, 228-9, 231-3, 234-9

Gorst, J. E., 157

Gray, William, 57

Green, B. L., 154

Greer, Thomas, 145-6

Grey, H. G., 183

Grosvenor, Lord Richard, 210-11

Grousset, Paschal, xiv

Hall, J. C., 231

Hall, Major W. J., 22

Hamilton, rt hon. Lord Claud, 53, 98-9, 135

Hamilton, Lord C. J., 62-3, 78

Hamilton, Lord E. W., 187, 191, 216, 237, 241, 251

Hamilton, Major James, 3

Hamilton, marquis of, later 2nd duke of Abercorn, 55, 104, 120-1, 128, 129, 131-2, 187, 199, 228, 242

Hanna, Rev. Hugh, 30, 227

Harbison, John, 23, 136, 138, 152

Harrington, Timothy, 166, 190, 202-3

Hartington, marquis of, 192, 233

Haslett, J. H., 188, 191, 215, 238, 242, 249

O'Laverty, Rev. James, 139
O'Neill, hon. Edward, 51-2, 71, 95-7, 139
O'Neill, hon. R. T., 170, 180, 191, 218, 250
O'Neill, Lord, 74
O'Reilly, Dr Francis, 133
O'Reilly, Rev. P., 118
O'Shea, Katherine, 210
O'Shea, Capt. W. H., 210-11
Orange order, xi, 7, 21, 31, 49, 52, 54, 60, 62, 71, 80, 83-9, 99-103, 106, 108-12, 115, 117, 123, 135, 137, 144, 154, 157, 162, 167, 178-92, 220, 222-3, 227,231, 240-3, 255, 257, 262-5
Orange and protestant working men's association, 109, 148, 188

Pakenham, Rev. A. H., 1
Pakenham, Lt col. T. H., 1
Palles, rt hon. Christopher, 82-3
Parnell, C. S., 8, 130, 152, 158, 161-5, 166-7, 173-4, 176, 202, 204, 208, 210-11, 213-5, 228, 232, 255-6
Party processions act, 49, 59
Peel, T. G., 48, 55, 70, 101, 119-20, 135, 156, 182-3, 207
People's Advocate, 37, 165, 167
Perry, Joseph, 96, 118, 170
Pinkerton, John, 196, 201, 216
Pirrie, W. J., 155
Portadown, 11
Portadown constitutional association, 183
Portadown liberal club, 156, 197, 238
Portadown working men's conservative association, 183
Porter, A. M., 163-5, 167
Porter, J. G. V., 54, 99-100, 136-7
Power Sir W. T., 103, 133
Presbyterians: numbers of, 15-18; socio-economic make up, 17-26; attitudes of, 29-31; objections to Church of Ireland, 31-2; good relations with catholics, 32-3; educational standards, 24, 33-4; links with newspapers, 34-7; proportion of electorate, 41-3

Presbyterian clergy, political role of, 61-3, 69, 95, 104, 111, 118, 122, 132-3, 135, 139, 201
Presbyterian constitutional association, 110
Presbyterian liberal association, 110
Pringle, Henry, 166-7

Quinn, J. C., 125, 158

Randalstown constitutional association, 157
Ranfurly family, 107, 147
Rea, John, 61, 84, 111, 155
Redistribution act (1885), 42, 173, 177, 258
Redmond, W. A., 164
Redmond, W. H. K., 206, 214, 217, 250
Registration, 44-5, 94, 105, 118, 131, 143-3, 150, 155, 177-8, 186, 191, 194, 200, 203, 209
Regium donum, 48, 52-55, 60, 69
Representation of the people (Ireland) act (1868), 39-40, 58, 60, 63, 65
Representation of the people act (1884), 39, 43, 174-5, 177, 179, 195, 209, 258
Representation of the people act (1918), 258
Reynolds, W. J., 206, 218, 245, 251
Richardson family (Bessbrook), 11
Richardson, J. N., 135, 150, 155, 166
Richhill constitutional association, 182
Ross, Sir John, 45, 47, 63, 187, 198
Rossmore family, Co. Monaghan, 57
Roughfort liberal association, 156, 196
Route farmers' and labourers association, 196, 228
Route reform association, 195-6
Route tenants' defence association, 5, 6, 94, 196, 239
Royal Belfast Academical Institution, 72
Russell, Charles, 133, 232
Russell, T. W., 238, 245-6
Russell, Thomas, 47
Rylett, Rev. Harold, 161-3

Salisbury, third marquis, 7, 217, 242
Saunders, R. C., 238, 243, 249